José Carlos Mariátegui

# José Carlos Mariátegui
*An Anthology*

*edited and translated by*
HARRY E. VANDEN *and* MARC BECKER

MONTHLY REVIEW PRESS
*New York*

Library of Congress Cataloging-in-Publication Data

Mariátegui, José Carlos, 1894–1930.

  [Selections. English. 2011]

  José Carlos Mariátegui : an anthology / edited and translated by Harry
E. Vanden and Marc Becker.

    p. cm.

  Includes bibliographical references and index.

  ISBN 978-1-58367-245-7 (pbk. : alk. paper) — ISBN 978-1-58367-246-4
(cloth : alk. paper)

  1. Communism—Latin America. 2. Nationalism and communism—Latin
America. 3. Indians of South America—Government relations. 4.
Communism—Peru. 5. Nationalism and communism—Peru. 6. Indians of
South America—Peru—Government relations. I. Vanden, Harry E. II.
Becker, Marc, Prof. III. Title.

  HX110.5.A6M294 2011

  335.43'48092—dc23

                       2011030558

Monthly Review Press

146 West 29th Street, Suite 6W

New York, NY 10001

www.monthlyreview.org

5  4  3  2  1

# Contents

Dedicated to all who have and will creatively use socialist thought and praxis to make the Americas a better place.

# Acknowledgments

This work springs from a profound conviction that José Carlos Mariátegui has much to say to English-language readers. His Complete Works (*Obras Completas*) have gone through numerous editions and have circulated widely throughout Latin America. His works have been translated into numerous languages, including not only French and Italian but also Russian and Japanese. Yet in English, translations of Mariátegui's works, especially his *Seven Interpretive Essays on Peruvian Reality*, were out of print by the time the world capitalist financial crisis hit in 2008.

Mariátegui's writings have much to say in the crisis period through which we are living. They represent the dynamic, creative vein in Marxist thought that can, we believe, best nourish cogent analyses and potent praxis. It is far from the dogmatic Marxism that came to dominate official thought in the Soviet Union and Eastern Europe. Both of us discovered Mariátegui's writing early on in our careers and we were much taken by the cogency and relevance of his writings. We hope that those who read this volume will discover the creative insights and current relevance that so impressed us.

We wish to thank the Mariátegui family, and in particular the late Javier Mariátegui, for gracefully receiving us and for granting access to many papers, documents, editions of Mariátegui's works, and a wealth of personal information that nourished our study of Mariátegui and his work. Special thanks also go to Michael Yates of Monthly Review Press for believing in this book, supporting us, and demonstrating that editors still exist who closely read and edit a manuscript. We also want to thank Erin Clermont for carefully copyediting this work.


HARRY E. VANDEN        MARC BECKER
Tampa, Florida         Madison, Wisconsin

# *Amauta*:
# An Introduction to the Life and Works
# of José Carlos Mariátegui

As we move into the twenty-first century, scholars and activists still debate the status and relevance of Marxism and Marxist thought. Some would argue that both are to be relegated to the back pages of history. Yet as this is said, world capitalism is suffering one of its worst setbacks in a century, and the very theoretical foundations on which neoliberal capitalism is based are being called into question as they prove inadequate to guide the modern world system. Whereas the rigid orthodox visions of Marxism that Joseph Stalin propagated when he had an inordinate influence on official Marxism have little to offer in this new reality, interest continues to grow in non-dogmatic, original Marxist thinkers like Antonio Gramsci and Rosa Luxemburg. Other writers outside of Europe also come to mind: Amílcar Cabral in Africa, Rabrindanath Tagore in India, or even Mao Tse-tung in China. Many find their analyses, insights, and formulations of considerable use in our current reality. Their thought combines well with more subtle forms of class, gender, cultural, and ecological analysis, and nourishes fresh visions for, and critiques of, our times.

In recent years, Latin America has emerged as an area that has challenged many neoliberal assumptions. As the region begins to restructure many of its internal class relations and foreign policies, it provides a fertile alternative to globalized neoliberal thought. In this context, it is worthwhile to turn to significant thinkers and writers who have contributed to the development of leftist thought in Latin America, whose work could successfully challenge the neoliberal cultural hegemony that the globalized world capitalist system has thrust upon the peoples of the global South as well as those of the global North. The intellectual atmosphere in Latin America has been nourished by leftist thought and has often embraced Marxist thinkers. Indeed, Marxism in Latin America is a rich and fascinating subject. As diverse as the Latin American people, it has reflected some of the most plodding and sectarian Latin American thought, but it also includes creative, innovative, and brilliant improvisations. Although Western philosophical traditions and political institutions have strongly influenced Latin America, it is part of the global South, and acknowledging this reality allowed some aspects of Marxist theory to develop in unique ways.

As we survey the Latin American intellectual landscape, one innovative thinker springs to the fore. He nourished the early Marxist thought of Ernesto Che Guevara, championed the causes of Indigenous peoples, realized the revolutionary potential of the peasantry, asserted a mature Marxist feminism, and even resisted the Stalinization of Latin American Marxist parties. This person is the Peruvian *Amauta* (Quechua for "wise teacher"), José Carlos Mariátegui (1894–1930). Mariátegui came from an impoverished family, yet he said that this allowed for wide exposure to Indigenous, *mestizo*, African, and European peoples in both Peru's *sierra* (Andean highlands) and coastal regions. He interacted with everyone, ranging from Lima's intellectual elite to Peru's proletariat, peasants, and miners. Mariátegui also enjoyed an extended stay in Europe, and engaged in political, literary, and even scientific discourse in three languages

(Spanish, Italian, and French). His thought was original and eclectic, and extended well beyond the narrow confines that came to characterize many Marxist thinkers from the 1930s to the 1960s.

Mariátegui left an unmistakable and lasting legacy not only on the political, social, and intellectual landscape of his native Peru, but on the entire continent. He energetically and actively engaged with European thought, working out new methods to analyze the problems of non-Western societies like his own. In the process he developed what subsequently become known as National Marxism, an approach that addressed the realities of a local situation within the context of Marxist theory. Mariátegui implemented a new theoretical framework that diverged from the doctrinaire ideology adopted by most of the Latin America Communist parties—an approach that attempted to apply a mechanical interpretation of Marxist strategy to a national reality. He broke from a rigid, orthodox interpretation of Marxism to develop a creative Marxist analysis that was oriented toward the specific historical reality of Peru and Latin America in the 1920s. Mariátegui did not believe that Marxism was a finished project. He favored a non-sectarian "open" Marxism and believed that "Marxist thought should be revisable, undogmatic, and adaptable to new situations."[1] Rather than a rigid reliance on objective economic factors to foment a revolutionary situation, Mariátegui also examined subjective elements such as the need for the political education and organization of the working-class proletariat, a strategy he believed could move a society to revolutionary action. He downplayed the passive economic determinism found in orthodox Marxism and followed a dynamic "voluntaristic conception of Marxism [that] did not allow him to wait for the economic conditions to force the peasants to act."[2] In addition, unlike orthodox Marxists who believed that peasants formed a reactionary class, Mariátegui looked to rural peasants and Indigenous peoples along with an industrialized urban working class to lead a social revolution that he believed would sweep across Latin America.

Even though Mariátegui's thought has retained central importance to ideological struggles in Latin America, in the English-speaking world few people are aware of his contributions. When Mariátegui died in 1930, his funeral turned into one of the largest processions of workers ever seen in the streets of Lima, but in the United States his death was hardly noticed. Waldo Frank, a U.S. writer and a close friend of Mariátegui, wrote in *The Nation* that Mariátegui's death plunged "the intelligentsia of all of Hispano-America into sorrow; and nothing could be more eloquent of the cultural separation between the two halves of the new world than the fact that to most of us these words convey no meaning."[3] Almost one hundred years later, Mariátegui's works still have relevance for those who seek to create radical thought and build a more humane and just world.

## JOSÉ CARLOS MARIÁTEGUI

José Carlos Mariátegui was born on July 14, 1894, in the small southern Peruvian town of Moquegua. He was the sixth child of a poor mestiza, María Amalia La Chira, who had lost her first three children shortly after childbirth. Mariátegui's father was Francisco Javier Mariátegui, a grandson of a liberal independence leader of the same name. Shortly after Mariátegui's birth, La Chira separated herself from her children's father and sought to shelter her children from his liberal influence. She eventually returned with her children to live with her parents in Sayán, a town frequented by travelers following the trade routes to and from the Peruvian highlands. There, Mariátegui spent countless hours in his grandfather's leather-working shop listening to the travelers recount their stories of their lives laboring as near serfs on the large landed highland estates called *latifundios*. At an early age he developed a tubercular condition, and when he was eight years old he hurt his left leg, which crippled him for life.

Mariátegui spent his adolescence on the outskirts of Lima. Because of a lack of financial resources and the need to support his family, he acquired only an eighth-grade education. At the age of fifteen, he began to work at the Peruvian newspaper *La Prensa*. Here he demonstrated a good deal of talent at journalism, and quickly moved from copy boy to writing and editing positions. Throughout his life, Mariátegui used his skills as a journalist to earn a living, as well as a means to express his political views. By the age of sixteen, his writings showed a socialist orientation. Together with his friend César Falcón, Mariátegui launched two short-lived papers, *Nuestra Epoca* and *La Razón*. Although these papers took a pro-labor stance, they did not espouse the revolutionary Marxism found in Mariátegui's later writings. Mariátegui's vocal support for the revolutionary demands of workers and students did, however, run afoul of the Peruvian dictator Augusto B. Leguía, who in October 1919 exiled Mariátegui and Falcón to Europe as Peruvian "information agents." Mariátegui's time in Europe strongly affected the development and maturation of his thought and solidified his socialist tendencies. Mariátegui later looked back on his early life as a journalist as his "Stone Age," in contrast to his later writings in the 1920s when he had matured as a Marxist thinker.

From 1919 to 1923, Mariátegui lived and studied in France and Italy where he found opportunities to meet with many European socialists. In France, he encountered Romain Rolland, Henri Barbusse, and others from the revolutionary *Clarté* group. Mariátegui spent three years in Italy where he met Benedetto Croce, Giovanni Papini, and others. The founding of the Italian Communist Party in 1921 deeply impressed Mariátegui with the revolutionary potential of a voluntarist approach to Marxism. By the time he returned to Peru in 1923, Mariátegui stated that he was "a convinced and declared Marxist."[4]

Soon after Mariátegui returned to Peru in 1923, he met student leader Víctor Raúl Haya de la Torre who had recently organized the Universidad Popular González Prada (González Prada Popular University) in Lima to educate Peruvian workers. Haya de la Torre invited him to give a series of lectures on world events that drew on the experiences and insights he had gained in Europe.[5] Mariátegui emphasized a working-class critique of recent European events in these lectures while demonstrating his broad comprehension of major political themes in postwar Europe. He was much better prepared than most of the other teachers at the university, and soon was one of the most popular lecturers.[6] Despite student requests, the public University of San Marcos refused to give him a professorship because he lacked the proper formal academic credentials. Although he was largely unschooled, he had a creative and brilliant mind. He loved to read and was, for the most part, self-educated. In short, Mariátegui was an intellectual who was at times at odds with the bourgeois intellectual world.

In 1924, Mariátegui lost his right leg, and this confined him to a wheelchair for the rest of his life. In spite of his failing health, Mariátegui increased the intensity of his efforts to organize a social revolution in Peru. In 1926, he founded *Amauta*, a journal intended as a vanguard voice for an intellectual and spiritual movement to create a new Peru. It would examine developments not only in the realm of politics but also philosophy, art, literature, and science, all with a clear political agenda. *Amauta* reached a wide audience not only in Peru but throughout Latin America.[7]

Because of its cost and vanguardist stance in art, literature, politics, and culture generally, *Amauta* did not find an ample audience among the Peruvian working class. As a result, in 1928 Mariátegui launched a less doctrinaire and more informative biweekly periodical called *Labor* as an extension of *Amauta*. *Labor*, which sought to inform, educate, and politicize the working class, survived less than a year before the Leguía dictatorship shut it down. Although the government never provided an official explanation for its closure, the newspaper was seen as a threat to Leguía's "increasingly unpopular and insecure regime."[8] *Amauta* continued publishing until shortly after Mariátegui's death in 1930.

During his lifetime, Mariátegui published many articles in various Peruvian periodicals, as well as two books, *La escena contemporánea* in 1925 and *7 ensayos de interpretación de la realidad peruana* in 1928. The first book, *La escena contemporánea* (The Contemporary Scene), is a compilation of articles he wrote for the popular Peruvian magazines *Variedades* and *Mundial*. In these essays he explores the current world political scene, including the rise of fascism, democracy, socialism, and anti-Semitism. His second book, translated into English in 1971 as

*Seven Interpretive Essays on Peruvian Reality*, was a critically acclaimed success for its original and creative insights into the Latin American reality. Mariátegui presents a brilliant analysis of Peruvian, and by extension Latin American, problems from a Marxist point of view. The book includes seven essays on the topics of economic development, Indigenous peoples, land distribution, the education system, religion, and literature. Intellectuals widely regard it as a fundamental work on Latin American Marxism.

Mariátegui's revolutionary activities were not to remain on a solely theoretical level. He made numerous demands that indicated the nature of the socialism he wished to construct in Peru, including labor and social reforms, an end to the hated *enganche* (debt peonage) system, implementation of an eight-hour workday, an increase in salaries, and the establishment of a minimum wage. In order to agitate for these changes, he founded the *Partido Socialista Peruano* (PSP, Peruvian Socialist Party) in 1928 and served as its first secretary general. In 1929, the PSP launched the *Confederación General de Trabajadores del Perú* (CGTP, General Confederation of Peruvian Workers), a Marxist-oriented trade union federation, as an effort of the party to organize the working class. Both the PSP and the CGTP were involved in an active internationalism, and participated in Communist International–sponsored meetings.

The exact extent and nature of Mariátegui's organizational activities is not entirely clear, though apparently he was actively involved in the organization of communist cells all over Peru. His activities were enough of a threat to the security of the Peruvian state that twice the Leguía dictatorship arrested and imprisoned him, although he was never convicted of any crime. The first arrest came in 1924 for his alleged subversive activity at the González Prada Popular University. The arrest triggered an immediate and strong international reaction, and he was soon released. The Leguía dictatorship arrested Mariátegui for a second time in 1927 and charged him with involvement in a communist plot. He was detained for only six days at a military hospital, but afterward he continued to be a victim of police harassment and surveillance. In September 1929, Mariátegui's working-class periodical

*Labor* was shut down, and in November of the same year the police raided his house and "kidnapped" him for three days. Mariátegui rejected the validity of the charges, and claimed they were politically motivated. "Naturally, they speak of a communist conspiracy," Mariátegui wrote to a friend. Mariátegui had published articles in both *Amauta* and *Labor* that were critical of the lack of safety measures and exploitative labor practices at Cerro de Pasco, a copper mine owned by a U.S. company. The Peruvian government feared that Mariátegui was "defending and inciting the workers to resistance." His support for the miners' organizational struggles and ensuing strike action alarmed the North American corporation, and the Peruvian government did not want to alienate powerful foreign economic interests.[9]

Although the political party and labor confederation he had helped to launch flourished, Mariátegui's health floundered. He planned to move to Argentina in search of a better climate, both for his health and his political work, when he died on April 16, 1930, at the age of thirty-six. After his death, the movement that Mariátegui had founded lost its vitality and its revolutionary potential.


IDEOLOGY


Mariátegui had the audacious attitude of a young reporter; using a wide diversity of life experiences and intellectual sources, he looked for the story wherever it could be found. Although he was a convinced international Marxist, his Peruvian and Latin American identity inclined his thinking in original ways. He was one of the first to develop revolutionary socialist thought from within the Latin American reality—*"pensar en América Latina,"* to think *in* Latin America—which Chilean philosopher Helio Gallardo suggested that committed Latin American intellectuals must do. Such "thinking" is a "practical sociohistorical activity," which "must be aware of its social-historic roots."[10] Such thought may be couched in general theory, but it is historic and thus fully conscious of the particularities that determine the reality at hand.

By thinking in context, Mariátegui was able to elucidate the Peruvian and Latin American reality in light of his Marxist method and the wealth of personal and intellectual experiences he had gained in Europe and Peru. He was striving for an original analysis of his own reality. The well-known Mexican thinker Leopoldo Zea cites Simón Bolívar's teacher Simón Rodríguez to the effect that Latin America must not imitate either Europe or the United States, but must be original. "The necessity for originality in culture and philosophy is especially great," Zea adds. One cannot slavishly imitate academic or philosophical systems that are imported from Europe or elsewhere. It is necessary to think, to analyze, to create from within one's own reality. Only in this way can formerly colonialized people affirm their own culture and Indigenous essence and contribute to universal philosophy and culture.[11] This argument—which parallels in many respects the thinking of Frantz Fanon and other Third World nationalists—is most applicable to Mariátegui.[12]

It is difficult to position Mariátegui in the historic epoch in which he was writing. A few Latin American Marxists, such as Aníbal Ponce, may have been much better versed in the classical categories of European Marxism and thus better able to frame their analyses in accepted Marxist terminology. As with many Marxists in Latin America, this classical Eurocentric Marxist view, however, would militate strongly against original analyses *in situ* (from *within* the Latin American contextual reality). It would not foster the creation of *Latin American* Marxist thought or analysis, but would permit Latin Americans to employ a European Marxism that (like previous philosophic and cultural systems) was not of their own making. This, it could further be argued, would only help to perpetuate Latin American cultural dependency in a new—albeit far more subtle—way. Mariátegui was applying an empirical method to penetrate the essential economic realities that predominated in Peru. The application of Marxist methodology, which focused on economic and class factors, caused many of his contemporaries to criticize his work for being a servile application of Marxism to the Peruvian and Latin American reality.[13] The applicability of his method and the clarity of his thought seem, however, to suggest the need for more realistic interpretations.

The pioneering analysis that Mariátegui undertook represents one of the first attempts by a Latin American intellectual to understand the peculiarities of the local reality by using the universal categories that the development of modern socialist thought provided. Although it is far from deterministic materialism, its primary focus is economic. Further, in that the analysis was being conducted *within* the Latin American reality, progressive Peruvian writers like César Antonio Ugarte, Hildebrando Castro Pozo, and Abelardo Solis strongly influenced its direction. They wrote their respective works on the economic history of Peru and the Indigenous communities in Peru within the Peruvian and Latin American context.[14] Mariátegui combined their work with that of other radical *indigenistas* (educated outsiders who defended the rights of Indigenous peoples) like Luis E. Valcárcel (who later became one of Peru's best-known anthropologists) to form the empirical basis for his study of the Peruvian reality. By enriching his Marxist approach with works like these, he was able to begin to see the particularistic (and native/Third World) aspects of his national reality in terms of world trends (like the growth of capitalism) and general Marxist theory. His analysis was a fascinating, if not completely resolved, synthesis between the perspective international Marxism provided and that of the radical, *indigenista* nationalism that was developing in Peru. Mariátegui was one of the first to use Marxism to reconstruct Latin American social and economic history so that the poverty and exploitation of the masses could be understood in terms of the economic relations that *outside* forces imposed on the region. It was a very Peruvian attempt to explain Peruvian problems in universal terms, and yet to do so from a Peruvian–Latin American perspective. Mariátegui was providing the background for future generations of Peruvian and Latin American thinkers and social analysts who would use the insights that modern thought provided to better understand the Latin American reality from *their* place within that reality.

Mariátegui's analysis was, then, far from dogmatic and was even considered—in a critical article by the Russian Miroshevsky—to be of questionable Marxist orthodoxy.[15] His analysis of Peruvian reality saw the simultaneous existence of three economic systems: the remnants of the original Andean Indigenous communities (which he viewed as a carryover from a primitive communist economy); the European feudalism that Spain implanted; and a modern capitalist economy (with concomitant imperialist linkages) in certain coastal areas that were relatively free from the feudal dominance of the *gamonal* (a Peruvianism meaning "landowner" or "local boss"). This was an original contribution by Mariátegui and provided an excellent means of viewing a difficult—if not otherwise confusing—national reality.

The linkages between different economic systems provide an outstanding example of how Mariátegui fused Marxist theory to the concrete national conditions he analyzed. The Peruvian thinker also believed that if the workers were to play an important role in a future (socialist) society they must have an adequate educational and cultural base.[16] Even more immediately, he felt that the revolutionary segments of the society must imbue the workers and the young with an education that would prepare them for the role they must play in any socialist revolution.[17] The mention he makes of the importance of establishing Marxist study groups in his letters and his plans for an "Office of Worker Self-Education" demonstrate the importance he assigned to this activity.[18] He was well aware of the educational and cultural preparation that even the most progressive and enlightened of the Peruvian workers would need to be able to participate effectively in a strong movement.

The Peruvian socialism that Mariátegui envisioned could not, however, be a lifeless copy of another socialist system or a dogmatic application of Marxist thought. It must be a "heroic creation"; Latin America's own reality must give it life.[19] Here we begin to see some of the special genius that gave Mariátegui's formulations such force and vigor. His vision of European socialism and the successes and failures of the European socialist revolution had imbued him with a deep understanding of the intricacies of formulating socialist doctrine and action for specific national conditions. From his historical situation, he understood that Peru and Latin America generally were distinct from the urbanized, industrialized European countries about which Marx wrote. He thought it was up to Marxist revolutionaries to creatively apply the revolutionary essence of Marx's doctrine (and Lenin's innovations) to the concrete historical situation at hand. Only in such a way could successful revolutionary socialist action be created.[20] He was very critical of dogmatic Marxism, to the point that writers connected with the Communist International condemned him as a "national populist."[21]

Mariátegui made his formulations on the basis of his own interpretations of works by Marx, Engels, and Lenin, and other European socialists. He did not—or could not—ignore his own Peruvian reality or national intellectual currents. González Prada, the Peruvian highlands, and the radical Indigenous movements beginning in Peru all influenced his thinking. It was, then, a combination of these factors that congealed to provide Mariátegui with a unique vision and enabled him to create a special Peruvian socialism.

If Mariátegui had made a strict application of classical Marxist theory, he would have left almost all the peasants outside of the potentially revolutionary laboring classes. Many miners might also have been excluded since they had close ties to their peasant origins and often worked in isolated rural communities. Perhaps the best summation of Mariátegui's position is set forth in the agreement reached at the Barranco meeting that marked the formation of the Socialist Party (see selection V.5). The third point states, "According to the *current conditions in Peru*, the Committee will establish a socialist party, based on the organized masses of workers and peasants."[22] The peasants (not to mention the miners) were essential to Mariátegui's plans for a socialist revolution as well as a Socialist Party. They were considered necessary for the success of the movement. Again, we see an excellent example of how Mariátegui was able to fuse Marxist doctrine to the concrete conditions that existed in Peru. His doctrinal orientation enabled him to conceive of the movement in Marxist terms, yet his flexibility, his innovative nature, and his respect for the concrete conditions allowed him to posit the program in original, creative terms. Although his ideas and political activity were clearly linked to classical Marxist sources and the European international socialist movement, he was creating a new kind of national Third World thought.

Unlike most other Latin American Marxists, Mariátegui realized that the indigenous peoples' culture, identity, and exploitation at the hands of the whites and *mestizos* could enable conscious organizers to incorporate them into the revolutionary movement. This emphasis was one of Mariátegui's most important and lasting influences on Latin American Marxism. This was borne out when Guatemalan revolutionary movements like the *Ejército Revolucionario de los Pobres* (ERP, Poor Peoples' Revolutionary Army) became one with Indigenous communities and respected Maya customs and culture. They found that the Indians soon began to see the Marxist-inspired revolutionary movement as a continuation of their own struggle. The success of these Guatemalan movements in the early 1980s was closely tied to massive indigenous involvement in the revolutionary struggle.

Indeed, Mariátegui felt that once Indigenous peoples had seized socialism, they would cling to it fervently, since it coincided with traditionally based communal feelings.[23] Such modern socialism would, however, be consistent with the new historic conditions and thus would incorporate modern Western science and technology.[24] It would be a way of fusing the legacy of "Inca communism" with modern socialist theory and modern Western technology.

Mariátegui reinterpreted the traditional, Third World realities in light of modern Marxist thought. If his reconstruction of Peru's precolonial "Golden Age" was not entirely accurate, his appreciation for some of the virtues in traditional communalism (if not traditional society itself) was groundbreaking. It was also a major step in affirming Peru's Third World essence and thus negating the basis for Eurocentric thought among Peruvian and Latin American intellectuals. Yet, such a Third World approach was not common. As Carlos Altamirano observed:

> All too frequently the Latin American disciples of Marx did not know how to elaborate or resolve the dialectical relationship between the national problematic and the world context. Consequently, and all too

frequently, their works seem to be more the echo or commentary of other formulations than the result of authentic intellectual creation.[25]

Other Latin American writers have made similar observations.[26] Jorge Abelardo Ramos expresses a similar view in *El marxismo de Indias*. He vehemently attacks the "disproportionate Europeanization of Marxism in Latin America," proposing a complete break with revolutionary phraseology that is copied from Europe and as a result is so lacking in substance that it actually creates an obstacle to the specific understanding of Latin American realities.[27]

As should be abundantly clear, Mariátegui was very much the exception among his contemporaries in breaking from a Eurocentric perspective. He focused on indigenous peoples, the peasants, a different type of party, and the importance of popular culture. Thus, for instance, Altamirano notes that Mariátegui was without doubt the most brilliant intellectual in the early history of Latin American Marxism.[28] He, like Ramos and many other subsequent Marxist intellectuals, recognized the importance of Mariátegui's efforts in adapting Marxism to their national realities precisely so that it could serve as a tool to understand better and eventually change that reality. "The road that Mariátegui chose shows us the only legitimate way to use Marxist thought and practice," Altamirano comments.[29]

Mariátegui had been able to creatively combine a wide range of intellectual and political trends at a crucial stage in the development of Latin American politics and ideas. He used his wide-ranging knowledge and experience to creatively fuse the most dynamic currents in Marxist thought and European culture to the growing national and Third World consciousness that was developing in Peru and Latin America. Although his Marxism did not coincide with the Russian Leninism that the Communist International began to project as the universal formula for socialist revolution, it proved to be extremely well adapted to national conditions. As such, it was an early—and perhaps unique—example of National Marxism in Latin America. It clearly was similar to Gramsci's Marxism and to later adaptations of socialist thought to the realities of Third World countries. In Latin

America, the subordination of a great deal of subsequent thought and praxis to an overly deterministic, European-oriented Marxism made adequate comprehension of Mariátegui's contribution difficult and did not allow many others to follow his path until much later. It took almost fifty years for most Latin American activists and leftist intellectuals to come to terms with the Peruvian *Amauta*'s unique contribution to social analysis and revolutionary thought. It was only after the Cuban and Nicaraguan revolutions, the "boom" in Latin American literature, and the implicit validation of a truly Latin American praxis and perception, that the full import of Mariátegui's endeavor could be understood. This volume includes a sampling of some of Mariátegui's most cogent works.

## HISTORY OF THE WORLD CRISIS

Upon Mariátegui's return from Europe, he gave a series of lectures on the "History of the World Crisis" at the newly formed González Prada Popular University in Lima. Now compiled as *Historia de la crisis mundial*, these lectures numbered seventeen in all and extended from June 1923 to January 1924. Complete texts for only nine of the lectures have survived. For the sixteenth, "La revolución Mexicana," only the newspaper account exists, although Mariátegui amply developed this theme in *Temas de nuestra América* and elsewhere.[30] For the remaining lectures, the editors of the *Obras Completas* presented the author's notes and newspaper accounts. Mariátegui develops many of the themes he initially presented as lectures more fully in *La escena contemporánea* and *Figuras y aspectos de la vida mundial*.[31] One of the principal aims of his lectures is to disseminate an understanding of the world crisis to the Peruvian proletariat. He notes that in Peru there is neither a press that would educate people politically nor socialist or union groups that could interest the proletariat in the world crisis. The only means of (revolutionary) education is that which the González Prada Popular University provided. To fulfill its mission, it must explain the profound malaise that affected the civilized peoples of the world.[32] Although, Mariátegui argues, the crisis is centered in Europe, it is a crisis of Western civilization. Capitalism has internationalized human life; internationalism is now a historical reality. Peru, like other countries, is also involved in the crisis, and these lectures are especially dedicated to the vanguard of the Peruvian proletariat. Mariátegui invites this vanguard "for various transcendental reasons" to study the process of the world crisis with him.[33] The proletariat, he continues, is no longer a spectator but a participant. Humanity is living in a revolutionary period. The world crisis is both economic and political, but above all ideological—it is a profound crisis of capitalist civilization. The tragedy of Europe is that capitalism no longer functions and socialism is not yet ready (*el capitalismo no puede más, y socialismo no puede todavía*).[34] By this time, Mariátegui's views had matured and reflected an understanding of the process of the internationalization of the Western capitalist system and the periodic crises that affect it so severely.

In these lectures, Mariátegui also dealt with national themes, as well as European and international events like the Versailles Peace Conference. He wanted to make his audience, which was mostly composed of workers, aware of the sweep of international events, their economic basis and interdependence, the capitalist crisis, the revolutionary movements and their potential, and the possibilities for Peru and the Peruvian proletariat. In the second lecture, which dealt with "War Literature," Mariátegui underlined the economic causes of the war and ended by noting that a few men and interests had involved the proletariat in the war and that the proletariat should consider whether it was worthwhile to reconstruct capitalist society so that another conflagration could occur in forty or fifty years, if not sooner.[35]

Mariátegui also discussed the Second International, noting that, despite the position of Lenin and Rosa Luxemburg, it was unable to take a definitive stand against the war, which was to cost the lives of so many workers, thus ensuring its own failure.[36] He would be even more biting in his criticisms of the Second International in his later writings. It is interesting to note that Mariátegui declared himself a partisan of "one proletarian front" (*frente unico proletariado*) and maintained that

before organizing themselves in sects or partisan groups, the workers
should group themselves in one federation, in which each would have
his or her own orientation but their common class credo would unite
all.[37] This seems to have been precisely the formula he followed when
he and his comrades organized the General Confederation of Peruvian
Workers in 1929.

Other lectures told the Peruvian workers and students of the revolutionary struggles in Germany and Hungary and made them aware of
proletarian heroes like Rosa Luxemburg and Bela Kun. He also nar-
rated the history of the Russian regime.[38] In these expositions, he
carefully noted that the Bolsheviks had their base in the industrialized
proletariat and that they had attracted the Russian peasants through
their program of peace and division of the land. At this time,
Mariátegui believed the peasants were not, however, prepared for
communism and might represent a possible threat to the regime in the
future.[39] Throughout his expositions (as with most of his writing), one
is struck by his realism and sensitivity to the dynamics of the political
process, as when he suggests that in formulating the New Economic
Program, "Soviet politics is based on reality and dictated by the facts
at hand."[40]

Mariátegui did not neglect Latin America's own revolution. In
his lecture on the Mexican Revolution, he developed its historical
trajectory, noted the importance of its agricultural significance, and
concluded by inviting the workers to salute the beginning of the
transformation of the Spanish American world.[41] The last of the seventeen lectures was dedicated to a eulogy of Lenin (who had recently died). In it, Mariátegui not only related Lenin's life but discussed
his role in the Russian Revolution and his writings, beginning with
*State and Revolution.*[42]

This series of lectures represents the beginning of Mariátegui's
efforts to educate and orient the working class in Peru. Workers (and
some students) attended the lectures, and for many of the participants
they provided the first exposure to international events. Up to that
time, there was very little socialist awareness. The Peruvian Socialist
Party that was founded in 1919 had by this time disappeared.

Anarchism, especially under González Prada's guidance, heavily influenced the workers.[43] The press was provincial and conservative. Many of the assembled workers even initially received Mariátegui with some hostility when he began his socialist expositions.[44] Anarchist thinking dominated the unions. Mariátegui approached this environment with his simple, lucid expositions of European and international themes. He clearly wanted to provide the "vanguard" of the Peruvian proletariat with some awareness of world events and the nascent socialist revolution that was in the air in Europe. It was at the Popular University that his simple manner and direct speeches began to attract a following among Peru's workers. He spoke clearly and used the second-person plural form of address (*vosotros*) in the tradition of socialist camaraderie. His explanations began to make many workers wonder what sort of (socialist) action they might begin in Peru.[45] They began to see the Bolshevik Revolution in a new light.

The Peruvian proletariat lacked a genuine class consciousness when Mariátegui arrived from Europe with his plans to form a communist movement.[46] Thus his first step was to begin a type of proletarian education that would sow the seeds from which consciousness could grow. It was no accident that he accepted an offer to teach in an environment where he could speak to the workers directly and intermix dialectics with didactics. He went to special pains to stress the international nature of capitalist exploitation—and the need for international socialist organization. He illuminated the struggles of the communists in Germany, Russia, and Hungary, and suggested that any loss the workers in Germany suffered was also a loss for their Peruvian comrades. He repeatedly stressed international ties and the need for an *international* socialist revolution. Although he did not discuss Peru directly (perhaps because of the Leguía dictatorship), he suggested that the European and American capitalists were living from exploitation throughout Asia, Africa, and Latin America (and thus Peru as well). His discussion of the Mexican Revolution and his invitation to the workers to salute it as the first step in a Latin American transformation suggested that there were indeed imminent possibilities for change in Latin America if not

Peru. Mariátegui's later writings and books would help to delineate the exact nature of these possibilities.

Somewhat anachronistically, the editors inserted an essay titled "Veinticinco años de sucesos extranjeros" (Twenty-five Years of Foreign Events), which Mariátegui wrote in 1929, at the end of the volume of his lectures. It is a succinct account of world events from 1904 to 1929 that the author supplied for the magazine *Variedades* to commemorate its twenty-fifth anniversary. Mariátegui gives a factual summary of important events, paying special attention to fascism in Italy, the revolution in China, the nationalist movement in India, and the Mexican Revolution.[47] Mariátegui treated many of the same themes in his lectures, but by 1929 he was much more aware of the changed situation in Europe and especially of the threat from fascism and other forms of reaction, such as what Primo de Rivera's fascism represented in Spain. In reference to Lenin, his exposition focused more strongly on Lenin's brand of international communism (which perhaps suggests less emphasis on the anarcho-sindicalist Georges Sorel). Indeed, this article was published March 6 and 13, 1929, just before Mariátegui sent the Peruvian delegation to the first meeting of Latin America's Communist parties with instructions to seek affiliation with the Third International.

## THE CONTEMPORARY SCENE

Most of the subjects touched on in the lectures assembled in *Historia de la crisis mundial* were elaborated in Mariátegui's first published work, *La escena contemporánea*. Issued by Editorial Minerva in 1925, this book is composed of articles that Mariátegui published in the Lima magazines *Variedades* and *Mundial* from 1923, when he returned to Lima, to 1925. He made only slight revisions to the essays to prepare them for publication in book form. In the preface to this work (see selection I.5), Mariátegui wrote that he did not endeavor to present an explanation of his time:

I do not think it is possible to imagine the entire panorama of the contemporary world in one theory. . . . We have to explore it and know it,
episode by episode, facet by facet. Our view and our imagination will
always be delayed in respect to the entirety of the phenomenon.
Therefore, the best way to explain and communicate our time is one
that is perhaps a little bit journalistic and a bit cinematographic.[48]

We find that Mariátegui, though a Marxist, had an appreciation for
the inadequacy of any theory to explain *all* facets of any phenomenon
as complex as the twentieth century. Indeed, reflecting on this quote
one can reach an appreciation for the agility of the thinker's mind.

Among the work's seven chapters, the one on fascism is among
Mariátegui's most penetrating essays. Mussolini is seen as the bellicose extremist he was. Mariátegui realized that the *Duce* was able to
attract the middle class only because of the maladies from which it
was suffering. He noted that the state of virtual civil war in Italy had
stimulated the growth of fascism and that the Italian socialists were
guilty of not using politics to help change middle-class ideas. Aware
of the diametrically opposed positions of fascism and socialism, he
noted that

in Italy, the reaction offers its maximum experiment, its maximum
spectacle. Italian fascism plainly represents the anti-revolution, or as
many prefer to call it, the counter-revolution. The Fascist offensive is
explained in Italy as a consequence of a revolutionary retreat, if not
defeat.[49]

In a brief but potent section, he examines Yankee democracy and
Yankee imperialism:

More than a great democracy the U.S. is a great empire. The growth
of the U.S. had to lead to an imperialist conclusion. American capitalism could not develop any more within the confines of the U.S. and
her colonies. It manifests, for this reason, a great force for expansion
and domination.[50]

This analysis would seem to suggest a direct import from Lenin. Indeed, Mariátegui remarks that "imperialism is, as Lenin said in a revolutionary pamphlet, the highest stage of capitalism."[51] Mariátegui relied on Lenin's *Imperialism: The Highest Stage of Capitalism* for his formulations on imperialism and the expansive nature of the U.S. economy. This influence is less clear in his lectures, although their abbreviated form and the scanty nature of Mariátegui's notes and the existing newspaper accounts make an exact determination impossible. It is, in any event, of considerable significance that as early as 1925 Mariátegui was conversant with Lenin's theory of imperialism, and that he was applying it to understand the nature of the U.S. empire and its relationship to Latin America. This further supports our earlier assertion that Mariátegui had begun to read Lenin while he was in Europe. Likewise, it helps to underline the fact that although Mariátegui called himself simply a Marxist or a socialist, much of his thought was more akin to Lenin's and the Third International's than to any less radical socialist ideology. These facts would also seem to give further credence to the assertion that Mariátegui was (pursuant to the plans he had adopted in his Genoa meeting with other advocates of Peruvian communism) helping to disseminate information and ideas that would give sustenance to a growing class-consciousness and would pave the way for the eventual formation of a class party in Peru.

In the chapter on the Russian Revolution, Mariátegui first discusses Trotsky and Lunacharsky and ends with a discussion of Zinoviev and the Third International: "The Second International was an organizational machine, the Third International is a combat machine."[52] Lenin, however, is mentioned only in relation to other themes. This is somewhat perplexing in that Lenin received a more prominent treatment in the lectures and would find prominence in most of Mariátegui's later writings. One possible explanation is that subsequent to Lenin's demise, Mariátegui wanted to focus attention on the new Soviet leaders. He had, as mentioned above, already underlined the importance of Lenin's thoughts on imperialism. The possibility also exists that he wanted to skirt the subject of Leninist internal politics and Communist Party organization because of his alliance with APRA (which was beginning to define itself as distinct from any communist movement) and because of the extremely repressive nature of the Leguía dictatorship, which might have equated a strong domestic focus on Lenin with subversive activity. Leguía was less alarmed about references to international events (and thus not national affairs), and Víctor Haya de la Torre was vehemently anti-imperialistic. Such a tactic would have encountered minimum resistance in both of these camps and would explain why only reference to Lenin's anti-imperialism would be permissible.

The chapter on the socialist crisis carries considerable import. Mariátegui is highly critical of the inability of European socialists to unify their forces. He argues, for instance, that France needed to liquidate the artificial differences that separated her socialist forces.[53] The Peruvian was also critical of the unrevolutionary nature of the Socialist Party. In a passage that is strangely reminiscent of Régis Debray[54] and many more current radicals, Mariátegui states that in France "the bureaucracy of the Socialist Party and the General Confederation of Workers (C.G.T.) lacks a revolutionary impulse. They are unable, then, to join the new International. A staff of orators, writers, bureaucrats, and lawyers . . . cannot be the leaders of a revolution."[55] (One is also here reminded of Roger Garaudy's criticisms of the French communists in the 1960s.)[56] Likewise, in Italy "the survival of the reformist spirit in the structure and leaders of the Italian proletariat . . . was evident," Mariátegui contended. "Leaders sabotaged the revolution."[57] He also notes that even the antifascist battle did not unify the Italian socialist forces.[58] The division markedly debilitated the socialist movement. Therefore, Mariátegui is quite pointed in his criticism of leftist factionalism. It seems clear that, as suggested previously, this assessment helped to influence his support for the *Frente Único* strategy in Peru and his decision to form a party that was socialist by name but integrated as many leftist groups as were consistent with its orientation. As one might imagine from his criticism of the timidity of the French and Italian socialists, he wanted such a unified Socialist Party to be revolutionary in its

stance and thus affiliated with the other revolutionary forces represented by the Third International.

In the chapter "La Revolución y la Inteligencia" (The Revolution
and the Intelligentsia), Mariátegui discusses intellectuals like Henri
Barbusse (who heavily influenced his thinking), Maxim Gorky, and
Filippo Marinetti, and sets forth his ideas on the possible role of the
intellectual in the revolution. "It is not possible to devote oneself
halfway to the revolution," Mariátegui wrote. "The intellectuals who
have a real revolutionary faith have no other choice than to accept a
place in collective action."[59] In a paragraph that might easily describe
his own traits, Mariátegui suggests that "intellectuals resist discipline,
program, or system. Their psychology is individualist, their thinking
is heterodox. . . . The individuality of the intellectual always feels
superior to the common rules."[60] He finally argues that the intellectual's intelligence creates a revolutionary obligation that the intelligentsia, being endowed with a creative function, cannot ignore.[61]

The penultimate chapter discusses "The Message from the
Orient" and, as was the case with the lectures, pays particular attention to India. Indeed, the argument is much the same as in his lectures,
but he is more specific in his objections to Gandhi as a politician. He
suggests that revolutionaries have to choose between suffering violence and using it,[62] and further argues that "if one does not wish spirit and intelligence to be commanded by force, one must resolve to put
force under the command of intelligence and spirit."[63]

*La escena contemporánea* numbers some 218 pages, but it does
indeed provide an excellent view of the forces that shaped world
events in the postwar period. Sections of the work—particularly
"Biología del fascismo" (Biology of fascism) —are remarkable for their
perceptiveness, even by today's standards.

## *AMAUTA*, THE WISE TEACHER

As a means of further disseminating his ideas and educating the reading public in Lima, Mariátegui had for some time thought he needed

his own magazine. In September of 1926, Mariátegui published the first issue of *Amauta*. As suggested in a letter from César Falcón, Mariátegui (like Gramsci and Barbusse) was especially interested in creating a progressive group of intellectuals as one element of the necessary class movement. He had considered the idea of such a magazine since his European stay and was finally able to bring it to fruition. As Mariátegui said in the introduction to the journal, "one would have to be very unwise not to realize that at this moment, an historical magazine is being born in Peru."[64] Indeed, Mariátegui wanted to use *Amauta* to attract intellectuals to the "vanguardist movement that the magazine represented."[65]

If *Amauta* had its tactical aspects, it was simultaneously a superb vehicle for disseminating ideas. Further, it was one of the outstanding literary magazines that Latin America produced during the first part of this century. In the "Presentación de *Amauta*" (Presentation of *Amauta*), Mariátegui clearly stated that the object of this magazine is "to raise, clarify and comprehend Peruvian problems from a scientific, doctrinaire point of view." He went on to say that "we will study all the great movements of political, artistic, literary, and scientific renovation. All that is human is ours."[66]

The first number opened with a selection from *Tempestad en los Andes* by Luis E. Valcarcel. It contained translations of selections from Sigmund Freud and sketches by George Grosz. José Sabogal's drawings and woodcuts were evident throughout. One finds poetry like that of José María Eguren interspersed among the essays. The indigenous theme finds frequent representation. Authors discuss the Mexican Revolution and the Spanish dictatorship, and it even includes a poem by Alberto Hidalgo, "Situating Lenin."[67] In the section "Books and Magazines" are artful reviews of important works like Unamuno's *L'agonie du christianisme*.

After carefully surveying the contents of the issue, one comes to appreciate Mariátegui's words in the "Presentación": "It is not necessary to expressly state that *Amauta* is not open to all spiritual currents.... We make no concession to the generally treacherous criteria of the tolerance of ideas. For us, there are good ideas and bad ideas."[68]

*Amauta* suggests its socialist criteria at an early stage. The magazine did, however, entertain articles, poems, and drawings from a variety of left-of-center sources. It included not only articles or selections from figures with a clear ideological definition like Marx or Lenin, but figures who were progressive in their applied thought (such as Freud), or in their aesthetic output (the Peruvian poet José María Eguren). Up until Mariátegui's break with Haya de la Torre in 1927, one even found articles and letters from Haya and Aprista intellectual Luis Alberto Sánchez. Several of Pablo Neruda's poems also appeared, and even a poem by Juana de Ibarbourou, which she wrote expressly for Mariátegui. The magazine contains several articles by and one letter from Miguel de Unamuno as well as a selection by José Ortega y Gasset. One issue began with a discussion of Peruvian art; another carried a delightfully illustrated section on Diego Rivera's work. Many Peruvian poets, including not only Eguren but César Vallejo and Magda Portal, submitted their poetry to the magazine. Mariátegui printed selections from José Vasconcelos's writings, in addition to several chapters of Mariano Azuela's *Los de abajo* (one of the most important novels from the revolutionary period in Mexico).[69] Mariátegui's North American friend Waldo Frank was also represented in the pages of the publication.

A whole generation of Peruvian writers found expression in *Amauta*'s pages. Atenor Orrego and Luis Valcárcel frequently submitted articles. Enrique López Albújar's work found its way to *Amauta*, as did that of Abelardo Solis. Jorge Basadre, who was then quite radical, penned several articles for the magazine. The later numbers of *Amauta* saw the increasing participation of clearly defined Marxists like Eudocio Ravines, Esteban Pavletich, and Ricardo Martínez de la Torre. César Falcón had participated from the first issue.

As the magazine developed, there was a change in orientation. In the tenth number of *Amauta* (the first to appear after it was closed down in 1927), Mariátegui wrote an editorial that he called "Second Act." Suggesting the genre of his magazine, he wrote the following lines: "When intellectual work is not metaphysical but *dialectic*, that is to say historic, it has its risks. Is it not obvious that there is a new kind of work accident in the contemporary world?"[70]

In this same number, Mariátegui began a section in *Amauta* entitled "La Vida Económica." In the presentation of this section, Mariátegui spoke of the importance of a "scientific and organic" study of Peruvian problems. Likewise, he stated that "in our time, economics explains the life of a country better than any other thing. Even those who do not accept historical materialism . . . are without a doubt convinced that economic factors singularly control the epoch in which we live." He further mentions the importance of "outlining the economic profile of Peruvian history with notes and data."[71]

The tenth issue also witnessed the intensification of other economic themes that had appeared from the beginning of the magazine. It includes an article on "The Problems of the Land," which Mariátegui later included as part of the *Seven Essays. Amauta* had previously published an article by Mariátegui that was also included in the *Seven Essays*. It dealt with the evolution of the Peruvian economy and regionalism and centralism. The fifth through the sixteenth issue carried a section entitled "The Process of the *Gamonal*" and contained a subsection called the "Bulletin of Indigenous Defense," which denounced the crimes and abuses of *gamonales* and their agents. This latter theme was related to the general *indigenista* orientation of the magazine—an orientation that Mariátegui focused on economic factors.

This dialectic orientation becomes more marked after the rupture with the Apristas (in the middle of 1928) and the development of an incipient classconsciousness among some intellectuals and workers. To celebrate *Amauta*'s second anniversary, Mariátegui wrote an extensive editorial that he called "Aniversario y balance" (Anniversary and Balance Sheet, see selection I.6). This is one of Mariátegui's more important public statements, and it definitively underlined the phenomenon of "concentration and polarization" that he had suggested in "Presentación de *Amauta*" might occur:[72]

On our banner, we inscribe one great, simple word: socialism. (With this slogan we affirm our absolute independence from the idea of a Nationalist Party, petty bourgeois and demagogic.) . . . In these two years, *Amauta* has been a magazine of ideological definition. . . . To us, the work of ideological definition seems completed. . . . *Amauta*'s first act has concluded. In the second act, it does not have to call itself a magazine of the "new generation," of the "vanguard," of "the left." To be faithful to the Revolution, it is enough to be a socialist magazine.

In this America of small revolutions, the same word Revolution frequently lends itself to misunderstanding. We have to reclaim it rigorously and intransigently. We have to restore its strict and exact meaning. The Latin American Revolution will be nothing more and nothing less than a stage, a phase of the world revolution. It will simply and clearly be the socialist revolution. . . . We certainly do not want socialism in Latin America to be a copy or imitation. It should be heroic creation. We have to give life to Indo-American socialism with our own reality, in our own language. Here is a mission worthy of a new generation.[73]

To celebrate this new orientation, *Amauta* began to publish a series of Mariátegui's articles that were called "Defense of Marxism." This series continued in *Amauta* through 1928, and ended with the June issue (number 24) of 1929. The collection of essays—which will be discussed in depth later—was subsequently collected in book form as *Defensa del marxismo* and is well represented in this anthology. *Amauta* also included doctrinaire articles by Marxists like Eudocio Ravines and even excerpts from Bukharin's "Notes on the Problem of the Theory of Historical Materialism."[74] By the late 1920s, *Amauta* had indeed defined its position.

Beginning with the seventeenth issue (September 1928), Mariátegui also inaugurated a section called "Panorama Móvil" (Mobile Overview). This heading was artfully employed not only to discuss economic conditions and to continue the discussions of the *gamonal* abuses but also to draw attention to union affairs and organizational drives by different workers' groups. *Amauta* had evolved (according to Mariátegui's plan) to become a class-centered publication with a manifest doctrinaire orientation. In the process, it had, however, maintained exceptional literary and aesthetic standards. The magazine ceased publication shortly after Mariátegui's death in 1930.


## SEVEN ESSAYS

Many of Mariátegui's essays on the economy and land printed in his journal *Amauta* were combined with other articles to form Mariátegui's best-known work, *7 ensayos de interpretación de la realidad peruana* (Seven Interpretive Essays on Peruvian Reality). The *Seven Essays* (Volume 2 of the *Obras Completas*) treats seven themes that Mariátegui had previously developed: "Outline of the Economic Evolution," "The Problem of the Indian," "The Problem of the Land," "Public Education," "The Religious Factor," "Regionalism and Centralism," and "Literature on Trial." In the words of the author, "this work is but a contribution to socialist criticism of the problems and history of Peru." Nor is Mariátegui "an impartial, objective critic." Rather, he explains, "My judgments are nourished by my ideals, my sentiments, my passions. I have an avowed and resolute ambition: to assist in the creation of Peruvian Socialism. I am far removed from the academic technique of the university."[75] Ever since Mariátegui's European experience, he had been trying to come to terms with his Peruvian reality. He wished to take advantage of European culture, praxis, theory, and the contribution of the new group of progressive Peruvian and Latin American intellectuals to better understand his own nation.

The *Seven Essays* and related writings are an original analysis of Peruvian problems based on a flexible Marxist analysis and essentially unique Peruvian conditions. Mariátegui later suggested that his analysis might be insufficiently rigorous for orthodox Marxists because of the importance he accorded to the Sorelian influence. He had, in any event, a well-defined perspective and a developed Marxist method. Likewise, he was well aware of the works of Peruvian writers like González Prada, Castro Pozo, Ugarte, and Valcárcel. He also relied heavily on the *Extracto estadístico del Perú*. With these influences he developed one of the most (if not the most) penetrating analysis of Peruvian reality yet to be published. Indeed, Harold Eugene Davis suggests that the *Seven Essays* is "one of the greatest Latin American books of the Twentieth Century."[76]

Mariátegui's best-known work begins with an outline of the economic evolution of the Peruvian nation. He skillfully utilizes an eclectic Marxist focus to better understand the economic forces that have shaped the development of Peru. Relying on statistics and other Peruvian writers to focus on the economic facts, he elucidates four stages of post-conquest history: the colonial economy, the early republican economy, the guano and saltpeter period, and the present economy. The analysis further suggests that the Inca economy was an adequate (socialist) mechanism that ensured the material well-being of the masses. The conquest, however, completely destroyed this productive organization and was unable to replace it. The colonizers' primary interest was in mining Peruvian gold and silver, not in caring for Indigenous peoples.

As is characteristic of his style throughout the work, Mariátegui sets aside the embellished descriptive narrative that had often characterized writing about the Peruvian nation. In a terse, almost cryptic style, he argues that the popularity of republican ideas from France or the United States is not due to the ideas of the Encyclopedists. Rather, "the needs of the development of the Western or, more precisely, capitalist civilization, determined South America's independence."[77] The new Peruvian Republic looked to the West for its needs and quickly became tied to the Western capitalist system. Further, Mariátegui reminds us that the incursion of British capital into Peru coincided with the sale of guano and saltpeter on the international market.[78] As more foreign capital arrived, the coastal economy began to evolve from feudal to capitalist modes of production. In his discussion of the contemporary Peruvian economy, the author argues that elements of three different economies existed simultaneously: the feudal economy (in the highlands); the capitalist economy (on the coast); and the Indigenous communistic economy (also in the highlands).[79] Much of Peruvian agriculture was still under a *latifundia* system that was semifeudal in nature. The landholding class was not yet transformed into a capitalist bourgeoisie; thus modern capitalism was not yet entirely dominant, although it was fast encroaching on the domain of the landowner.

The work contains Mariátegui's most cogent discussion of the Indigenous question (chapter 2). "Any treatment of the problems of the Indian," Mariátegui writes, "that fails or refuses to recognize it as a socioeconomic problem is but a sterile, theoretical exercise destined to be completely discredited."[80] He, like González Prada before him, believed that the economic condition of the Indians was essential to any understanding—or liberation. Indeed, Mariátegui remarked that the socialist critic defines the problem by looking for its causes in the country's economy.[81] Indigenous impoverishment is a result of the land tenure system. One cannot talk of changing the lot of the Indian without changing the feudal landholding system. The influence of González Prada's "Our Indians" is readily apparent in Mariátegui's writings.[82] Not surprisingly, Mariátegui believes that the solution must come from Indigenous peoples and not from any attempts to moralize or educate them by well meaning, but confused, liberal idealists or missionaries.[83]

In the following chapter of the *Seven Essays*, "El problema de la tierra" (The Problem of the Land; see selection I.2), Mariátegui sharpens his analysis of the problems that the land-tenure system occasioned in Peru. He sets aside the apostolic position of Bishop Bartolomé de las Casas, a colonial bishop well known for his defense of Indigenous peoples in Spanish America, in order to establish the economic nature of the problems. The most worrisome inheritance from colonial Spain, he argues, was the feudal economic regime, which did not permit the development of a modern capitalist class. The old landholding class—still feudal in nature—had maintained its hold on the country. The feudal economy that Spain imposed on Peru was less efficient than the Inca "communism." The latter could at least supply the ten million inhabitants of Tawantinsuyu (the Inca Empire) with sufficient sustenance. Even the republic's liberal constitution had allowed the feudal landholders to encroach continually on the *comunidades* (the communal landholding of the Indigenous communities). The communal feelings of the people had, however, continued into the present day.

Neither the War of Independence nor the republic that followed attacked the *latifundio*. The aristocratic landholders, Mariátegui reminds us, remained the dominant class. As a result, the necessary elements for a capitalist economy hardly existed in Peru at the time of independence.[84] A new legal and economic order could not be the work of a strongman (*caudillo*). Rather, a class must create it. Since a bourgeoisie did not exist in Peru, a bourgeois regime did not exist. The feudal regime remained operative and was especially well entrenched among the *latifundios* in the highlands.

On the coast, Mariátegui continues, the *latifundio* had evolved from feudal to capitalist techniques. This was not the case in the highlands, where "the large landholdings have fully retained its feudal character, pitting a much stronger resistance than the community to the development of the capitalist economy."[85] In the feudal haciendas, the state's laws were not valid. Everything was subject to the landowner's control inside the estate. Scholars commonly contend that Inca communism was not the same as the modern industrial communism that Marx and Sorel envisioned. Different historical epochs produce different kinds of communism.[86] Thus certain aspects of Inca communism are incompatible with our epoch, although this was not the case with the agrarian civilization that then existed. However, the "community" that is the present-day carryover from early Inca communism "is a system of production that keeps alive in the Indian the moral incentives that stimulate him to do his best work."[87] Indeed, the "communities" can be changed into cooperatives (and therefore form a rural base for modern Peruvian socialism).[88]

In the last part of this chapter, Mariátegui develops one of the more interesting aspects of his economic analysis and anticipates much of the subsequent neo-Marxist and dependency literature:

> Peru's economy is a colonial economy. Its movement, its development
> are subordinated to the interests and the necessities of the markets in

London and New York. . . . Our *latifundistas*, our landowners, whatever their illusions of independence, are in reality only intermediary
agents of foreign capitalism.[89]

Mariátegui realizes that the remnants of the feudal *latifundio* system are tied to the international capitalist system through the sale of
export commodities. Although many of the internal relations were
feudal in nature, the external ties to the international capitalist system through the mechanisms of the international commodities market establish the dependent nature of the Peruvian economy. This
also explained why much of the rich coastal land that was once
devoted to the production of foodstuffs for the local population was
now used to produce cash crops such as cotton. Mariátegui argues
that the subjugation of coastal agriculture to the interests of British
and United States capital kept it from organizing and developing
according to the specific needs of Peru's economy. Further, he
believes that the laissez-faire policy that had been so sterile in Peru
should be definitely replaced by a social policy of nationalizing the
great sources of wealth.[90]

Mariátegui also examines other aspects of Peru's dependent relationship. In the fourth essay, Mariátegui outlines the ideological and
political basis of public education in Peru. He explains that in public
education, as in other aspects of the national life, one finds the super-
imposition of foreign elements without the necessary adaptation to
local conditions. Three successive foreign cultures heavily influenced
education in Peru: the Spanish legacy, the French influence, and
influence from North America. The Spanish influence, however,
remained dominant in Peru. Others were only grafted onto the
Hispanic framework without substantially altering it.[91] Peruvian education was therefore devoid of a national spirit or sufficient national
identity. This same Spanish influence ensured the persistence of a literary, rhetorical orientation.

The French period of influence coincided with the coming of the
republic that, Mariátegui adds, only intensified existing problems.
The 1920 reform movement (which was initiated in Córdoba in 1918)

heralded the rise of the North American democratic influence. However, the resultant educational system only reached a small fraction of the population even at the primary level. The doors of higher education were closed to the poor. The colonial aristocracy created economic and political systems that had long kept the Latin American university under the tutelage of the oligarchy and their supporters. The purpose of the university was chiefly to provide lawyers and other professionals for the ruling class.[92]

In concluding the chapter, Mariátegui argues that education must be considered as an economic and social problem. Accordingly, Peruvian education was increasingly dependent on the evolving class interests of the bourgeois economy in which, because of their different economic bases, feudal and modern bourgeois interests would clash and would be challenged by the growing class consciousness of the urban proletariat.[93]

In the fifth essay, Mariátegui develops a fascinating analysis of the "Religious Factor" in Peru. "The times of *a priori* anticlericalism are long gone," he writes. "Revolutionary criticism no longer demeans the service to humanity or the place in history that religion or churches play."[94] Though at variance with the usual interpretation of Marx's writings on religion, this section allows considerable insight into Mariátegui's focus on the religious factor in the development of human society and is quite clearly compatible with the Theology of Liberation movement that became so popular in Latin America in the early 1980s.[95] It also suggests the extent to which his analysis was rooted in his own reality and life experiences.

The penultimate essay (chapter 6) focuses on "Regionalism and Centralism." Here, Mariátegui applies his analysis to move beyond the inherent limitations in most discussions of this conflict, pointing out that in the traditional polemic between federalism and centralism, the solution is not to be found in federalism. Rather, "our economic and political organization needs to be totally examined and transformed."[96] Decentralism, for instance, would not signify any progress toward the solution of the problem of the Indian. Indeed, decentralism would increase the power of *gamonalismo*. "Government form is

no longer of paramount concern," Mariátegui suggests by way of conclusion. "We live in an era where economics only too obviously dominates and absorbs politics. In every country of the world, discussion
of the economic bases of the state no longer takes precedence over
reform of its administrative machinery."[97]

The last and the longest of the seven essays concerns Mariátegui's
evaluation of national literature. Our focus on political matters does
not warrant a lengthy discussion of this interesting exposition. Certain
aspects of this essay should, nonetheless, be underlined. Firstly, this is,
to our knowledge, one of the first times (if not the first) that Peruvian
literature was judged from a national proletarian point of view. That is
to say, Mariátegui was applying his own analysis, which was heavily
imbued with his Marxist perspective, to Peruvian literature. He was, in
effect, putting literature on trial to see if it had fulfilled its mission of
nationalizing the culture and creating some consciousness of national
conditions. Let us allow Mariátegui to speak for himself:

> I do not pretend to be an impartial or agnostic critic, which in any
> event I do not believe is possible. Philosophical, political, and world
> concerns influence any critic. . . .
>
> The human spirit is indivisible and it must be so to achieve plen-
> ty and harmony. I declare without hesitation that I bring to literary
> exegesis all my political passions and ideas, although in view of the
> way this word has been misused, I should add that my politics are
> philosophy and religion. . . .
>
> This does not mean that I judge literature and art without refer-
> ence to aesthetics, but that in the depth of my consciousness, the aes-
> thetic concept is so intimately linked to my political and religious
> ideas that, although it does not lose its identity, it cannot operate
> independently or differently. . . .
>
> I confront his [Riva Agüero's] unacknowledged *Civilista* and
> Colonialist bias with my avowed revolutionary and socialist sympa-
> thies. I do not claim to be a temperate and impartial judge; I declare
> myself a passionate and belligerent adversary.[98]

Secondly, Mariátegui's position is not simply that of one who is blindly wedded to a class analysis. His exposure to European critics like Croce made for a wider vision:

> I shall not use the Marxist classification of literature as feudal or aristocratic, bourgeois or proletarian. In order not to strengthen the impression that I have organized my case along political or class lines, I shall base it on aesthetic history and criticism. This will serve as a method of explanation rather than as a theory that *a priori* judges and interprets works and their authors.[99]

It should not surprise us to find that Mariátegui criticizes the fact that, with few exceptions, the Peruvian writers have almost never felt any tie with the common people. Nor is he critical of Manuel González Prada for not evolving beyond his anarchism to a more scientific socialism. But neither should we be given pause when we find that one of the Peruvian's most unusual eulogies is reserved for José María Eguren—a "pure poet" without any political orientation. Such, then, were Mariátegui's literary views.

## THE DEFENSE OF MARXISM

As conditions were changing in Peru, Mariátegui was evolving in more doctrinaire directions. Starting in September 1928, *Amauta* began to publish a series of Mariátegui's articles entitled "Defensa del marxismo." With these, Mariátegui launched a prolonged critique of revisionist tendencies in Europe and a defense of revolutionary Marxism as interpreted by Lenin and other modern revolutionaries. The series continued consecutively through June 1929, but was only published in book form posthumously.[100] The sixteen essays, which were originally published in *Amauta*, cover only one hundred and seven pages. A second section composed of related writing ("Teoría y práctica de la reacción," or Theory and practice of the reaction) comprised another thirty-five pages.

Mariátegui begins the essay (see selection III.4) by suggesting that Henri de Man is far from correct when he asserts in *Beyond Marxism* that not only the revision but the liquidation of Marxism is at hand. Nor, Mariátegui continues, is de Man alone in this assertion. There have been a series of similar reactions to Marxism. Within the camp of those who reacted to Marx's original formulations, there are groups of revisionists who, like de Man and Eduard Bernstein, have been more influenced by the reformist spirit of Lassalle than by the revolutionary thoughts of the author of *Das Kapital*.[101] Mariátegui argues that

> The true revision of Marxism, in the sense of the renovation and continuation of the work of Marx, has been done, in theory and practice, by another category of revolutionary intellectual—George Sorel, in studies that separate and distinguish what is essential and substantive in Marx from that which is formal and contingent. In the first two decades of the current century . . . he represented the return of the dynamic and revolutionary conception of Marx and his insertion in the new intellectual, organic reality. Through Sorel, Marxism assimilates the substantial elements and acquisitions of philosophic currents after Marx. . . . And Lenin appears incontestably in our epoch as the most energetic and profound restorer of Marxist thought, whatever doubts plague the disillusioned author of *Beyond Marxism*. Whether the reformists accept it or not, the Russian Revolution constitutes the dominant accomplishment of contemporary socialism.[102]

Although all sections of the work are not so unambiguous, these quotations are representative of the main arguments of the work. They suggest Mariátegui's disdain for the social democratic "reformism" that Henri de Man represents. Likewise, Mariátegui had a high regard for revolutionary Marxism and those whom he considered to be its leaders. He was particularly attuned to Georges Sorel (*Reflections on Violence*) and V. I. Lenin, both of whom he thought had helped to keep Marxism developing in the dynamic revolutionary tradition that Marx set down.

Throughout the work, one finds a dialectical assertion of a revolutionary Marxism, that Lenin and events in the Soviet state influenced.

Mariátegui develops arguments for revolutionary Marxism that are the product of the refutation (negation) of parliamentary socialist positions like those of the Belgian Social Democrat Henri de Man. One then must read through Mariátegui's criticism to find the assertion. Such indirect assertions had a much better chance of being printed in a press that the Leguía dictatorship maintained under constant surveillance. The government had already closed *Amauta* once for six months; Mariátegui had already been imprisoned on the pretext of being part of a "communist plot." Conditions were such as to suggest caution, at least in articles on Marxism that would enjoy wide circulation.

Mariátegui suggests that many intellectuals tend to exaggerate Marxist determinism, though in reality "Marxism, wherever it has shown itself to be revolutionary—that is, where it has been Marxist— has never obeyed a passive and rigid determinism."[103] He further argued that Marx's political realism saw that when the capitalist process is most vigorous, it leads to socialism. But Mariátegui observes that Marx always understood that "a spiritual and intellectual preparation of the proletariat was necessary to realize it."[104] Further, the voluntary (*voluntarista*) character of socialism is truly not less evident, although less understood by the critics, than its determinism. "In the development of the proletarian movement," Mariátegui writes, "every word, every Marxist act resounds with faith, will, heroic and creative conviction, whose impulse it would be absurd to seek in a mediocre and passive determinist sentiment."[105] The influence of Mariátegui's Italian experience and exposure to Gramsci and Barbusse no doubt heavily influenced this aspect of his thought.

In the section on "Freudianism and Marxism," Mariátegui suggests that the Marxist dialectical principle does not reduce human action to a mechanical economy that would exclude psychological factors.[106] On the contrary, Mariátegui does not find the teachings of Marx incompatible with those of Freud.

The second section, "Teoria y practica de la reacción," was not originally published as part of "Defensa del marxismo" in *Amauta*, but was destined instead for inclusion in an edition of the work that

Mariátegui envisioned during his lifetime.[107] The following quotes (see selection IV.6) suggest the clarity and prescience of Mariátegui's analysis and the evolution of his thought:

> There is slight reason not to believe that Anglo-Saxon Capitalism will be the last one to speak for the bourgeoisie in the conflict between Roman law and Soviet law. . . . [108]

> All these facts indicate that the seat, the axis, the center of capitalist society is now found in North America. Yankee industry is best equipped for mass production at a lower cost.[109]

> The two poles of contemporary history are Russia and North America: capitalism and communism, both universalist although very different and distinct.[110]

Interestingly, the essays in this latter section were first published in 1927. Mariátegui's ability to view U.S. development and expansion in such Leninist terms would seem to indicate a rather mature Marxist understanding of the increasing competition between the standard-bearers of socialism and capitalism. Further, it suggests the continuity of Leninist and revolutionary Marxist thought throughout Mariátegui's written work.


IDEOLOGY AND POLITICS

Lamentably, no work published during Mariátegui's lifetime brings together the full force of the Peruvian's ideological writings. In an introductory note to the *Seven Essays*, Mariátegui mentions a book on the political and ideological evolution of Peru that he was writing.[111] He makes a second reference to this work in the autobiographical note that he sent to the First Latin American Communist Conference in 1929.[112] The originals of this work were, it seems, sent to César Falcón in Madrid for publication in Spain, but were somehow lost before any of them appeared in print.[113] By way of compensation, the editors of Biblioteca Amauta published a volume of doctrinaire theses and union speeches that correspond to such themes. A posthumous compilation, *Ideología y política*, is probably one of the best sources for an understanding of Mariátegui's political thought. It contains the Peruvian thinker's writings that are most closely linked to his political activity.

The work itself numbers 260 pages, and contains five sections: Ideological Theses, Political and Union Writing, Polemic Themes, editorials from *Amauta,* and from Mariátegui's short-lived working-class newspaper, *Labor*. Many of the pieces contained in this work were never published during Mariátegui's lifetime and generally pertain to the 1928–1929 period in which his public statements were taking a decidedly more doctrinaire orientation.

The first section contains three papers that Mariátegui prepared for the Montevideo meeting of the Constituent Congress of the Latin American Union Confederation (May 1929) and the First Latin American Communist Conference, which met in Buenos Aires in June 1929. The first of these, "El problema de las razas en la América Latina" (The Problem of Race in Latin America; see selection V.2) was presented at both meetings as a sort of position paper to generate discussion and help orient both conferences toward an evaluation that would give sufficient weight to the specific Latin American historical conditions. Although several sections of this thesis are included in *Ideología y política*, Mariátegui only wrote the first, "Planteamiento de la cuestión" (Framing the Question). Dr. Hugo Pesce, Mariátegui's confidant and personal representative to the Buenos Aires meeting, developed the remainder of the exposition. Although it was based in large part on Mariátegui's notes, it also included additional information and points of view that other delegations presented at the meeting, or that Pesce added himself. Therefore, we shall focus on the first section.

Mariátegui begins by suggesting that in Latin America the racial problem often serves to hide, if not ignore, the real problems of the continent. "Marxist criticism has a vital duty to establish it in real terms, ridding it of any sophistic or pedantic misrepresentation,"

Mariátegui argues. "Economically, socially, and politically, the problem of the races, as with that of land, is fundamentally one of the liquidation of feudalism."[114]

He sees the problem as economic and thus springing from the feudal landholding system that Spain implemented in her colonies. Further, he finds that the bourgeoisie in Latin America often proved to be too weak to break the feudal hold. As a result, large segments of the population remained in servitude.

> Feudal and bourgeois elements in our countries have the same contempt for the Indians, as well as for blacks and mulattos, as do the white imperialists. . . . The native lord or bourgeois have nothing in common with their pawns of color. Class solidarity is added to racial solidarity or prejudice.[115]

Mariátegui does not accept the thesis of racial inferiority for either Indigenous or black peoples, and cites Nikolai Bukharin (*The Theory of Historical Materialism*) to the effect that the theory of racial inferiority is completely at variance with the facts.[116]

Although Mariátegui notes that it is not common to all of Latin America, in countries like Peru, Bolivia, and to a lesser extent Ecuador, where the greater part of the population is Indigenous, their rights became the dominant social and popular vindication.[117] A precise socialist political realism, based on an appreciation of the facts with which one must operate in these countries, should convert the racial factor into a revolutionary factor.[118] A revolutionary consciousness may take some time to form, "but once Indians have made the socialist idea their own, they will serve it with a discipline, a tenacity, and strength that few other proletarians from other milieus will be able to surpass."[119] Mariátegui believes this was because of Indigenous peoples' natural inclination toward socialism, which resulted from the communal work and property-owning habits that were a carryover from the Inca Empire. As such, they represent Mariátegui's implicit acknowledgment of the importance of cultural norms.

The second of the three theses to appear in this section deals with the Alianza Popular Revolucionaria Americana (APRA, American Revolutionary Popular Alliance) and anti-imperialism. It carries the title "Punto de vista antiimperialista" (Anti-imperialist Point of View) and Julio Portocarrero presented it at the Buenos Aires conference (see selection IV.2). Here Mariátegui argues that the Latin American republics may be compared to other semicolonial countries in that their economic condition is semicolonial and thus subject to growing imperialist penetration. Further, the state, or better said, the dominant class, would not miss a developed national autonomy, and might preserve little more than the illusion of national sovereignty.[120]

Focusing on the APRA, Mariátegui notes the case of the Kuomintang in China that illustrated the limitations of trusting the national revolutionary sentiments of the bourgeoisie. APRA, then, is a kind of Latin American Kuomintang.[121] And "anti-imperialism does not constitute, or can it constitute by itself, a political program;" it "does not annul antagonisms between classes." Rather, Mariátegui continued, "our mission is to explain and demonstrate to the masses that only socialist revolution can permanently and truly oppose the advance of imperialism."[122] Even if a populist demagogic movement were to take power, this would never represent the conquest of power by the proletarian masses, by socialism. The exposition ends with this often quoted and now famous paragraph: "In conclusion, we are anti-imperialists because we are Marxists, because we are revolutionaries, because we oppose capitalism with socialism as adversarial systems, called to succeed it."[123]

The third of the theses, "Antecedentes y desarrollo de la acción clasista" (Class Action in Peru; selection II.5), which was presented at the Montevideo Congress in 1929, is a brief chronology of how class action developed in Peru. This document provided an excellent presentation of Mariátegui's focus on labor organizing, but unfortunately covers such action only through 1928.

The second section of *Ideologia y política*, "Escritos politicos y sindicales" (Political and Union Writings), includes Mariátegui's writings on unions or workers' organizations as well as a few other writings, such as the "Principios programáticos del Partido Socialista" (Programmatic Principles of the Socialist Party; selection III.5). This section also includes the "Manifiesto a los trabajadores de la república lanzado por el Comité Pro 1º de Mayo" (Manifesto to the Workers of the Republic launched by the Pro 1st of May Committee) and the "Manifiesto de la Confederación General de Trabajadores del Perú a la clase trabajadora del país" (Manifesto of the General Confederation of Peruvian Workers to the Peruvian Working Class; selection V.7). Labor leaders, including Avelino Navarro and Julio Portocarrero, wrote these documents, although with Mariátegui's approval and perhaps direction and subsequent revision.

"Motivos polémicos" (Polemic Themes), the third section of the book, mainly includes Mariátegui's polemic essays against APRA. Principal among these are his replies in the polemic with Luis Alberto Sánchez that was printed in *Mundial* and *Amauta* in February and March of 1927: "Intermezzo polémico" (Polemical intermezzo), "Réplica a Luis Alberto Sánchez" (Reply to Luis Albert Sánchez; selection III.1), "Respuesta al señor Escalante" (Response to Mr. Escalante), and "Polémica finita" (Final polemic). In these, Mariátegui defends himself against Sánchez's accusation of being a "Europeanizer" and goes on to define his ideology in his defense of the radical *indigenista* movement:

> The *indigenismo* of the vanguardist does not seem sincere to Luis Alberto Sánchez. . . . In Peru, the masses—the working class—are four-fifths Indian. Our socialism would not be Peruvian—nor would it be socialism—if it did not establish its solidarity principally with the Indian's vindications.
>
> Do not call me, Luis Alberto Sánchez, "nationalist," "*indigenista*," nor "pseudo-*indigenista*." These terms are not necessary to classify me. Call me simply, Socialist.[124]

The following section, on *Amauta,* contains the famous editorials: "Presentación de *Amauta*" (Presentation of *Amauta*), "Segundo acto" (Second Act), and "Aniversario y balance" (Anniversary and Balance

Sheet; selection I.6). The fifth and last section, on *Labor,* contains four important editorials from Mariátegui's short-lived working-class newspaper, *Labor*: "Presentación de *Labor*" (Presentation of *Labor*), "*Labor* continua" (*Labor* Continues), and "*Labor* interdicta" (*Labor* Interdicted). In "*Labor* Continues," Mariátegui states:

> *Labor* represents the interests and aspirations of all the productive class; industrial and transport workers; agricultural workers, miners, Indian communities, teachers, [white-collar] employees, etc. It is not an organ for one category or group; rather, it is a class organ. The intellectuals and students who bind themselves to the proletariat without reserve have their platform here. Educational workers fighting for the renovation of schools can count on these pages for their vindication. The defense of the [white-collar] employee, and the rights and interests of this kind of worker, will also find space in *Labor*'s columns.[125]

Brief mention should also be made of an essay subsequently added to the *Obras Completas.* It is a written interview in which Mariátegui clarifies his position on the manifestations of Peruvian feudalism and capitalism, and on the particular form the initial stage of socialism would take in Peru. He argues that socialism in Peru may have to accomplish some of the tasks that theoretically belong to capitalism.[126]

Mariátegui's correspondence was not included in his *Obras Completas* and was not published until 1984. It offers substantial insight into his thought and helps to clarify many issues raised in *Ideología y política.* Apart from the cited letters in the Mariátegui family archive, there is a series of letters addressed to Samuel Glusberg (Enrique Espinoza) of *La Vida Literaria* (Buenos Aires). Glusberg published most of these in his book *Trinchera.* One, dated September 30, 1927, offers a particularly interesting insight into Mariátegui's thinking:

> I am politically opposed to [Leopoldo] Lugones. I am a revolutionary. . . . I shall never understand the other political sector: that of

mediocre reformers, of domesticated socialism, of farcical democracy. Furthermore, if the revolution demands violence, authority, discipline, then I am for violence, authority, discipline. I accept them as a block with all their terrors, and without cowardly reservations.[127]

Adding these to the writings included in *Ideología y política*, one gains a better idea of how Mariátegui's political thought was evolving and what sort of material might have been contained in the work that was lost.

### PERUVIANIZING PERU

Mariátegui wrote most of the essays published in *Peruanicemos al Peru* over a five-year period (1924–1929) for a section similarly titled "Peruanicemos al Peru" of the periodical *Mundial* that Gaston Roger (Ezequiel Balarezo Pinillos) started and Mariátegui later took over. Writing under this rubric, Mariátegui published most of the articles that now appear in this work, as well as some that were included in the *Seven Essays*. These essays treat themes like "El hecho económico en la historia peruana" (The Economic Factor in Peruvian History; selection I.3), "El progreso nacional y el capital humano" (National Progress and Human Capital), "Nacionalismo y vanguardismo" (Nationalism and Vanguardism), "Economía colonial" (Colonial Economy; selection I.7), and "Principios de política agraria nacional" (The Beginnings of a National Agrarian Policy). Through them, Mariátegui developed his ideas on Peruvian nationalism and national problems. He argues, in fact, for a study of "Peruvian problems" that necessarily takes into account not only things Peruvian but contemporary world currents as well.[128] Indeed, he argues for Peruvian economic and sociological studies and bemoans the lack of available statistics.[129] His is a call for the type of pioneering study that the *Seven Essays* represents. Such an interpretation would creatively fuse an assiduous consideration of the existent national empirical data to a theoretical overview that would help to place social and productive forces in proper perspective. It would carefully study all aspects of the national reality in light of the theoretical and philosophical insights that Marx, Lenin, and other contemporary Marxist and non-Marxist thinkers and writers provide. In "Hacia el estudio de los problemas peruanos" (Toward the Study of Peruvian Problems), Mariátegui argues that current researchers are obliged to penetrate the national problematic much more deeply. He looks to writers like López Albújar, Luis E. Valcárcel, and Jorge Basadre to show the way. Such "new" Peruvians would employ scientific research and intelligent interpretation of the facts to elucidate the national panorama and assist in the process of making Peru truly belong to the Peruvians.[130] They must study and comprehend their own reality to reclaim it.


## THE ANTHOLOGY

Most of the writings in this anthology come from Mariátegui's *Obras Completas* (Complete Works) that contain sixteen volumes of his essays and four secondary works about him. Mariátegui's four sons and his wife organized the collection, and Biblioteca Amauta in Lima began publishing his complete works in 1957 and finished the project in 1970. The volumes have gone through numerous editions since then. This anthology is divided into nine sections that reflect the major areas in which Mariátegui wrote:[131]

I.      On Studying the Peruvian and Indo-American Reality
II.     Peru and *Indigenismo*
III.    Marxism and Socialism
        (including most chapters from *Defensa del marxismo*)
IV.     Imperialism
V.      Politics, Organization, Peasants, Workers, and Race
VI.     Women
VII.    Myth and the Optimism of the Ideal
VIII.   Aesthetics
IX.     Latin America

The volumes we have used are the following:

Vol. 1    *La escena contemoránea* (4th ed.), 1970.
Vol. 2    *7 Ensayos de interpretación de la realidad peruana*
          (12th ed.), 1967.
Vol. 3    *El alma matinal* (4th ed.), 1970.
Vol. 4    *La novela y la vida* (4th ed.), 1970.
Vol. 5    *Defesa del marxismo* (3rd ed.), 1967.
Vol. 6    *El artista y la época* (lst ed.), 1967.
Vol. 7    *Signos y obras* (2nd ed.), 1967.
Vol. 8    *Historia de la crisis mundial* (3rd ed.), 1971.
Vols. 9 and 10 are secondary works (see Luis Nieto et al., *Poemas
          a Mariátegui*, and María Wiesse, *José Carlos Mariátegui*)
Vol. 11   *Peruanicemos al Perú* (2nd ed.), 1972.
Vol. 12   *Temas de nuestra América* (lst ed.), 1960.
Vol. 13   *Ideología y política* (3rd ed.), 1971.
Vol. 14   *Temas de educación* (1st ed.), 1972.
Vol.15    *Cartas de Italia* (2nd ed.), 1970.
Vols. 16, 17, and 18   *Figuras y aspectos de la vida mundial* (3 vols.),
          1970.
Vols. 19 and 20 are secondary works about Mariátegui (see Alberto
          Tauro, *Amauta y su influencia*, and Armando Bazán,
          *Mariátequi y su tiempo*).

We have endeavored to choose a representative sampling of
Mariátegui's writings, and to provide the reader with adequate materials to appreciate the nature of his Marxist thought and the breadth of
his wide-ranging intellect.

### NOTES

1.    Sheldon B. Liss, *Marxist Thought in Latin America* (Berkeley: University
      of California Press, 1984), 129–30.
2.    Harry E. Vanden, *National Marxism in Latin America: José Carlos Mariátegui's
      Thought and Politics* (Boulder: Lynne Rienner Publishers, 1986), 68.

3. Waldo Frank, "A Great American," *The Nation* 130/3389 (June 18, 1930): 704.

4. José Carlos Mariátegui, "The Problem of Land," *Seven Interpretive Essays on Peruvian Reality*, trans. Marjory Urquidi, with an Introduction by Jorge Basadre (Austin: University of Texas Press, 1971), 42.

5. Vanden interview with Víctor Raúl Haya de la Torre, Lima, December 3, 1973.

6. Vanden interview with Julio Portocarrero, Lima, August 25, 1974. Portocarrero first heard and then met Mariátegui through the González Prada Popular University.

7. David O. Wise, "Mariátegui's *Amauta* (1926–30), A Source for Peruvian Cultural History," *Revista Interamericana de Bibliografía* 29/3–4 (1979): 288.

8. David O. Wise, "*Labor* (Lima 1928–1929), José Carlos Mariátegui's Working-Class Counterpart to *Amauta*," *Revista de Estudios Hispanicos* 14/3 (October 1980): 125.

9. Letter from José Carlos Mariátegui to César Alfredo Miro Quesada in *José Carlos Mariátegui: Correspondencia* (Lima: Biblioteca Amauta, 1984), 2:677.

10. Hello Gallardo, *Pensar en America Latina* (Heredia, Costa Rica: Editorial de la Universidad Nacional, 1981), 18.

11. Leopoldo Zea, *La filosofía americana como filosofía sin más*, Colección Mínima, no. 30 (México: Siglo Veintiuno Editores, 1969), 32–33.

12. See Frantz Fanon, *The Wretched of the Earth* (New York: Grove Press, 1963).

13. See especially, in this respect, the "Catholic" criticism of the 7 *Ensayos* (Seven Essays) that Víctor Andrés Belaúnde makes in *La realidad nacional* (París: Editorial "Le Livre libre," 1931).

14. See also César Antonio Ugarte, *Bosquejo de la historia económica del Perú* (Lima: Imp. Cabieses, 1926), cited in chap. 3 of the 7 *Ensayos* (Seven Essays); Hildebrando Castro Pozo, *Nuestra comunidad indígena* (Lima: Editorial: "El Lucero," 1924), see hapters 2 and 3 of the 7 *Ensayos*; and Abelardo Solis, *Ante el problema agrario peruano* (Lima, Perú: Impresiones encuadernaciones "Perú," 1928).

15. See V. Miroshevsky, "El populismo en el Perú, papel de Mariátegui en la historia del pensamiento social latino-americano," *Dialéctica* 1/1 (May–June 1942): 41–59.

16. José Carlos Mariátegui, "La crisis mundial y el proletariado peruano," *Historia de la crisis mundial: conferencias (años 1923 y 1924)*, in *Obras Completas*, 3rd ed. (Lima: Biblioteca Amauta, 1971), 8:15.

17. José Carlos Mariátegui, *Defensa del marxismo: polémica revolucionaria*, in *Obras Completas*, 3rd ed. (Lima: Biblioteca Amauta, 1967), 5:95 (the youth) and 57 (the workers).

18.   Letter to N. de la Fuente, June 20, 1929; José Carlos Mariátegui, *Ideología y política*, in *Obras Completas*, 3rd ed. (Lima: Biblioteca Amauta, 1971), 13:156–58.

19.   Mariátegui, "Aniversario y balance," *Ideología y política*, 249.

20.   Mariátegui, "Manifesto a los trabajadores de la república," *Ideología y política*, 123; see also Harry E. Vanden, "The Peasants as a Revolutionary Class: An Early Latin American View," *Journal of Inter-American Studies and World Affairs* 20/2 (1978): 191–209; and Harry E. Vanden, "Marxism and the Peasantry in Latin America: Marginalization or Mobilization?" *Latin American Perspectives* 9/4 (35) (Fall 1982): 74–98.

21.   See Miroshevsky, "El populismo en el Perú."

22.   "La Reunión del Baranco," in Ricardo Martínez de la Torre, *Apuntes para una interpretación marxista de la historia social del Perú* (Lima: Empresa Editora Peruana, 1947–49), 2:17. Emphasis added.

23.   Mariátegui, "El problema de las razas," in *Ideología y política*, 46.

24.   Mariátegui, "Principios programáticos del partido socialista," *Ideología y política*, 161.

25.   Carlos Altamirano, *El marxismo en la América Latina* (Buenos Aires: Centro Editor de América Latina, 1972), 7.

26.   See, for instance, Espartaco (Aníbal Pinto Santa Cruz), *Crítica de la izquierda latinoamericana* (Montevideo: ARCA, 1965), and José Aricó, *Marx y América Latina* (Lima: Centro de Estudios para el Desarrollo y la Participación, 1980).

27.   Jorge Abelardo Ramos, *El marxismo de Indias* (Barcelona: Editorial Planeta, 1973), 7–8.

28.   Altamirano, *El marxismo*, 9.

29.   Ibid.

30.   See José Carlos Mariátegui, "México y la revolución," in *Temas de nuestra América, Obras Completas*, 1st ed. (Lima: Biblioteca Amauta, 1960), 12:39–43.

31.   Mariátegui, *Historia de la crisis mundial*, 7–8. This may explain why the collection of lectures is published as vol. 8 of the *Obras Completas*, even though written after the *Cartas de Italia* (vol. 15). Lamentably, the *Obras Completas* generally do not follow any set chronology.

32.   Mariátegui, "La crisis mundial y el proletariado peruano," in *Historia de la crisis mundial*, 13.

33.   Ibid., 16–18.

34.   Ibid., 19–24.

35.   Mariátegui, "Literatura de guerra," in *Historia de la crisis mundial*, 2.

36.   Mariátegui, "El proceso de la segunda internacional," in *Historia de la crisis mundial*, 33–36.

37.   Ibid., 33.

38.   Mariátegui, "Exposición y crítica de las instituciones del régimen ruso" (author's notes), in *Historia de la crisis mundial*, 148–52.

39. Ibid.,149–50. Mariátegui's thoughts on the revolutionary potential of the peasantry would, however, change considerably by the late 1920s.

40. Ibid., 152.

41. Mariátegui, "La revolución mexicana," in *Historia de la crisis mundial*, 166.

42. Mariátegui, "Elogio de Lenin," in *Historia de la crisis mundial*, 168–69.

43. Vanden interview with Julio Portocarrero, Lima, August 25, 1974.

44. Vanden interview with Víctor Raúl Haya de la Torre, Lima, December 3, 1973.

45. Vanden interview with Florenzio Chávez, Lima, September 2, 1974. Chávez was a worker at this time and was attracted to the proletarian movement through his contact with Mariátegui.

46. Autobiographical letter, published in *La Vida Literaria* (Buenos Aires).

47. Mariátegui, "Veinticinco años de sucesos extranjeros," in *Historia de la crisis mundial*, 200.

48. José Carlos Mariátegui, *La escena contemporánea*, *Obras Completas*, 4th ed. (Lima: Biblioteca Amauta, 1970), 1:9.

49. Ibid.

50. Ibid., 82–87.

51. Ibid., 82.

52. Ibid., 113.

53. Ibid., 122.

54. Régis Debray, *Revolution in the Revolution? Armed Struggle and Political Struggle in Latin America* (New York: Monthly Review Press, 1967).

55. Mariátegui, *La escena contemporánea*, 125.

56. See Roger Garaudy, *The Crisis in Communism: The Turning-Point of Socialism* (New York: Grove Press, 1970), and Roger Garaudy, *Marxism in the Twentieth Century* (New York: Scribner, 1970).

57. Mariátegui, *La escena contemporánea*, 138.

58. Ibid., 142.

59. Ibid., 153.

60. Ibid., 154.

61. Ibid., 158.

62. Ibid., 198.

63. Ibid., 199.

64. "Presentación de Amauta," *Amauta* 1/1 (September 1926): 1.

65. Vanden interview with Antonio Navarro Madrid, Lima, April 10, 1974.

66. "Presentación de Amauta," 1.

67. Alberto Hidalgo, "Ubicación de Lenin," *Amauta* 1/1 (September 1926): 12.

68. "Presentación de Amauta," 1.

69. *Amauta* 11 (January 1928): 30–31. See Mariano Azuela, *The Underdogs* (New York: Penguin, 1963).

70. "Segundo acto," *Amauta* 10 (December 1927): 1. The work accident was, of course, imprisonment. Emphasis added.

71. *Amauta* 10 (December 1927): 37.
72. "Presentación de Amauta," 1.
73. José Carlos Mariátegui, "Aniversario y balance," *Amauta* 3/17 (September 1928): 3.
74. See *Amauta* 23 (May 1929) and *Amauta* 24 (June 1929).
75. Mariátegui, *Seven Interpretive Essays on Peruvian Reality*, xxxvi.
76. Harold Eugene Davis, *Latin American Thought* (Baton Rouge: Louisiana State University Press, 1972), 189.
77. José Carlos Mariátegui, *7 ensayos de interpretación de la realidad peruana*, in *Obras Completas*, 12th ed. (Lima: Biblioteca Amauta, 1967), 2:7.
78. Mariátegui, *7 ensayos*, 10–11.
79. Ibid., 18–21.
80. Ibid., 22.
81. Ibid.
82. Manuel González Prada, "Nuestros indios," in *Horas de lucha*, 2nd ed. (Callao: Tip. "Lux," 1924).
83. Mariátegui, *7 ensayos*, 24–27.
84. Ibid., 45–46.
85. Ibid., 59.
86. Ibid., 74–75.
87. Ibid., 61.
88. Ibid., 24–27.59.
89. Ibid., 80.
90. Ibid., 82.
91. Ibid., 85.
92. Ibid., 104.
93. Ibid., 121.
94. Ibid., 128.
95. Gustavo Gutiérrez shows considerable interest in Mariátegui and cites him directly in his book *Theology of Liberation* (Maryknoll, NY: Orbis Books, 1973), which points to Mariátegui's strong influence on the origins of the Peruvian priest's theology.
96. Mariátegui, *7 ensayos*, 154.
97. Ibid., 170.
98. Ibid., 183–86. *Civilista* refers to a Peruvian political movement of the late nineteenth and early twentieth centuries that opposed military control of the government.
99. Mariátegui, *7 ensayos*, 190–91.
100. Biblioteca Amauta published the first complete edition in 1959. A 1934 Santiago edition carries the same title, but is incomplete and contains writings from other works.
101. Mariátegui, *Defensa del marxismo*, 15.
102. Ibid., 16–17.

103. Ibid., 56.

104. Ibid., 57.

105. Ibid., 58.

106. Ibid., 58.

107. Letter to Samuel Glusberg, dated March 10, 1928, in Enrique Espinoza (pseud. Samuel Glusberg), *Trinchera* (Buenos Aires: Biblioteca Argentina de Buenas Ediciones Literarias (BABEL), 1932), 53.

108. Mariátegui, *Defensa del marxismo*, 113.

109. Ibid., 126.

110. Ibid., 129.

111. Mariátegui, *Seven Interpretive Essays on Peruvian Reality*, iiiv.

112. Mariátegui, *Ideología y política*, 15.

113. Martínez de la Torre, *Apuntes*, 2:404.

114. Mariátegui, *Ideología y política*, 21.

115. Ibid., 27.

116. Ibid., 29.

117. Ibid., 32.

118. Ibid., 33.

119. Ibid., 46.

120. Ibid., 87.

121. Ibid., 90.

122. Ibid., 91.

123. Ibid., 95.

124. Ibid., 217. This entire polemic is reprinted in Manuel Aquézolo Castro, ed., *La polémica del indigenismo* (Lima: Mosca Azul, 1976).

125. "Labor continua," Mariátegui, *Ideología y política*, 227–28.

126. Mariátegui, "Acerca del carácter de la sociedad peruana." This is the text of the interview that appeared in the magazine *La Sierra* (May 29, 1929). In the early 1970s, it was republished in a limited edition, *Acerca del carácter de la sociedad peruana* (Lima: Editorial Popular, 1973), and is now included in *Ideología y política*. See "On the Character of Peruvian Society," selection III.6 in this volume.

127. Enrique Espinoza, *Trinchera*, 45–46.

128. José Carlos Mariátegui, "Hacia el estudio de los problemas peruanos," *Peruanicemos al Perú*, in *Obras Completas*, 2nd ed. (Lima: Biblioteca Amauta, 1972), 11:50–53.

129. Mariátegui, "Hacia el estudio de los problemas peruanos," 54–58; Mariátegui, "El problema de la estadística," *Peruanicemos al Perú*, 88–91.

130. Mariátegui, "El problema de la estadística," *Peruanicemos al Perú*, 50–53; see selection I.4.

131. For an excellent anthology in Spanish, see Francisco Baez, ed., *José Carlos Mariátegui Obras*, Colección Pensamiento de Nuestra América, 2 vols. (Havana: Casa de las Americas, 1982).

# PART 1

# On Studying the Peruvian and Indo-American Reality

. . .

IN THIS SECTION, José Carlos Mariátegui breaks from more impressionistic quasi-historical studies of Peru to bring his well-honed Marxist analysis to bear on careful, empirically based studies of the problems plaguing the Peruvian and Latin American reality. These selections come primarily from the collection of essays published as *Peruanicemos al Peru*, volume 11 in the *Obras Completas*. We also include in this section "The Land Problem," a key chapter from *Seven Essays* in which Mariátegui builds a strong argument that persistent problems of Indigenous marginalization will not be solved through liberal reforms, but only through profound structural changes in the land.

# 1 – Toward a Study of Peruvian Problems

Among the attributes of our generation, one can and should note a certain virtuous and meritorious attitude: a growing interest in things Peruvian. The Peruvians of today are showing themselves to be more attuned to their own people and their own history than the Peruvians of yesterday. But this is not a consequence of their spirit being closed or confined within our borders. It is precisely the contrary. The contemporary Peruvians have more contact with global ideas and emotions. Little by little humanity's desire for renovation is taking charge of its new men. And an urgent, diffuse aspiration to understand Peruvian reality is born of this desire for renovation.

Past generations are not only characterized by a scant understanding of our problems, but also by a weak connection to their own historical epoch. As it ends, we note a fact: the epoch was different. After a long revolutionary period, a regime and an order that then seemed more or less definitive were established and developed in the West. On the other hand, the world was not so articulated as now. Peru did not seem as incorporated in history or as much in the orbit of Western civilization as it is today.

The greater part of the intellectuals constitutes an obedient clientele of heirs or descendants of colonial feudalism. This caste's interests do not allow it to descend from its disdainful and frivolous Parnassus to the deep reality of Peru. Nor do those who rebel instinctively and consciously against these class interests, immerse their view in social and economic realities either. Their ideology—or their phraseology—is nourished by the abstract literature of the *Declaration of the Rights of Man and the Citizen.*

Radicalism, for example, ends in a pamphleteering verbalism, not without merit, but condemned to sterility. Pierolism,[1] which arrived to power supported by the masses, showed itself to be even less solid in its doctrine. Piérola, on the other hand, constructed a civilian-oriented [*civilista*][2] government in his four years of being the constitutional president. His party, because of this commitment, spiritually separated from the class that it seemed to represent in its first days.

In *Le Péru Contemporain,* Francisco García Calderón studied Peru with a more realistic criterion than that of previous intellectual generations. But García Calderón avoided all bold research, all audacious examination. His book limited itself to noting, with *civilista* optimism, the existence of progressive forces in Peru. The conclusion of this study did not take into account what I insist on calling Peru's deep reality. In 1906 García Calderón was happy to prescribe government by an enlightened, practical oligarchy, and in proposing that we prepare ourselves to accustom our life to the advantages of a Pan-American railroad that his foresight then judged would soon connect the continent from north to south, and that twenty years later still seems like a far-off vision. Before the Pan-American railroad other avalanches had to pass through Peru's history.

Víctor Andrés Belaúnde, in his youth, reacted a little against the mediocrity of the university, and reclaimed a more realistic and more Peruvian orientation in higher education. But Balaúnde did not persevere on this path. After some skirmishes, he desisted in this belligerent attitude. Today the *Mercurio Peruano*[3] does not say any of the things about the university that Belaúnde said in his youth. Moreover, he felt obliged to say in the margin of an article of mine that one should not suppose he was supportive of a phrase about San Marcos. (A superfluous declaration since it did not occur to the public to suspect in

*Mercurio Peruano* concurrence or solidarity with my ideas. The public knows well that the responsibility for my ideas is totally mine. This responsibility does not compromise in any way the magazines that graciously and courteously count me among their collaborators.)

The tendency to penetrate things and problems Peruvian, with greater *élan,* belongs to our epoch. This movement is covered first in literature. Valdelomar,[4] his literary elitism and aristocratism notwithstanding, extracts his most delicate themes and emotions from the humble and rustic native land. Unlike the prudish literary figures of yesteryear, in his literature he does not ignore plebeians or things that come from them. On the contrary, he looks for them and he loves them in spite of his decadent inspiration and a tinge of D'Annunzio.[5]

One day the Plaza of the Market was the theme of his humor and literature. Later, in his *Plantel de Inválidos,* César Falcón gathered various delightful sketches of Peruvian life. And, like Valdelomar, he knew how to show a happy disdain for "distinguished" themes. In this way literature acquires even more of a focus on Indigenous peoples. The books of López Abujar, of Luis E. Valcárcel and Augusto Aguirre Morales, about which I plan to soon write, equally document this interesting phenomenon.

In scientific research, in theoretical speculation, the same tendency is seen. César Ugate, with his sagacity and intelligence, is preoccupied with the agrarian problem. Julio Tello penetratingly studies race. Honorio Delgado, according to my information, has proposed undertaking a methodical study of Indigenous psychology. Jorge Basadre and Luis Alberto Sánchez have abandoned the routine use of anecdote and chronicle in their historical studies. They are concerned with the interpretation of the facts, not their purposeless relating. Jorge Basadre is author of a study about road gang conscription that shows a way and a method to his comrades in the university vanguard. And recently a course in the Social History of Peru was inaugurated in the Popular University; it is an original course, a new course, in which an aptitude for research and interpretation will be put to the test. And in regard to the Popular University, it should not be forgotten that Haya de la Torre, one of our new men, has given the greatest service to the study of "Peru's deep reality" in creating this cultural center. The internationalist feels, more than many nationalists, the Indigenous, the Peruvian; that the things Indigenous, Peruvian are not the *esprit* of the Jirón de la Unión or the Lima soireés, rather something much deeper and more transcendent.

—*Mundial*, Lima, 10 July 1925

NOTES

Source: "Hacia el estudio de los problemas peruanos," in *Peruanicemos al Péru,* in *Obras Completas,* 11th ed. (Lima: Biblioteca Amauta, 1988), 11:69–73.

1. From José Nicolás de Piérola y Villena who was a prominent Peruvian politician, finance minister, and twice (from 1879 to 1881 and 1895 to 1899) president of the republic.
2. *Civilista* refers to a Peruvian political movement of the late nineteenth and early twentieth centuries that opposed military control of the government.
3. *Mercurio Peruano* was a Peruvian intellectual magazine that Víctor Andrés Belaunde founded in 1918.
4. Abraham Valdelomar, vanguardist Peruvian poet and writer.
5. Gabriele D'Annunzio (March 12, 1863–March 1, 1938) was an Italian poet, journalist, novelist, dramatist, and adventurer whose political activism influenced Italian politics in the 1920s.

# 2—The Land Problem

*The Agrarian Problem and the Indian Problem*

For those of us who study and identify the problem of the Indian from a socialist point of view, we began by declaring humanitarian or philanthropic views that, as an extension of the apostolic battle of Father Bartolomé de las Casas, supported old pro-Indigenous campaigns as absolutely outdated. Our first effort is to establish its character as a fundamentally economic problem. First, we protest against the instinctive and defensive tendency of the *creole* or *mestizo* to reduce it to a purely administrative, pedagogical, ethnic, or moral problem in order to avoid at all costs its economic aspects. Therefore, it would be absurd to accuse us of being romantic or literary. We assume the least romantic and literary position possible by identifying it primarily as a socioeconomic problem. We are not content with demanding the Indians' right to education, culture, progress, love, and heaven. We start by categorically demanding their right to land. This thoroughly materialistic demand should be enough for us not to be confused with the heirs or imitators of the evangelical language of the great Spanish friar, who, on the other hand, our materialism does not prevent us from fervently admiring and esteeming.

And this problem of the land, whose solidarity with the problem of the Indian is overly evident, does not allow us to mitigate or diminish it opportunistically. Quite the contrary. For my part, I will try to present it in absolutely uncertain and clear terms.

The agrarian problem is first and foremost the problem of the liquidation of feudalism in Peru. This liquidation should have already been done by the democratic bourgeois regime that was formally established by the independence revolution. But in Peru, we have not had in one hundred years as a republic a true bourgeois class, a true capitalist class. The old feudal class, camouflaged or disguised as a republican bourgeoisie, has kept their positions. The policy of confiscation of agricultural property, initiated by the independence revolution as a logical consequence of its ideology, did not lead to the development of small properties. The old landowning class had not lost its dominance. The survival of a large landholder regime led, in practice, to the maintenance of large estates. It is well known that the confiscation of agricultural property attacked communities instead. And the fact is that during a century of republican rule, the large agrarian properties have been strengthened and enlarged in spite of the liberal theory of our constitution and the practical necessities of the development of our capitalist economy.

There are two expressions of feudalism that survive: large estates and servitude. They are inseparable and the same expressions whose analysis leads us to the conclusion that one cannot eliminate the servitude that weighs on the Indigenous race without eliminating the large estates.

When the agrarian problem in Peru is presented this way it is not easily distorted. It appears in its full magnitude as a socioeconomic, and therefore political, problem under the domain of men who work on this level of facts and ideas. And it is useless to convert it, for example, into a technical-agrarian problem for agronomists.

Everyone knows that the liberal solution to this problem would be, according to the individualist ideology, breaking up the large landholdings to create small properties. But there is so much ignorance of the principal elements of socialism everywhere around us that it is worthwhile repeating that this formula of breaking up large estates in favor of small properties is neither utopian, nor heretical, nor revolutionary, nor Bolshevik, nor vanguardist, but orthodox, constitutional, democratic, capitalist and bourgeois. It has its origins in the liberal ideals that inspired the constitutional laws of all democratic bourgeois states. And the countries of Central and Eastern Europe (Czechoslovakia, Romania, Poland, Bulgaria, etc.), have enacted agrarian laws that restrict, in principle, land ownership, to a maximum of 500 hectares. This is where the crisis of the war led to the pulling down of the last ramparts of feudalism. Since then, Western capitalism used precisely this group of countries to oppose Russia in an anti-Bolshevik bloc of countries.

In keeping with my ideological position, I think that the time to attempt the liberal method, the individualistic formula, in Peru has already passed. Aside from doctrinal reasons, I believe that our agrarian problem has a fundamental indisputable and concrete factor that gives it a special character: the survival of the community and elements of practical socialism in Indigenous agriculture and life.

But those who remain within the democratic-liberal doctrine, if they are truly looking for a solution to the problem of the Indian, which will above all redeem them from servitude, can turn their gaze to the Czech or Romanian experience, since the Mexican example seems dangerous as an inspiration and as a process. For them it is still time to advocate the liberal formula. If they did, they would at least ensure that the discussion of the agrarian problem pushed by the new generation would not entirely lack the liberal thinking that, according to written history, governs the life of Peru since the founding of the republic.

### Colonialism-Feudalism

The land problem clarifies the vanguard or socialist attitude toward the remains of the viceroyalty. The literary *perricholismo*[1] does not interest us except as a sign or reflection of economic colonialism. The colonial legacy we want to eliminate is not, fundamentally, one of veils and lattices, but that of the feudal economic regime, whose expressions are those of *gamonalismo*, large estates, and servitude. The colonial literature, nostalgic evocation of the viceroyalty and its splendor, for me is only the product of a mediocre spirit engendered and nourished by that regime. The viceroyalty does not survive in the *perricholismo* of some troubadours and chroniclers. It survives in a feudalism that contains, even without imposing its own law, a latent and incipient capitalism. We do not so much reject the Spanish legacy as the feudal legacy.

Spain brought us the Medieval Ages: the Inquisition, feudalism, etc. Later it brought the Counter-Reformation: a reactionary spirit, a Jesuit method, a scholastic casuistry. We have painfully freed ourselves from most of these things through the assimilation of Western culture, sometimes obtained from Spain itself. But we are still not freed from its economic foundations, which are rooted in the interests of a class whose hegemony was not destroyed by the independence revolution. The roots of feudalism are intact. Their livelihood is responsible, for example, for the delay of our capitalist development.

The ownership of land determines the political and administrative system of any nation. The agrarian problem, which the republic has not yet been able to resolve, dominates all of our problems. Democratic and liberal institutions cannot prosper nor function in a semi-feudal economy.

For special reasons, the subordination of the Indigenous problem to the land problem is even more absolute. The Indigenous race is a race of farmers. The Inca people were a rural people, normally devoted to agriculture and pasturing animals. Industries and the arts had a domestic and rural character. The principle that "life comes from the earth" was truer in the Peru of the Incas than anywhere else. The most admirable public works and collective works of Tawantinsuyu had a military, religious, or agricultural purpose. The highland and coastal irrigation channels, and the agricultural terraces in the Andes, are the best evidence of the degree of economic organization reached by Inca Peru. All of the dominant features characterize their civilization as an agricultural civilization. "The land," Valcárcel writes in his study of the economic life of Tawantinsuyu,

> in native tradition, is the common mother: not only food but man himself comes from her womb. Land provides all wealth. The cult of the Mama Pacha, Mother Earth, is on par with the worship of the sun, and such as the sun does not belong to anyone in particular, neither does the planet. Agrarianism was born from the twin concepts of aboriginal ideology of communal ownership of land and the universal religion of the sun.[2]

Inca communism, which cannot be denied or disparaged, developed under the autocratic rule of the Incas, is therefore designated as an agrarian communism. The fundamental characteristics of the Inca economy, according to César Ugarte, who carefully defines the general features of our development, were:

> Collective ownership of cultivatable land by the *ayllu* or set of related families, although it was divided into individual and non-transferable lots; collective ownership of water, pasture land, and forests by the *marka* or tribe (the federation of *ayllu*s settled around the same village); cooperative labor; individual appropriation of harvests and produce.[3]

The destruction of this economy, and hence the culture that nourished it, is one of the colony's least discussed results of colonialism, not for comprising the destruction of autochthonous forms, but for not having replaced them with superior forms. The colonial regime disrupted and annihilated the Incas' agricultural economy without replacing it with an economy of higher yields. Under an Indigenous aristocracy, the natives made up a nation of ten million men, with an efficient and organic state who ruled all its territory. Under a foreign aristocracy, the natives were reduced to a scattered and chaotic mass of a million men reduced to servitude and peonage.

The demographic data are, in this respect, the most authoritative and decisive. Against all the criticisms based on the modern liberal concepts of freedom and justice that can be made against the Inca system, is the positive and material historical fact that they ensured the survival and growth of a population that, when the conquistadors arrived in Peru, amounted to ten million, and that after three centuries of Spanish domination fell to a million. This fact condemns colonialism, and not from an abstract or theoretical or moral perspective of justice, or however one wants to qualify it, but from the practical, concrete, and material point of view of utility.

Colonialism, powerless to organize in Peru even a feudal economy, introduced elements of a slave economy in this.

### The Politics of Colonialism: Depopulation and Slavery

It is easy to explain why Spanish colonial rule was unable to organize a pure feudal economy in Peru. It is not possible to organize an economy without a clear understanding and sure appreciation of it, at least its needs if not its principles. An Indigenous, organic, native economy develops alone. It alone spontaneously determines its institutions. But a colonial economy is established on bases that are in part artificial and foreign, and subordinated to the interests of the colonizer. Its development depends on the colonizer's ability either to adapt to environmental conditions or to transform them.

The Spanish colonizers conspicuously lacked this ability. They had a rather exaggerated idea of the economic value of natural wealth, but almost no idea about any of the economic value of people.

The practice of exterminating the Indigenous population and the destruction of their institutions, often in conflict with the laws and orders of the metropolis, impoverished and bled the fabulous country earned by the conquistadors for the King of Spain, to an extent they were not able to perceive and appreciate. Formulating an economic principle for his time, a South American statesman of the nineteenth century was to say later, impressed by the sight of a semi-deserted continent: "To govern is to populate." The Spanish colonizers, infinitely far away from these criteria, introduced to Peru a depopulation scheme.

The persecution and enslavement of Indians rapidly consumed a capital that had been dramatically underestimated by the colonists: human capital. The Spanish increasingly found that they were in need of labor for the exploitation and use of the wealth they had conquered. They resorted to the most antisocial and primitive colonization system: the importation of slaves. On the other hand, the colonizers thereby gave up the undertaking for which the conquerors previously thought possible: the assimilation of the Indian. They brought the black race for, among other reasons, to reduce the demographic imbalance between the whites and Indians.

The greed for precious metals, quite logical in a century during which distant lands could hardly send any other products to Europe, drove the Spanish to engage mainly in mining. Their interests led to the conversion of miners who, under the Incas and even before, had been engaged in agriculture. From this was born the need to subject Indians to the harsh law of slavery. Within a naturally feudal system, agricultural labor would have converted the Indians into serfs linked to the land. Labor in the mines and cities would make them slaves. With the *mita*, the Spanish established a system of forced labor that uprooted Indians from their soil and customs.

The importation of African slaves who supplied labor and domestic servants to the coastal Spanish population where the viceroyal court was located meant that Spain was not aware of its economic and political mistake. Slavery was injected into the regime, corrupting and weakening it.

Professor Javier Prado, writing in a study on the social status of colonial Peru and from a perspective that of course I do not share, arrived at conclusions that contain precisely one aspect of this failure of the colonial enterprise. "Blacks," he says,

> are considered a commercial merchandise, and were imported to America as machines for human labor needed to irrigate the land with the sweat of their brow, but without making it fertile or productive. It is the same pattern of elimination that civilization has always followed throughout human history. Slaves are unproductive in their labor, in

the Roman Empire and as has been the case in Peru. It is a cancer on the social body that corrupts national feelings and ideals. Accordingly, slaves have disappeared in Peru but without leaving cultivated fields behind. They took revenge on the whites, mixed their blood together, and in this collusion lowered the moral and intellectual criterion of those who initially were their cruel masters, and later their godfathers, companions, and siblings.[4]

Today one cannot charge colonialism with the responsibility of having brought an inferior race; this was the essential reproach of sociologists half a century ago. Rather it is that they brought slavery with the slaves, a system destined to fail as a means of economic exploitation and organization of the colony, while strengthening a regime based only on conquest and force.

The colonial nature of coastal agriculture, which still has not rid itself of this defect, comes largely from the slave system. Large coastal estates asked for labor rather than men to fertilize their land. Thus when they ran out of African slaves they sought a substitute in the Chinese coolies. This other importation was typical of a regime of *encomenderos* that, as with that of blacks, conflicted with the normal formation of a liberal economy consistent with the political order established by the independence revolution. César Ugarte acknowledges this in his previously mentioned study of the Peruvian economy, arguing strongly that what Peru needed was not labor but men.[5]

## The Spanish Colonizers

The inability of colonialism to organize the Peruvian economy on its natural agricultural bases can be explained by the type of colonizer we had. Whereas in North America colonization planted the seeds of a spirit and an economy then growing in Europe and to which the future belonged, the Spanish brought to America the effects and methods of a declining spirit and economy that belonged to the past. This thesis may seem too simplistic to those who consider only its economic aspect, and who are unknowingly survivors of the old scholastic rhetoric. They show a lack of an ability to understand economic reality, something that is a key defect of those among us who study history. I am pleased to have found José Vasconcelos's recent book *Indología*, whose opinion has the value of coming from a thinker who cannot be accused of too much Marxism or too little Hispanicism. Vasconcelos writes:

> If there were not so many other causes of moral and physical order that perfectly explain the apparently reckless spectacle of the tremendous progress of the Saxons of the North and the slow disoriented pace of southern Latinos, only the comparison of the two property systems would be sufficient to explain the reasons for the contrast. The North did not have kings who disposed of each other's land as if it were their own. Without special favors from its monarchs, and furthermore in a certain state of moral rebellion against the English monarch, the northern colonizers were able to develop a system of private property in which each person paid the price for their land and only occupied as much as they could cultivate. As a result, instead of *encomiendas* there was cultivation. And instead of a warrior and agriculture aristocracy with a sense of royal lineage descended from a servile and murderous nobility, an aristocracy emerged with an aptitude toward what is called democracy, a democracy that at first recognized precepts none other than those of the French motto: liberty, equality, fraternity.
>
> The northern men were conquering the virgin forest, but the victorious general in the fight against the Indians was not allowed to take control, as in our ancient tradition, "as far as the eye can see." The newly conquered lands were neither at the hands of the sovereign to distribute according to his wishes and thereby create a nobility with a contradictory morality: a lackey of the sovereign and an insolent oppressor of the weakest. In the North, the republic coincided with the great expansionist movement, and the republic gave away a large amount of good land, and created vast reserves barred to private business. It did not use them to create duchies or to reward patriotic

services, but to promote popular education. And so, in the midst of a growing population, rising land values assured the provision of educational services. And every time a new city arose in the middle of the desert, there was no favoritism in the distribution of land concessions but rather a public auction of the lots that previously had been subdivided according to a plan for the future city. This also came with the limitation that no one person could buy many lots at once. From this wise and just social system emerged the great North American power. Because we did not proceed in a similar fashion, we have been proceeding backwards.[6]

Feudalism is, in the opinion of Vasconcelos, a defect that is the result of colonialism. Countries that, after independence, have managed to cure themselves of this defect are those that have progressed. Those that have not yet managed to do so are backwards. We have already seen how the defect of feudalism is joined with the defect of slavery.

The Spanish did not have the Anglo-Saxons' conditions of colonization. The creation of the United States is considered to be the work of the pioneer. After the epic of the conquest, Spain sent us almost nothing but nobles, clergy, and villains. The conquistadors were of heroic stock; the colonizers were not. The conquistadors were gentlemen, not pioneers. Those who thought that Peru's richness lay in its precious metals, under the practice of *mitas*, turned mining into a factor of annihilation of human capital and the decline of agriculture. Even in *civilista* literature we find these accusations. Javier Prado writes that "the state of agriculture in the Viceroyalty of Peru is quite unfortunate because of the absurd economic system maintained by the Spaniards," and that the depopulation of the country was due to this exploitative regime.[7]

The colonizers who worked the mines rather than the fields had the psychology of gold prospectors. They were not, therefore, creators of wealth. An economy and a society are the work of those who colonize and bring the land to life, not those who precariously extract treasures out of its subsoil. The history of the growth and decay of

many colonial highland towns, driven by the discovery and abandonment of mines that were quickly depleted or discarded, strongly illustrates this law of history to us.

Perhaps the only real phalanges of true colonizers that Spain sent
us were the Jesuit and Dominican missions. Both congregations,
especially the Jesuits, created in Peru a number of interesting centers
of production. The Jesuits introduced religious, political, and economic factors into their enterprise—not to the same extent as in
Paraguay where they carried out their most famous and extensive
experiments, but along the same principles.

This function of the congregations not only conformed to the policies of the Jesuits in Spanish America, but also to the same tradition of
monasteries in the Middle Ages. The monasteries had an economic
role, among others, in medieval society. In an era of warriors and mystics, they were in charge of saving the techniques of arts and crafts,
refining and cultivating elements on which the bourgeois industry
would later be established. Georges Sorel is one of the modern economists who in his study of the Benedictine order as the prototype of
the monastery-industrial enterprise best outlines and defines the role
of the monasteries in the European economy. Sorel points out that

> Finding capital at that time was a very difficult problem to solve. For
> the monks it was a simple matter. Very quickly the donations of
> wealthy families lavished them with huge amounts of precious metals.
> This greatly facilitated the primitive accumulation of capital.
> Moreover, convents spent little and the strict economy that the orders
> imposed recalls the frugal habits of the early capitalists. For a long
> time the monks were in a position to undertake excellent operations
> to increase their fortune.

Sorel expounds on how "after having rendered outstanding services
to Europe that everyone recognizes, these institutions declined rapidly,"
and how the Benedictines "ceased to be workers grouped in an almost
capitalist workshop and became a bourgeoisie withdrawn from business
who thought only to live in a sweet idleness in the countryside."[8]

That aspect of colonization, as with many others of our economy, has not yet been studied. It has fallen to me, a convicted and confessed Marxist, to report these findings. I believe this study is essential for the economic justification of the measures that future agricultural policy will take to the estates of monasteries and congregations, because it will conclusively establish that their rights of ownership and the royal titles on which they rest have expired.

## The Community under Colonial Rule

The Laws of the Indies protected Indigenous property and recognized its communist organization. The legislation relating to Indigenous communities adapted to the need not to attack the institutions and customs that were not opposed to the religious spirit and the political character of colonialism. The agrarian communism of the *ayllu*, once the Inca state was destroyed, was not incompatible with either one. Quite the contrary; the Jesuits took advantage of Indigenous communism in Peru, Mexico, and on an even larger scale in Paraguay, for their purposes of religious instruction. The medieval system, in theory and in practice, reconciled feudal property with community property.

The recognition of communities and their economic customs by the Laws of the Indies did not only illustrate the realistic wisdom of colonial policy but absolutely conformed to feudal theory and practice. The provisions of the colonial laws on community, which maintained its economic mechanism without any problem, logically reformed, of course, customs contrary to Catholic doctrine (trial marriage, etc.), and tended to convert the community into a cog in administrative and fiscal machinery. The community could and should survive for the greater glory and benefit of the king and the church.

We know well that this law remained largely on paper. Because of colonial practices, Indigenous property could not be sufficiently protected. All evidence agrees on this point. Ugarte makes the following observations:

Not Toledo's forward-thinking measures, nor those that were attempted at different times, prevented that a large portion of Indigenous property passed either legally or illegally into the hands of the Spaniards or *creoles*. One of the institutions that facilitated this plunder was the *encomienda*. Under the legal concept of the institution, the *encomendero* was charged with collecting the taxes and the organization and Christianization of its tributaries. But in reality he was a feudal lord, master of life and estates, because he controlled the Indians as if they were trees from the forest. If they died or disappeared he took over their lands by one means or another. In short, the colonial agrarian regime resulted in the substitution of a large number of Indigenous agricultural communities with large individually owned estates cultivated by Indians organized in a feudal manner. These large fiefdoms, far from being divided over time, became concentrated and consolidated into few hands because the real estate was subject to innumerable obstacles and perpetual encumbrances that immobilized it, like primogeniture, religious bequests and payments, and other entailments on the property.[9]

Feudalism similarly let rural communes continue in Russia, a country with which parallels are always interesting because its historical process is more similar to that of agricultural and semifeudal countries than that of Western capitalist countries. Eugène Schkaff, in his study of the evolution of the *mir*[10] in Russia, writes:

> Since landlords were responsible for taxes, they wanted each peasant to have more or less the same amount of land so that each one would contribute with their work to pay taxes. In order to assure their effectiveness, they established a solidarity responsibility. The government extended this to the other peasants. Land was redistributed as the number of serfs varied. Feudalism and absolutism gradually transformed the communal organization of the peasants into an instrument of exploitation. In this context, the emancipation of the serfs did not provide any change.[11]

Under the manorial system of ownership, the Russian *mir*, as with the Peruvian community, underwent a complete distortion. The amount of land available to the community was increasingly inadequate, and their distribution increasingly defective. The *mir* did not guarantee peasants the amount of land necessary for their livelihood. On the other hand, it guaranteed the landowners the provision of the necessary labor for working their estates. When in 1861 slavery was abolished, the landowners found ways of reducing lots granted to peasants to such a small size that they could not survive on their own products. Russian agriculture thus retained its feudal character. The large landholders used reform for their benefit. They had already noticed that it was in their interest to grant the peasants a lot, provided that they were not large enough to provide subsistence for them and their families. There was no better way to link the peasant to the land, and at the same time keep their emigration to a minimum. Peasants were forced to serve the landowner who forced them to work on the estate. As if the poverty on the tiny plots was not enough, the landowner also held dominance over meadows, forests, mills, waters, etc.

The existence of community and large estates in Peru is thus fully explained not only by the characteristics of the system of colonialism but also by the experience of feudal Europe. But the community, under this regime, was tolerated rather than protected. The large estates imposed their law of despotic force without the control of the state. The community survived, but under a system of servitude. Previously it had been the very nucleus of the state, which ensured the necessary dynamism for the welfare of its members. Colonialism petrified it within the large estates, which were the basis of a new state alien to its destiny.

Liberalism of the laws of the republic, powerless to destroy feudalism and establish capitalism, later denied the protection that the absolutism of colonial laws had granted.

## *The Independence Revolution and Agrarian Property*

Let us now examine the problem of land under the republic. To clarify my views on the agrarian question during this period, I must insist on a concept that I have expressed regarding the nature of the independence revolution in Peru. The revolution found Peru to be backwards in the formation of its bourgeoisie. The elements of a capitalist economy in our country were more embryonic than in other American countries where the revolution had a less hidden and incipient bourgeois.

If the revolution had been a movement of the Indigenous masses or had championed their cause, it would necessarily have had an agrarian face. It is already well demonstrated how the French Revolution particularly benefited from the rural class, on which it had to rely to prevent the return of the old regime. This phenomenon, furthermore, seems in general to be true of the bourgeois as well as socialist revolution, judging from the better defined and more stable elimination of feudalism in central Europe and in Russia czarism. Directed and performed mainly by the urban bourgeoisie and the urban proletariat, both revolutions brought immediate benefits to the peasants. Particularly in Russia, it was this class that has reaped the first fruits of the Bolshevik Revolution, because there had not been a bourgeois revolution to destroy feudalism and absolutism and put in its place a liberal democratic regime.

But for the liberal democratic revolution to have these effects, two premises have been necessary: the existence of a bourgeoisie conscious of the consequences and the interests of its action, and the existence of a revolutionary spirit in the peasant class, and, above all, its claim to the right of land in defiance of the power of the landowning aristocracy. In Peru, less so than in other American countries, the independence revolution did not meet these conditions. The revolution had triumphed because of the forced continental solidarity of peoples who rebelled against Spanish domination, and because the political and economic circumstances of the world worked in their favor. The continental nationalism of the Spanish American revolutionaries combined with the forced pooling of their destinies to put the people who were most advanced in their march to capitalism with those who were most backwards.

In his study of the Argentine and therefore Latin American wars of independence, Echeverría classified society as follows:

> American society was divided into three conflicting classes of interest, without any moral and political social bonds. The first was composed of lawyers, the clergy, and authorities; the second those enriched by monopolies and good fortune; the third rustics, known as "gauchos" and "compadritos" in the Río de la Plata, "cholos" in Peru, "rotos" in Chile, "leperos" in Mexico. The Indigenous and African castes were slaves and lived outside of society. The first class enjoyed life without producing anything and had the power and privileges of nobility; they were the aristocracy, composed primarily of Spaniards and very few Americans. The second also lived in comfort, quietly engaged in their industry and commerce; it was the middle class that sat on the municipal council. The third, the only producer of manual work, was composed of artisans and proletarians of all kinds. The American descendants of the first two classes who received some education in America or on the Iberian Peninsula were the ones who raised the banner of the revolution.[12]

Rather than a conflict between the landowning nobility and commercial bourgeoisie, in many cases the Latin American revolutions resulted in their collaboration, either because of the indoctrination of liberal ideas as the aristocracy claimed, or because in many cases they did not see this revolution as anything more than a liberation movement from the Spanish crown. The rural population, which in Peru was Indigenous, did not have a direct or active presence in the revolution. The revolutionary program did not represent their grievances.

But this program was based on liberal ideology. The revolution could not dispense with principles that supported agrarian demands based on the practical needs and theoretical justice of freeing the land from its feudal shackles. The republic inserted these principles into its statutes. Peru did not have a bourgeois class to implement them in accordance with its economic interests and political and legal doctrine. But the republic, because this was the course and the dictates of history, should be established on liberal and bourgeois principles. Only the practical consequences of the revolution as they related to agricultural property could not fail to be stopped by the limits set by the interests of the large landowners.

Therefore the policy of decoupling of agricultural property imposed by the political foundations of the republic did not attack the system of large landholdings. And, although the new laws ordered the division of lands to Indigenous peoples, it also attacked the community in the name of liberal principles.

Thus was inaugurated a regime that, irrespective of its principles, to some extent worsened the condition of the Indigenous peoples rather than improved it. And this was not the fault of the ideology behind the new policy and which, applied correctly, should have ended feudal control of the land and converted the Indigenous peoples into small landholders.

The new policy formally abolished the *mita*, *encomienda*, etc. It included a series of measures that meant the end of Indigenous serfdom. But since it left the power and force of feudal property intact, it contradicted its own measures to protect the small landowner and farmer.

Even if the landowning aristocracy in principle gave up its privileges, in fact it retained its position. In Peru it continued to be the dominant class. The revolution had not really brought a new class to power. The professional and commercial bourgeoisie was too weak to govern. The abolition of serfdom, therefore, never became more than a theoretical statement because the revolution had not touched the landholding system. Servitude is only one aspect of feudalism, but not feudalism itself.

## The Republic's Agrarian Policy

A liberal policy on land ownership could not naturally develop or be formulated during the period of military strongmen that followed the

independence revolution. Military strongmen were the natural product of a revolutionary period that had not been able to create a new
governing class. In this context, power was exercised by soldiers of the
revolution who, on one hand, enjoyed the prestige of their wartime
achievements and, on the other, were able to stay in government
through the force of their weapons. Of course, these strongmen could
not escape the influence of class interests or of opposing historical
forces. They were supported by the inconsistent liberalism and rhetoric of urban *demos* or the colonial conservatism of the landowner
caste. They were inspired by the clientele of the tribunes and lawyers
of the city's democracy, or by the writers and orators of the landholding aristocracy. Because, in the conflict of interests between liberals
and conservatives, there was no direct and active presence of rural
demands that would oblige the former to include the redistribution of
agrarian property in its agenda.

This basic problem would have been definitely noticed and appreciated by a better statesperson. But none of our military chieftains of
this period were like that.

The military strongmen, moreover, seem organically incapable of
reform on this scale, which requires more than anything, clear legal
and economic criteria. Their violence produces an atmosphere
adverse to experimentation with the principles for a new legal and
economic system. Vasconcelos makes the following observation:

> On an economic level, the strongmen are always the main support of the
> landholding system. Although sometimes they proclaim themselves to
> be enemies of property, there is hardly any strongman who does not end
> up as a wealthy estate owner. The fact is that military power inevitably
> leads to the crime of appropriation of land ownership. Whether called a
> soldier, military strongman, king or emperor, despotism and large land-
> holdings are correlative terms. And of course economic, as well as polit-
> ical rights, can only be preserved and defended within a regime of free-
> dom. Absolutism inevitably leads to the misery of many, and opulence
> and abuse of power for the few. Only democracy, despite all its short-
> comings, has been able to take us close to the best achievements of social

justice, at least democracy before it degenerates into the imperialism of republics that are too wealthy and are surrounded by decadent people. Anyway, among us the strongmen and the military government have cooperated with the development of large estates. Even a superficial examination of property deeds of our large landowners is enough to show that almost all of their wealth initially came from the Spanish Crown, and afterward from concessions and illegitimate favors granted to the influential generals of our false republics. At each step, the grants and concessions have been awarded without taking into account the rights of entire populations of Indigenous peoples or *mestizos* who have no power to assert their ownership.[13]

[This opinion, which is true in regard to the relations between military caudillos and agrarian property in America, is not equally valid for all times and historical situations. It is not possible to subscribe to it without this specific qualification.]*

A new legal and economic order cannot be, in any case, the work of a strongman but of a class. When the class exists, the strongman acts as its interpreter and trustee. It is not his personal whims, but a set of collective interests and needs that decides his policy. Peru lacked a bourgeois class capable of organizing a strong and efficient state. Militarism represented an elementary and provisional order that as soon as it stopped being indispensable had to be replaced by a more advanced and integrated order. It was unable to understand or even consider the agrarian problem. Rudimentary and immediate problems absorbed its limited action. Castilla was the military strongman at its best. His shrewd opportunism, his acute malice, his crudeness, and his absolute empiricism prevented him from adopting a liberal policy until the end. Castilla realized that the liberals of his time were a clique, a group, not a class. This led him to avoid cautiously any act seriously opposed to the interests and principles of the conservative class. But the merits of his policy lie in his reformist and progressive tendency. His most significant

---

*Observations in brackets are found in Mariátegui's original footnotes and are included here to present a more comprehensive understanding of this work.—Eds.

historical acts, the abolition of African slavery and forced tribute payments from Indigenous peoples, represent his liberal attitude.

Since the enactment of the Civil Code, Peru has entered a period of gradual organization. There is almost no need to remark that this signified, among other things, the decline of militarism. The code, inspired by the same principles as the first decrees of the republic on land, reinforced and continued the policy of disentailment and redistribution of agricultural property. Ugarte, noting the progress of this national legislation with regard to land, notes that the code "confirmed the legal abolition of Indigenous communities and of the entailments; it introduced new legislation establishing occupation as one of the ways to acquire property without an owner; in the rules on inherence, it tried to encourage small property holdings."[14]

Francisco García Calderón attributes effects to the Civil Code that it actually did not have, or at least were not of the radical and absolute scope that he believed. "The constitution," he writes,

> had destroyed the privileges and the civil law divided the property and terminated the rights of equality in families. The consequences of this provision were, in the political realm, the death of the entire oligarchy, of the entire landholding aristocracy. Socially, it led to the rise of the bourgeoisie and of racial mixing. . . . Economically, the equal partition of inheritances favored the formation of small property holdings previously blocked by the great landholding estates.[15]

This was certainly the intention of the legal codifiers in Peru. But the Civil Code is only one of the instruments of liberal politics and capitalist practice. As Ugarte recognized, Peruvian law "is intended to promote the democratization of land ownership, *but by the purely negative means* of removing obstacles rather than providing positive protection to the farmers."[16] Nowhere has the division of agricultural property, or rather its redistribution, been possible without special expropriation laws that have transferred ownership of land to the class that works it.

Notwithstanding the code, small property has not flourished in Peru. To the contrary, the large estates have been consolidated and extended. And the property of the Indigenous community has been the only one that has suffered the consequences of this deformed liberalism.

## Large Property and Political Power

The two factors that kept the independence revolution from engaging and addressing the agrarian problem in Peru—the extremely incipient nature of the urban bourgeoisie and the extra-social situation of the Indigenous peoples, as Echeverría defines it—later prevented governments during the republic from developing a policy somehow aimed at a less unequal and unjust distribution of land.

During the period of military strongmen, rather than strengthening the urban *demos* the landholding aristocracy was strengthened. The emergence of a vibrant urban bourgeoisie was not economically possible with trade and finance in foreign hands. Spanish education, radically distant from the ends and needs of industrialism and capitalism, did not train businesspeople or technicians, but lawyers, writers, theologians, etc. Unless they felt a special vocation for Jacobinism or demagoguery, they joined the clientele of the landowning caste. Business capital, almost entirely foreign, could not do anything other than to come to an understanding with and be associated with this aristocracy, which, moreover, tacitly or explicitly retained its political dominance. In this way, the landholding aristocracy and its adherents became the beneficiaries of the fiscal policy and the exploitation of guano and nitrate. In this way, this caste was compelled by its economic role to assume in Peru the role of the bourgeois class, but without losing its colonial and aristocratic vices and prejudices. So, finally, the urban bourgeoisie, professionals, and businesspeople were absorbed by *civilismo*.

The power of this class, *civilistas* or "neogoths," has come largely from the ownership of the land. In the early years after independence, it was not exactly a capitalist class but a class of owners. Their status as an ownership rather than educated class allowed them to merge their interests with those of foreign business owners, and to use this title to deal with the state and public wealth. Land ownership granted by the viceroyalty meant that during the republic they gained access to business capital. The privileges of the colony engendered the privileges of the republic.

It was, therefore, natural and instinctive that this class holds the most conservative attitudes toward land ownership. The persistence of the extra-social status of Indigenous peoples, on the other hand, meant that there were no conscious peasant masses ready to oppose feudal landholding interests.

These were the main factors in the preservation and development of large landholdings. The liberalism of the republican legislation, passive in the face of feudal landholdings, was only active toward communal landholdings. Although it could not do anything against the large landholdings, it could do a lot to communities. In a people with communist traditions, dissolving the community did not mean creating small properties. A society cannot be artificially transformed, much less a peasant society deeply attached to its tradition and legal institutions. Individualism has never had its origin in a country's constitution or civil code. Its formation has always been a more complicated and spontaneous process. Destroying communities did not mean converting Indigenous peoples into small landholders or even into free salaried workers, but the surrendering of their lands to *gamonales* and their clientele. This made it easier for large landholders to tie Indigenous peoples to large estates.

It is claimed that the key to the concentration of land ownership on the coast has been the need of owners to gain access peacefully to a sufficient water supply. According to this argument, irrigated agriculture in river valleys formed by shallow rivers has led to the flourishing of large properties and the suffocation of medium and small properties. But this is a specious argument, and only in small part accurate. Because technical or material reasons overestimate it, it influences the concentration of ownership only because of the establishment and development of vast industrial crops on the coast. Before this prosperous success, before coast agriculture acquired a capitalist organization, the risk factor was too weak to determine the concentration of ownership. It is true that the shortage of irrigation water that resulted because of the difficulties of its distribution among multiple irrigators favors the large property. But it is not true that this is what keeps that property from being subdivided. The origins of large coast landholdings date back to colonial rule. The depopulation of the coast as a result of colonial practices is one of the consequences and one of the reasons for the presence of large landholdings. The problem of laborers, the only one that coastal landowners have faced, has all its roots in the large landholding system. Landowners wanted to resolve it with African slaves in colonial times, with Chinese coolies during the republic. It was a futile endeavor. The earth cannot be peopled with slaves. Above all, it does not make the land. Due to this policy, the large landowners on the coast have all the land they can hold, but they do not have enough men to enliven and exploit it. This is the defense of large property, but it is also its misfortune and weakness.

The agrarian situation in the highlands shows, moreover, the fallacy of the above argument. The highlands do not have a water problem. Abundant rainfall allows large landowners, the same as the communal farmer, to grow the same crops. Nevertheless, in the highlands the phenomenon of the concentration of land ownership also exists. This fact points to the essentially sociopolitical nature of the problem.

The development of industrial crops for agricultural export on coastal haciendas is entirely dependent on the economic colonization of Latin America by Western capitalism. British businesspeople and bankers became interested in the exploitation of these lands when the possibility of using them profitably, first for the production of sugar and later for cotton, was proven. A large part of agricultural land has long been mortgaged to the control of foreign firms. The landowners, in debt to foreign businesses and bankers, served as intermediaries, almost as *yanaconas* to Anglo-Saxon capitalism to ensure that cultivated fields would be worked at minimal cost by enslaved and wretched laborers, bent to the ground under the whip of the colonial slave drivers.

But the large estates on the coast have reached a more or less advanced technical capitalist level, even though their exploitation still relies on feudal practices and principles. The production yields for cotton and sugarcane are those of the capitalist system. The companies have access to powerful capital, and the land is worked with modern machinery and procedures. Powerful industrial plants work to process the products. Meanwhile, in the highlands, production figures from large landholdings generally are no higher than those of community landholdings. And if the justification for a production system is in its outcome, as objective economic criteria demand, this fact alone irremediably condemns the landholding system in the highlands.

### The Community under the Republic

We have already seen how the formal liberalism of republican legislation has only been active against Indigenous communities. Arguably, the concept of individual property has assumed an almost antisocial role in the republic because of its conflict with the livelihood of the community. Indeed, if its expropriation and dissolution was ordered and carried out by capitalism in a vigorous and autonomous growth, it would appear as if it were a casualty of economic progress. Indians would have moved from a mixed system of communism and servitude to a system of free wage. This change would have somewhat denaturalized them, but it would have also positioned them to organize and emancipate themselves as a class, the same as proletariats throughout the world. Meanwhile, the expropriation and gradual absorption of the community into large landholdings on the one hand sunk them deeper into bondage, and on the other destroyed the economic and legal institution that helped safeguard the spirit and substance of their ancient civilization.

[If the historical evidence of Inca communism does not appear incontestable, the community, the specific body of communism, should be sufficient to dispel any doubt.[17] The "despotism" of the Incas, however, has offended the liberal scruples of some of the minds of our time. I want to reaffirm here the defense that I made of Inca communism, and refute the argument of its latest challenger, Augusto Aguirre Morales, author of the novel *El Pueblo del Sol* (The People of the Sun).[18]

Modern communism is different from Inca communism. This is the first thing that a scholarly man who explores Tawantinsuyu needs to learn and understand. The two kinds of communism are products of different human experiences. They belong to different historical eras. They were developed by different civilizations. The Inca civilization was agrarian. That of Marx and Sorel is an industrial civilization. In the former, man submitted to nature. In the latter, nature sometimes submits to man. It is absurd, therefore, to compare the forms and institutions of one communism to the other. The only thing that can be compared is their material and essential likeness, within the essential material difference in time and space. For this comparison we need a little bit of historical relativism. Otherwise one runs the risk of falling into the same serious errors into which Víctor Andrés Belaúnde fell when he attempted this type of comparison.

The chroniclers of the conquest and the colonial period viewed the Indigenous panorama with medieval eyes. Their testimony certainly cannot be accepted at face value.

Their judgments strictly corresponded to their Spanish and Catholic points of view. But Aguirre Morales is also a victim of a false point of view. His position in the study of the Inca empire is not a relativist position. Aguirre considers and examines the empire with liberal and individualistic prejudices. And he believes that the Inca people were an enslaved and unhappy people because they lacked freedom.

Individual freedom is one aspect of a complex liberal phenomenon. A realistic critic could define it as the legal basis of capitalist civilization. (Without free will there would be no free trade, or free competition, or free industry.) An idealist criticism may define it as an acquisition of the human spirit in the modern age. In no case did this freedom fit the Inca life. The man of Tawantinsuyu absolutely did not feel any need for individual freedom, just as he felt absolutely no need, for example, for freedom of the press. The freedom of the press can be useful to Aguirre Morales and to me, but the Indians could be happy without knowing or even conceiving it. The life and spirit of the Indians were not tormented by the desire for speculation and intellectual creation. They were not subordinated to the need for commerce, to make contracts, or to travel. What use, therefore, could this freedom invented by our civilization serve the Indian? If the spirit of freedom was revealed to the Quechua, it was undoubtedly in a formula or, rather, in an emotion different from the liberal, Jacobin, and individualistic formula of freedom. The revelation of freedom, as the revelation of God, varies with age, peoples, and climates. To believe that the abstract idea of freedom, with the concrete image of liberty with a Phrygian cap, the daughter of Protestantism and the Renaissance and the French Revolution, is to be trapped by an illusion that depends perhaps on a mere, though not disinterested, philosophical astigmatism of the bourgeoisie and its democracy.

Aguirre's argument that denies the communist nature of Inca society rests entirely on a misconception. Aguirre begins with the idea that autocracy and communism are two irreconcilable terms. The Inca regime, he says, was despotic and theocratic; then he says it was not a communist regime. But historically communism does not assume individual freedom or the popular vote. Autocracy and communism are incompatible in our time, but they were not in primitive societies. Today a new order cannot give up any of the moral progress of modern society. Contemporary socialism (other times have had other types of socialism that history has labeled with different names) is the antithesis of liberalism, but it was born from its womb and is fed by its experience. It does not disdain any of its intellectual conquests. It only flouts and vilifies its limitations. It appreciates and understands everything that is positive in the liberal idea: it only condemns and attacks what is negative and selfish in it.

The Inca regime was certainly theocratic and despotic. But this is a common feature of all ancient regimes. All monarchies in history have relied on the religious sentiments of their peoples. The divorce of temporal and spiritual power is a new development. And more than a divorce, it is a separation. Until William of Hohenzollern, monarchs have invoked their divine right.

It is not possible to speak abstractly of tyranny. Tyranny is a concrete fact. And it is real only to the extent that it represses the will of an oppressed people, or otherwise suffocates their vital impulses.

Often in ancient times, an absolutist and theocratic regime has embodied and represented, on the contrary, that will and force. This seems to have been the case for the Inca empire. I do not believe in the supernatural powers of the Incas. Their political capacity is clearly evident, but I judge it to be no less clear that its work consisted of building the empire with human materials and moral elements amassed over the centuries. The *ayllu*, the community, was the nucleus of the empire. The Incas unified and created the empire, but they did not create its nucleus. The legal state organized by the Incas undoubtedly reproduced the natural preexisting state. The Incas did not disrupt anything. Their work should be praised; the millenarian expression and myriad elements of which this work is but an expression and consequence should not be scorned and disparaged.

The part of this work that belongs to the masses should not be depreciated, much less denied. Aguirre, an individualistic writer, is content to ignore the role of the masses in history. His romantic gaze only looks for the hero.

The vestiges of Inca civilization unanimously stand against the statements of Aguirre Morales. The author of *El Pueblo del Sol* cites the testimony of thousands of *huacos* that have passed before his eyes. And so those *huacos* say that Inca art was a popular art. And the best document of Inca civilization is perhaps its art. A crude and barbarous people could not have produced these stylized, synthetic ceramics.

James George Frazer, spiritually and physically very distant from the colonial chroniclers, wrote:

> Nor, to remount the stream of history to its sources, is it an accident that all the first great strides towards civilisation have been made under despotic and theocratic governments, like those of Egypt, Babylon, and Peru, where the supreme ruler claimed and received the servile allegiance of his subjects in the double character of King and a god. It is hardly too much to say that at this early epoch despotism is the best friend of humanity and, paradoxical as it may sound, of liberty. For after all there is more liberty in the best sense—liberty to think our own thoughts and to fashion our own

destinies—under the most absolute despotism, the most grinding
tyranny, than under the apparent freedom of savage life, where the
individual's lot is cast from the cradle to the grave in the iron mould
of hereditary custom.[19]

Morales Aguirre said that there was no theft in Inca society
because of a simple lack of imagination for evil. But this sentence of
witty literary humor does not destroy a social reality that proves precisely what Aguirre insists on denying: Inca communism. The
French economist Charles Gidj believed that more accurate than
Proudhon's famous formula is the following: "Theft is property."
Inca society had no theft because there was no property. Or, if you
will, because there was a socialist organization of property.

We dispute and, if necessary, reject the testimony of colonial
chroniclers. But it is the case of Aguirre's theory that it seeks support
precisely in the medieval interpretation of those chroniclers on the
form of distribution of land and products.

The fruits of the soil cannot be hoarded. It is not plausible, therefore, that two-thirds were reserved for the consumption of the officials
and priests of the empire. Much more plausible is that the crops that
were supposedly reserved for the nobility and Inca leader were
intended for state storehouses. And that they represent, in sum, an act
of social providence, typical and characteristic of a socialist order.]

During the republican period, national writers and legislators have
shown a more or less uniform tendency to condemn the community as
the residue of a primitive society or a survival of the colonial organization. This attitude has sometimes been due to the interests of the
landowning *gamonales* and sometimes to other individualist and liberal thought that automatically dominated an overly literary and emotional culture.

A study by Dr. M. V. Villarán, one of the intellectuals who, with
the most critical skills and greatest doctrinal coherency, represent
this thought during our first century. His study marks the beginning
of a careful revision of his findings regarding the Indigenous community. Dr. Villarán theoretically maintains his liberal position in

advocating the principle of individual ownership of property, but in practice he accepts the protection of communities against large landholdings by recognizing that they had a function the state should protect.

But the first integrated and documented defense of the Indigenous community had to draw on socialist thought based on a concrete study of its nature and carried out according to the research methods of modern sociology and economics. Hildebrando Castro Pozo's book *Nuestra Comunidad Indígena* does this. In this interesting study, Castro Pozo approaches the issue free of liberal preconceptions. This allows him to address the problem of the community with a mind able to appreciate and understand it. Castro Pozo not only reveals that the Indigenous community, despite the attacks of liberal formalism placed at the service of a system of feudalism, is still a living organism, but also that despite the hostile environment that suffocates and deforms it, it also spontaneously manifests obvious possibilities for evolution and development.

Castro Pozo argues that "the *ayllu* or community has preserved its natural idiosyncrasy, its character as almost a family institution within which its main constituent factors continued to persist after the conquest."[20] Here he is in agreement with Valcárcel, whose propositions in regard to the *ayllu* seem to some to be overdominated by the ideal of Indigenous resurgence.

What are and how do the communities currently function? Castro Pozo believes that they can be classified in the following way:

First—agricultural communities; Second—livestock farming communities; Third—communities with pasture lands and water; and Fourth—communities that have use of the land. It must be taken into account that in a country like ours, where a single institution acquires different characteristics according to the medium in which it has developed, no one type from this classification is in reality so distinct and different from the others that it alone can be held up as a model. On the contrary, the first type of agricultural communities contains characteristics that correspond to the others, and in the others some similar to the first. But since a set of external factors has been imposed on each of these

groups, a certain kind of life in their customs, habits, and work systems
in their properties and industries, each group has predominant characteristics. These define it as agricultural, livestock, livestock farmers
with communal pastures and water, or only the last two, and those that
absolutely or relatively lack ownership of land and the usufructuary of
it by the *ayllu* that, undoubtedly, was its sole proprietor.[21]

These differences have not been developed by natural evolution or
degeneration of the ancient community but as a result of legislation
aimed at the individualization of property and, above all, as a result of
the expropriation of communal lands in favor of large landholdings.
They demonstrate, therefore, the vitality of Indigenous communism
that invariably promotes various forms of cooperation and association
for the aboriginals. Indians, despite the laws of one hundred years of
the republican regime, have not become individualistic. And this does
not come from resistance to progress, as is simplistically claimed by
detractors. Rather, it is because individualism under a feudal regime
cannot find the conditions necessary to gain strength and develop.
Communism, on the other hand, has continued to be the only defense
for the Indians. Individualism cannot flourish, or even effectively
exist, except in a system of free competition. Indians have not felt less
free than when they have felt alone.

Therefore, in Indigenous villages where families are grouped and
bonds of heritage and communal work have been extinguished,
strong and tenacious habits of cooperation and solidarity that are the
empirical expression of a communist spirit still exist. The community draws on this spirit. It is their body. When expropriation and redi-
vision seem about to liquidate the community, Indigenous socialism
always finds a way to reject, resist, or evade it. Communal labor and
property are replaced by cooperation in individual work. As Castro
Pozo writes: "Customs have been reduced to *mingas* and *ayllu* meetings to help some community member with a wall, irrigation ditch, or
house. Tasks proceed to the music of harps and violins, the consumption of several arrobas[22] of sugarcane aguardiente, packs of cigarettes,
and chewing coca." These customs have led Indigenous peoples to

the naturally incipient and rudimentary practice of the collective contract rather than the individual contract. They are not isolated individuals who offer their labor to a landowner or contractor; they are all the able people of the area who cooperatively do so.

## The Community and the Large Estate

The defense of the Indigenous community is not based on abstract principles of justice or sentimental traditionalist considerations, but on concrete and practical reasons of economic and social order. In Peru, communal property does not represent a primitive economy that has been gradually replaced by a progressive economy founded on individual property. No, the communities have been stripped of their land for the benefit of the feudal or semifeudal large landholdings that are constitutionally incapable of technical progress. [Writing this paper, I find in Víctor Raúl Haya de la Torre's book *Por la emancipación de la América Latina* (For the Emancipation of Latin America) concepts that coincide absolutely with mine on the agrarian question in general and the Indigenous community in particular. We start with the same views, so it is imperative that our findings are also the same.][23]

On the coast, from the viewpoint of cultivation, the large landholdings have evolved from a feudal routine to a capitalist technique, while the Indigenous community has disappeared as a communist exploitation of the land. But in the highlands, the large landholdings have fully retained its feudal character, pitting a much stronger resistance than the community to the development of the capitalist economy. The community, in fact, when it is connected by the railroad to a commercial system and central transportation routes, has spontaneously transformed itself into a cooperative. Castro Pozo, who as head of the Indigenous Affairs section in the Ministry of Development collected extensive data on the life of communities, points to the highlights of the fascinating case of the settlement of Muquiyauyo, which, he says, represents the characteristics of production, consumption, and credit cooperatives.

As owner of a magnificent power plant on the banks of the Mantaro River, which provides electrical power to the small industries in the districts of Jauja, Concepción, Mito, Muqui, Sincos, Huanpampa, and Muquiyauyo, it has been transformed into a community institution par excellence. Instead of neglecting its Indigenous customs, the community has taken advantage of them to carry out the work of the company. It has used the money saved on the manual labor done by the settlement to purchase heavy machinery. The same is true for the building of a common house, which used *mingas* in which even the women and children were useful participants in carrying construction materials.[24]

Large landholdings compare unfavorably with the community as an enterprise for agricultural production. Within the capitalist system, large properties replace and dislodge small farms because of the ability to intensify production through the use of advanced production techniques. The industrialization of agriculture leads to the concentration of land ownership. The large property appears justified by the interest of production, which are both identified, at least theoretically, with the interest of society. But large landholdings do not have the same effect, nor do they respond to an economic necessity. Except in cases of sugarcane plantations, which are engaged in the production of aguardiente destined for the poisoning and brutalization of Indigenous peasants, the production of highland estates is generally the same as that of communities. And the production figures are no different. The lack of agricultural statistics does not permit an exact accounting, but all available data point to the fact that crop yields in the communities are not, on average, lower than those of large estates. The only production statistic for the highlands is for wheat and it bears out this conclusion. Castro Pozo, summarizing statistical data for 1917–18, writes the following:

> The harvest was, on average, 450 and 580 kilos per hectare for communal and individual property, respectively. If we take into account that the best land has come under the control of the large landowners, since the struggle for it in the southern departments has reached the point of removing Indigenous landholders through violence or

massacres, and that the communal farmers' ignorance leads them to
hide data concerning the exact amount of the harvest, understating
the figures out of fear of new taxes or assessments by minor political
authorities or their agents, it can be easily inferred that the difference
in output per hectare that favors individual property is not accurate,
and that reasonably it should be understood as negligible. Therefore,
in terms of the means of production and cultivation, both types of
properties are identical.[25]

In feudal Russia of the past century, large estates had higher
returns than small properties. The figures in hectoliters per hectare
were as follows: for rye, 11.5 to 9.4; for wheat, 11 to 9.1; for oats, 15.4
to 12.7; for barley, 11.5 to 10.5; for potatoes, 92.3 to 72.[26] The large
highland estates in Peru, therefore, are below the execrable large landholdings of Tsarist Russia in terms of factors of production.

The community, however, on the one hand leads to an effective
capacity for development and transformation, and on the other hand
is presented as a system of production that keeps alive in the Indians
the moral stimuli needed for their maximum performance as workers.
Castro Pozo makes a very accurate observation when he writes

> The Indigenous community retains two major economic and social
> principles that until the present neither sociological science nor the
> empiricism of the great industrialists has been able to resolve satisfac-
> torily: the multiple labor contract and the ability to have the labor
> preformed with less physiological wear and in a friendly and support-
> ive environment.

[The author has some interesting comments on the spiritual elements of the communal economy. He points out

> The energy, perseverance and interest with which a community
> member reaps and sheaf wheat or barley, *quipicha* [*quipichar*: to
> carry on one's back—a widespread Indigenous custom throughout
> the highlands: porters and stevedores on the coast shoulder their

loads] and rapidly proceeds to the threshing floor, joking with his companion or suffering the tugging on his shirt from behind, present a very profound and decisive difference compared to the indolence, indifference, apathy, and apparent fatigue with which the *yanaconas* labor in identical or other similar workplaces. Since at first sight what jumps out is the deep difference in value of both psychological and physical states, and since the first question implied in spirit is what influence does its objectification and concrete and immediate purpose have on the process of labor?][27]

By dissolving or abandoning the community, the system of large feudal estates has not only attacked an economic institution, but also and most importantly, a social institution that defends Indigenous traditions, which preserves the role of the rural family and translates that popular legal philosophy so highly valued by Proudhon and Sorel. [Sorel, who has devoted much attention to the ideas of Proudhon, and Le Play on the role of the family in the structure and spirit of society, has studied with shrewd insight "the spiritual part of the economic environment." If anything has been missing in Marx, it has been an insufficient legal spirit, although it is agreed that this aspect of the production did not escape Treves's dialectic. "We know," he writes in his *Introduction à L'Economie Moderne*, "that to observe the customs of the families on the Saxon plain, made a deep impression on Le Play at the beginning of his travels and had a decisive influence on his thinking. I have wondered if Marx had not thought of these ancient customs when he accused capitalism of turning the proletarian into a man without a family." With regard to the observations of Castro Pozo, I want to recall another concept from Sorel: "Work depends to a very large degree on the feelings that the workers have about their task."][28]

### The Work System: Servitude and Salaried Work

In agriculture, the work system is determined primarily by the property system. It is therefore not surprising that to the extent large feudal estates survive in Peru, servitude also survives in various forms and with different names. The difference between agriculture on the coast and agriculture in the highlands appears to have less to do with the labor system than with its technique. Agriculture on the coast has evolved more or less quickly toward a capitalist technique of soil cultivation and the processing and sale of crops. But in contrast, it has remained overly static in its attitude and conduct with regard to labor. In terms of the laborer, the large colonial estates have not renounced their feudal habits except when circumstances demand it do so.

This phenomenon is explained not only because the old feudal lords have retained ownership of the land, but as intermediaries of foreign capital they have adopted the practice but not the spirit of modern capitalism. This also explains the colonial mentality of this caste of owners who are accustomed to consider work with the criterion of slave owners and traders. In Europe, the feudal lord embodied, to some extent, the primitive patriarchal tradition, so that in respect to his servants he naturally felt higher, but not ethnically or nationally different from them. The landowning aristocrats in Europe found it possible to accept a new concept and a new practice in their dealings with the agricultural worker. In colonial America, meanwhile, the white person's arrogant and deep-rooted belief in the inferiority of people of color has stood in the way of this development.

On the Peruvian coast, when the agricultural worker has not been an Indian he has been an African slave or Chinese coolie who is, if possible, held in more contempt. Coastal estate owners have simultaneously assumed the feelings of a medieval aristocrat and a white colonizer saturated with racial prejudices.

The *yanaconazgo* and indenture are not the only more or less feudal expressions that still persist in coastal agriculture. The estate is run as a baronial fief. State laws are not applied on the large estates without the tacit or formal consensus of the large landowners. The authority of political or administrative officials is in fact subject to the authority of the landowners in the territory of their domain. Landowners practically consider their estates to be outside the jurisdiction of the state, and they are not the least bit worried about the civil rights of the people who live within the boundaries of their property. They collect excise taxes, grant monopolies, and impose sanctions restricting the freedom of the laborers and their families. Within the state, transportation, business, and even customs are subject to the control of the landowner. And frequently the huts for the workers are not significantly different from the sheds that housed the slave population.

The large coastal landowners are not legally entitled to their feudal or semi-feudal rights, but their ruling-class status and unlimited hoarding of land in an area without industries or transportation grants them an almost uncontrollable power. Through indenture [*enganche*] and *yanaconazgo*, large landowners resist the establishment of a free-wage system, a functional necessity to a liberal and capitalist economy. Indenture deprives laborers of the right to dispose of their person and labor until they fulfill the contractual obligations with the landowner, and is unmistakably descended from the semi-slave traffic in coolies. The *yanaconazgo* is a kind of a system of bondage through which feudalism has been extended into our capitalist age among politically and economically backward peoples. The Peruvian system of *yanaconazgo*, for example, is similar to the Russian system of *polovnischestvo* under which in some cases crops would be equally split between the landlords and the peasants, and in other cases only receive a third part.[29]

The small population on the coast creates a constant threat of a labor shortage for agricultural enterprises. *Yanaconazgo* ties the small local population to the land, because without the minimal guarantee of the use of land they would tend to diminish and migrate. Indenture ensures coastal agriculture a supply of highland laborers who, though they find themselves on foreign land and in a strange environment on coastal estates, at least receive better pay for their work.

This indicates that, despite everything and although perhaps only superficially or partially, the situation of the workers on the coastal estates is better than of those in the highlands where feudalism remains all-powerful. (One should not forget that highland workers suffer on the hot and unhealthy coast. Highland Indians almost surely contract malaria, which weakens them and leaves them vulnerable to tuberculosis. Nor should we forget the deep attachment of Indians to their homes and surroundings. On the coast they feel like exiles, like *mitimaes*.) Coastal landowners are forced to accept, albeit in a restricted and attenuated form, the system of free wages and labor. The capitalist character of their businesses constrains the competition. The laborers retain, if only relatively so, their freedom to emigrate and to refuse to work for bosses who are too abusive. The vicinity of ports and cities, the access to modern transportation and business routes offer, on the other hand, the possibility for laborers to escape their rural destiny and to try another means of earning a livelihood.

If agriculture on the coast would have had a more progressive, more capitalist character, it would have sought a logical solution to the labor problem that has been talked about so much. More enlightened landowners would have realized that large estates, as they function now, are agents of depopulation and that therefore the labor problem is one of its most clear and logical consequences. [One of the most important findings to this topic is how closely our agrarian problem is linked with our population problem. The concentration of land in the hands of the *gamonales* is a cancer that stops the growth of the national population. Only when this obstacle to Peruvian progress is broken is it actually possible to adopt the South American principle: "To govern is to populate."]

In the same measure as capitalist techniques progress in coastal agriculture, wage labor replaces *yanaconazgo*. Scientific farming—the use of equipment, fertilizer, etc.—is incompatible with a labor system that belongs to a routine and primitive agricultural system. But the demographic factor, the "labor problem," presents a serious resistance to this process of capitalist development. The *yanaconazgo* and its variations are used to keep a population base in the valleys that ensures enterprises the minimum number of workers necessary for the permanent work. The immigrant day laborer does not offer the same assurances of continuity in work that the native settler or native *yanacona* enjoy. The latter represents, moreover, the roots of a peasant family, whose oldest children will be more or less forced to rent out their labor to the landowner.

Finding this out now leads those same large landowners to consider the desirability of, slowly and cautiously without any possibility of compromising their interests, establishing colonies or clusters of small landowners. Part of the irrigated land in the Imperial Valley has been reserved for small farms. There is a proposal to apply the same principle in other irrigated zones. A rich, intelligent, and experienced landowner who talked with me recently told me that the existence of small farms next to large estates was essential for the formation of a rural population, otherwise working the land would always be at the mercy of the possibilities of migratory indentured workers. The program of the Agricultural Subdivision Company is another expression of an agrarian policy aimed at the gradual establishment of small farms. [The project that the government conceived to create small agrarian property was inspired by a liberal and capitalist economic approach. Along the coast its implementation, subject to the expropriation of estates and the irrigation of uncultivated lands, can still correspond to the more or less extensive opportunities for colonization. In the highlands its effects would be much more limited and uncertain. All attempts at land allocation over the course of our republican history are characterized by prescinding the social value of the community and its timidity before large landholders who safeguard their interests with expressive zeal. It is not possible in highland regions where a market monetary economy does not exist to set the payment for a parcel of land in cash or in twenty annual payments. Payment in such cases should be provided not in cash but in goods. The state's system to acquire estates to distribute among the Indians manifests its extreme concern for the wealthy landowners who are offered the opportunity to sell unproductive or run-down estates for a profit.]

But since this policy systematically avoids expropriation, or, more precisely, large-scale expropriation by the state for reasons of public utility or distributive justice, and since its limited possibilities for development for the moment are confined to a few valleys, it is not likely that small farms will quickly or widely replace *yanaconazgo* in its demographic function. In valleys where the indenture system of highland workers is not capable of supplying sufficient labor on advantageous terms for the large landowners, *yanaconazgo* will continue to coexist for some time in its many varieties with wage labor.

The forms of *yanaconazgo*, tenancy, or renting vary on the coast and in the highlands according to regions, practices, or crops. They also have different names. But within their variety they can generally be identified with precapitalist methods of working the land as observed in other countries with semifeudal agriculture. For example, in tsarist Russia. The Russian system of *otrabotki* has all the varieties of paying for rent by work, money, or crops as exist in Peru. This can be confirmed by reading what Schkaff writes about such a system in his documented book on the agrarian question in Russia:

> Between the old bonded labor in which violence or coercion plays a large role, and free labor in which the only constraint that remains is a purely economic coercion, there extends a transitional system of extremely varied forms that combine the features of *barchtchina* and the wage earner. It is the *otrabototschnaía* system. Wages are paid either in cash where services are contracted, or in products, or in land. In this last case (*otrabotki* in the strict sense of the word), the landowner gives his land to the farmers instead of a wage for the work they do on his estate. . . . The payment for work in the *otrabotki* system is always lower than the wages of capitalist free contracting. The payment in produce makes landowners more independent of the variations in prices in the wheat and labor markets. They find local farmers to be a cheaper labor source, and thus enjoy a true local monopoly. . . . The rent paid by the farmer takes many forms. Sometimes, in addition to work, the farmer must give money and products. If one receives a *deciatina* of land, that person commits to work one and a half deciatina of the landowner's estate, to give ten eggs and one hen. That farmer will also deliver manure from his livestock because everything, including manure, is used for payment. Often the farmer is even required "to do all that the landowner requires of him," to transport crops, cut firewood, and carry loads.[30]

These traits of feudal property and work are particularly and precisely found in highland agriculture. The free labor system has not been developed there. The landowner does not care about the productivity of the land. He only cares about its profitability. For him, the factors of production are almost reduced to only two: the land and the Indian. Land ownership allows him unlimited use of Indian labor. The usury practiced on this labor force, which results in the misery of the Indian, is added to the rent charged for the land, calculated at the usual rate of tenancy. The landowner retains the best land and distributes the less productive land among his Indigenous laborers who are forced to work the first without pay and to live off the fruits of the second. The Indian pays rent for the land in labor or crops, very rarely in money (the Indian's labor has more value to the owner), most commonly in mixed or combined forms. Among other reports, I have seen a study by Dr. Ponce de León of the University of Cuzco that presents firsthand documentation of all the varieties of rental agreements and *yanaconazgo* in this vast department. It presents a fairly objective picture, despite the author's conclusions in respect to the landowners' privileges of the feudal exploitation. Here are some of his findings:

> In the province of Paucartambo the property owner grants the use of his land to a group of Indigenous peoples with the condition that they do all the required work for the cultivation of the estate lands that have been reserved for the owner. Generally they work three alternating days a week throughout the year. The tenants, or *"yanaconas"* as they are known in this province, also are obliged to transport the landowner's crops to this city with their own beasts without payment, and to serve as *pongos* [providers of domestic service] on the same estate, or more commonly in Cuzco where the owners prefer to live.... The same thing happens in Chumbivilcas. Tenants cultivate as much land as they can, and in exchange work for the owner as often as he requires. This form of lease can be simplified as follows: the property owner proposes to the tenant to use as much land as "you can," with the condition of working for me whenever I need it.... In the province of Anta the owner grants use of his land under the following conditions: the tenant furnish-

es the capital (seed, fertilizer) and the labor needed for cultivation until
the end (harvest). Once completed, the tenant and the landowner
equally divide all products. That is, each one takes 50 percent of production without the owner having done anything except to grant the
use of his lands without even fertilizing it. But that is not all. The
*aparcero* [tenant] is required to attend personally to the work of the
landowner but with the usual payment of 25 *centavos* a day.[31]

A comparison of this information with that of Schkaff is enough to
demonstrate that none of the dark aspects of precapitalist property
and work are lacking in the feudal highlands.


### The "Colonialism" of Our Coastal Agriculture

The degree of development achieved by the industrialization of agriculture under a capitalist system and technique on the coastal valleys
has as its principal factor the interest of the UK and U.S. in the production of sugar and cotton in Peru. The extension of these crops is
not primarily due to the ability or the industrial capacity of the capitalist landowners. They dedicate their land to cotton production and
sugarcane that powerful export firms funded or authorized.

The best lands on the coastal valleys are planted with cotton and
sugarcane, not so much because they are suited only for those crops,
but because they are the only ones that currently matter to English and
Yankees businesses. Agricultural credit, totally subordinated to the
interests of these firms until a national agricultural bank is established,
does not promote any other crop. Food crops for the domestic market
are generally in the hands of small landowners and tenant farmers.
Only in the valleys of Lima, because of their proximity to major urban
markets, are there large estates whose owners engage in the production of food crops. Cotton and sugar estates often do not grow enough
food crops to feed their own rural population.

The same small landowner or small tenant is pushed to cultivate cotton by this trend that does not take the needs of the national economy

into account. The shift from traditional food crops to cotton on coastal farms where small property owners remain has been one of the most visible causes in the rise of food prices in coastal towns.

The farmer finds commercial facilities almost exclusively for the cultivation of cotton. From top to bottom, loans are reserved almost exclusively for cotton farmers. Cotton production is not governed by any concern for the national economy. It is produced for the world market, without providing any control to protect this economy from the potential drops in prices resulting from periods of industrial crisis or the overproduction of cotton.

A cattle rancher recently told me that though the credit one can get on a cotton crop is limited only by price fluctuations, a loan on a herd or a ranch is completely conventional or uncertain. Coastal ranchers cannot secure substantial bank loans to develop their businesses. Other farmers face the same situation if they are unable to offer cotton or a sugarcane crop as collateral for their loans.

If domestic consumption needs were met by the country's agricultural production, this phenomenon would certainly not be so artificial. But it is not so. But the soil does not yet produce all that the population needs for subsistence. The greatest area of our imports is that of foodstuffs: 3,620,235 Peruvian pounds in the year 1924. This statistic, with a total import of 18 million pounds, reveals one of the problems with our economy. It is not possible to cease all our importation of foodstuffs, but the most significant could be stopped. The largest of all is the importation of wheat and flouer, which in 1924 increased to more than 12 million *soles*.

For some time, the Peruvian economy's interest clearly and urgently required that the country produce the wheat necessary for its population's bread. If this objective had been achieved, Peru would not have to pay twelve or more million *soles* annually for the import of the wheat consumed in its coastal cities.

Why has this problem for our economy not been resolved? It is not only because the state has not yet worried about making a subsistence policy. Nor is it because the cultivation of sugarcane and cotton is best suited to the soil and climate on the coast. Just one of the Inter-

Andean plains—that a few kilometers of railroad and road would open to traffic—could more than abundantly supply wheat, barley, etc. to the population of Peru. On the same coast, the Spanish cultivated wheat in the early colonial years until cataclysm changed the coastal weather conditions. There was no subsequent scientific and organic study of the possibility of cultivation. The experiment conducted in the north, on the lands of Salamanca, shows that varieties of wheat resistant to pests that attack this cereal on the coast exist, and until this experiment the lazy *creoles* appeared to be resigned to defeat. [Experiments that the Commission for the Promotion of Wheat Cultivation recently performed in different parts of the coast have had, according to their announcements, satisfactory success. They have obtained substantial income from the rust-immune "Kappli Emmer" variety, even in semiarid areas.]

The obstacle, the resistance to a solution, is found in the very structure of the Peruvian economy. Peru's economy is a colonial economy. Its movement, its development, are subordinated to the interests and the necessities of the markets in London and New York. These markets see Peru as a primary product deposit and a market for their manufactured goods. Because of this, Peruvian agriculture only receives investment credit and transportation for the products that Peru offers to the big markets on favorable terms. Foreign finance is interested in rubber one day, cotton on another, and another day in sugar. The day that London can get a product at a better price from India or Egypt it will instantaneously leave its suppliers in Peru to their own fate. Our *latifundistas*, our landowners, whatever their illusions of independence, are in reality only intermediary agents of foreign capitalism.

## Final Propositions

To the key propositions already set out in this study on the current aspects of the agrarian question in Peru, I should add the following:

1. The nature of agricultural property in Peru is one of the greatest obstacles to the development of national capitalism. Large or medium-size tenants farm a very high percentage of land that belongs to landowners who have never managed their own estates. These landowners, completely absent from agriculture and its problems, live from their property income without providing any work or intelligence to the country's economic activity. They correspond to the category of the aristocrat or the rentier who are unproductive consumers. By their hereditary property rights they receive a rental income that can be seen as a feudal privilege. The tenant farmer, however, is more like the head of capitalist enterprise. Within a true capitalist system, a company's capital gain should benefit this industrialist and the capital that finances his work. The domination of the land by a class of rentiers imposes a heavy burden of sustaining a rental income that is not subject to potential declines in the value of agricultural products. In this system, rentiers usually do not encounter all the stimuli necessary for carrying out improvements to increase the value of land, their crops, and facilities. The fear of an increase in rental payments when a lease expires is a motivation to keep investment to a minimum. The tenant farmer's ambition is, of course, to become the owner, but his own efforts contribute to a rise in the value of agricultural property that benefits the landowners. Emerging conditions of agricultural credit in Peru prevent a stronger capitalist expropriation of land for this class of industry. Capitalist and industrial exploitation of land that requires for its free and full development the elimination of all feudal privileges develops very slowly in our country. This is a problem, evident not only to socialist but also to capitalist critics. Formulating a principle that is embedded in the agrarian program of the French liberal bourgeoisie, Edouard Herriot says, "The land requires the actual presence."[32] In this respect, the West is certainly no more advanced than the East given that Mohammedan law provides that, as Charles Gide observes, "The land belongs to the one who makes it fertile and gives it life."

2.  The subsistence of the large estate system in Peru, on the other
    hand, is the most serious barrier to white immigration. For obvi-
    ous reasons, the immigration we can expect is of farmers from
    Italy, Central Europe, and the Balkans. The Western urban pop-
    ulation migrates on a much smaller scale and, moreover, industri-
    al workers are aware they have very little to do in Latin America.
    And that is true. The European farmer does not come to America
    to work as a laborer except in cases where high salaries would
    permit large savings. And this is not the case in Peru. Not even
    the most miserable peasant from Poland or Romania would
    accept the terms of our daily workloads on the sugarcane and
    cotton plantations. His aspiration is to become a small landown-
    er. In order for our fields to attract this immigration it is essential
    to provide land complete with houses, animals, and tools, and
    connected with railways and markets. A fascist official or propa-
    gandist who visited Peru about three years ago told local newspa-
    pers that our system of large property holdings was incompatible
    with a program of colonization and immigration capable of
    attracting the Italian peasant.

3.  The subordination of agriculture on the coast to the interests of
    British and American capital and markets prevents not only its
    organization and development according to the specific needs of
    the national economy, that is, to first make sure of a food supply for
    the population, but also its ability to test and adopt new crops. The
    largest undertaking of this order in recent years, that of the tobac-
    co plantations of Tumbes, has been possible only with state inter-
    vention. This fact proves better than any other argument that the
    liberal laissez-faire policy that has given such poor results in Peru
    should definitely be replaced by a social policy of nationalization
    of the major sources of wealth.

4.  Agricultural property on the coast, despite the prosperous times
    it has enjoyed, has not been able to meet the challenges of rural
    health to the extent that the state requires, which is certainly a

modest goal. The large landowners still have not complied with the requirements of the Office of Public Health in the current provisions against malaria. There has not even been a general improvement in housing. There is evidence that the rural population on the coast shows the highest rates of mortality and morbidity in the country. (Except, of course, for the extremely unhealthy regions of the jungle.) Demographic statistics from the rural district of Pativilca from three years ago showed a higher death rate than birth rate. Irrigation works, as the engineer Sutton notes about the Olmos project, provide possibly the most radical solution to the problem of marshes or swamps. But without the work of harnessing the surplus water from the Chancay River carried out in Huacho by Antonio Graña, who also has an interesting plan of colonization, and without projects to exploit underground water carried out in Chiclín and some other projects in the North, the action of private capital in the irrigation of the Peruvian coast would be truly negligible.

5. In the highlands, the survival of agrarian feudalism shows its total ineptitude in creating wealth and progress. Except for livestock businesses that export wool and other products, large estates in highland valleys and tablelands produce almost nothing. The crop yields are very low, the working methods are primitive. A local publication once said that in the Peruvian highlands the *gamonal* appears to be relatively as poor as the Indian. This argument, which is completely invalid in terms of relativity, far from justifying the *gamonal*, unquestionably condemned him. For the modern economy, understood as an objective and concrete science, the only justification for capitalism and its captains of industry and finance is in its role as a creator of wealth. In economic terms, the feudal lord or *gamonal* is the first one responsible for the low value of his lands. We have already seen how this estate owner does not care about productivity, but only the profitability of the land. We have also seen how, despite owning the best lands, their production figures are not higher than those obtained by the Indians with

their primitive farming tools and meager communal lands. The *gamonal*, as an economic factor, is thus completely disqualified.

6. As an explanation for this phenomenon it is said that the economic situation of highland agriculture depends entirely on roads and transportation. Those who believe this undoubtedly do not understand the organic, fundamental difference that exists between a feudal or semifeudal economy and a capitalist economy. They do not understand that the patriarchal, primitive type of feudal landowner is substantially different from a modern company manager. On the other hand, *gamonalism* and large landholdings also appear as an obstacle to the implementation of the state's present road program. The abuses and interests of the *gamonales* are totally opposed to a straightforward application of the law of road conscription. The Indian instinctively regards it as a weapon of *gamonalism*. Under the Inca regime, road construction service was duly established as an obligatory public service, fully compatible with the principles of modern socialism. Under the colonial regime of large landholdings and servitude, the same service acquires the hated character of the *mita*.

## NOTES

Source: José Carlos Mariátegui, *7 ensayos de interpretación de la realidad peruana*, 13th ed. (Lima: Biblioteca Amauta, 1968), 42–84.

1. *Perricholismo* refers to María Michaela Villegas y Hurtado (Lima, September 18, 1748–1819), a famous Peruvian actress known as La Perricholi. Mistress to the Viceroy Manuel de Amat y Juniet (1761 to 1776), she was renowned for her showmanship and role as a nascent *gran diva* in numerous plays.

2. Luis E. Valcárcel, *Del ayllu al imperio: la evolución politico-social en el antiguo Perú y otros estudios*, Serie "El inkario" (Lima: Editorial Garcilaso, 1925), 166.

3. César Antonio Ugarte, *Bosquejo de la historia económica del Perú* (Lima: Imp. Cabieses, 1926), 9.

4. Javier Prado, "Estado Social del Perú durante la dominación española," in *Anales Universitarios del Perú*, 22:125–26.

5.   Ugarte, *Bosquejo de la Historia Económica del Perú*, 64.
6.   José Vasconcelos, *Indología una interpretación de la cultura ibero-america-na* (París: Agencia Mundial de Librería, 192?).
7.   Prado, "Estado Social del Perú durante la dominación española," 37.
8.   Georges Sorel, *Introduction a l'économie moderne* (Paris: M. Rivière, 1922), 120, 130.
9.   Ugarte, *Bosquejo de la Historia Económica del Perú*, 24.
10.  The *mir* was a form of communal landholding in peasant villages in Russia.
11.  Eugène Schkaff, *La question agraire en Russie* (Paris: Rousseau & cie, 1922), 118.
12.  Esteban Echeverría, "Antecedentes y primeros pasos de la revolución de Mayo," *Obras completas de D. Esteban Echeverria* (Buenos Aires: C. Casaralle, 1874), 5:247.
13.  José Vasconcelos, "El Nacionalismo en la América Latina," *Amauta* no. 4 (December 1926): 15.
14.  Ugarte, *Bosquejo de la Historia Económica del Perú*, 57.
15.  Francisco García Calderón, *Le Pérou contemporain: étude sociale* (Paris: Dujarric et cie, 1907), 98, 99.
16.  Ugarte, *Bosquejo de la Historia Económica del Perú*, 58.
17.  Mariátegui included the following section as a footnote to this essay, but because of its length and importance we have moved it to the main text.
18.  Augusto Aguirre Morales, *El Pueblo del Sol* (Lima: Editorial Garcilaso, 1924).
19.  James George Frazer, *The Golden Bough*, abridged edition (London: Macmillan & Co., 1954), 48.
20.  Hildebrando Castro Pozo, *Nuestra comunidad indígena* (Lima: Editorial: El Lucero, 1924).
21.  Ibid., 16 and 17.
22.  One *arroba* is the equivalent of about 25 gallons.
23.  Víctor Raúl Haya de la Torre, *Por la emancipación de la América Latina* (Buenos Aires: M. Gleizer, 1927).
24.  Castro Pozo, *Nuestra comunidad indígena*, 66 and 67.
25.  Ibid., 434.
26.  Schkaff, *La question agraire en Russie*, 188.
27.  Castro Pozo, *Nuestra comunidad indígena*, 47.
28.  Sorel, *Introduction a l'économie moderne*.
29.  Schkaff, *La question agraire en Russie*, 135.
30.  Schkaff, *La question agraire en Russie*, 133–35.
31.  Francisco Ponce de León, *Sistemas de arrendamiento de terrenos del culti-vo en el departamento del Cuzco y el problema de la tierra* (Cuzco: Rozas, 1934).
32.  Edouard Herriot, *Créer* (Paris: Payot, 1920).

# 3—The Economic Factor
in Peruvian History

Interpretive essays on the history of the Peruvian Republic that lie on the shelves of our libraries generally coincide in their disdain or ignorance of the economic trauma that comes from politics. Our people suffer an obstinate inclination not to explain Peruvian history in other than romantic and novelistic terms. In each episode, in each act, the main character is sought. They do not strive to understand the interests or passions that the player represents. Mediocre bosses, vulgar managers of *creole* politics are taken as movers and shakers of a reality in which they have been minimal and opaque instruments. The mental laziness of the *creoles* becomes easily accustomed to missing the argument of Peruvian history: they are content with the recognition of its *dramatis personae.*

The study of the phenomena of Peruvian history suffers from its lack of realism. Belaúnde, with his excess optimism, believes that national thought has been markedly positivist during a long period. He labels the university generation that preceded his own as positivist. But in large part one is obliged to correct his judgment by acknowledging that this university generation adopted the most feeble and ethereal part of positivism—its ideology—and not its most solid and valid—its method. We have not even had a positivist generation. To adopt an ideology is not just to manipulate its most superfluous commonalities. We must distinguish the ideas of a philosophical current or school from the phraseology.

Because of this, even a merely speculative criticism would be satisfied by the growing support that historical materialism enjoys in the new generation. This ideological direction would be fertile even if it only serves to allow the Peruvian mentality to adapt to the perception and understanding of economic facts.

Nothing is more evident that the inability to understand, without the help of economics, phenomena that dominate the process of formation of the Peruvian nation. Economics probably does not explain the totality of the phenomenon and its consequences. But it does explain its roots. This is clear, at least in our epoch. And if for some reason the epoch seems rigid, that undoubtedly would be because of the logic of economics.

The conquest of Peru destroyed economic and social forms that were born spontaneously from the Peruvian land and people. These were fully nourished by an Indigenous sense of life. The complex work of the creation of a new economy and a new society began during the colonial period. Spain, too absolutist, rigid, and medieval, was unable to complete this process under its rule. The Spanish monarchy thought it held all the keys to the colonial economy in its hands. The development of the new economic forces in the colony broke this link.

This was the primary root cause of the independence revolution. The ideas of the French Revolution and the U.S. Constitution found a climate favorable to their diffusion in South America because in South America there still existed a bourgeoisie, albeit an embryonic one, that because of its needs and economic interests could and would be infected with the revolutionary ideas of the European bourgeoisie. Certainly the independence of Spanish America would not have been achieved if it had not been able to count on a heroic generation that, sensitive to the emotions of their epoch, had the ability and will to activate a real revolution among their peoples. Independence, in this respect, is presented as a romantic enterprise. But this does not contradict the thesis of the economic foundation of the independence revolution. The leaders, the *caudillos*, the ideologues of this revolution were not above or more important than the economic premises and reasons for this event. The intellectual and sentimental act did not precede the economic act.

Economic factors similarly hold the key of all the other phases of republican history. In the early days of independence the struggle of factions and military chiefs appears, for example, as a consequence of the lack of an organic bourgeoisie. Though less defined and more backward than elsewhere in Latin America, one finds liberal and bourgeois elements in Peru at the time of the revolution. For this order to function more or less embryonically, a vigorous capitalist class needed to constitute itself. While this class was organizing itself, power was at the mercy of the military caudillos. These caudillos, descendants of the rhetoric of the independence revolution, sometimes temporarily supported the claims of the masses and did so without any ideology in order to win or at least maintain their power against the conservative and reactionary sentiments of the descendants of and successors to the Spanish *encomenderos*. Castilla,[1] for instance, the most interesting and representative of these military leaders, effectively raised the flag in favor of the abolition of the taxation of Indigenous peoples and the end of African slavery. Although once in power, of course, he needed to adopt his program to a political situation dominated by the interests of the conservative caste, which he indemnified with state funds for the damage caused to them by the emancipation of the slaves.

Furthermore, Castilla's government marked the phase of the capitalist class's consolidation. State concessions and the benefits of guano and saltpeter created capitalism and a bourgeoisie. This class, which was later organized on a civilian basis, moved quickly to take complete power. The war with Chile interrupted its domination. It reestablished for a time the conditions and circumstances of the first years of the republic. But the economic evolution of our postwar period little by little gradually returned to the same path.

The war with Chile also had an economic basis. The Chilean plutocracy, who coveted the profits of Peruvian businesses and tax proceeds, was preparing to conquer and plunder the country. An incident, appropriately of an economic nature, provided the pretext for the aggression.

It is not possible to understand Peruvian reality without examining the economic facts. Perhaps the new generation does not clearly understand this history. But it feels it very strongly. It realizes that Peru's fundamental problem of the Indian and land is above all a problem of the Peruvian economy. The current economy, current Peruvian society, suffers from the original sin of the conquest. This is the sin of having been born and having been formed without the Indian and against the Indian.

—*Mundial*, Lima, 14 August 1925


NOTES

Source: "El hecho económico en la historia peruana," in *Peruanicemos al Péru* in *Obras Completas*, 11th ed. (Lima: Biblioteca Amauta, 1988), 11:79–83.

1.    Ramón Castilla was a Peruvian political leader and president from 1845 to 1851.

# 4—The Problem of Statistics

## I.

When studying any of the national problems, one is invariably faced with an obstacle that has to be categorized as a problem: the lack of statistics. In Peru we do not know, for example, how many people are in our country. That is, we do not even have basic information about our country. For those who want to know the current population of Peru, the only available information is the census of 1876 or the calculations of the Geographical Society from 1896. In addition to only being estimates, the latest figures available are now thirty years old.

Because this figure is not the result of an official census, it cannot be accepted by anyone without the benefit of an inventory. Geographic studies of Peru from the last twenty years set a lower figure. This does not mean that in the estimate of its authors that the population of Peru has declined, but rather that the calculation of the Geographical Society seems too insecure.

A new census was ordered some time ago. I am not exactly asking for a new census; that will be discussed soon enough. I am not looking here at the census, but rather at the broader problem of statistics.

The day, no doubt coming soon, that will involve a complicated mobilization of wealthy men, so that we will have a census, but we still will not have sufficient statistics. In countries without statistics there is no need to register people to know how many there are. In Peru, even after registering everyone, we still will not know exactly how many we are. That is because nomadic jungle tribes about which geographers have for a long time have not been able to provide an accurate report remain out of the census.

## II.

Need I note that a country that does not know their demographic reality does not know its economy situation either? One cannot know what a country produces, consumes, and saves if it does not know one fundamental thing: the population. All studies, all the forecasts for countries like Germany, France, Italy, etc., before making any prognoses, before advocating any policy direction, first verify changes in the population.

In a country where one cannot count the people, it is even less able to count production. It does not know the most important factors: the human factor, the labor factor.

For several years in Peru we have a Department of Statistics that, of course, is functioning. Thanks to the work of this department it now produces an annual *Statistical Abstract of Peru*. But this publication cannot physically include more information than what we are able to generate. A Department of Statistics cannot demand miracles. It has to work with its limited resources. And, above all, its purpose is not to create statistics but to compile and organize them.

The *Statistical Abstract* does not tell us in 1925 the population of Peru, but rather reports what the Geographical Society said in 1896. For the most part the information it includes is fragmentary. Its lacunae do not ring true.

We lack statistics on the labor force and productive industries. There are few agricultural statistics, and what we have refers almost exclusively to the production of sugarcane, cotton, and rice. Not only small producers but almost all of the production of the highlands and

Amazon are not included in the reports. There is no statistical break-down of agricultural lands into large, medium, and small landowners. The *Statistical Abstract* does not even provide basic information. It does not provide an index of the cost of living. It barely provides demographic information on a couple of cities.

## III.

This lack of statistical information is a result, no doubt, of Peru still being, as Maúrtua Victor wrote several years ago, "an inorganic country." Statistics require precisely what Maúrtua, in his insightful opinion, noted what Peru most lacks: organicity. Statistics are an effect, a consequence, a result. They cannot be produced artificially. They represent a level of organicity and organization.

In an organized and organic country, each community operates as a living cell of the state. It is not possible, therefore, that the state ignores anything related to population, labor, production, consumption. What is missing from its control is very insignificant and descriptive.

But in Peru we all well know what municipalities are and to what extent one can speak of municipalities. The state controls only a part of the population. Regarding Indigenous people, its authority passes through the hands of feudalistic landowners. And feudalism itself, if it holds the Indians in servitude, cannot provide them with any form of organization. If one explores the highlands, one immediately discovers the surviving forms and institutions of a regime or an order that is considered absolute and definitively cancelled since the time of Spanish domination.

The problem with statistics is that it is not an easier problem to solve than other national problems. One cannot make much progress in solving this problem while progress is not being made in finding fundamental solutions to other more serious problems. This problem, as with everything, is not an isolated one. When other fundamental problems of our organization are resolved, then these will be resolved in an integral manner. And not before that.

It is evident, however, that a lot more could be done. What is known statistically of Peru is far from what we could know. Just as it is possible, for example, to carry out a census, many other things are also possible. Nothing excuses the lack of population figures for all of the cities. Nothing excuses the lack of indexes of the cost of living, at least in the main areas. At a minimum, the major centers of production, labor, and trade in Peru should already have a true statistic analysis.

—*Mundial*, Lima, 1 January 1926

NOTE

Source: "El problema de la estadística," in *Peruanicemos al Perú*, in *Obras Completas*, 11th ed. (Lima: Biblioteca Amauta, 1988), 11:121–25.

# 5—Theory

As a result of the benevolent insistence of some of my friends, I decided to put together in a book some of my articles from the past two years about figures and aspects of the worldwide life.

Coordinated and grouped in one volume under the title of *The Contemporary Scene*, these are not intended to be quick and fragmented impressions, something comprising an explanation of our times. Rather, they contain the primary elements of a sketch or an interpretative essay on this era and its stormy problems that I dared to try to make into a more organic book.

I do not think it is possible to imagine the entire panorama of the contemporary world in one theory. It is not possible, above all, to set in theory its movement. We have to explore it and know it, episode by episode, facet by facet. Our view and our imagination will always be delayed in respect to the entirety of the phenomenon.

Therefore, the best way to explain and communicate our time is one that is perhaps a little bit journalistic and a bit cinematographic.

This is another reason to bring these items to print. Almost all have been published in *Variedades*. Only five of this series have appeared in *Mundial*.

I have not touched the substance of these articles in reviewing and correcting them. I have limited myself to some formal amendments, including the deletion of reference points that were only relevant to the moment in which they were written. To facilitate and manage their reading, I have organized them according to subject matter.

I know that my vision of the era is not very objective or anastigmatic. I am not an indifferent spectator of the human drama. In contrast, I am a man with an affiliation and a faith. This book has no more value than that of loyally reflecting the spirit and sensibilities of my generation. For this reason, I dedicate it to the new men, to the young men of Indo-Iberian America.

—JOSÉ CARLOS MARIÁTEGUI
Lima, MCMXXV


NOTES

This short piece formed the preface to Mariátegui's first book, *La escena contemporánea*, published in 1925.

Source: José Carlos Mariátegui, "Advertencia," *La escena contemporánea*, in *Obras Completas*, 14th ed. (Lima: Biblioteca Amauta, 1987), 1:10–11.

# 6—Anniversary and Balance Sheet

With this issue, *Amauta* reaches its second birthday. Before its first birthday it was on the verge of going under with the ninth issue. Unamuno's warning—"a magazine that gets old degenerates"—would have been the epitaph for a vibrant but ephemeral work. But *Amauta* was not born to last for only one episode, but to be and to make history. If history is the creation of men and ideas, we can face the future with hope. Our strength comes from men and ideas.

The primary objective of all work that the likes of *Amauta* have imposed is this: to last. History is endurance. The isolated cry, no matter how large its echo, is not valid; the constant, continual persistent sermon is what matters. Ideas that are perfect, absolute, abstract, indifferent to the facts, to changing and moving reality do not work; ideas that are germinal, concrete, dialectic, workable, rich in potential and capable of movement do. *Amauta* is neither a diversion nor a game of pure intellectuals; it professes a historic idea, it confesses an active, mass-based faith, it obeys a contemporary social movement. In the struggle between two systems, between two ideas, it does not occur to us to feel like spectators or to invent a third way. Extreme originality is a literary and anarchic preoccupation. On our banner, we inscribe one great, simple word: socialism. (With this slogan we affirm our absolute independence from the idea of a nationalist party, petty bourgeois and demagogic.)

We have wanted *Amauta* to have an organic, autonomous, distinct, national development. Because of this we began by looking for a title in Peruvian tradition. *Amauta* should not be a plagiarized term or a translation. We took an Inca word to create it anew. So that Indian Peru, Indigenous America might feel that this magazine was theirs. And we presented *Amauta* as the voice of a movement and of a generation. In these two years, *Amauta* has been a magazine of ideological definition that has gathered in its pages the propositions of whoever has wanted to speak with sincerity and competency in the name of this generation and this movement.

To us, the work of ideological definition seems completed. In any case, we have already heard categorical and solicited opinions being expressed. All debate is opened up for those who opine, not for those who remain silent. *Amauta*'s first act has concluded. In the second act, it does not have to call itself a magazine of the "new generation," of the "vanguard," of "the left." To be faithful to the Revolution, it is enough to be a socialist magazine.

"New generation," "new spirit," and "new sensibility" are all terms that have grown old. The same must be said of these other labels: "vanguard," "left," "renovation." They were new and good in their moment. We have made use of them to establish provisional demarcations, for reasons contingent on topography and orientation. Today they have already become too generic and dubious. Gross counterfeits enter under these labels. The new generation will not effectively be new unless it finally knows itself to be adult and creative.

In this America of small revolutions, the same word, revolution, frequently lends itself to misunderstanding. We have to reclaim it rigorously and intransigently. We have to restore its strict and exact meaning. The Latin American Revolution will be nothing more and nothing less than a stage, a phase of the world revolution. It will simply and clearly be the socialist revolution. Add all the adjectives you want to this word according to a particular case: "anti-imperialist," "agrarian," "national-revolutionary." Socialism, supposes, precedes, and includes all of them.

It is only possible to effectively oppose a capitalist, plutocratic, imperialist United States with a socialist Latin or Iberian America. The epoch of free competition in the capitalist economy has ended in all fields and all aspects. We are in the age of monopolies, that is to say, empires. The Latin American countries arrived late to capitalist competition. The first positions are already definitively assigned. In the capitalist order, the destiny of these countries is that of simple colonies. The tension between languages, races, spirits has no decisive meaning. It is ridiculous to still speak of the contrast between a materialist Anglo-Saxon America and an idealist Latin America, between a blond Rome and a pallid Greece. These are all definitively discredited topics. Rodó's myth[1] no longer touches souls in a useful or productive manner, nor has it ever done so. We inexorably discard all these caricatures and semblances of ideology and do a serious, frank accounting of reality.

Socialism is certainly not an Indo-American doctrine. But no doctrine, no contemporary system is or could be. And although socialism, like capitalism, may have been born in Europe it is not specifically or particularly European. It is a worldwide movement in which none of the countries that move within the orbit of Western civilization are excluded. This civilization drives toward universality with the force and means that no other civilization possessed. Indo-America can and should have individuality and style in this new world order, but not its own culture or fate that is unique. One hundred years ago we owed our independence as nations to the rhythm of Western history, whose compass has inexorably moved us since colonization. Liberty, Democracy, Parliament, Sovereignty of the People—all the great words that our men of that time pronounced, came from the European repertoire. History, however, does not measure the greatness of these men for the originality of these ideas, but for the efficacy and genius with which they served them. And the peoples who have marched farthest in the continent are those where these ideas took root best and most quickly. The interdependence, the solidarity of peoples and continents, however, was in that time much less than in this. Socialism, finally, is in the American tradition.

The most advanced primitive communist organization that history records is that of the Incas.

We certainly do not want socialism in Latin America to be a copy or imitation. It should be a heroic creation. We have to give life to Indo-American socialism with our own reality, in our own language. Here is a mission worthy of a new generation.

In Europe, parliamentary degeneration and socialist reformism have imposed specific categories after the war. In those peoples where this phenomenon has not occurred because socialism appeared recently in the historic process, the old, great word conserves its greatness intact. It will maintain it in history, in the future, when the contingent, conventional demarcations that today separate practices and methods have disappeared.

Capitalism or Socialism. This is the problem of our epoch. We do not anticipate the syntheses, the transactions that can only operate through history. We think and feel like Gobetti[2] that history is reformist on the condition that the revolutionaries act as such. Marx, Sorel, Lenin, these are the men who make history.

It is possible that many artists and intellectuals will note that we absolutely revere the authority of masters irrevocably involved in the process of "*la trahison des clercs.*"[3] We confess, without scruple, that we are in the domain of the temporal, the historic, and that we have no intention of abandoning them. We leave the spirits incapable of accepting and understanding their epoch to their sterile afflictions and tearful metaphysics. Socialist materialism encompasses all the possibilities of spiritual, ethical and philosophical ascension. And never have we felt more rabid, more efficacious and more religiously idealist than when we solidly place our ideas and our feet on that which is material.

### NOTES

Source: "Aniversario y Balance," *Amauta* no. 17, September 3, 1928; repr. in *Ideología y Política*, in *Obras Completas,* 18th ed. (Lima: Editorial Amauta, 1988), 13:246–50.

1.  Mariátegui here refers to the theories of José Enrique Rodó, as expressed in his eulogy of Latin America's blithe spirit, *Ariel*. See José Enrique Rodó, *Ariel* (Austin: University of Texas Press, 1988).

2.  Piero Gobetti, an influential Italian writer of the day who espoused a radical liberalism.

3.  Julien Benda, *La trahison des clercs* (Paris: B. Grasset, 1927), available in English as Julien Benda, *The Treason of the Intellectuals* (New Brunswick, NJ: Transaction Publishers, 2007). Benda was a French philosopher and novelist whose polemical work gained him notoriety for arguing that Europeans had lost the ability to reason dispassionately about political and military matters, instead becoming apologists for crass nationalism, warmongering, and racism.

# 7—Colonial Economy[1]

The economic year of 1925 has reminded us anew that all of the coastal economy and thus of all Peru born of the conquest rests on two bases that physically could not appear more solid to anyone: cotton and sugar. For practical men this confirmation lacks value. But the vision of practical men is always too dominated by superficial things to be really profound. And in some things, theory penetrates more deeply than experience.

Besides, theory intervenes much more than is thought in concepts that are apparently empirical and objective. The world, for example, believes in the solidity of the British economy not so much because of what its commercial statistics say but because the base of this economy is coal. And confidence in the recovery of the German economy surely has analogous motives. The proof is that this confidence was only broken when one of Germany's foundations, that of coal and steel, was threatened or undermined.

The metaphor that is, evidently, more of a necessity than just a pleasure has led us to represent ourselves, a society, a state, an economy, etc., as a building. This explains the inevitable preoccupation with foundation.

In the discourse of 1925, on the other hand, it has been nature, not theory, which has revealed the weak consistency of sugar and cotton as bases for an economy. Excessive rain has caused the economic life of the country to dissolve. A series of things that many people have become used to seeing as definitively acquired by Peruvian progress have ended up being dependent on the price of sugar and cotton in the markets in New York and London.

Peru's economic dependency is felt throughout the nation. For example, even with a favorable foreign trade balance with monetary circulation solidly guaranteed in gold, Peru does not have the money it should have. In spite of the surplus in foreign trade, in spite of guarantees for fiduciary issue, the Peruvian pound is quoted at a discounted rate of 23 percent or 24 percent. Why? In this, as with all else, the colonial character of our economy becomes apparent. The most minimal analysis of the foreign trade balance shows it to be a fiction. The European nations have "invisible importations" that equalize their commercial trade balance: immigrant remittances, profits from foreign investments, earnings from the tourism industry, etc. On the other hand, in Peru as in all countries with colonial economies, there are "invisible exports." The profits from mining, commerce, transportation and such do not stay in Peru. They mostly go outside the country in the form of dividends, interest, etc. To get these profits back, the Peruvian economy needs to ask for them in loans.

And so, in each difficult moment, in each episode in the historical experience we are completing, we always find ourselves facing the same problem: Peruvianizing, nationalizing, emancipating our economy.

NOTES

Source: José Carlos Mariátegui, "Economía colonial," in *Peruanicemos al Perú*, in *Obras Completas,* 11th ed. (Lima: Biblioteca Amauta, 1988), 11:127–31.

1.    A section dealing with the historic colonial economy was not included because it is included as part of the Land Problem (1.2) as published in the *Seven Essays.*

# PART II

# Peru and "Indigenismo"

. . .

THIS SECTION DEVELOPS Mariátegui's understanding of Peru and its Indigenous peoples, and also strongly draws on the essays in *Peruanicemos al Peru*. The economic context in which he treats Indigenous issues is clear. Mariátegui was among a group of intellectuals who were carefully studying the original peoples in this Andean country. Referred to as *indigenistas*, they realized the importance of Peru's Indigenous people and their culture and were hard at work studying it and recasting it in a positive postcolonial light. They valued, rather than disparaged, the Inca empire and the descendants of the original population. In "Peru's Principal Problem" (II.1), Mariátegui writes: "The Indian is the foundation of our nationality in formation. . . . Those who impoverish and repress the Indian impoverish and repress the nation. Indians cannot be creators of wealth if they are exploited, mocked, and stultified. Devaluing and depreciating someone as a person is equivalent to devaluing and depreciating that person as a producer. Only when Indians gain the value of their work will they acquire the quality of consumer and producer that a modern nation's economy needs from all of its members. When one speaks of Peruvianness, one should begin by investigating whether this Peruvianness includes the Indian. Without the Indian no Peruvianness is possible."

# 1 — Peru's Principal Problem

Before one turns off the echoes of the celebration of the figure and the work of Clorinda Matto Turner,[1] before the delegates of the fourth congress of the Indigenous race disperse, we turn our eyes to the fundamental problem, to Peru's principal problem. We say something that Clorinda Matto Turner would certainly say if she were still alive. This is the best tribute that the new men, the young men from Peru, can pay to the memory of this singular woman who, at a time more complicated and cooler than our own, nobly rose up against the injustices and crimes of the exploiters of the Indigenous race.

The *creole* people, the metropolitan people, did not like this tough issue. But their tendency to ignore, to forget, should not be spread. The gesture of an ostrich that hides its head in the sand when threatened is too dumb. Refusing to see a problem does not make it go away. The problem of the Indians is the problem of four million Peruvians. It is the problem of three-quarters of the Peruvian population. It is the problem of the majority. It is the problem of the nationality. The unwillingness of our people to study it and approach it honestly is a sign of mental laziness and, above all, moral insensitivity.

The viceroyalty, from this and other points of view, appears to be less responsible than the republic. Originally the full responsibility for the misery and depression of the Indians fell to the viceroyalty. But in those inquisitorial days, a great Christian voice, that of Fray Bartolomé de Las Casas, vigorously defended the Indians against the brutal methods of the colonizers. There has not been so stubborn and effective an advocate of the aboriginal race during the republic.[2]

While the viceroyalty was a medieval and foreign regime, the republic is formally a Peruvian and liberal regime. The republic, therefore, had a duty the viceroyalty did not have. The republic has the responsibility to raise the status of the Indian. And contrary to this duty, the republic has impoverished the Indians. It has compounded their depression and exasperated their misery. The republic has meant for the Indians the ascent of a new ruling class that has systematically taken their lands. In a race based on customs and an agricultural soul, as with the Indigenous race, this dispossession has constituted a cause for their material and moral dissolution. Land has always been the joy of the Indians. Indians are wed to the land. They feel that life comes from the earth and returns to the earth. For this reason, Indians can be indifferent to everything except the possession of the land which by their hands and through their encouragement is religiously fruitful. *Creole* feudalism has behaved, in this respect, worse than Spanish feudalism. Overall, the Spanish *encomendero* often had some of the noble habits of feudal lords. The *creole encomendero* has all the defects of a commoner and none of the virtues of a gentleman. The servitude of the Indian, in short, has not decreased under the republic. All uprisings, all of the Indian unrest, have been drowned in blood. Indian demands have always been met with a military response. The silence of the puna afterward guards the tragic secret of these responses. The republic has in the end restored, under the title of the road labor draft, the system of *mitas*. Our nationalists, of course, have protested against this restoration. Jorge Basadre,[3] a young avant-garde writer, has been one of the few who have felt the duty to denounce, in a moderate and discreet study that nevertheless has a tremendous result, the true nature of the road conscription. The rhetoric of nationalism has not followed his example.

In addition, the republic is also responsible for the lethargic and weak energies of the race. The Túpac Amaru insurgency proved, in the viceroyalty's seat, that the Indians were still able to fight for their freedom. Independence weakened this capability. The cause of the redemption of the Indians became under the republic a demagogic speculation of some caudillos. *Creole* parties have signed up for their program. And thus the Indians lost their will to fight for their demands.

But by postponing the solution of the Indian problem, the republic has postponed the realization of its dreams of progress. A policy that is truly national in scope cannot dispense with the Indian; it cannot ignore the Indian. The Indian is the foundation of our nationality in formation. Oppression makes the Indian an enemy of civilization. It practically annuls an element of progress. Those who impoverish and repress the Indian, impoverish and repress the nation. Indians cannot be creators of wealth if they are exploited, mocked, and stultified. Devaluing and depreciating someone as a person is equivalent to devaluing and depreciating that person as a producer. Only when Indians gain the value of their work will they acquire the quality of consumer and producer that a modern nation's economy needs from all of its members. When one speaks of Peruvianness, one should begin by investigating whether this Peruvianness includes the Indian. Without the Indian no Peruvianness is possible. People of a truly bourgeois, liberal democratic, and nationalist ideology should particularly appreciate this truth. The motto of all nationalisms, beginning with the nationalism of Charles Maurras and L'Action Française, says: "All that is national is ours."

The problem of the Indian, which is the problem of Peru, cannot find its solution in an abstract humanitarian formula. It cannot be the result of a philanthropic movement. The patronage of Indigenous *caciques* and phony lawyers are a mockery. Leagues of the type of the former Pro-Indigenous Association provide a voice clamoring in the wilderness. The Pro-Indigenous Association did not arrive on time to become a movement. Their action was gradually reduced to the generous, selfless, noble, personal actions of Pedro S. Zulen and Dora

Mayer. As an experiment, the Pro-Indigenous Association was a failure. It served to contrast and measure the moral callousness of a generation and an era.

The solution to the problem of the Indian must be a social solution. It must be worked out by the Indians themselves. This concept leads to seeing the meeting of Indigenous congresses as a historical fact. The Indigenous congresses have not yet formed a program, but they do represent a movement. They indicate that the Indians are beginning to gain a collective consciousness of their situation. The least important aspect of the Indian Congress is its deliberations and its votes. The transcendent, historic aspect is the congress itself. The congress is an affirmation of the will of the race to make their own claims. But the Indians lack a national presence. Their protests have always been regional. This has contributed in large part to their defeat. Four million peoples, conscious of their numbers, do not despair of their future. These same four million people, though they are nothing more than an inorganic mass, a dispersed crowd, are unable to decide its historical course.[4] In the Indian Congress, the Indian from the North has met the Indian from the center and the Indian from the South. The Indian in congress, moreover, has been in contact with vanguard leaders in the capital. This vanguard treats them as brothers. Their accent is new, their language is also new. Indians recognize in them their own emotions. These emotions widen with this contact. This is something that is still very vague, very confused, something outlined in this human nebula, which probably, surely, contains the seeds of the future of Peruvian nationality.

—*Mundial*, Lima, 9 December 1924

NOTES

Source: José Carlos Mariátegui, "El problema primario del Perú," in *Peruanicemos al Perú*, in *Obras Completas*, 11th ed. (Lima: Biblioteca Amauta, 1988), 11:41–46.

1.  Clorinda Matto Turner was a Peruvian feminist *indigenista* writer of the
    late nineteenth century. Her most famous work is *Aves sin nido*, a novel of
    Indigenous life and priestly oppression in Peru. See *Birds Without a Nest*
    (Austin: University of Texas Press, 1996).

2.  This paragraph and the following two largely repeat part of "On the Indian
    Problem."

3.  Jorge Basadre was Mariátegui's contemporary who became one of Peru's
    best-known intellectuals and historians.

4.  This paragraph to this point is also found in "Aspects of the Indian
    Problem" in *Seven Essays*.

# 2—On the Indigenous Problem: Brief Historical Review

The population of the Inca empire, according to conservative estimates, was at least ten million. Some people place it at twelve or even fifteen million. The conquest was, more than anything, a terrible carnage. The Spanish conquerors, with their small numbers, could not impose their domination, but only managed to terrorize the Indigenous population. The invaders' guns and horses, which were regarded as supernatural beings, created a superstitious impression. The political and economic organization of the colony, which came after the conquest, continued the extermination of the Indigenous race. The viceroyalty established a system of brutal exploitation. Spanish greed for precious metals led to an economic activity directed toward mines that, under the Incas, had been worked on very small scale because the Indians, who were largely an agricultural people, did not use iron and only used gold and silver as ornaments. In order to work the mines and *obrajes* (sweatshops) where weaving was done, the Spanish established a system of forced labor that decimated the population. This was not only a state of servitude, as might have been the case had the Spanish limited the exploitation to the use of land and retained the agricultural character of the country, but was in large part a state of slavery. Humanitarian and civilizing voices called for the King of Spain to defend the Indians. More than anyone, Father Bartolomé de Las Casas stood out in their defense. The Laws of the Indies were inspired by the purpose of protecting the Indians. It recognized their traditional organization into communities. But in reality the Indians continued to be at the mercy of a ruthless feudalism that destroyed the Inca economy and society without replacing it with something that could increase production. The tendency of the Spanish to settle on the coast drove away so many aboriginals from the region that it resulted in a lack of workers. The viceroyalty wanted to solve this problem through the importation of African slaves. These people were appropriate to the climate and challenges of the hot valleys and plains of the coast and, in contrast, inappropriate for work in the mines in the cold sierra highlands. The African slave reinforced the Spanish domination that in spite of the Indigenous depopulation was still outnumbered by the Indians who, though subjugated, remained a hostile enemy. Blacks were devoted to domestic service and other jobs. Whites easily mixed with blacks, producing a mixture of a type characteristic of the coastal population that has greater adherence to the Spanish and resists Indigenous influences.

The independence revolution was not, as is known, an Indigenous movement. It was a movement of and for the benefit of *creoles* and even Spanish living in the colonies. But it took advantage of the support of the Indigenous masses. Furthermore, as illustrated by the Pumacahua, some Indians played an important role in its development. The liberal program of the revolution logically included the redemption of the Indian as an automatic consequence of the implementation of its egalitarian principles. And so, among the first acts of the republic, were several laws and decrees in favor of the Indians. They ordered the distribution of land, the abolition of forced labor, and so on. But the revolution in Peru did not bring in a new ruling class, and all of these provisions remained on paper without a government capacity to carry them out. The colony's landholding aristocracy, the owner of power, retained their feudal rights over land and, therefore, over the Indians.

All provisions apparently designed to protect them have not been able to do anything against feudalism even today.

The viceroyalty seems less to blame than the republic. The full responsibility for the misery and depression of the Indians originally belongs to the viceroyalty. But in those inquisitorial days, a great Christian voice, that of Fray [Friar] Bartolomé de Las Casas, vigorously defended the Indians against the brutal methods of the colonizers. There has never been as stubborn and effective an advocate of the aboriginal race during the republic.

While the viceroyalty was a medieval and foreign regime, the republic is formally a Peruvian and liberal regime. The republic, therefore, had a duty the viceroyalty did not have. The republic has the responsibility to raise the status of the Indian. And contrary to this duty, the republic has impoverished the Indians. It has compounded their depression and exasperated their misery. The republic has meant for the Indians the ascent of a new ruling class that has systematically taken their lands. In a race based on customs and an agricultural soul, as with the Indigenous race, this dispossession has constituted a cause for their material and moral dissolution. Land has always been the joy of the Indians. Indians are wed to the land. They feel that "life comes from the earth" and returns to the earth. For this reason, Indians can be indifferent to everything except the possession of the land, which by their hands and through their encouragement is religiously fruitful. *Creole* feudalism has behaved, in this respect, worse than Spanish feudalism. Overall, the Spanish *encomendero* often had some of the noble habits of feudal lords. The *creole encomendero* has all the defects of a commoner and none of the virtues of a gentleman. The servitude of the Indian, in short, has not decreased under the republic. All uprisings, all of the Indian unrest, have been drowned in blood. Indian demands have always been met with a military response. The silence of the puna[1] afterward guards the tragic secret of these responses. In the end, the republic restored, under the title of the road labor draft, the system of *mitas*.

In addition, the republic is also responsible for the lethargic and weak energies of the race. The cause of the redemption of the Indians became under the republic a demagogic speculation of some strong-men. *Creole* parties have signed up for their program. And thus the Indians lost their will to fight for their demands.

In the highlands, the region mostly inhabited by the Indians, the most barbaric and omnipotent feudalism remains largely unchanged. The domination of the earth in the hands of the *gamonales*, the fate of the Indigenous race, falls to an extreme level of depression and ignorance. In addition to farming, which is car-ried out on a very primitive level, the Peruvian highlands also have another economic activity: mining, almost entirely in the hands of two large U.S. companies. Wages are regulated in the mines, but the pay is negligible, there is almost no defense for the lives of the work-ers, and labor laws governing accidents are ignored. The system of *enganche*, which through false promises enslaves workers, puts the Indians at the mercy of these capitalist companies. The misery of agrarian feudalism is so great that Indians prefer the lot offered by the mines.

The spread of socialist ideas in Peru has resulted in a strong move-ment reflecting Indigenous demands. The new Peruvian generation knows that Peru's progress will be fictitious, or at least will not be Peruvian, if it does not benefit the Peruvian masses, four-fifths of whom are Indigenous and peasant. This same trend is evident in art and in national literature in which there is a growing appreciation of Indigenous forms and affairs, which before had been depreciated by the dominance of a Spanish colonial spirit and mentality. *Indigenista* literature seems to fulfill the same role of Mujika literature in pre-revolutionary Russia. Indians themselves are beginning to show signs of a new conscious-ness. Relationships between various Indigenous settlements which before were out of contact because of great distances grow day by day. The regular meeting of Indigenous congresses that are sponsored by the government initiated these linkages, but as the nature of their demands became revolutionary they were denatured as advanced ele-ments were excluded and the representation was made apocryphal. *Indigenista* currents press for official action. For the first time the gov-ernment has been forced to accept and proclaim *indigenista* views, and has decreed some measures that do not touch *gamonal* interests and are ineffective because of this. For the first time the Indigenous problem, which disappears in the face of ruling-class rhetoric, is posed in its social and economic terms and is identified more than anything as a land problem. Every day more evidence underscores the conviction that this problem cannot find its solution in a humanitarian formula. It cannot be the result of a philanthropic movement. The patronage of Indigenous chieftains and phony lawyers are a mockery. Leagues of the type of the former Pro-Indigenous Association provide a voice clamoring in the wilderness. The Pro-Indigenous Association did not arrive in time to become a movement. Their action was gradually reduced to the generous, selfless, noble, personal actions of Pedro S. Zulen and Dora Mayer. As an experiment, the Pro-Indigenous Association served to contrast, to measure, the moral callousness of a generation and an era.[2]

The solution to the problem of the Indian must be a social solution. It must be worked out by the Indians themselves. This concept leads to seeing the meeting of Indigenous congresses as a historical fact. The Indigenous congresses, misled in recent years by bureaucratic tendencies, have not yet formed a program, but their first meetings indicated a route for Indians in different regions. The Indians lack a national organization. Their protests have always been regional. This has contributed in large part to their defeat. Four million people, conscious of their numbers, do not despair of their future. These same four million people, though they are nothing more than an inorganic mass, a dispersed crowd, are unable to decide its historical course.

## NOTES

José Carlos Mariátegui wrote this "Brief Historical Review" at the request of the Tass News Agency in New York, and it was translated and published as "The New Peru," in *The Nation* 128 (January 16, 1929). It was reprinted in *Labor* (Year I, No. 1, 1928) with the title "On the Indian Problem: Brief Historical Review." An editorial note from Mariátegui preceded it indicating that these notes "in a sense complement a chapter on 'The Problem of Indian' in *Seven*

*Interpretive Essays on Peruvian Reality*." For this reason, the editors of *Obras Completas* added it to this essay beginning with the third edition, April 1952.

Source: José Carlos Mariátegui, "Sobre el problema indígena," *Labor: Quincenario de información e ideas* 1/1 (November 10, 1928): 6.

1.    Cold, desolate highland region.
2.    The Asociación Pro-Indígena (Pro-Indigenous Association) was a moderate Peruvian association dedicated to advancing Indigenous rights. It operated in the first part of the twentieth century.

# 3—Aspects of the Indigenous Problem

Recently Dora Mayer de Zulen, whose intelligence and character are not yet sufficiently appreciated and admired, has made, with the honesty and restraint that distinguishes her, the evaluation of the interesting and worthwhile experiment that culminated in the Pro-Indigenous Association.[1] The usefulness of this experiment is fully demonstrated by anyone who was, in a partnership and skillful solidarity with the generous spirit and precursor of Pedro S. Zulen, its heroic and stubborn leader. The Pro-Indigenous Association was useful in making a series of key statements on the process of *gamonalismo*, identifying and specifying their tremendous and unpunished responsibilities. It served to promote in coastal Peru a pro-Indigenous current that preceded the attitudes of later generations. It served, above all, to ignite a hope in the Andean darkness, stirring the dormant Indigenous consciousness.

But, as the very same Dora Mayer acknowledges with her usual candor, this experiment was more or less completed. It gave all, or nearly all, the fruits it could give. It showed that the Indigenous problem could not find its solution in an abstract humanitarian formula in a purely philanthropic movement. From this point of view, as I once said, the Pro-Indigenous Association, in a way, was a failure because its main result was to register or to verify the moral insensitivity of past generations.

This experiment has permanently closed the hope, or rather the utopia, that the solution to the Indigenous problem will be made possible by a class joined to *gamonalismo*. The *Patronato de la Raza* [Patronage of the Race], established by the state, is there as a testimony to the experiment's sterile presence.

The solution to the problem of the Indian must be a social solution. It must be worked out by the Indians themselves. This concept leads to seeing, for example, the meeting of Indigenous congresses as a historical fact. The Indigenous congresses, misled in recent years by bureaucratic tendencies, have not yet formed a program, but their first meetings indicated a route for Indians in different regions. The Indians lack a national organization. Their protests have always been regional. This has contributed in large part to their defeat. Four million people, conscious of their numbers, do not despair of their future. These same four million people, though they are nothing more than an inorganic mass, a dispersed crowd, are unable to decide its historical course.

This evaluation of the Indigenous problem is outlined with stammering and confusing claims, that are each time more extensive and concrete than those made by Indigenous peoples. Dora Mayer is substantially in agreement with me when she writes: "It is time that the race took up its own defense because otherwise it will never be saved if it is unable to act on behalf of its own salvation." And, in her assessment of the value of the Pro-Indigenous Association, she also accepts my main point of view when she says, "On the basis of cold concrete practical information, the Pro-Indigenous Association means for historians what Mariátegui assumes: an experiment to rescue the backward and enslaved Indigenous race through an outside protector body which for free, through legal means has sought to serve as an advocate of their claims to the powers of the State."

I no longer think it is time to try again the method thus defined. Other paths are necessary. And this does not affirm only the concepts but also the events that now require our consideration. The Indigenous claims, the Indigenous movement, which until two years ago had an extraordinary leader in the form of a dark Indian, Ezekiel

Urviola, rejected the humanitarian and philanthropic formula. Valcárcel wrote: "Pro-Indigenous, Patronato, always a gesture from the lord for the slave, always in the air the protector in the form of those who have dominated for five centuries: Never the severe gesture of justice, never a word of justice, never the virile word of the honest man, never the thunder of biblical indignation. Not even the few apostles who were born in the land of Peru preached the holy word of regeneration. In a feminine spasm of compassion and mercy for the poor oppressed Indian, it passed over life and generations. There is no virile soul that screams a sure Indian savior. Once and for all the crying literature of the *indigenistas* ends. The peasants of the Andes despise the words of consolation."

The Indigenous problem cannot, therefore, be regarded today with the same criteria as only a few years ago. History appears to be passing quickly in our country, as in the rest of the world, for a decade in this part. Many ideas, good and valid until only yesterday, are today almost worthless. The whole question is posed in radically new terms, from the day the clamoring has come to claim first place in its debate.

—*Mundial*, Lima, 17 December 1926

NOTES

Source: José Carlos Mariátegui, "Aspectos del problema indígena," in *Peruanicemos al Perú*, in *Obras Completas*, 11th ed. (Lima: Biblioteca Amauta, 1988), 11:145–48.

1.    Dora Mayer de Zulen's article, "Lo que ha significado la pro-indígena" was published in *Amauta* 1/1 (September 1926): 20.

# 4—National Progress and Human Capital

## I.

Those who, arbitrarily and simplistically, reduce Peruvian progress to a problem of golden capital, reason and run as if there did not exist an issue of human capital that is entitled to priority in the debate. They ignore or forget that historically man is above money. This conceptualization of progress aims to be North American and positivist in nature. But, precisely, there is no better example of total ignorance than the case of the Yankees.

The enormous material development of the United States does not prove the power of gold, but rather the power of man. The wealth of the United States is not in its banks or in their markets; it is in its people. History teaches us that the roots and the spiritual and physical impulses of the North American phenomenon are found entirely in its biological material. It also teaches us that in this material, numbers have been less important than quality. The power of the United States has been its Puritans, its Jews, its mystics. These were the migrants, the exiles, the persecuted of Europe. From the ideological mysticism of these men descended the mysticism of action recognized by the great North American captains of industry and finance. The North

American phenomenon appears, in its origin, not only as quantitative but also as qualitative.

But this is another issue. I am not interested at the moment in anything other than to denounce the unreal false start of materialism that, though crude and utopian, seems to imagine that money has invented a civilization but it is incapable of understanding that civilization has invented money. And the crisis and the contemporary decline began precisely when civilization began to depend almost entirely on money and subordinated its spirit and motion to money.

The error and sin of the prophets of Peruvian progress and its programs have always resided in their resistance or inability to understand the primacy of the biological factor; the human factor is the most important and is more important than all other factors which are, if not artificial, secondary. This is, moreover, a common defect in all nationalisms that fail to communicate or represent anything but oligarchic and conservative interests. This nationalism, of fascist nature, conceives of the nation as an abstract reality that appears better and distinct from the concrete and lived reality of its citizens. And, therefore, they are always willing to sacrifice man to myth.

In Peru we have had a much less intellectual nationalism, much more rudimentary and instinctive than Western nationalisms that defined the nation. But its practice, its theory, was naturally the same. Peruvian politics—bourgeois on the coast, feudal in the mountains—has been characterized by an ignorance of the value of human capital. Its rectification, in this area as in all others, begins with the assimilation of a new ideology. The new generation feels and knows that Peruvian progress will be fictitious, or at least will not be Peruvian, as long as its work does not contribute to the welfare of the Peruvian people, which is four-fifths Indigenous and peasant.

## II.

One of the substantive aspects of the problem of human capital is the medico-social aspect. Among the few things written on the subject we have to note an interesting book. The book is *Studies on the Pathology and Medical Geography of Peru.*[1] Its authors are Sebastián Lorente and Raul Flores Córdova, two intelligent and hardworking doctors who are also health officials. This book, with its more than six hundred pages of dense data and figures, provides a detailed study of the medical and social realities of Peru.

The authors are, of course, optimistic in their effort and hope. But their positive approach does not provide, based on their research, deceptive illusions. The truth of our health situation emerges in a precise and categorical fashion in the book. The rates of mortality and morbidity in Peru are excessive. Human capital remains nearly stationary. On the coast, malaria and tuberculosis; in the mountains, typhus and smallpox; in the jungle, all the problems of the tropics and marshes erode the meager population of the republic. We do not have exact population figures. But the commonly accepted figure of five million is enough to see the weakness and slowness of our population growth. Infant mortality is one of its most terrible and tragic brakes on growth. In Lima and Callao one quarter of the children die before reaching one year of age. In the small rural villages of the coast the rate of infant mortality is even higher. I am looking at population statistics from the Pativilca district from the first half of this year that shows a higher mortality than birth rate.

In the preface to their book, doctors Lorente and Córdova Flores write that "the medical and social scene presents its full scope and severity in our health problems." Their study did not exaggerate the reality in any way; perhaps, instead, it understates the problem. What clouds the mind when reading this volume, which will, we hope, arrive in the hands of those who are so easily misled about the hierarchy or gradation of national problems, is not the trials, always modest, of the authors, but the bare facts, the objective observation, the undistorted findings.

## III.

I have not addressed the theoretical merit or the scientific value of these *Studies on the Pathology and Medical Geography of Peru*. That analysis belongs exclusively to professionals, to the authorities. But, without encroaching on areas of criticism of others, I would point out its usefulness and importance as a current and authoritative document on the "deep reality" of Peru. It seems clear to me, moreover, that doctors Lorente and Flores Córdova have written a systematic and calculating study that is uniquely meritorious in a context such as ours, where it is difficult for scholars to engage in speculations of this magnitude.

The Lorente and Flores Córdova book is not intended only for professionals. It will be of interest to all scholars. Their work is a journey through a less picturesque Peru, but one more real than other books which describe or disguise us.

## IV.

Doctors Lorente and Córdova Flores are not content in their book to collect, compare, and classify precious data. They demand, formally and urgently, that more attention be given to the problem of human capital. "The problem for which Peru requires most urgently an organic and effective solution," they write, "is the health problem. This is not only because each day the concept of public health advocacy is more prevalent and rooted in today's conscience as a primary duty of every modern state, but primarily because no other term more accurately reflects the pressing and obvious demands of the Peruvian reality."

This is true, but incomplete. The health problem cannot be considered separately. It is linked and confused with other deep Peruvian problems that are the domain of sociologists and politicians. The ills, the morbidity of the mountains and the coast, feed mainly on poverty and ignorance. The problem, inasmuch as it is studied, becomes an economic, social, and political problem. But the distinguished hygienists, authors of *Medical Geography of Peru*, did not touch on this type of analysis. The shortcomings of their diagnosis are the result of only being doctors.

—*Mundial*, Lima, 9 October 1923

NOTES

Source: José Carlos Mariátegui, "El progreso nacional y el capital humano," in *Peruanicemos al Perú*, in *Obras Completas*, 11th ed. (Lima: Biblioteca Amauta, 1988), 11:91–96.

1.    Sebastián Lorente and Raúl Flores Córdova, *Estudios sobre geografía médica y patología del Perú* (Lima: Impr. Americana, 1925).

# 5—Class Action in Peru

The first manifestations of revolutionary ideological propaganda in Peru are those raised at the beginning of this century by the radical thinking of González Prada.[1] Shortly after González Prada definitively separated himself from the politics of the day and the Radical Party experiment failed, the first libertarian groups appears. Some workers who are interested in these ideas come into contact with González Prada, whose disillusionment with political struggles led him to an anarchist position. They create small libertarian groups that are limited to spreading propaganda with his ideas without proposing any other action at this time. González Prada collaborated under a pseudonym or without attribution in what would become anarchist fliers: *Los Parias*, *El Hambriento* [The Outcasts, The Hungry]. Some radicals and freemasons, friends of González Prada, sympathize with this propaganda, without immediately committing themselves to it. Other ephemeral fliers appear: *Simiente Roja* [Red Seed], etc. The only one that has any permanence is *La Protesta* [The Protest] that gives its name to the first persistent anarchist group.

The Bakers' Federation "Star of Peru" was the first guild to be influenced by revolutionary ideas. It is at an action by the bakers that González Prada gave his May 1, 1905, speech on intellectuals and the Proletariat that was reprinted in issue No. 8 of *Labor*.

The Billinghurst movement[2] gains membership from some participants in these initial ideological skirmishes, the most important of them
is an ex-libertarian, Carlos del Barzo, an artisan later involved in the
attempt to organize a Socialist Party and who had been a workers' candi-
date for a neighborhood district in Lima. Billinghurism also had at its
side the leader of port strikes at that time, Fernando Vera, but he capitu-
lated and became a "sellout." Under the government of Billinghurst, the
yellow mutualism in the service of all the governments, took a cordial attitude toward Chilean workers. A commission of these workers' groups
sponsored by the government visited Chile where they exchanged words
of reconciliation and friendship with more or less false representatives of
one proletariat or another. The Peruvian anarchist group that was working at that time to give life to a Regional Federation of Peruvian Workers
sent to Chile, without the awareness of the official delegation endorsed
by Billinghurism, the worker Otazu, who was received by workers of the
same affiliation in the southern country. One can say that the first expressions of Peruvian internationalism date to this time. We must always take
into account in the first instance the character of statements connected to
the policy of the Foreign Ministry in its dealings with its counterparts in
Chile to settle the question of Tacna and Arica.

Once Billinghurst was overthrown, González Prada publishes a
weekly against Benavides's military government: *La Lucha* [The
Struggle]. Carlos del Barzo publishes *El Motín* [The Mutiny]. But
both newspapers only represent a protest against the military regime, a
corrective against its abuses. Because of the ideological affiliation, the
papers' leaders ally nonetheless with the social movement. Del Barzo is
imprisoned and deported; González Prada is tried in the press.

Under the government of Pardo, the effects of the European war on
the economic situation have an influence on social upheavals and in
ideological orientations. A labor group dominates anarchists in the
work among the masses. Barzo directs some shoemaker strikes and
organizes the union of workers in this industry in the capital. Anarcho-
syndicalist propaganda penetrates the Huacho countryside, producing
unrest that is bloodily suppressed by Pardo's government. The struggle for the 8-hour day in 1918 consists of anarcho-syndicalists inten-

sively taking their propaganda to the masses. The textile union, leader of this struggle, acquires an influential role in the class action. Already several students have come into contact with advanced workers' groups. Faced with the struggle for the 8-hour day the Student Federation produces an official statement of sympathy with the workers' demands. The student masses did not have the vaguest idea of the scope of these claims, and believe that the role of university students was to guide and direct the workers.

At this time the opposition daily *El Tiempo* began to publish. It was very popular then, an effort to give life to a group of socialist propaganda and concentration. The direction of the newspaper, linked to opposition political groups, is foreign to this effort, which exclusively represents the orientation toward socialism of some young non-political writers who tend to give the newspaper campaigns a social character. These writers are César Falcón, José Carlos Mariátegui, Humberto del Águila, and some other associated young intellectuals. In mid-1918 they publish a combative periodical: *Nuestra Época* [Our Time]. An anti-armament article by Mariátegui causes a violent protest by the army officers who, in large group, invaded the editorial offices of *El Tiempo*, where the writer works, to attack him. *Nuestra Época* does not have a socialist agenda, but it appears as an ideological and propaganda effort in this regard. After two issues it stops publishing, deprecated by the newspaper industry to which its main writers had lent their services. But they continue in their efforts to create a Socialist Propaganda Committee. They join with another editor of *El Tiempo*, Luis Ulloa, from the old Radical Party, who came into contact with unions during his newspaper's campaign against "those who keep the people hungry." A committee is constituted with the participation of Del Barzo and some workers close to him, and the two groups of students (some already professionals) take part even to the point of labor agitation. The group tends to assimilate all the elements capable of claiming socialism, without excluding those from the González Prada radical group who keep away from political parties. A part of the included group, led by Luis Ulloa, proposes the immediate transformation of the group into a party. The other part includes precisely the founders and initiators who claim that they should maintain the Committee of Socialist Propaganda and Organization while their presence has no roots in the masses. The time is not right for socialist organization. Some of the members of the committee edited a newspaper, *Germinal*, that adheres to Leguía's movement. Mariátegui, Falcon, and their companions finally leave the group that agreed to its appearance as a party on May 1, 1919.

At the same time as these efforts, some people associated with Billinghurst and others on behalf of an ex-Democrat presumptive nominee for the presidency of the republic press to create a Labor Party. They propose to the socialist committee to merge the two groups, but the socialists reject the idea. The opening ceremony of the Labor Party is set for May 1, 1918. But at a people's assembly meeting, convened by the promoters of this party at a theater in the capital, the union orator Gutarra denounces the backroom electoral politics of their efforts and leads the crowd to the street in a class-based demonstration.

The attempt of the Socialist Party fails because the May 1, 1919, demonstration followed the large general strike of the same month (see *El Movimiento Obrero en 1919* by Ricardo Martínez de la Torre[3]) in which the leadership of that group avoids any action, abandoning the masses and, moreover, taking an attitude contrary to its revolutionary action. With Luis Ulloa absent from the country and Carlos del Barzo dead, the committee of the party is dissolved without leaving any trace of their activity on the workers' consciences.

The student university reform movement, in the same way as in other Latin American countries, brings the student vanguard to the proletariat. The First Congress of Students of Cuzco, held in 1919, agrees to the creation of popular universities. In 1921 the vanguard group from this conference, led by Haya de la Torre, founds the González Prada Popular University in Lima and Vitarte. The Workers' Congress in Lima approves a vote to join in the popular culture works of these universities. But workers do not have much confidence in the perseverance of the students, and in order not to arouse any suspicion the popular universities refrain from any work of ideological orientation for the proletariat. On the other hand, most students of the popular universities lack this orientation. In terms of the social question, they are going to learn rather than teach alongside the proletariat. Change starts with the May 23 action directed and led by the popular university with the help of organized labor. Mariátegui returns from Europe at this time with the aim of working toward organizing a class party. The popular universities that are in their heyday during the days of May 23 offered their platform and he accepts it. He develops a course of lectures on the global crisis in which he explains the revolutionary nature of this crisis. The anarchists show themselves to be hostile to this propaganda, especially the defense of the Russian Revolution to which they are in part opposed. But Mariátegui gains sympathy from the popular university and its most enthusiastic supporters of workers' organizations. *Claridad* [Clarity] begins to publish in April 1923 as an organ of free youth but more precisely of the popular university. Its orientation is "*clartista.*" It corresponds, above all, to the spirit of student unrest. Haya de la Torre is deported upon discovery of a conspiracy by the supporters of Don Germán Leguía y Martínez that serves as a pretext to punish its May 23 action, falsely accusing it of having a relationship with politicians of the old regime. In the days during which they boxed up issue 4 of *Claridad*, Mariátegui assumed its leadership. Issue 5 exhibits the principle of a frank doctrinarian orientation in which *Claridad* abandons the student tone. After that number, *Claridad* appears as an organ of the Local Workers' Federation. Chased by the police, the organized proletariat wants to protect it with its formal solidarity. Mariátegui begins organizing a workers' editorial society for the publication of the magazine with a view to publishing a newspaper, but at this time he becomes seriously ill and escapes death at the cost of the amputation of his right leg.

From late 1924 to early 1925, the repression of the student vanguard grows. The most active members of the popular university and the Federation of Students are deported: Bustamante, Rabines, Hurwitz, Terreros, Lecaros, Seoane, Heysen, Cornejo, Pavietich, etc. The secretary of the Local Federation of Arcelles and two of the leaders of the Indigenous organization are also deported. The activities of the popular university, however, are maintained by a spirited and persevering group. At this time discussions are begun to found APRA, at the behest of the originator Haya de la Torre, who from Europe leads the Peruvian vanguard in this regard. These elements accept, in principle, APRA, which even in its title is presented as an alliance or united front.[4]

In September 1926, *Amauta* appears as an organ of this movement, as a forum for "ideological definition." The Local Workers' Federation convenes a second Labor Congress. Mariátegui, director of *Amauta*, in a letter to this Congress which lacks a serious work of preparation, warns of the untimeliness of a discussion of doctrinal trends, proposing the organization of workers with a program of "proletarian unity," the founding of a national central labor federation based on the principle of "class struggle." But the tendencies bring their points of view to the Congress, leading to a disorderly discussion concerning the class doctrine to which the organized proletariat should adhere. This is the moment that the current Minister of Government, interested in increasing his political importance and threatened by rivalries in its circles, with a big performance chooses to engage in large-scale repression. On the night of June 5, the workers' society publication *Claridad* is surprised in a meeting which one of the newspapers has described as normal. That same night the best-known and most active militants of the workers' organizations and some intellectuals and university students are seized in their homes. An official notice carried in all of the newspapers announces the arrest of these people in a meeting they characterized as clandestine. The Minister of Government, Manchego Muñoz, says, without shame, that they have discovered nothing less than a communist plot. The *civilista* publication *El Comercio*, reduced to silence since the early days of the Leguía government and known for its links to the plutocracy of the old regime, editorially approved this repression and the steps to follow: closure of *Amauta*, closure of the Editorial Minerva shops where the writers-editors printed their material, detention of José Carlos Mariátegui who, given his health conditions, is taken to the San Bartolomé Military Hospital. About 50 militants were brought to the island of San Lorenzo. Many more suffered brief detention in police cells, and others who were pursued had to hide. The police notified those who remained at large that the Workers' Local Federation, the Textile Federation, and other organizations of the same character should be considered dissolved and that any union activity was severely prohibited. They did not miss the opportunity to applaud these measures, and as the *El Comercio* had done, did not hesitate to express delight at the suppression of *Amauta*. Yellow mutualists, unconditionally under orders of this as of all governments, as well as a presumptively brand-new "labor party," founded by some suspended and self-serving employees with the cooperation of a few craftsmen, acted similarly. But it was so disproportionate in respect to the vagaries and individual roles that it sought to document the kind of "communist conspiracy to destroy the social order" that is nonetheless slowly closing off all newspapers to impartial information. The publications that those initial moments created vanished. All that was found in the press was a brief letter Mariátegui sent from the military hospital, roundly and clearly denying all parts of the police invention.

Two professors at the popular university, Carlos M. Coxy and Manuel Vásquez Díaz, were deported to the north. Magda Portal and Serafín Delmar had previously been sent there. And four months later when the issue was no longer receiving public attention and there was no vestige of memories of the plot, the San Lorenzo prisoners were freed. In December 1927, *Amauta* reappeared, which otherwise would have resumed publication in Buenos Aires.

Among other effects, the repression in June has the result of pushing for a review of methods and concepts, and an elimination of the weak and disoriented in the social movement. On one hand it accentuates the tendency in Peru for organization, outside of the remnants of anarcho-syndicalism purged of "subversive bohemians"; on the other hand the diversion of APRA clearly appears. One group of deported Peruvians in Mexico advocates the establishment of a Nationalist Liberator Party; Haya defined APRA as the Latin American Kuomintang. There is a discussion in which the doctrinaire socialist tendency definitively states its aversion to any form of demagogic and inconclusive populism, including personalistic caudillos. The attached documents show the terms and outcomes of this debate, from which the Peruvian leftist movement enters a stage of definitive orientation. *Amauta*, in its issue No. 17 on its second anniversary declared that it had completed the process of "ideological definition," categorically affirming its Marxist nature. In November 1928, *Labor* appears as a newspaper extension of the work of *Amauta* to convert itself gradually into an organ of union reorganization.

## NOTES

This paper was presented to the Constituent Congress of the Labor Confederation of Latin America, Montevideo, May 1929. Reprinted in Ricardo Martinez de la Torre, ed., *Apuntes para una Interpretación Marxista de Historia,* 2:404–9.

Source: José Carlos Mariátegui, "Antecedentes y desarrollo de la acción clasista," in *Ideología y política*, in *Obras Completas,* 19th ed. (Lima: Biblioteca Amauta, 1990), 13:96–104.

1.  Manuel González Prada (January 6, 1844–July 22, 1918) was a Peruvian politician and anarchist, literary critic, and director of the National Library of Peru.
2.  Guillermo Enrique Billinghurst Angulo (July 27, 1851–June 28, 1915) was a millionaire business owner and populist mayor of Lima before being elected president of Peru from 1912 to 1914. He implemented reformist legislation such as an 8-hour workday before being overthrown in a military coup.
3.  Ricardo Martínez de la Torre, *El movimiento obrero en 1919: apuntes para una interpretacion marxista de historia social del Peru* (Lima: Ediciones "Amauta," 1928).
4.  Víctor Raúl Haya de la Torre founded the Alianza Popular Revolucionaria Americana (APRA; Popular Revolutionary Alliance of America) in 1924.

# PART III

# Marxism and Socialism

. . .

MARIÁTEGUI'S MARXIST THOUGHT was of the most original of its day. As the Peruvian thinker said after he returned from his stay in Italy, "I married a woman and some ideas." His affiliation was socialist and for him (Marxist): "socialism is a method and a doctrine, a system of ideas and a praxis." He flirted with more utopian versions of socialist thought before he went to Europe, but by the time he returned in 1923, he was a "convinced socialist of conviction." His Marxist socialism ranged broadly and incorporated not only Marx and Lenin, but a myriad of diverse thought and thinkers, from Rosa Luxemburg to Antonio Gramsci to the communal socialism practiced by the original Americans in the remnants of the Inca empire. It was to be based on the facts, not speculation, and through its method could bring problems into sharp focus. It was not dogmatic or narrow and, as Mariátegui said in "Anniversary and Balance Sheet" (see I.6), "We do not want American socialism to be a copy or imitation, it should be a heroic creation. We must give life to Indo-American socialism with our own life, in our own language." Indeed, as suggested in selection III.2, "Marxism is a method and a doctrine, a way of formulating ideas, and a type of practical political action." Further, "Marxism is the only method for improving on Marx."

Much of this section is made up of key chapters of what was to be Mariátegui's book on Marxism: *Defensa del marxismo*, which is discussed in the introductory note for the section "Defense of Marxism" (see III.4).

# 1—Reply to Luis Alberto Sánchez

Luis Alberto Sánchez[1] declares that he is delighted to see me enter into a polemical debate, because, among other things, "my monologue was becoming a little insipid." But if my monologue were what I have been writing for the last two years in this journal [*Amauta*] and others, we would have to call it a polemical monologue. One could say, then, that upholding new ideas brings with it the necessity of confronting and opposing the old ones, that is to say, disputing them to proclaim their shortcomings and fallacies. When I study or write a study of a question or a national theme I necessarily engage in polemics with the ideas or phraseology of past generations. This is not for the pleasure of polemicizing, but because I consider, as is logical, each question, each theme, according to different principles, which is what drives me to different conclusions, avoiding the risk of being a renovator by etiquette and conservative by content. My normal attitude is polemical, even although I polemicize little with individuals and a great deal with ideas.

Your condition as a spectator is ratified immediately, Luis Alberto. But, fortuitously, it follows from your own words that you accept this unfortunate position. You have no other choice, you say, "while Maese Pedro moves his marionettes in the workshop." But when these disappear, Sánchez promises "to go back to his first steps of combatant, of struggler," perhaps even under my flags, that is, under the flags of Peruvian socialism. I have to understand, then, the darts that are shot at me from Luis Alberto's trench, that until yesterday I rightfully thought were friendly, as an effect of his bad humor as an obligatory spectator. The constant repression of his desire to combat those on the right puts him in the situation of expending it on those who are on the left, those who, of course, are the ones to whom he feels closest.

I will not follow my colleague on the road of bibliographic anecdotes that, going beyond doctrinal polemics, he takes in the first part of his article. I believe it is not yet the time for the public to take interest in the "parallel lives" that Sánchez outlines to show that though at other times I have walked exotic and Europeanizing routes, he has not strayed from the Peruvian and nationalist path. These seem as minutiae to this same Luis Alberto, when, further along, he says, "It is not worth it to have to start a dialogue to air more or less personal questions."

Nor would I here confute your judgment about *Amauta* because— despite the hospitality that *Mundial* affords my writing, I think that the place for this rebound is in the very magazine I direct and that Luis Alberto occasionally and summarily judges. Because of the mistake that it might generate, I would only rectify, in passing, that the concept which is most mine is in *Amauta*. I feel that what I write in this magazine, and in any other, is equally mine, and no duality is more unpleasant than writing for the public and writing for myself. As obliged, I do not bring to this magazine topics that are at odds with the selection in which the director of *Mundial* has wanted to place my studies and notes about national themes, and even less do I bring an agitator's harangues or a catechist's sermons; but this does not mean to say that I diminish my thought here, rather that I respect the limits of the generous hospitality that *Mundial* allows me and which my discretion would never allow me to abuse.

It is not my fault that while my writings clearly show my socialist affiliation, one cannot deduce with equal facility the same of Luis Alberto Sánchez from his writings. It is Sánchez himself who has defined himself, terminally, as a "spectator." The merits of his labor as a student of national themes—which are not under discussion—are not enough to define a position in the contrasting doctrines and interests. To be "nationalist" because of the genre of studies does not require the same for one's political attitude, in the same limited or specific sense that foreign nationalists have defined this term. Sánchez, like me, repudiates precisely this nationalism that hides or disguises a simple conservatism, decorating it with ornaments of a national tradition.

And, arriving at this point, I want to specify another aspect of the nexus that Luis Alberto has not discovered in my socialism of some years—all those of my youth, that has no reason to feel responsible for the literary episodes of my adolescence and my "very recent nationalism." The nationalism of the European nations—where nationalism and conservatism are identified and consubstantiate—proposes imperialist ends. It is reactionary and anti-socialist. But the nationalism of the colonial peoples—yes, economically colonial, although they boast of their political autonomy—has a totally different origin and impulse. In these peoples, nationalism is revolutionary, and therefore ends in socialism. In these peoples the idea of the nation has not yet run its trajectory nor exhausted its historical mission. And this is not theory. If Luis Alberto Sánchez does not confide in theory, he will show no lack of confidence in experience, even less if the experience is under his scrutinizing eyes as a scholar. And I will be content with advising him that he direct his gaze to China, where the nationalist movement of the Kuomintang gets its most vigorous impulse from Chinese socialism.

At the end of his article, Luis Alberto Sánchez asks me—in the discourse in which his thought marauds through the borders of the subject of this dialogue, without going to the crux— how those of us who are militants under the banners of renovation propose to resolve the Indigenous problem. Above all, I would respond to him with my affiliation. Socialism is a method and a doctrine, a system of ideas and a praxis. I invite Sánchez to study them seriously, and not only in the books and actions but in the spirit that animates and engenders them.

The questionnaire that Sánchez puts before me is—permit me to say so—very ingenious. How can Sánchez ask me if I reduce all of the Peruvian problems to the opposition between coast and highlands? I have noted the duality born of the conquest to affirm the historic necessity of resolving it. My ideal is not a colonial Peru or Inca Peru, but an integrated Peru. Here we are, as I have written on founding a doctrinal and polemic magazine, people who want to create a new Peru in the new world. And how can Sánchez ask me if I do not invoke the *cholo* movement? And if this cannot be a movement of total and non-exclusive vindication, I have the right to believe that Sánchez not only does not take into consideration my socialism, but that he judges and contradicts me without having read me.

The vindication that we argue for is that of work. It is that of the working classes, without distinction between coast and highlands, Indian or cholo. If in the debate—that is in the theory—we distinguish the problem of the Indian, it is because in practice it is also differentiated in the facts. The urban worker is a proletarian; the Indian peasant is still a serf. The vindication of the first—for whom in Europe the struggle has not stopped—represents the fight against the bourgeoisie, whereas the vindication of the second represents the fight against feudalism, whose expressions of solidarity are two: latifundium and servitude. If we do not recognize the priority of this problem, yes it would be right, then, to accuse us of not being tied to Peruvian reality. These are, theoretically, things that are too elementary. I am not to blame that in Peru—in plain ideological debate—it is still necessary to explain them.

And now to put an end to this polemical interlude. I will continue polemicizing but, as before, more with ideas than with people. The polemic is useful when it endeavors, truly, to clarify theories and facts. And when what it brings are clear ideas and motives.

—*Mundial*, Lima, 11 March 1927,
and in *Amauta* no. 7 (March 1927), 38–39

## NOTES

Source: José Carlos Mariátegui, "Réplica a Luis Alberto Sánchez," in *Ideología y Política*, in *Obras Completas*, 19th ed. (Lima: Biblioteca Amauta, 1990), 13:219–23.

1. Luis Alberto Sánchez (October 12, 1900–February 6, 1994) was a Peruvian writer, lawyer, jurist, philosopher, historian, politician, and Aprista Party leader. In this polemic between two of Peru's most accomplished intellectuals of the time, Sánchez increasingly takes on a nationalist position and tries to paint any introduction of Marxist analysis or Marxist theory by Mariátegui as a foreign, European influence.

# 2—The Process of Contemporary French Literature

*This excerpt on socialism and Marxist dogma is part of Mariátegui's response to revisionist writers and parliamentary socialists of the time like the Belgian Henri de Man and his work* Beyond Marxism. *This helps to set the stage for the other chapters from* Defensa del marxismo *(see III.4).*

Having fulfilled the Dada and Surrealist experiment, a group of great artists, whose absolute aesthetic modernity no one would dispute, has realized that on the social and political plane, Marxism incontestably represents Revolution. André Breton finds it useless to rail against the laws of historical materialism and declares false "any enterprise of social explanation different to that of Marx."

Dogma is here understood as a doctrine of historical change. And as such, while change happens, it is so only while dogma is not filed away in an archive or becomes an ideological law of the past; there is nothing like dogma to guarantee creative liberty, the germinative function of thought. The intellectual needs to take on a belief, a principle that makes him a factor in history, in progress. [Bernard] Shaw intuits this when he says, "Karl Marx made a man of me. Socialism made a

man of me." Dogma did not impede Dante, in his day, from being one
of the greatest poets of all time; dogma, if that is what you wish to call
it, expanding the acceptance of the term, did not impede Lenin from
being one of the greatest revolutionaries and one of the greatest statesmen. Someone who is dogmatic like Marx or Engels has more influence in accomplishments and ideas than any great heretic or any great
nihilist. This fact alone ought to annul all apprehension, all fear in
regard to the limitation of dogma. The Marxist position, for the contemporary, non-utopian intellectual, is the only position that offers a
road of liberty and advance. Dogma allows a course, a geographic
map: it is the only guarantee of not, under the illusion of advancing,
covering the same ground twice, and of not landing in an impasse
because of bad information. The extreme free thinker is generally condemned to the narrowest of servitudes: his speculation revolves at a
crazy speed but without any fixed point. Dogma is not an itinerary but
a compass on the journey. To think with freedom, the first condition is
to abandon the preoccupation of absolute liberty. Thought has a strict
need for direction and objective. Thinking well is, in large part, a question of direction or orbit. Sorelism, as a return to the original sentiment of class struggle, as a protest against parliamentary pacification,
bourgeoisfied socialism, is a type of heresy that is incorporated into
dogma. And in Sorel we acknowledge an intellectual who, outside of
party discipline but true to a superior discipline of class and method,
serves the revolutionary ideal. Sorel managed an original continuation
of Marxism, because he began by accepting all the premises of
Marxism, not by repudiating them a priori en bloc, like Henri de Man
in his vainglorious adventure. Lenin proves to us, with the irrefutable
testimony of a revolution, that Marxism is the only means of following
and surpassing Marx.


NOTE

Source: *Defensa del Marxismo,* in *Obras Completas,* 3rd ed. (Lima: Editorial
Amauta, 1967), chap. 15, 5:103–5.

# 3—Message to the Workers' Congress

The First Workers Congress of Lima, with its available resources, achieved its essential objective, which was to give life to the Local Labor Federation that provides the cell, nucleus, and cement for the working class of Peru. Its natural program, modest in appearance, was reduced to this step. The development, the work of the Local Labor Federation these five years, shows that in this assembly the vanguard workers in Lima, through uncertain attempts, knew how to finally find their road.

The time of the Second Congress has come. It has taken a little time, but it would not be fair to blame this on its organizers. And its ends are, logically, new and their own. Now it concerns taking another step and you have to know how to do it with resolve and success.

The experience of five years of union work in Lima should be studied and used. Proposition and debates that in 1922 would have been premature and inopportune today can be broadened with the precise elements of wisdom that were disputed in this period of struggle. The diffusion of orientations, of praxis, is never so sterile as when it solely rests on abstractions. The history of the last years of world crisis, so pregnant with reflections and lessons for the proletariat, requires realistic criteria from its leaders. You have to radically shed old dogmatisms, discredited prejudices, and outdated superstitions.

Marxism, of which all speak but few know or above all comprehend, is a fundamentally dialectic method. It is a method that is completely based in reality, on the facts. It is not, as some erroneously suppose, a body of principles of rigid consequences, the same for all historical climates and all social latitudes. Marx extracted his method
from history's very guts. Marxism, in every country, in every people,
operates and acts on the environment, on the medium, without
neglecting any of its modalities. Because of this, after more than half a
century of struggle, its strength is shown to be ever increasing. The
Russian Communists, the British Labourites, the German Socialists,
etc., all equally claim Marx. This fact alone is enough to counter all the
objections about the validity of the Marxist method.

Revolutionary syndicalism, whose greatest teacher is Georges
Sorel—less known by our workers than his imitative and mediocre
replicators, phraseologists, and falsifiers—absolutely does not deny
the Marxist tradition. On the contrary, syndicalism completes and
expands it. In its impulse, in its essence, in its foment, revolutionary
unionism constituted exactly a rebirth of the revolutionary spirit, that
is to say Marxist, caused by the parliamentary and reformist degeneration of the socialist parties. (Of the socialist parties, not of socialism.)
George Sorel felt as far from the domesticated parliamentary socialists
as from the incandescent anarchists of sporadic revolts and violence.

The revolutionary crisis opened by the war has fundamentally
modified the terms of the ideological debate. The opposition between
socialism and unionism does not exist now. The old revolutionary
unionism, in the same country where it sought to be more purely and
faithfully Sorelian—France—has aged and degenerated no more and
no less than the old parliamentary socialism, against which he reacted
and rebelled.

One part of this socialism is now so reformist and is as bourgeoisfied as right-wing socialism, with which it tenderly collaborates. No
one ignores the fact that the postwar crisis broke the CGT
(Confédération générale du travail) into two factions, one of which
works on the side of the Socialist Party and the other with the
Communist Party. Old union leaders who until recently filled their

mouths with the names Pelloutier and Sorel, now cooperate with the most domesticated reformist socialist politicians.

The new situation has brought, then, a new break, or better, a new schism. The revolutionary spirit is not represented by those who represented it before the war. The terms of debate have changed totally. George Sorel, before dying, had time to salute the Russian Revolution as the dawn of a new age. One of his last writings was *Defense of Lenin*.

To repeat the commonplaces of prewar unionism, in a situation that is essentially different, is to persist in an attitude that has been surpassed. It is to act with absolute foreknowledge of the accelerated and convulsive process of the historic process of the last years. Above all, when the commonplaces that are repeated are not those of the real Sorelian unionism, but of the bad Spanish, or better said, Catalan translation. (If there is something to learn from the anarchic syndicalism of Barcelona, it is without doubt the lesson of its failure.)

The programmatic debate among us does not have any reason to get lost in theoretical deviations. The union organization does not need etiquette, but spirit. I have already said in *Amauta* that this is a country of labels. And I want to repeat it here. To get lost in sterile debates about principles in a proletariat whose principles are so weakly rooted does not serve to do anything for the workers but disorganize them, when precisely the issue is about organizing them.

The motto of the Congress should be *proletarian unity*.

Theoretical disagreements do not impede agreement on a program of action. The workers' united front is our objective. In the work of building it the vanguard workers have the obligation to set an example. In the work for today, nothing divides us: everything unites us.

The Union should not require anything of its affiliates but the acceptance of the classist principle. In the Union, there is room for reformist socialist exiles like unionists, like communists, like libertarians. The Union fundamentally and exclusively constitutes a *class organ. Praxis, tactics* depend on the current that predominates in its bosom. And there is no reason not to confide in the instinct of the majorities. The mass always follows the creative, realist, sure, heroic spirits. The best prevail when they really know how to be the best.

There is not, then, effective difficulty in understanding about the program of worker organization. All the Byzantine arguments about remote goals are not needed. The vanguard proletariat has, right before it, concrete questions of national working-class organization, class solidarity with indigenous demands, the defense and foment of institutions of popular culture, the cooperation with the daily laborers and *yanaconas* in the haciendas, development of a working class press, etc., etc.

These are questions that should principally concern us. Those that provoke schisms and dissidents, in the name of abstract principles, do not bring anything to the study and solution of these concrete problems. They consciously or unconsciously betray the proletarian cause.

The task of establishing the bases for a general confederation of labor fell to the Workers' Congress that united all of the republic's unions and workers' associations that adhered to a classist program. The objective of the first congress was local organization; that of the second ought to be, as is possible, national organization.

It is necessary to create a class consciousness. The organizers know well that most workers have a spirit of cooperation and mutualism. This spirit should be developed and educated until it is converted into a class spirit. The first thing that must be overcome and defeated is the anarchoid, individualistic, egoistic spirit, which besides being profoundly antisocial, does not constitute anything but the exacerbation and degeneration of the old bourgeois liberalism; the second thing that must be overcome is the spirit of corporatism, of a trade, of job category.

Class consciousness does not translate into addled, eviscerated harangues. (It is extremely comic to hear, for example, protests of extreme and delirious internationalism toward a man, pre-scripted with freewheeling revolutionarism, who at times has not, in his conduct and practical vision, liberated himself from sentiments and motives of the church bell tower or village.)

Class consciousness translates into solidarity with all the fundamental demands of the working class. And it translates, furthermore, into discipline. There is no solidarity without discipline. No great human work is possible without the union that leads even to the sacrifice of the men who attempt to organize it.

Before concluding these lines, I want to say to you that it is necessary to give the vanguard proletariat, along with a realist sense of history, a heroic will for creation and implementation. The desire for betterment, the appetite for well-being, are not enough. The defeats, the failures of the European proletariat have their origin in the mediocre positivism with which timid union bureaucrats and bland parliamentary teams cultivate a Sancho Panza mentality and a lazy spirit in the masses. A proletariat without more of an ideal than a reduction of the work hours and a salary raise of a few cents will never be capable of a grand historic enterprise. And as it is necessary to rise above a visceral and grotesque positivism, you have to also rise above negative, destructive nihilist interests. The revolutionary spirit is a constructive spirit. And the proletariat, the same as the bourgeoisie, has its dissolvent, corrosive elements that unconsciously work for the dissolution of its own class.

I will not discuss the program of the congress in detail. These lines of salutation are not a guideline, but an opinion. They are the opinion of an intellectual comrade who is trying to meet his duty, without easy demagogic orations, with an honored sense of responsibility and in a disciplined way.

NOTES

Published for the Second Workers' Congress of Lima, in *Amauta* 2/5 (January 1927): 35–36.

Source: José Carlos Mariátegui, "Mensaje al congreso obrero," in *Ideología y Política*, in *Obras Completas*, 19th ed. (Lima: Biblioteca Amauta, 1990), 13:111–16.

# 4—Defense of Marxism

*The Defense of Marxism* was one of the three books that José Carlos Mariátegui prepared for publication during his lifetime (*The Contemporary Scene* and *Seven Interpretive Essays on Peruvian Reality* are the other two). Unlike the first two and a third manuscript on ideological and political themes that was sent to Spain but lost, *Defense of Marxism* was published posthumously in a Chilean edition in 1934 and finally published in its original form as part of the *Obras Completas* by Editorial Amauta in 1967. It has the bulk, though not all, of Mariátegui's writings on Marxism and makes very clear his revolutionary yet non-dogmatic approach to the doctrine.

Mariátegui's longtime friend, comrade in their early struggles, and companion in his European exile, Jorge Falcón, provided one of the best descriptions of Mariátegui's Marxism in the presentation of this work which the Mariátegui family published in the *Obras Completas* edition with the Editorial Amauta. Falcón notes that Mariátegui was positioned far from leftist sectarianism and rightist revisionism long before he wrote *Defense of Marxism*. He goes on to remind the reader that *Defense* was written as a direct refutation of the criticism of revolutionary Marxism by the likes of Belgian revisionist writer and parliamentarian Henri de Man, as found in de Man's book *Beyond Marxism*

(*Zur Psychologie des Sozialismus*, published in Jena in 1926 and translated into French in 1927 as *Au delà du marxisme*). He reminds the reader that Mariátegui clearly states: "Marxism, where it has shown itself to be revolutionary—that is to say where it has been Marxism—has never obeyed a passive and rigid determinism." And that "socialism cannot be an automatic consequence of a bankrupt enterprise; it has to be the result of a tenacious and belabored work of ascension." He further reminds the readers, by quoting Mariátegui, that they should keep in mind that "the classes that have emerged in the domination of society have always disguised their material motives with a mythology that credits the idealism of their conduct." De Man ends by suggesting that such an approach will give a correct interpretation of the objective reality of a society and locate the routes of its historic process, unifying, as had Mariátegui, practice and theory.

The following selections (indicated with the letters a through j) contain most but not all of the sixteen chapters of *Defense of Marxism* and allow Mariátegui to present his arguments in full force. Chapter 2, "The Tentative Revisionism of *Beyond Marxism*"; 5, "Features and Spirit of Belgian Socialism"; 11, "The Position of British Socialism"; 14, "The Myth of the New Generation"; and 15, "The Process of Contemporary French Literature," do not seem as germane to Mariátegui's main arguments on Marxism and so are not included here. We do include, however, sections of chapter 15 on dogma in III.2 that set the stage for the discussion of this defense of Marxism.

# 4.a—*Henri de Man*
## *and the* Crisis of Marxism[1]

In a tome that perhaps strives to achieve the same resonance and diffusion as the two volumes of *The Decline of the West* by Spengler,
Henri de Man goes beyond Eduard Bernstein's endeavor of a quarter
of a century ago, and would not only "revise" Marxism, but "liquidate" it. . . .

But neither Bernstein nor the rest of the "revisionists" of his school
were able to expunge the citadel of Marxism. Bernstein, who has not
tried to sustain a secessionist current but to reconsider circumstances
not foreseen by Marx, operated within a German social democracy
that was more influenced by the reformist spirit of Lasalle than by the
revolutionary thought of the author of *Capital*.

It is not worth it to enumerate other minor offenses. . . .

The true revision of Marxism, in the sense of the renovation and
continuation of the work of Marx, has been done, in theory and practice, by another category of revolutionary intellectual—Georges
Sorel, in studies that separate and distinguish what is essential and
substantive in Marx from that which is formal and contingent. In the
first two decades of the current century, he represented more than the

reaction of the classist sentiment of the unions against the parliamen-tary and evolutionist degeneration of socialism. He represented the return of the dynamic and revolutionary conception of Marx and his insertion in the new intellectual, organic reality. Through Sorel, Marxism assimilates the substantial elements and acquisitions of philosophic currents after Marx. . . . And Lenin appears incon-testably in our epoch as the most energetic and profound restorer of Marxist thought, whatever doubts plague the disillusioned author of *Beyond Marxism*. Whether the reformists accept it or not, the Russian evolution constitutes the dominant accomplishment of con-temporary socialism. It is to this accomplishment, of which the his-torical reach cannot yet be measured, that one must go in order to find the new stage of Marxism. . . .

Active, living Marxism of today has very little to do with the deso-late proofs offered by Henri de Man.

NOTES

Source: *Defensa del marxismo*, in *Obras Completas*, 3rd ed. (Lima: Editorial Amauta, 1967), chap. 1, 5:15–19.

1.   The reference to the crisis of Marxism comes from Henri de Man's critical writings on Marxism, especially *Au delà du marxism*, (Paris: F. Alcan, 1929) and *La crisis del Socialismo* (Madrid: no publisher given, 1929).

## 4.b—*Liberal and Socialist Economics*

The revision—and much less the liquidation—of Marxism cannot be conceived unless it endeavors to be an original and documented rectification of the Marxist economy before anything else. Henri de Man, however, is content in this area with jokes like "why didn't Marx derive social evolution from geological or cosmological evolution," instead of ultimately making it depend on economic causes. De Man does not offer us either a critique or any conception of the contemporary economy. . . .

Henri de Man entertains himself by joking about the extent of Marx's predictions that the development of mechanization would make skilled labor obsolete. . . .

De Man is sure that Taylorism[1] will be discredited, as it is proven that "it causes psychological consequences that are so unfavorable to production, that they cannot be compensated by the economic benefits of labor and salaries that are theoretically possible." Moreover, in this and other speculations, his reasoning is based on psychology and not economics. Industry now obeys Ford's reasoning much more than that of Belgian socialists. The capitalist method of rational organization radically ignores Henri de Man. Its objective is reduction of cost through the employment of machines and unskilled workers. . . .

Neo-revisionism is limited to a few superficial empirical observations that do not comprehend the course the economy has taken, or explain the feeling of postwar crisis. The most important of Marxist predictions—the concentration of capital—has been accomplished. . . .

But de Man thinks that capitalism is more a mentality than a type of economy, and reproaches Bernstein for the deliberate limits of his revisionism, which, instead of debating the philosophical hypotheses from which Marxism came, labors to employ the Marxist method and continue his inquiries. One must, then, look elsewhere for his motivations.

## NOTES

Source: *Defensa del marxismo,* in *Obras Completas,* 3rd ed. (Lima: Editorial Amauta, 1967), chap. 3, 5:27–33.

1.    Taylorism was a theory of scientific management that Frederick Taylor (1856–1915) pioneered to analyze and synthesize industrial work flows with the goal of improving economic efficiency and labor productivity. It provides a fundamental rationale for the routinization of labor into simple, repetitive tasks.

# 4.c—*Modern Philosophy and Marxism*

Using the language of the Bible, in 1919 the poet Paul Valéry expressed a genealogical line in this way: "And it was Kant who begot Hegel, who begot Marx, who begot . . ."[1] Although the Russian Revolution was already in progress, it was still too soon not to prudently content oneself with these ellipses in discussing Marx's descendants. But in 1925, C. Achelin replaced them with the name of Lenin. And it is probable that Paul Valéry himself would not find this too bold a manner of completing his thought.

Historical materialism recognizes three springs as its source: classical German philosophy, English political economy, and French socialism. This is precisely Lenin's concept. Kant and Hegel precede and engender first Marx, and later, Lenin (whom we now add) in the same way that capitalism precedes and gives rise to socialism. To such conspicuous representatives of idealist philosophy as the Italians Croce and Gentile, who have dedicated themselves to the philosophical background of Marx's thought, this obvious affiliation to historical materialism is certainly not foreign. The transcendental dialectic of Kant is a prelude to the Marxist dialectic in the history of modern thought.

But this affiliation does not signify any subjugation of Marxism to Hegel or his philosophy, which, according to the famous phrase, Marx turned on its feet against the intent of its author, who left it standing on its head. In the first place, Marx never proposed the elaboration of a philosophical system of historical interpretation to serve as an instrument for carrying out his political and revolutionary ideas. His work is in part philosophical, because this type of speculation is not, properly speaking, reducible to systems in which, as Benedetto Croce warns—anyone's thought with a philosophical character is a philosophy—even though at times one only encounters external manifestations. Marx's materialist conception is born, dialectically, as the antithesis of Hegel's idealist conception. And this very relationship does not seem clear even to critics as sagacious as Croce. "The connection between these two conceptions," says Croce, "seems to me more psychological than anything else, because Hegelianism was the pre-culture of the young Marx, and it is natural that everyone ties new ideas to old as development, as correction, as antithesis."[2]

The efforts of those, such as Henri de Man, who summarily condemn Marxism as a simple product of nineteenth-century rationalism, could therefore not be more hasty or capricious. Historical materialism is precisely not metaphysical or philosophical materialism, nor is it a philosophy of history left behind by scientific progress. Marx had no reason to create anything more than a method of historical interpretation of modern society. Refuting Professor Stamler, Croce claims that "the presupposition of socialism is not a Philosophy of History, but a historical conception determined by the present conditions of society and the manner in which they have appeared."[3] Marxist criticism studies capitalist society concretely. As long as capitalism has been transformed definitively, Marx's canon remains valid. Socialism or, rather, the struggle to transform the social order from capitalist to collectivist, keeps this critique alive, continues it, confirms it, corrects it. Any attempt to categorize it as a simple scientific theory is in vain since it works in history as the gospel and method of a mass movement. Because, Croce goes on to say, "Historical materialism arose from the need to be aware of a particular social configuration, not as a research design for studying the factors of historical existence; and it was developed in the minds of political leaders and revolutionaries, not those of cold and plodding library learned wisemen."[4]

Marx lives in the struggle to attain socialism unleashed throughout the world by the innumerable multitudes animated by his doctrine. The fate of the scientific or philosophical theories he used, surpassing and transcending them as elements of his theoretical work, do not in any way compromise the validity and relevance of his ideas. It is radically different from the mutable fortunes of the scientific and philosophical ideas that accompany or immediately precede them in time.

Henri de Man formulated his criticism in the following manner: "Marxism is a child of the nineteenth century. Its origins go back to the epoch in which the reign of intellectual knowledge, which was begun by humanism and the Reformation, reached its apogee in the rationalist method. This method took its religion from the precise natural sciences, to which it owed the progress of productive technique and communications; and it consists of transporting the principle of mechanical causality, which manifests itself in technology, to the interpretation of psychic actions. It sees in rational thought, which modern psychology recognizes only in its function as organizer and inhibitor of the psyche, as the ruler of all human desire and all social development." And he immediately adds that "Marx made a psychological synthesis of the philosophical thought of his era" (agreeing that it was "so singularly new and vigorous in the sociological realm itself that it is illicit to doubt its brilliant originality"), and that "what is expressed in Marx's theories is not the movement of ideas, which have only arisen from the depths of working-class life and social practice since his death; it is the causal materialism of Darwin and the teleological idealism of Hegel."[5]

The irrevocable sentences against Marxist socialism pronounced, on the one hand, by futurism and, on the other, by Thomism are not very different. Marinetti lumps Marx, Darwin, Spencer, and Comte together to execute them more rapidly and implacably, without taking account of the distance that might separate their equally nineteenth-century, and therefore easy to dispense with, ideas. And the neo-Thomists, coming from the opposite extreme—the vindication of the medieval against modernity—find in socialism the logical conclusion of the Reformation and all Protestant, liberal, and individualist heresies. Thus de Man lacks even the merit of originality in his perfectly reactionary attempt to catalog Marxism among the most particular mental processes of the "stupid" nineteenth century.

It is unnecessary to defend that century against the contrived and superficial diatribes of its detractors to refute the author of *Beyond Marxism*.[6] Nor is it necessary to show that Darwin, like Spenser and Comte, in any case, corresponds in different ways to the capitalist method of thought; that like Hegel, from whom he descends—with the same apparent revolutionary rationalism of Marx and Engels—there is the conservative rationalism of historians who apply the formula "Everything that is rational is real" as a justification for despotism and plutocracy. If Marx could not base his political plans or his historical theories on De Vries's biology, or Freud's psychology, or Einstein's physics, then, none other than Kant would have had to content himself with Newtonian physics and the sciences of his era in elaborating his philosophy. Marxism in its later development—or rather, its intellectuals—has not failed to continually assimilate the most substantive and relevant of post-Hegelian or post-rationalist philosophical and historical speculation. Georges Sorel, so influential in the spiritual formation of Lenin, illuminated the revolutionary socialist movement—with a talent that Henri de Man certainly does not ignore, although his book omits any reference to the author of *Reflections on Violence* in light of Bergsonian philosophy, continuing the work of Marx, who fifty years earlier had elucidated this in light of the philosophy of Hegel, Fichte, and Feuerbach. Revolutionary literature does not abound, as de Man would like it to, in erudite publications of psychology, metaphysics, aesthetics, etc., because it must attend to the concrete objectives of agitation and criticism. But outside the official party press, in journals like *Clarté* and *La Lutte des Classes* in Paris, *Unter den Banner des Marxismus* in Berlin, etc., one will find expressions of philosophical thought much more serious than in his revisionist attempt.

Vitalism, activism, pragmatism, relativism: none of these philosophical currents, insofar as what they bring to the Revolution, have remained marginal to the Marxist intellectual movement. William James is no stranger to Sorel's theory of socialist myth, which, on the other hand, is so markedly influenced by Vilfredo Pareto.[7] And the Russian Revolution, in Lenin, Trotsky, and others, has created a type of thoughtful, active person, which should give something to think about to certain cheap philosophers, full of all the rationalist prejudices and superstitions of which they imagine themselves purged and immune.

Marx gave birth to this type of man of action and thought. But this ideologue-actor appears with a clearer profile in the leaders of the Russian Revolution. Lenin, Trotsky, Bukharin, and Lunacharsky philosophize in theory and praxis. Lenin leaves, along with his works on the strategy of class struggle, *Materialism and Emperiocriticism*. In the midst of the difficulties of the civil war and the party discussion, Trotsky found time for his meditations on *Literature and Revolution*. And was not Rosa Luxemburg always both a fighter and artist? Who among the professors that Henri de Man so admires live with more fullness and intensity of ideas and creativity? A time will come, despite the conceited academics who now monopolize the official representation of culture, when the amazing woman who wrote such marvelous letters from prison to Luisa Kautsky will inspire the same devotion and find the same recognition as a Theresa de Avila. A spirit, active and contemplative at the same time, more philosophic and modern than the pedantic crowd that ignores her, infused the tragic poetry of her life with a heroism, beauty, agony, and joy taught in no school of knowledge.

Instead of accusing Marxism of backwardness or indifference with respect to modern philosophy, it would be more appropriate to accuse the latter of a deliberate and fearful incomprehension of the class struggle and socialism. A liberal philosopher like Benedetto Croce—a real philosopher and a true liberal—had already opened this issue in unassailably just terms before another philosopher, Giovanni Gentile, also an idealist and liberal and the continuator and interpreter of Hegelian thought, accepted a position in the brigades of fascism, in the promiscuous company of the most dogmatic neo-Thomists and the most incandescent anti-intellectuals (Marinetti and his patrol).

The bankruptcy of positivism and scientism as a philosophy in no way compromises the position of Marxism. Marx's theory and politics are invariably cemented to science, not scientism. And as Benda observes, all political programs now wish to base themselves on science, even the most reactionary and anti-historical. And today, as Benda observes, all the political programs—including the most reactionary and anti-historic—want to rest on science. Does not Brunetière, who proclaims the bankruptcy of science, hope to wed Catholicism and positivism? And does not Maurras also claim to be a child of scientific thought? As Waldo Frank thinks, the religion of the future, if a belief has to ascend to the category of a real religion, will rest on science.

## NOTES

Source: *Defensa del marxismo*, in *Obras Completas*, 3rd ed. (Lima: Editorial Amauta, 1967), chap. 4, 13:35–42.

1.   Paul Valéry was a well-known French poet, writer, and philosopher in the first part of the twentieth century.
2.   Benedetto Croce, *Historical Materialism and the Economics of Karl Marx* (London: George Allen & Unwin, 1922), chap. 1; originally published in Italian in 1900.
3.   Rudolph Stammler was a professor at the University of Halle, in Leipzig. This quote comes from the first pages of the second chapter of Croce, *Historical Materialism and the Economics of Karl Marx* .
4.   Ibid.
5.   Ibid.
6.   Henri de Man
7.   Vilfredo Pareto (1848–1923) was an Italian thinker known for his work in economics and sociology.

# 4.d—*Ethics and Socialism*

The way Marxism is reproached for its supposed anti-ethicism, for its moveable materialism, for the sarcasm with which Marx and Engels treat bourgeois morality in their polemical pages, is not new. Neo-revisionist critiques do not say in this respect anything that the utopians and phrase-makers of all kinds have not already said. But the vindication of Marx from an ethical point of view has also already been done by Benedetto Croce. He is one of the most authoritative representatives of idealist philosophy, whose dictum will seem much more decisive than that of any Jesuit deploring petite bourgeois intelligence. In one of his first essays about historical materialism, in which he disapproves of the anti-ethical thesis about Marxism, Croce wrote the following:

This current has been principally determined by the necessity in which Marx and Engels found themselves, facing the multiple types of utopians, to affirm that what has been called the social question is not a moral question (that is, as it has been interpreted, it is not resolved with sermons and with what could be called moral means) and by their acerbic criticism of class ideologies and hypocrisies. Later, it has been helped, it seems to me, by the Hegelian origins of Marx and Engels's thought. It is well known that Hegelian philosophy and ethics lose the rigidity that Kant might give and that Herbart conserves. And, finally, the denomination of "materialism" is not lacking in efficacy, as it immediately makes one think of well-understood interests and the calculation of pleasures. But it is evident that the ideality and the absolute of the moral, in the philosophical sense of such words, are of course a necessary motive of socialism. Is it not perhaps a moral or social interest, as one might want to say, that moves us to construct a concept of surplus value? Does not the proletariat sell its labor for what it is worth, given its situation in the present society? And without this motive, how would one explain, together with Marx's political action, the tone of the violent indignation or the bitter satire that is noticed in each page of *Capital*? (*Materialismo Storico ed Economía Marxísta*)[1]

It has fallen to me to appeal to this judgment by Croce, in regard to some of Unamuno's phrases in *The Agony of Christianity*, writing that, in truth, Marx was not a professor but a prophet.

Croce has ratified more than once these quoted words. One of his critical conclusions about the matter is precisely "the negation of the intrinsic amorality or of the intrinsic anti-ethicalism of Marxism."[2] And in the same work, he marvels that no one "might have thought to call Marx, as an honorary title, the Machiavelli of the proletariat." One must find the ample and definitive explanation of his concept in his defense of the author of *The Prince,* also so persecuted by the disapproval of his posterity. On Machiavelli, Croce has written, "He discovers the necessity and the autonomy of politics that is beyond good and moral evil, that has its laws against which it is futile to rebel and which one cannot exorcise or drag from the world with holy water."[3] In Croce's opinion, Machiavelli is "as divided as soul and mind about politics, and of which he has discovered autonomy and that it now appears to him as a sad necessity of debasing one's hands by having to have it out with brutish people, now as a sublime art of founding and sustaining that grand institution that is the State" (*Elimenti di politica*).[4] Croce himself has expressly indicated the similarity between the two cases in these terms:

A case, analogous in certain aspects to that of the discussions about the ethics of Marx, is the traditional critique of Machiavelli: a criticism that was surpassed by De Sanctis (in the chapter about Machiavelli in his *Storia della letteratura*), but that continually returns in the work of Professor Villari, who finds the imperfection of Machiavelli in this: in that he did not consider the moral question. And it has always occurred to me to ask myself by what obligation, by what agreement, Machiavelli should treat all manner of questions, including those which did not interest him and those about which he had nothing to say. It would be the same to reproach someone among those who do research in chemistry for not going back to general metaphysical research about the principles of what is real.

The ethical function of socialism—with respect to that which fearlessly induces the hurried and summary excesses of some Marxists like Lafargue—should be sought not in grandiloquent Decalogues, nor in philosophic speculations that by no means constitute a necessity in Marxist theorizing, but in the creation of a producers' moral for the very process of anticapitalist struggle. Kautsky said, "It is in vain to look to use moral sermons to inspire in British workers a more elevated conception of life—the sentiment of noble effort. The ethic of the proletariat emanates from its revolutionary aspiration; it is they who give it its force and elevation. It is the idea of the revolution that has saved the proletariat from once again being strongly driven down." Sorel adds that for Kautsky the moral is always subordinated to the idea of the sublime and, although not in agreement with many official Marxists who paint the moralists with extreme paradox and ridicule, they agree that "Marxists have a particular reason to be doubtful of all that has to do with ethics; the party-going propagandists, the utopians and democrats had made such an abuse of justice that they had a right to view all dissertations along these lines as an exercise in rhetoric or a sophistry that was destined to mislead the people who were concerned with the workers' movement."

We owe an apology about this ethical function of socialism to the Sorelian socialist thought of Eduard Berth. Daniel Harvey, says Berth, seems to believe that the exaltation of the producer should prejudice that of the man; he attributes to me a totally American enthusiasm for an industrial civilization. It absolutely is not that way; the life of the free spirit is as dear to me as to him, and I am far from believing that there is nothing more than production in the world. It is always, ultimately, the old reproach made to Marxists, who are accused of being morally and metaphysically materialists. There is nothing more false; historical materialism does not impede in any way the highest development of what Hegel called the free or absolute spirit; it is, on the contrary, its preliminary condition. And our hope is, precisely, that in a society seated on an adequate economic base, composed of a federation of workshops where free workers will be motivated by a lively enthusiasm for the production of art, religion, and philosophy that can take in an enormous impulse and the same ardent, frenetic rhythm, will transport them to the heights.[5]

The wisdom, not exempt from the fine French irony of Luc Durtain, sustains this ascendant religiosity of Marxism, in the first country to have a constitution consistent with its principles. Historically it was already understood, through the Western socialist struggle, that the sublime of the proletariat is not an intellectual utopia or a propagandistic hypothesis.

When Henri de Man, reclaiming in socialism an ethical content, forces himself to show that class interest cannot be by itself a sufficient motor, it absolutely does not go "beyond Marxism," nor repair things that have not been foreseen by revolutionary criticism. His revisionism attacks reformist syndicalism, wherein class interest is content with satisfying limited material aspirations. A producer's morality, as Sorel conceives it and as Kautsky would conceive it, does not mechanically flow from economic interest: it forms in class struggle—liberated by heroic animus possessed of passionate will. It is absurd to look for the ethical sentiment of socialism in the bourgeoisified unions—in which a domesticated bureaucracy has debilitated class consciousness—or in the parliamentary groups, spiritually assimilated to the enemy through their combat through speeches and motions. Henri de Man says something

perfectly useless when he affirms "class interest does not explain everything. It does not create ethical motives."[6] These affirmations can
impress a certain type of nineteenth-century intellectuals who noisily
ignore the history of class struggle. They, like Henri de Man, exceed the
limits of Marx and his school. The ethic of socialism is formed in class
struggle. In order that the proletariat fulfills its historic mission in regard
to moral progress, it is necessary to assume its existing class interest,
though class interest by itself is not enough. Long before Henri de Man,
the Marxists have felt and understood it. It is precisely from this that
they start their steeled criticisms against facile reformism. "Without revolutionary theory there is no revolutionary action," Lenin submitted,
alluding to the yellow tendency to forget revolutionary finality by only
paying attention to present circumstances.

The struggle for socialism elevates the workers, who with extreme
energy and absolute conviction take part in it, to an asceticism, to
which it is totally ridiculous to berate its materialist creed in the name
of a morality of theorizers and philosophers. Luc Durtain, after visit-
ing a Soviet school, asked if he could not find a lay school in Russia,
because the Marxist teaching seemed religious. The materialist, if he
professes and serves his faith religiously, even if only for linguistic convention, can be opposed and distinguished from the idealist. (Already
Unamuno touched another aspect of the opposition between idealism
and materialism when he said that "as materialism is nothing more for
us than an idea, materialism is idealism.")

The worker, indifferent to class struggle, content with his tenor of
life, satisfied with his material well-being, can arrive at a mediocre bourgeois morality, but will never manage to elevate himself to a socialist
ethic. And it is false to pretend that Marx wanted to separate the worker from his work, deprive him of what spiritually tied him to his work,
so that the demon of class struggle could better take hold of him. This
conjecture is only conceivable to those such as Lafargue, the apologist
for the right to slothfulness, who adhere to marxist speculations.

The shop, the factory, affects the worker psychologically and mentally. The union, the class struggle, continues and completes the work
that is begun there. "The factory," Gobetti notes,

gives the precise vision of the coexistence of social interests: work solidarity. The individual becomes assumed to being part of a productive process, an indispensable part of the same means of production that is lacking. Here you have the most perfect school for pride and humility. I will always remember the impression I had of the workers, when it occurred to me to visit the Fiat factory, one of the few Anglo-Saxon, modern, capitalist establishments that exist in Italy. I felt in the workers an attitude of domination, an unassuming security, a contempt for all types of dilettantism. Whoever lives in a factory has the dignity of work, the habit of sacrifice and fatigue. The rhythm of life is based strongly on the spirit of tolerance and interdependence that accustoms one to punctuality, to rigor, to continuity. These virtues of capitalism are resisted by an almost arid asceticism; but on the other hand such suffering feeds, through exasperation, the courage of struggle, and the instinct of political defense. Anglo-Saxon maturity, the capacity to believe in precise ideologies, to confront dangers by making them stand out, the rigid resolve of practicing the political struggle with dignity, are born in this novitiate, which signifies the greatest revolution to come after Christianity.[7]

In this severe atmosphere of persistence, of effort, of tenacity, the energies of European socialism have been tempered, even in the countries where parliamentary socialism prevails over the masses; it offers an admirable example of continuity and duration to the Indo-Americans. The socialist parties, the union masses, have suffered a hundred defeats in these countries. However, each new year will always find increased and obstinate elections, protests, and any ordinary or extraordinary mobilization. Renan recognized the religious and mystical in this social faith. Labriola correctly exalts German socialism: "This truly new example is imposing in terms of social pedagogy, that is, in a large number of workers and petit bourgeois a new conscience is formed, one in which the governing sentiment of the economic situation, which induces class struggle, equally coincides with socialist propaganda, understood as goal and arrival point."[8] If socialism should not be realized as a social order, it would be enough as a work of education and elevation to be justified in history. De Man himself admits this concept when he says, although for a different reason, that "the essential in socialism is the struggle for it," a phrase that reminds us a lot of Bernstein advising the socialists to worry about the movement, not its goal. He was saying, according to Sorel, something much more philosophical than the revisionist leader imagined.

De Man did not ignore the spiritual, pedagogical function of unionism and the factory, even though his experience might be that of mediocre social democracy. "The union organizations," he observes, "contribute to strengthening the ties that bind the worker to his work much more than most of the workers and almost all the bosses suppose. They obtain this result almost without knowing it, trying to sustain a professional aptitude and develop industrial teaching, organizing the worker's right to inspection and to democratize workplace discipline, by means of a system of delegates and sections, etc. In this way they give the worker a much less problematic service, considering him a citizen of a future city, before looking for the remedy in the disappearance of all the psychic relations between the worker and the environment of the workshop." But the Belgian neo-revisionist, his idealistic boasts notwithstanding, finds the advantage and the merit of this in the growing apogee of the worker in his material well-being and in the extent to which this makes him a philistine. Paradoxes of petit bourgeois idealism!

## NOTES

Source: *Defensa del marxismo,* in *Obras Completas,* 3rd ed. (Lima: Editorial Amauta, 1967), chap. 6, 5:47–54.

1.   Mariátegui was well acquainted with Benedetto Croce's work and had copies of four of his books, including a fourth edition of *Materialismo storico ed economia marxista* (Historical Materialism and the Economics of Karl Marx) (Bari: Guiseppe Laterza, 1921), in which these themes are discussed at some length. See the first two chapters of *Historical Materialism;* and H.

E. Vanden, *Marátegui, influencias en su formación idelógica* (Lima: Editorial Amauta, 1975), and *National Marxism in Latin America, José Carlos Mariátegui's Thought and Politics* (Boulder, CO: Lynne Rienner, 1986).

2.   See the first two chapters of *Historical Materialism*.

3.   Ibid.

4.   Benedetto Croce, *Elimenti di politica* (Bari: G. Laterza & figli, 1925).

5.   From Èdouard Berth, a French socialist writer best known for *Les Méfaits des intellectuels* (The Misdeeds of the Intellectuals). Published in Paris in 1914 with a preface by Georges Sorel.

6.   From the Spanish thinker and writer Miguel de Unamuno.

7.   From Piero Gobetti.

8.   From Antonio Labriola (1843–1904), an Italian Marxist thinker who influenced Beneditto Croce and Antonio Gramsci.

## 4.e—*Marxist Determinism*

Another frequent attitude of intellectuals who entertain themselves by denigrating Marxist bibliography is to self-interestedly exaggerate the determinism of Marx and his school, with the aim of declaring them a product of the mechanistic mentality of the nineteenth century, which is incompatible with the heroic, voluntaristic conception of life to which the modern world has been inclined since the war. These reproaches do not accord with a critique of the rationalist and utopian superstitions and the mystical foundation of the socialist movement. But Henri de Man could not miss the opportunity to support the argument that wreaks havoc even among twentieth-century intellectuals, who are seduced by the reactionary snobbism against the "stupid nineteenth century." The Belgian revisionist observes a certain prudence in this regard. "One must point out that Marx," he declares, "does not merit the reproach that is frequently directed against him, that of being a fatalist, in the sense that he might deny the influence of human will in historical development; actually, he considers this will to be predetermined." He adds, "Marx's disciples are right when they defend their teacher from the reproach of having preached this type of fatalism." But none of this keeps him, however, from accusing them of their "belief in another sort of fatalism, that of categorical, inevitable ends," since "according to

the Marxist conception, there is a social will, subject to laws, which is
fulfilled by means of the class struggle and is the inevitable result of an
economic evolution that creates opposed interests."[1]

In substance, neo-revisionism adopts the idealist critique that reaf-
firms the action of the will and spirit, although with discreet amendments. But this critique only pertains to social democratic orthodoxy,
which, as we have already established, is not and was not Marxist, but
rather, Lasallean, a fact proven by the vigor with which the slogan
"Back to Lasalle" is disseminated inside German social democracy
today. For this critique to be valid, it would have to begin by proving
that Marxism is social democracy, an effort that Henri de Man avoids
attempting. On the contrary, he recognizes the Third International as
the heir to the International Working Men's Association, in whose congresses one could breathe a mysticism quite close to that of the
Christianity of the catacombs. And he corroborates this explicit judgment in his book: "The vulgar Marxists of communism are the real
usufructs of the Marxist heritage. Not in the sense that they understand
Marx better in reference to his era, but because they more effectively
use it for the tasks of their own era, to realize their objectives. The
image of Marx that Kautsky offers us appears more like the original
than the one Lenin popularized among his disciples. But Kautsky has
commented on a politics that Marx never influenced, while the words
that Lenin took from Marx after his death as his saint and sign are his
very politics, and they continue creating new realities."

In his *The Agony of Christianity,* Unamuno praises a phrase attributed to Lenin, pronounced in contradicting someone who observed
that his efforts went against reality: "So much the worse for reality!"
Marxism, where it has shown itself to be revolutionary—that is, where
it has been Marxist—has never obeyed a passive and rigid determinism. The reformists resisted revolution during the postwar agitation for
the most rudimentary economic determinist reasons—reasons that
were, in essence, identified with the conservative bourgeoisie and that
denounced the absolutely bourgeois and non-socialist character of
such determinism. To the majority of its critics, the Russian Revolution
appears, on the other hand, as a rationalist, romantic, anti-historical

effort of utopian fanatics. All caliber of reformists primarily rebuked the revolutionaries' tendency to force history, censuring the tactics of the Third International's parties as "Blanquist" and "putschist."

Marx could only conceive or propose realistic politics, and he therefore carried to extremes his demonstration that the processes of the capitalist economy lead to socialism to the extent that they are fully and energetically realized. But he always understood the spiritual and intellectual capacity of the proletariat to create a new order through class struggle as a necessary condition. Before Marx, the modern world had already reached the moment when no political and social doctrine could appear in contradiction to history and science. The decline of religion has its quite visible origin in its increasing alienation from historical and scientific experience. And it would be absurd to ask a political idea like socialism, so eminently modern in all its aspects, to be indifferent to this order of consideration. As Benda observes in his book *The Treason of the Intellectuals,* all contemporary political movements, starting with the most reactionary, are characterized by their efforts to attribute to themselves a strict correspondence with the course of history. For the reactionaries of Action Française, who are literally more positivist than any revolutionary, the whole period inaugurated by the liberal revolution is monstrously romantic and anti-historical. The limits and function of Marxist determinism have been fixed for some time. Critics alien to any party criteria, such as Adriano Tilgher, subscribe to the following interpretation:

> Socialist tactics, to lead to success, must take into account the historical situation in which they must operate, and where this is still too immature for the installation of socialism, they must certainly take good care not to have their hand forced. But on the other hand, they must not Quietistically[2] give up during the course of events, but rather, insert themselves in this flow to orient these events in a socialist sense so as to make them ripe for the final transformation. Marxist tactics are thus as dynamic and dialectical as Marxist theory itself. Socialists do not agitate in a vacuum, do not disregard the preexisting

situation, do not delude themselves that they can change things with
calls to humanity's better emotions, but adhere solidly to historical
reality, without resigning themselves passively to it. Rather, they
always react more energetically against historical realities with the
goal of economically and spiritually reinforcing the working class,
accentuating its consciousness of conflict with the bourgeoisie, until,
having reached the limit of exasperation, and with the bourgeoisie
having reached the end of the power of the capitalist regime, it
becomes an obstacle for the productive forces, and they can be use-
fully overthrown and replaced by a socialist regime to everyone's
advantage. (*La Crisi Mondiale e Saggi critice di Marxismo e
Socialismo*)

The voluntarist character of socialism is, in truth, no less evident—
even if less understood by its critics—than its determinist foundation.
To give it its true value, though, it is nevertheless enough to follow the
development of the proletarian movement from the actions of Marx
and Engels in London at the beginning of the First International to the
present, dominated by the first experience of a socialist state: the
USSR. In this process, every word, every Marxist act, resounds with
faith, will, heroic and creative conviction, whose impulse it would be
absurd to seek in a mediocre and passive determinist sentiment.

## NOTES

Source: *Defensa del marxismo,* in *Obras Completas,* 3rd ed. (Lima: Editorial
Amauta, 1967), chap. 7, 5:55–58.

1.    Henri de Man, *Au delà du marxisme* (Paris: Alcan, 1929; repr., Paris: Éd.
      du Seuil, 1974).
2.    Referring to Quietism, a form of religious mysticism focusing on passive
      meditation.

## 4.f—*The Heroic and Creative Sense of Socialism*

All those, like Henri de Man, who preach and proclaim an ethical socialism based on humanitarian principles, instead of contributing in some way to the moral elevation of the proletariat, unconsciously and paradoxically work against its affirmation as a creative and heroic force, that is, against its civilizing role. By way of "moral" socialism and its anti-materialist conversations, one can only manage to fall back into the most sterile and lachrymose humanitarian romanticism, the most decadent, "pariah-like" apologetics, and the most sentimental and useless plagiarism of evangelical epigrams about the "poor in spirit." And this is the equivalent of returning socialism to its romantic, utopian period, when its demands were, in grand part, nurtured by the sentiments and ramblings of this aristocracy that, after having entertained itself in an idyllic, eighteenth-century way by dressing as shepherds and shepherdesses and being converted to the *Encyclopédie* and liberalism, strangely dreamed of nobly leading a revolution of the shirtless and the helots. Obeying a tendency to sublimate one's sentiments, this type of socialist—whose services no one thinks of denying, and among whom some extraordinary and

admirable spirits rise to great heights—pulled from the gutter the sentimental clichés and demagogic images of the era of *sansculottes* so as
to inaugurate a paradisiacally Rousseauean age throughout the
world. But, as we have known for some time, this was absolutely not
the road to socialist revolution. Marx discovered and taught that one
had to begin by understanding the necessity and, especially, the value
of the capitalist stage. Socialism, beginning with Marx, appeared as
the conception of a new class, as a theory and movement that had
nothing in common with the romanticism of those who repudiated
the work of capitalism as an abomination. The proletariat succeeded
the bourgeoisie in the work of civilization. And it assumed this mission, conscious of its responsibility and capacity—gained in revolutionary activity and the capitalist factory—when the bourgeoisie, having fulfilled its destiny, ceased being a force for progress and culture.

For this reason, Marx's work has a certain tone of admiration for
the work of capitalism, and *Capital,* as it lays the bases for socialist science, is the best history of the epoch of capitalism (something that
seemingly does not escape Henri de Man's view, but that does in its
deeper sense).

Ethical, pseudo-Christian, humanitarian socialism, which
anachronistically tries to oppose itself to Marxist socialism, might be
the more or less lyric and innocuous exercise of a tired and decadent
bourgeoisie, but not the theory of a class that has reached its adulthood, overcoming the greatest objectives of the capitalist class.
Marxism is completely foreign and contrary to these mediocre, altruistic, and philanthropic speculations. We Marxists do not believe that
the job of creating a new social order, superior to the capitalist order,
falls to an amorphous mass of oppressed pariahs guided by evangelical preachers of goodness. The revolutionary energy of socialism is
not nurtured by compassion or envy. In the class struggle, where all
the sublime and heroic elements of its ascent reside, the proletariat
must elevate itself to a "producers' morality," quite distant and distinct
from the "slave morality" that its gratuitous professors of morals, hor-
rified by its materialism, officiously attempt to provide. A new civilization cannot arise from a sad and humiliated world of miserable helots

with no greater merits or faculties than their servility and misery. The proletariat only enters history politically, as a social class, at the moment it discovers its mission to build a superior social order with elements gathered by human effort, whether moral or amoral, just or unjust. And it has not gained this ability miraculously. It has won it by situating itself solidly on the terrain of the economy, of production. Its class morale depends on the energy and heroism with which it operates on this terrain, and the amplitude with which it understands and masters the bourgeois economy.

De Man touches upon this truth at times, but he generally takes care not to adopt it. He thus writes, for example, "The essential part of socialism is the struggle for it. According to the formula of a representative of the German Socialist Youth, the purpose of our existence is not paradisiacal, but heroic." But this is not exactly the conception that inspires the thought of the Belgian revisionist, who, a few pages before, confesses, "I feel closer to reformist than extremist practice, and I value a new sewer in a working-class neighborhood or a flower garden in front of a worker's house more than a new theory of class struggle." In the first part of his book, de Man criticizes the tendency to idealize the proletariat, just as the peasant, the primitive, simple man, was idealized in the age of Rousseau. And this indicates that his speculation and practice are almost solely based on the humanitarian socialism of intellectuals.

There is no doubt that, until now, this humanitarian socialism has been propagated a little among the working masses. The *Internationale*, the hymn of the revolution, addresses itself in its first verse to the "poor of the earth," a phrase clearly reminiscent of the gospels. If one remembers that the author of these verses is a popular French poet of a purely bohemian and romantic stripe, the vein of his inspiration becomes clear. The work of another Frenchman, the great Henri Barbusse, is impregnated with this same sentiment: the idealization of the masses—the timeless, eternal mass, the caryatidic masses—upon which the glory of heroes and the burden of culture weigh oppressively. But this mass of people is not the modern proletariat, and its generic demands are not revolutionary and socialist.

The exceptional merit of Marx consists, in this sense, in having discovered the proletariat. As Adriano Tilgher writes, "Marx stands before history as the discoverer, one could almost say the *inventor,* of the working class. He, in effect, not only gave the proletarian movement the consciousness of its nature, its legitimacy and historical necessity, of its internal laws, the ultimate goal toward which it is moving, and in this way has thus imbued the working class with the consciousness it had previously lacked; he has created, one could say, the very notion, and behind the notion, the reality of the proletariat as the class essentially antithetical to the bourgeoisie, and the true and sole bearer of the revolutionary spirit in modern industrial society."

NOTES

Source: *Defensa del marxismo*, in *Obras Completas,* 3rd ed. (Lima: Editorial Amauta, 1967), chap. 8, 5:59–62.

## 4.g— *The Liberal Economy and the Socialist Economy*

Those phases of the economic process that Marx did not foresee—and it is necessary to desist in consulting the fecund volumes of criticism and theory in which he espouses his method of interpretation as if these were the memoirs of a fortune-teller—do not minimally affect the fundamentals of Marxist economics. It is precisely the increasingly severe and profound events that have rectified the practice of capitalism during the last century that have forced, in line with specific cases, protectionism over free trade and intervention over laissez-faire policies, but they have not challenged the fundamentals of the liberal economy that provide the theoretical bases of the capitalist order. Today, in the time of worldwide standardization of services and enterprises, the leader of the Republican Party and President-elect of the United States claims these individualist principles to be essential to the prosperity and development of that nation. This comes in light of the tendency of the opposition party to over reward the state with business functions as part of its attack on the most vital force of the Yankee economy. No matter how much the Republican regime keeps the Yankee state in its classical economic line, reserving business and production for private enterprise, a pro-trust policy, and monopoly practices, it represents the derogation of the old principles that Hoover proclaims so vigorously. But if these principles are in the last analysis reduced to the principle of private property, capitalism will not retain anything with which it can ideologically oppose socialism. Although the facts restrict and, in certain cases, annul its validity—as corresponds to an economy that has served its mission—these principles, which constitute the substance of the liberal economy, cannot be denied by these developments and, consequently, by its statesmen or politicians. . . .

"Liberal political economy," Sorel observes,

> has been one of the best examples of utopia that can be cited. They have imagined a society in which everything can be reduced to commercial patterns under the most complete laissez-faire laws possible. Today this society would be as difficult to achieve as that of Plato. But great modern ministers have owed their glory to the efforts they have made to introduce something of this commercial liberty in industrial legislation.

Croce for his part does not explain under which rubric the liberal economists censure socialism as utopian, when it is evident that

> the socialists can return the same censure to liberalism, if they were to study it as it is now and not how it was years ago, when Marx conjured his critique. Liberalism directs its exhortations to an entity that, at least now, does not exist: the national or general interest of a society; because present society is divided in antagonistic groups and knows the interest of each of these groups but not, or only weakly, of a general interest.[1]

And it cannot be said, on the other hand, that Marxism as a praxis currently relies on the data and premises of Marx's economy studies, because the theses and debates of all its congresses are not anything other than a continual reintroduction of the economic and political problems, according to the new aspects of reality. The Soviets, who in this respect can invoke a varied and extensive experience, have sustained in the last European Economic Conference the principle of the legitimate coexistence of states with a socialist economy with those states with a capitalist economy. For this coexistence that is given in history today as a fact, they reclaim it as a right, in order to achieve the legal and economic organization of their relations. In this proposition, the first socialist state shows itself to be much more liberal than the formally liberal states. This confirms the conclusion to which liberal thinkers arrive when they affirm that the historic and philosophical function of liberalism has passed to socialism, and that liberalism today, being a principle of incessant evolution and progress, is less liberal than the old parties of this name.

NOTES

Source: *Defensa del marxismo,* in *Obras Completas,* 3rd ed. (Lima: Editorial Amauta, 1967), chap. 9, 5:63–66.

1.    Benedetto Croce, *Materialismo Storico ed Economía Marxista,* 4th ed. (Bari: Guiseppe Laterza, 1921), 96.

# 4.h—*Freudianism and Marxism*

The recent book by Max Eastman, *The Science of Revolution*, coincides with that of Henri de Man in a tendency to study Marxism with data from the new psychology. But Eastman, resentful of the Bolsheviks, is not exempt from revisionist motives. He comes from a different point of view than the Belgian writer, and in varied ways brings a more original contribution to the critique of Marxism. Henri de Man is a heretic from reformism or social democracy and Max Eastman is a heretic from revolution. His super-Trotskyite intellectual criticism divorced him from the Soviets, whose leaders, especially Stalin, he attacked violently in his book *After Lenin's Death*.[1]

Max Eastman is far from believing that contemporary psychology in general, and Freudian psychology in particular, diminishes the validity of Marxism as a practical science of revolution.[2] To the contrary: he affirms that it reinforces it and shows interesting affinities between the essential discoveries of Marx and the discoveries of Freud, and similarly in the reactions provoked in official science by one and the other. Marx shows that the classes idealized and masked their motives and that behind their ideologies, that is, in their political, philosophical or religious principles, their interests and economic necessities were operating. This assertion is formulated with the rigor and the absolutism that each revolutionary theory always has when it begins, and that for polemical reasons is accentuated in the debate with those who contradict it. It profoundly injures the idealism of the intellectuals, who until now were unwilling to admit any scientific notion that implies a negation or a reduction of the autonomy or majesty of thought, or, more exactly, of the professionals or functionaries of thought.

Freudianism and Marxism, even though the disciples of Freud and Marx are not yet those with the greatest propensity to understand it and notice it, are related in their distinct dominions not only for their theories of "submission," as Freud says, because of the idealist conceptualizations of humanity, but for the methods used to confront the problems considered. "To cure individual upheavals," Max Eastman observes, "the psychoanalyst pays particular attention to the deformations of conscience produced by repressed sexual motives. The Marxist who tries to cure the upheavals of society pays particular attention to the deformations engendered by hunger and egoism." Marx's term "ideology" is simply a name that serves to designate the deformations of social and political thought produced by repressed motives. This term translates the idea of the Freudians when they speak of rationalization, of substitution, of transference, of displacement, of sublimation. The economic interpretation of history is not anything more than a generalized psychoanalysis of the social and political spirit. From it we have a sample of the spasmodic and unreasonable resistance against the patient. Marxist diagnosis is considered more as an outrage than as a scientific answer. Instead of being embraced with a truly comprehensive critical spirit, it runs into rationalizations and "defensive reactions" of the most violent and infantile character.[3]

Freud, examining the resistance to psychoanalysis, has already described these reactions, which neither the physicians nor the philosophers have attributed to properly scientific or philosophical reasons. Psychoanalysis was objected to because, more than anything, it contradicted and stirred up a thick layer of sentiments and superstitions. Its affirmations about the subconscious, and especially about the libido, inflict on men a humiliation as severe as that felt with Darwin's theory and with the discovery of Copernicus. Freud may have added a third precedent to biological and cosmological humiliation: that caused by economic materialism just as idealist philosophy was at its full apogee.

The accusation of pan-sexuality that Freud's theory encounters has an exact equivalent in the accusation of pan-economism that Marx's doctrine still encounters. Apart from the fact that the concept of economy in Marx is as broad and deep as Freud's concept of the libido, the dialectical principle on which all of the Marxist conception is based excludes the reduction of the historical process to a purely mechanical economics. And the Marxists can refute and destroy the accusation of pan-economism with the same logic with which Freud, defending psychoanalysis, said, "They reproach his pan-sexualism, even though the psychoanalytic study of the instincts might have always been rigorously dualist and might never have failed to acknowledge, with regard to sexual appetites, other rather strong motives for rejecting sexual instinct."[4] Likewise, in the attacks on psychoanalysis there has been no greater influence on the resistance to Marxism than the anti-Semitic sentiment. And many of the ironies and reserve with which psychoanalysis is received in France, because it comes from a German whose nebulousness is little related to Latin and French civility, seems surprising in terms of those that Marxism has always encountered. This is not only the case among the anti-socialists in this country where unconscious nationalism has habitually inclined people to see the thought of Marx as that of a dark, metaphysical Boche.[5] The Italians, for their part, have not spared the same epithets nor have they been less extremist and jealous in opposing, as the case may be, Latin idealism and positivism to Marx's German materialism or abstraction.

To motives based on class and intellectual education that stiffen the resistance to the Marxist method, as Max Eastman says, Freud's own disciples—inclined to consider revolutionary attitude as a simple neurosis—do not, among men of science, manage to exclude themselves. Class instinct determines this fundamentally reactionary judgment.

The scientific, logical value of Max Eastman's book—and this is the curious conclusion to which one arrives after reading it and recalling the antecedents in *After the Death of Lenin* and his noisy excommunication by the Russian Communists—is very relative, if one does a little research on the sentiments that inevitably inspire it. Psychoanalysis, from this perspective, could be prejudicial to Max Eastman as part of his Marxist critique. For the author of *The Science of Revolution* it would be impossible to prove that his neo-revisionist personal reasoning, in his heretical position, and above all in his conceptions about Bolshevism, are not minimally influenced by his personal resentments. Sentiment is too frequently imposed on the reasoning of this writer, who so passionately tries to situate himself on objective and scientific ground.

NOTES

Source: *Defensa del marxismo,* in *Obras Completas,* 3rd ed. (Lima: Editorial Amauta, 1967), chap. 10, 5:67–70.

1.    The original title in English was *Marx and Lenin: The Science of Revolution,* first published in 1926, following the publication of *After the Death of Lenin* (1925). Mariátegui used and cited a French edition, *Depuis la mort de Lénine* (Paris: Librairie Gallimard, 1925). For this essay, written in 1929, Mariátegui evidently used a Spanish translation of *Marx and Lenin: The Science of Revolution.* See *La ciencia de la revolución* (Barcelona: Librería Catalonia, 1928).

2.    Max Eastman (1883–1969) was one of the most prolific leftist writers in the United States and masterful editor of *Masses,* until government censorship closed it. After a year's stay in the Soviet Union and befriending Leon Trotsky, he became increasingly critical of Stalin and eventually of Soviet Communism.

3.    Eastman, *Marx and Lenin: The Science of Revolution.*

4.    Ibid.

5.    Ibid.

# 4.i—*Materialist Idealism*

A friend and comrade whose intelligence I greatly value writes to me that, in his judgment, the merit of Henri de Man's work is as an effort to spiritualize Marxism. In his dual role as intellectual and academic, my friend should have been scandalized more than once by the simplistic and elemental materialism of orthodox catechists. I know many of these cases, and I myself had this experience in the early stages of my investigations into the revolutionary phenomenon. But even without advancing practically with this investigation, it is enough to consider the nature of the ingredients with which such a judgment contents itself to see its uselessness. My friend would find a pretension of claiming to understand and appraise Catholicism through the sermons of a parish priest absurd. He would insist on a serious and profound treatment of scholasticism and mysticism in such a critique. And any honest investigator would join him in such a demand. How, then, can he agree with the first philosophy student who has just picked up a dislike and disdain for Marxism from a phrase by his professor about the need to spiritualize this theory, too gross for the academic palate as it is understood and propagated by its public vulgarizers?

Above all, what kind of spiritualization do we want? If capitalist civilization, in decadence similar to that of Roman civilization in so many ways, renounces its own philosophic thought and abdicates its own scientific certitude to search for drug-like Oriental occultism and Asian metaphysics, then the best sign of the health and power of socialism as the source of a new civilization is undoubtedly its resistance to all these spiritualist ecstasies. In comparison with the return of the decadent and menaced bourgeoisie to mythologies that did not trouble the bourgeoisie in its youth, the most solid affirmation of the creative power of the proletariat would be its resounding rejection, its smiling deprecation of the anguish and the nightmares of a menopausal spiritualism.

Against the sentimental—nonreligious raptures—the other worldly nostalgias, of a class that senses its mission to be concluded, a new ruling class disposes of no more valid defense than its confirmation of the materialist principles of its revolutionary philosophy. What would distinguish socialist thinking from the most senile and rotten capitalist thinking if it shared all its hidden tastes? No, nothing is more insincere than to suppose that the incipient tendency of a professor or banker to revere Krishnamurti, or at least to show himself able to understand his message, is a sign of superiority. None of his clients asks the same banker, no one in his audience asks the same professor, that they show themselves similarly capable of understanding Lenin's message.

What person who follows the development of modern thought with critical lucidity can fail to note that the return to spiritualist ideas, the retreat to Asian paradises, has clearly decadent causes and origins? Marxism, as philosophical reflection, discovers the work of capitalist thought at the point where it abandons its forward march and begins its retreat, vacillating before its extreme consequences, a vacillation that precisely corresponds, on the economic and political plane, to a crisis of the liberal bourgeois system. Its mission is to continue this work. Revisionists like Henri de Man, who, according to the phrase of Vandervelde, "de-bone" Marxism for fear of appearing backward in relation to philosophical attitudes of a clearly reactionary impulse, intend nothing other than an apostate rectification in which socialism would attenuate its materialist premises to the point of making them acceptable to spiritualists and theologians for the frivolous purpose of adapting itself to current fashion.

The first false position in this meditation is that of supposing that a materialist conception of the universe is not suitable for producing great spiritual values. The theological—and not philosophical—prejudices that act as residue in minds that imagine themselves free of vanquished dogmatisms lead them to attach an untamed existence to materialist philosophy. History contradicts this arbitrary concept through innumerable historical testimonies. The biographies of Marx, Sorel, Lenin, and a thousand other protagonists of socialism find nothing to envy as to moral beauty and the full affirmation of the power of the spirit in the biographies of those heroes and ascetics who had earlier worked in accord with a spiritual or religious conception, in the classical sense of these words. The USSR combats bourgeois ideology with the most extreme weapons of materialism. The work of the USSR nevertheless tests the current limits of rationalism and spirituality in its declarations and objectives, if the object of rationalism and spiritualism is to improve and ennoble life. Do those who aspire to a spiritualization of Marxism believe that the creative spirit is less present and active in the actions of those who struggle for a new world order than it is among those New York moneylenders and industrialists who, marking the moment of capitalist exhaustion, disown potent Nietzschean ethics—the sublimated morality of capitalism—to flirt with fakirs and occultists? Just as Christian metaphysics have not kept the West from great material accomplishments, Marxist materialism, as I have affirmed on other occasions, encompasses all of our era's possibilities for moral, spiritual, and philosophical ascent.

Piero Gobetti, a disciple and heir of Crocean idealism, drawing on the doctrine's purity and active orientation, has considered this problem in admirably proper terms. "Christianity," Gobetti writes,

> reached the world of truth inside us, in the intimacy of spirit, it pointed out to humanity a duty, a mission, a redemption. But having abandoned Christian dogma, we have found richer, more conscious, more actionable spiritual values. Our problem is moral and political: our

philosophy sanctifies the value of practice. Everything is reduced to a criterion of human responsibility; if the earthly struggle is the only reality, everyone has value insofar as they work, and it is all of us who make our own history. This is progress because ever richer new experiences unfold. It is not a matter of reaching a goal or denying oneself through an ascetic renunciation; it is a matter of always more intensely and consciously being oneself, of overcoming the chains of our weakness in a perennial superhuman effort. The new criterion of truth is work that is adequate to each person's responsibility. We are in the kingdom of struggle (the struggle of man against man, of class against class, of state against state), because only through struggle are capabilities tempered and everyone, intransigently defending their position, collaborates in the vital process that has transcended the death of Greek asceticism and objectivism.

A Latin mind could not find a more classically precise formula than this: "Our philosophy sanctifies the value of practice."

The classes that have succeeded in dominating society have always disguised their material interests with a mythology that credits the idealism of its conduct. Since socialism, consistent with its philosophical premises, renounces this anachronistic garb, all spiritualistic superstitions rebel against it, in a conclave of international Pharisaism, whose holy decisions timid intellectuals and ingenuous academics feel obliged to consider.

But because bourgeois philosophical thought has lost the security and stoicism with which it wished to be characterized in its affirmative and revolutionary era, should socialism imitate its withdrawal to the Thomist cloister or its pilgrimage to the pagoda of the living Buddha, following the Parisian itinerary of Jean Cocteau or the touristic itinerary of Paul Morand? Who are more idealistic in the higher, abstract sense of the word, the idealists of the bourgeois order or the materialists of the socialist revolution? And if the word *idealism* is discredited and compromised by its service to systems that signify all the old class interests and privileges, what historical need has socialism of taking on its protection? Idealist philosophy, historically, is the philosophy of liberal society and the bourgeois order. And we already know the results that it has theoretically and practically given since the bourgeoisie became conservative. For every Benedetto Croce who loyally develops this philosophy and denounces the inflamed conspiracy of academia against socialism, which is unrecognized as an idea that arises from the development of liberalism, how many Giovanni Gentilis[1] serve a party whose ideologues are sectarian supporters of a spiritual restoration of the Middle Ages who repudiate modernity in toto? During the era when the formula "All that is real is rational" sufficed against egalitarian rationalism and utopianism, the historicist and evolutionist bourgeoisie dogmatically and forcibly disposed of almost all "idealists." Now that the myths of History and Evolution no longer serve to resist socialism, they become anti-historicist, reconcile with all religions and superstitions, favor the return to transcendence and theology, adopt the principles of the reactionaries who fought it most furiously when they were revolutionary and liberal, and once again discover the solicitous suppliers of all sermons useful for the rejuvenation of the oldest myths in the ranks and leading circles of a "bonne à tout faire" idealist philosophy (neo-Kantian, neo-pragmatist, etc.), whether dandies and gallants like Count Keyserling or pamphleteers and provincials à la Léon Bloy, like Domenico Giulliotti.

It is possible that those of the university who are vaguely sympathizers of Marx and Lenin but more particularly of Jaures and Macdonald feel the lack of a feverishly spiritual socialist theory or literature with abundant citations from Keyserling, Scheller, Stammler, and even Steiner and Krishnamurti.[2] It is logical that Henri de Man's revisionism, and others of lesser distinction, would find disciples and admirers among such elements who are often lacking any serious knowledge of Marxism. Few among them will bother to find out if the ideas of *Beyond Marxism* are at least original, or if, as Vandervelde himself certifies, they add nothing to the older revisionist critique. Both Henri de Man and Max Eastman draw their best arguments from the critique of the materialist conception of history formulated some years ago in the following terms by Professor Brandenberg: "It wishes to base all the *variations* of the collective life of humanity in the changes that take place in the realm of productive forces, but it cannot explain why the latter must constantly change, and why this change must necessarily occur in the direction of socialism." Bukharin responds to this criticism in an appendix to *Historical Materialism*. But it is easier and more convenient to content oneself with reading Henri de Man than to investigate his sources and inform oneself of the arguments of Bukharin and Professor Brandenberg, which are circulated less widely by news distributors.

On the other hand, the following proposition is peculiar and exclusive to Henri de Man's attempt to spiritualize socialism: "Living values are superior to material ones, and among living values, the highest ones are spiritual. Eudemonistically, this could be expressed as follows: Under equal conditions, the most desirable satisfactions are those which one feels in one's conscience when reflecting what is most enduring in the reality of the self and the medium that surrounds it." This arbitrary categorization of values has no other purpose than to satisfy those pseudo-socialists who wish to be furnished a formula equivalent to that of the neo-Thomists: "the primacy of the spirit." Henri de Man could never satisfactorily explain how living values differ from material ones. And to distinguish material from spiritual values would require a reliance on the most archaic dualism.

In the appendix to his book on historical materialism, Bukharin passes judgment on a tendency in which one could place de Man:

> According to Marx, the relations of production are the material base of society. Nevertheless, among numerous Marxist (or, rather, pseudo-Marxist) groups, an irresistible tendency to spiritualize this material base exists. The progress of the psychological school and method in bourgeois sociology could not fail to "contaminate" Marxist and semi-Marxist milieus. This phenomenon went hand in hand with the growing influence of idealist academic philosophy. The Austrian school (Bohm-Bawerk, L. Word, and all the rest) began to remake Marx's construction, introducing the "ideal" psychological base into the material base of society. The initiative in this task fell to Austro-Marxism, theoretically in decline. They began to treat the material

base in the spirit of the Pickwick Club. The economy, the mode of production, became a category inferior to that of psychological reactions. The solid cement of the material disappeared from the social edifice.

Let Keyserling and Spengler, those sirens of decadence, remain on the margins of Marxist thought. More harmful and disturbing to socialism at its current stage is the fear of not seeming intellectual and spiritual enough to academic critics. "Men who have received an elementary education," Sorel wrote in the introduction to his *Reflections on Violence*,

> are generally imbued with a certain reverence for the educated world, and they readily attribute genius to the people who attract the attention of the literary world to any great extent; they imagine that they must have a great deal to learn from authors whose names are so often mentioned with praise in the newspapers; they listen with singular respect to the commentaries that these literary prize winners present to them. It is not easy to fight against these prejudices, but it is very useful work; we regard this task as being absolutely of the first importance, and we can carry it to a profitable conclusion without ever attempting to direct the working-class movement. The proletariat must be preserved from the experience of the Germans who conquered the Roman Empire; the latter were ashamed of being barbarians, and put themselves to school with the rhetoricians of the Latin decadence; they had no reason to congratulate themselves for having wished to be civilized.[3]

This warning, from the man of thought and learning who took for socialism the best parts of Bergson's teachings, has never been as relevant as during these interim periods of capitalist stabilization.

## NOTES

Source: *Defensa del marxismo*, in *Obras Completas*, 3rd ed. (Lima: Editorial Amauta, 1950), chap. 13, 5:83–90.

1.   Giovanni Gentilis (1875–1944) was an Italian neo-Hegelian idealist philosopher.

2.   Jiddu Krishnamurti (1895–1986) was an Indian-born writer and speaker on philosophical and spiritual issues.

3.   Georges Sorel, *Reflections on Violence,* trans. T. E. Hulme and J. Roth (Glencoe, IL: Free Press, 1950), 61–62.

# 4.j—*The Science Of Revolution*

*The Science of Revolution* by Max Eastman is almost reduced to the assertion that Marx never managed to emancipate himself from Hegel in his thought. If this incurable Hegelianism had persisted only in Marx and Engels the author of *The Science of Revolution* would be little worried. But as it is found living in Marxist theorizing and those who continue it and, above all, dogmatically professed by the ideologues of the Russian Revolution, Max Eastman considers it urgent and essential to denounce and combat it. One must consider his fixing of Marx as reparations of Marxism.

But what *The Science of Revolution* demonstrates rather than the impossibility of Marx emancipating himself from Hegel is the inability of Max Eastman to emancipate himself from William James. Eastman shows himself particularly loyal to William James in his anti-Hegelianism. William James, after recognizing Hegel as one of few thinkers who propose a comprehensive solution to dialectic problems, pressures himself to add that Hegel "wrote so abominably that I cannot understand him" (*Introduction to Philosophy*).[1] Max Eastman did not force himself to understand Hegel any more. In his offensive against the dialectical method, all his North American resistances come into play—the proclivity for a flexible and individualist practicality, permeated with pragmatic ideas—against German panlogism,[2] against the system of a utilitarian and dialectical conception. At first glance, the "Americanism" of Max Eastman's thesis is in his belief that revolution does not need a philosophy, only a science, a technique. At the bottom, however, it is truly in its Anglos Saxon tendency to reject, in the name of pure "good feeling," all ideological construction that jars his pragmatic education.

Max Eastman on reproaching Marx for not having liberated himself from Hegel, reproaches him in general for not having liberated himself from all metaphysics, all philosophy. Not taken into account is if Marx, with the tediousness of a German expert, had only proposed and achieved the scientific elucidation of the problems of the revolution, as they were empirically presented in his time, he would not have achieved his most effective and valuable scientific conclusions. Moreover, he would not have elevated socialism to the level of an ideological discipline and political organization that converted it into the constructive force for a new social order. Marx could be an expert on revolution the same way Lenin was precisely because he did not belabor the elaboration of some strictly verifiable recipes. If he had rejected or been afraid to confront the "difficulties" of the creation of a "system," so as not to disgust the irreducible pluralism of Max Eastman later, his theoretical work would not be any better than that of Proudhon and Kropotkin[3] in its historical transcendence.

Nor does Max Eastman note that without the theory of historical materialism, socialism would not have advanced beyond the low point of philosophical materialism, and in the inevitable aging of this, by its lack of understanding of the necessity to fix the laws of evolution and movement, it would have been more easily contaminated by all derivatives of reactionary "idealisms." For Max Eastman, Hegelianism is a demon that must be forced to exit the body of Marxism, exorcising it in the name of science. What are the reasons for supporting his thesis to affirm that the work of Marx continually is at variance with the most metaphysical and Teutonic Hegelianism? In truth, Max Eastman does not have any more proof of this conviction than those who in times past were believers in the presence of demons in someone's body that had to be exorcised. Here is his diagnosis of the case of Marx:

Upon happily declaring that there is no such idea, that there is not any such empirical order that occupies the center of the universe, that the ultimate reality is not the spirit, but materialism, he put aside all sentimental emotion, and in a disposition that seemed completely realist, he put himself to write the science of the proletarian revolution. But in spite of this profound emotional transformation that he experienced, his writings continue to have a metaphysical and essentially animist character. Marx had not examined this material world the same way an artisan examines his materials, in order to be able to get the best out of them. Marx examines the material world the same way a priest examines the ideal world, with the hope of finding his own creative aspirations in it, and in the contrary case, to see how to transplant them in it. In his intellectual system, Marxism does not represent the passage of utopian socialism to scientific socialism; it does not represent the substitution of a non-practical evangelization for a better world by a practical plan, helped by a study of actual society, and indicating the means of replacing it with a better society. Marxism constitutes the passage of utopian socialism to socialist religion, a scheme destined to convince the believer that the universe itself automatically engenders a better society and that he, the believer, does not have to do anything more than follow that universe.[4]

The propositions that Eastman himself copies in *The Science of Revolution* from *Thesis on Feuerbach* are not enough for him as a guarantee of the totally new and revolutionary sense found in Marx when the dialectic is employed. He does not remember at any time this definitive affirmation of Marx: "The dialectic method not only differs in regard to Hegel's essence, rather it is totally contrary. For Hegel the process of thought, that he transforms under the name of ideal, into an independent subject, is the *demiurg* (creator) of reality, this last not being more than its exterior manifestation. For me, on the contrary, the idea is not anything but the material world translated and transformed by the human brain."[5] Without doubt, Max Eastman will try to maintain that his criticism does not concern the theoretical exposition of historical materialism but a spiritual and intellectual Hegelianism—in certain mental conformity to a professor of metaphysics—and that in his judgment Marx never knew how to get off the ground in spite of historical materialism whose signs one has to look for in the dominant tone of his speculation and sermonizing. And here we touch on his fundamental error: his repudiation of philosophy itself, his mystical conviction that everything, absolutely everything, is reducible to science, and that socialist revolution does not need philosophers, but technical experts. Emmanuel Berl definitively ridicules this tendency, although without distinguishing it, as is de rigueur, from the authentic expressions of revolutionary thought. "This same revolutionary agitation," Berl writes,

> ends up being represented as a special technique that can be taught in a central school. Conclusions can be obtained in examples of the study of advanced Marxism, the history of revolutions, and more or less real participation in diverse movements that can emerge at any point from which one can extract abstract formulas that cannot be applied automatically where ever a revolutionary possibility emerges. At the side of the Commissar of Rubber, the Commissar of Propaganda, both multifaceted technical experts.

The scientism of Max Eastman is not rigorously original either. In the times that the positivists still pontificated, Enrico Ferri[6] gave the term "scientific socialism" a strict and literal acceptance. He also thought that something like a Science of Revolution was possible. Sorel was greatly amused by this, at the expense of the learned Italian, whose contributions to socialist speculation were never taken seriously by the heads of German socialism. Today the times are less favorable than before to attempt it again, not from the point of view of the positivist school, but rather from that of Yankee practicality. Besides, Max Eastman does not represent any of the principles of the Science of Revolution. In this respect, the intention of his book, which coincides with that of Henri de Man in its negative character, never gets past the title.

## NOTES

Source: *Defensa del marxismo,* in *Obras Completas,* 3rd ed. (Lima: Editorial Amauta, 1967), chap. 16, 5:107–11.

1. William James, *Some Problems of Philosophy: A Beginning of an Introduction to Philosophy* (New York: Longmans, Green, 1911), 92.
2. In philosophy, panlogism is a Hegelian doctrine that holds that the universe is the act or realization of Logos.
3. Proudhon and Kropotkin were anarchist thinkers.
4. Max Eastman, *Marx, Lenin and the Science of Revolution* (London: G. Allen & Unwin, 1926).
5. Ibid.
6. Enrico Ferri (February 25, 1856–April 12, 1929) was an Italian socialist and editor of the daily socialist newspaper *Avanti*.

# 5—Programmatic Principles of the Socialist Party

*In October 1928, the Organizing Committee of the Peruvian Socialist Party placed José Carlos Mariátegui in charge of drafting this program outline.*

The program should be a doctrinal declaration that affirms:

1. The international character of the contemporary economy, which does not allow any country to escape the transformations flowing from the current conditions of production.

2. The international character of the revolutionary proletarian movement. The Socialist Party adapts its practice to the country's specific circumstances, but it follows a broad class vision and its national context is subordinated to the rhythm of world history. The independence revolution more than a century ago was a movement in solidarity with all peoples subjugated by Spain. The socialist revolution is a movement of all the peoples oppressed by capitalism. If the liberal revolution, nationalist in nature, could not be achieved without a close union between South American countries,

it is easy to understand that the historical law in an era of stronger linkages and interdependence of nations requires that the social revolution, internationalist in its nature, operates with a much more disciplined and intense coordination of proletarian parties. Marx and Engels's *Communist Manifesto* condenses the first principle of the proletarian revolution in the historic phrase: "Workers of the world, unite!"

3. The sharpening of contradictions in the capitalist economy. Capitalism has emerged in a semi-feudal context such as ours, and at a stage of the liberal ideologies of monopolies and imperialism that corresponds to the stage of free competition, which has ceased to be valid. Imperialism does not allow any of these semicolonial peoples, whom it exploits as a market for capital and goods and as a source for raw materials, to have an economic program of nationalization and industrialization. This process requires specialization and monoculture (petroleum, copper, sugar, cotton in Peru). The crisis arises from this rigid determination of national production created by forces of the world capitalist market.

4. Capitalism is in its imperialist stage. It is the capitalism of monopolies, of finance capital, of imperialist wars for the plundering of markets and providing sources of raw materials. The practice of Marxist socialism in this period is that of Marxism-Leninism. Marxism-Leninism is the revolutionary method in the stage of imperialism and monopoly. The Peruvian Socialist Party takes it as its method of struggle.

5. The precapitalist economy of republican Peru, because of the absence of a strong bourgeois class and the national and international conditions that have caused the country's slow progress on the capitalist road, cannot be liberated under a bourgeois regime subjugated to imperialist interests. It colludes with *gamonal* and clerical feudalism, and suffers from the defects and vestiges of colonial feudalism.

The colonial fate of the country determines its process. The emancipation of the country's economy is possible only by the action of the proletarian masses in solidarity with the global anti-imperialist struggle. Only proletarian action can stimulate and then perform the tasks of the bourgeois-democratic revolution that the bourgeois regime is incapable of developing and delivering.

6. Socialism finds the same elements of a solution to the land question in the livelihoods of communities, as it does in large agricultural enterprises. In areas where the presence of the *yanaconazgo* sharecropping system or small landholdings require keeping individual management, the solution will be the exploitation of land by small farmers, while at the same time moving toward the collective management of agriculture in areas where this type of exploitation prevails. But this, like the stimulation that freely provides for the resurgence of Indigenous peoples, the creative manifestation of its forces and native spirit, does not mean at all a romantic and anti-historical trend of reconstructing or resurrecting Inca socialism, which corresponded to historical conditions completely bypassed, and which remains only as a favorable factor in a perfectly scientific production technique, that is, the habits of cooperation and socialism of Indigenous peasants. Socialism presupposes the technique, the science, the capitalist stage. It cannot permit any setbacks in the realization of the achievements of modern civilization, but on the contrary it must methodically accelerate the incorporation of these achievements into national life.

7. Only socialism can solve the problem of an effective democratic and egalitarian education, under which all members of society receive the education that is their right. Only the socialist education system can fully and consistently implement the principles of the school system, the work school, the school communities, and more generally all of the ideals of the contemporary revolutionary pedagogy. These are incompatible with the privileges of the capital-

ist school, which condemns the poor to a cultural inferiority and makes higher education a monopoly of the wealthy.

8. Completing its bourgeois-democratic phase, the revolution becomes in its objectives and in its doctrine a proletarian revolution. The proletariat party, trained in the struggle for control of power and developing its own program, at this stage performs the tasks of the organization and defense of the social order.

9. The Peruvian Socialist Party is the vanguard of the proletariat, the political force that assumes the task of guiding and leading the struggle for the realization of its class ideals.

### Immediate Demands

- Recognize freedom of labor organization, assembly, and press.

- Recognize the right of all workers to strike.

- Abolish roadwork conscription.

- Replace the vagrancy law with the articles that specifically considered the issue of vagrancy in the draft Criminal Code introduced by the state, with the sole exception of those items that are incompatible with the spirit and criminal criteria of the special law.

- Establish state-funded social security and social welfare systems.

- Comply with the laws of worker's compensation, protection of the rights of working women and minors, and protection for the eight-hour day in agricultural tasks.

- Add malaria in the coastal valleys to the list of work-related diseases that landowners are responsible for treating.

- Establish a seven-hour day in the mines and in places that are unhealthy, dangerous, and harmful to the worker's health.

- Require mining and oil companies to permanently and fully recognize all the rights guaranteed to their workers by law.

- Increase wages in industry, agriculture, mining, sea and land transport, and on the guano islands, in proportion to the cost of living and the right of workers to a higher standard of living.

- Complete abolition of all forced or unpaid labor. Abolish or penalize semi-slave labor in the eastern forest region.

- Break up lands belonging to large *latifundia* and distribute them among the estates' workers in proportion necessary to meet their needs.

- Expropriate without payment all estates belonging to monasteries and religious congregations in order to give them to rural communities.

- Obtain legal rights for *yanacona* sharecroppers, tenants, etc., who work a plot for more than three consecutive years to continue to use the plots, with annual rents not to exceed 60 percent of the current standard. Discount this rent by at least 50 percent for those who remain as tenants.

- Award cooperatives and poor peasants with land put into agricultural production through irrigation projects.

- Maintain everywhere the rights granted to employees by law. Regulate pension rights with a parity commission that does not result in the slightest reduction of those rights as established by law.

- Introduce pay and minimum wage.

- Ratify freedom of religion and religious education, at a minimum following the guidelines of the constitutional article and subsequent repeal of the last decree against non-Catholic schools.

- Make education free at all levels.

We will immediately fight for these main demands of the Socialist Party. All are urgent demands for the material and intellectual emancipation of the masses. All demands have to be actively supported by the proletariat and by conscious elements of the middle class. The very act of the public establishment of this group lays claim to the rights of the freedom for the party to act lawfully and openly under the Constitution and to claim the guarantees it grants citizens to access press freedoms without restrictions and to hold congresses and debates. Closely associated groups to those that today address the public through this statement resolutely assume, through the consciousness of a duty and a historic responsibility, the mission to defend and propagate its principles and to maintain and enhance its organization, at the expense of any sacrifice. And the working masses of the city, the countryside, mining camps, and Indigenous peasants, whose interests and aspirations we represent in the political struggle, will embrace these claims and ideas, will fight persistently and vigorously for them, and will find, through each struggle, the road that leads to the final victory of socialism.

## NOTES

Reprinted from Ricardo Martínez de la Torre, *Apuntes para una Interpretación Marxista de Historia Social del Perú* (Lima: Empresa Editora Peruana SA, 1948), 2:398–402.

Source: "Principios programáticos del Partido Socialista," *Ideología y política*, in *Obras Completas*, 19th ed. (Lima: Biblioteca Amauta, 1990), 5:159–64.

# 6—On the Character
of Peruvian Society

*This selection, composed of Mariátegui's responses to a questionnaire in the Andean magazine* La Sierra *(no. 29, May 1929), provides some of his most penetrating analyses of Peru and its feudal and capitalist development. As such, it makes clear the originality of Mariátegui's application of Marxism, and his insistence on using the journal to penetrate to the essence of national problems in such a way as to maximize the possibility of changing conditions. The manuscript that Mariátegui refers to was evidently lost and never published, but most of it was eventually included in editions of* Ideología y Política. *This translation is taken from a previous book,* Acerca del Carácter de la Sociedad Peruana, Articulo Inédito de José Carlos Mariátegui *(Lima: Editorial Popular, 1973), for which the well-known Peruvian leftist journalist and Mariátegui scholar César Lévano wrote the Preface.[1]*

My answer to some of these questions is in *Seven Interpretive Essays on Peruvian Reality*. And I treat the purely political questions in a book on which I am now working that Historia Nueva will publish in a few months in Madrid. I believe that these types of questionnaires are not really useful unless concrete, precise, data, and fact-based research is being proposed. The general themes cannot be covered effectively in a few pages, no matter how great a study's power of synthesis. I am going to limit myself to a few schematic propositions that the "Seminar of Peruvian Culture" will find more fully developed in other studies.

### 1. What are the manifestations of the survival of feudalism?

The survival of feudalism certainly should not be looked for in political or juridical institutions and structures that persist from the feudal order. Formally, Peru is a republican and democratic-bourgeois state. Feudalism or semifeudalism survives in the structure of our agrarian economy. And in that Peru is a principally agricultural country, the conditions of its agrarian economy, in which the colonial inheritance is still visible, are decisively reflected in its political practice and institutions. The same would certainly not occur if industry, commerce, the metropolis were stronger than agriculture. Latifundism is not the only proof of agrarian feudalism or semifeudalism. In the *sierra*[2] we have definitive proof of its typical economic expression: servitude. In relations of production and work, a paid salary indicates the transition to capitalism. Properly speaking, no capitalist regime exists where there is no salary regime. Capitalist concentration also creates latifundism with the absorption of the small properties by large enterprises. But the capitalist *latifundio*, exploited according to a principle of production and not profitability, requires salaried labor, a fact that definitively differentiates it from a feudal *latifundio*. In the study and the classification of the forms and variations of servitude one does find the material for a possible and practical survey. The value of the hacienda does not depend on anything more than its population, its own labor force. The *latifundio* has the peasant masses because it has the land. The instrument of capital is sick. The day laborer who receives a poor piece of land with the obligation to work the lord's land without any additional pay is nothing more than a serf. And does not servitude subsist in the crude and characteristic form of the subordinated Indian servant [*pongazo*]? Certainly no law authorizes servitude. But the servitude is there, evidently almost intact. Nonpaid services have been abolished many times, but nonpaid services persist, because feudalism has not been abolished economically. Señor Luis Carranza proposes a capitalist method that, strictly applied, would have ruined feudal *gamonalism*: the fixing of a daily minimum salary of one sol for the highland haciendas. The *latifundio* would not have been able to accept this measure. If the state were to have imposed it, the *latifundio* would have rebelled, claiming its absolute right to property. The landless Indians would have seen themselves compelled by the threat of hunger, to occupy the *latifundios* through force. We would have had our agrarian revolution. All of this is by way of hypothesis, because in this history, which of the governments in this republican century would have felt strong enough to attack *gamonalism* so resolutely?

Salaried labor prevails on the coastal haciendas. Production techniques and labor systems indicate that our sugar and cotton haciendas are capitalist enterprises. But the *hacendado* [landowner] feels no less absolute in his domain. Inside his fief, he judges, controls, and regulates commerce, governs the collective life. The population on the *latifundio* lacks civil rights. Socially speaking, it does not constitute a town or a community, but rather all the peon labor of the hacienda. Obedience to the laws and authority of the state is totally subordinated to the will of the hacendado. The workers do not have the right to organize as citizens in communes or municipalities; and much less do they have the right to organize proletarian unions. State authority barely reaches the *latifundio*. The *latifundio* conserves the spirit of the *encomendero*. Preserving its peasant masses from all contamination by doctrines or proletarian vindications, caring for the health of their souls in his own way, trafficking in provisions by means of sellers and contractors, he cares for the health of their bodies. The *yanacongazo* and the *enganche* also maintain a certain character of feudal throwback in the coastal haciendas.

## 2. Historically, is the establishment
## of a formal capitalism possible?

A formal capitalism is already established. Even though the liquidation of feudalism has not been achieved, and our incipient, mediocre bourgeoisie has shown itself incapable of achieving it, Peru is in a period of capitalist growth.

Upon politically emancipating itself from Spanish rule, Peru was a country with an agrarian, feudal economy. Its mining, to which Peru owed its fame for fabulous wealth, found itself in crisis. The Spaniards had dedicated great effort to the exploitation of the mines, but they were unable to organize them technically and financially in a way that ensured their development. They allowed centers of production that, for geographic reasons, ceased to be the easiest and most advantageous to exploit, to be extinguished. The enormous distance that separated Peru from the European markets made it difficult for the old continent to exploit other Peruvian products. England, without doubt, had already taken its first commercial and financial steps. In London, the first small loans to the republic were made. Peru's republican beginnings emerged in the midst of fiscal tightness. The exploitation of guano and saltpeter deposits on the southern coast quickly opened an era of abundance in midcentury. The state began to enjoy bountiful resources. But Peru did not know how to administer its treasury prudently: it felt itself rich, compromised its credit, and having no choice began to use government loans, squandered its resources, and as a result created disorder. The exploitation of guano and saltpeter  enriched a number of speculators and contractors, who in part came from the old colonial caste. This group was transformed, by the addition of more than a few nouveaux riches, into a capitalist bourgeoisie. The War of the Pacific, in which Peru lost the saltpeter territory to Chile, caused a surprise for the country when, overwhelmed by the service on the public debt, which it had tried to regularize through a contract with the French firm Dreyfus, the public treasury found itself in profound crisis.

With the war, Peru's economy was completely prostrate. Fiscal resources were reduced to the scarce yield produced by customs and consumption taxes. The service on the public debt could not be taken care of at all; bankruptcy resulted in the loss of state credit. The foreign debt in large part ended up in the hands of English creditors, who entered into negotiations with the government to get an agreement. After these negotiations the Grace Contract was made, passing management of the state railways and guano islands to a company that held the national debt, the Peruvian Corporation. The exchequer agreed on its own to begin the service on the national debt with plated coins whose value was later fixed at 80,000 pounds sterling.

In this period, the cultivation of sugar began to acquire importance in the hot coastal valleys, which even before the war were susceptible to development. Peru had secure markets for sugar production in Chile and Bolivia, and had an extremely advantageous position for England.

The Peruvian Corporation, fulfilling its contractual obligations, completed the rail lines in the center first and in the south later, with the former favoring the exploitation of the mines in Junín. An American company, the Cerro de Pasco Mining Company, later changed to the Cerro de Pasco Copper Corporation, was established in Cerro de Pasco and Morococha [the two principal mining centers in the department of Junín]. With the establishment of this company and the petroleum company, a subsidy of Standard Oil and owner of the Negritos oilfield in northern Peru, the large-scale penetration by Yankee capitalism began. It was initially closely linked to the activity of English capitalism, dominant in the Peruvian economy through the Peruvian Corporation and the principal import-export houses.

At the dawn of the present century, the principal registered export products for Peru were sugar and cotton (whose cultivation was extended because of the stimulus of good prices for the coastal haciendas), copper and other minerals, petroleum and wools. Rubber had its period of prosperity at the beginning of the century, before the English developed the cultivation of rubber trees in their colonies. Extracted from forest regions that are difficult to access, Peruvian rubber was soon seen as an impractical competitor with the rubber from the English colonial plantations. Petroleum, on the other hand, continued to develop in an ascendant line. The

International Petroleum Company, the principal producer, offspring of Standard Oil, had a conflict with the state because of the taxes the Brea and Pariñas oilfields paid, which for some time was improperly recorded at much less than the true value. This enterprise should have paid the exchequer a sum much greater, but with the threat of suspending the work and with the collaboration of government officials and legislators the company managed a transaction that was favorable to their interests.

The European war made Peruvian capitalism move from a moratorium on the issuing of banknotes, for which it faced some resistance because of the unpleasant memory of treasury notes, to a period of investment and excess profits. But the national bourgeoisie, which constituted the base of an aristocracy tending toward idleness and dominated by prejudice, had always lacked a true capitalist spirit. They scorned this opportunity to use unexpected resources to ensure a more independent situation, and a more secure and stable position, and did so in the face of lenders and foreign experts and the eventual declining prices of the export products. It was thought that excess profits would not end and that cotton and sugar prices would remain at high levels indefinitely. The value of the cultivatable coastal land increased; the hacendados carelessly extended the land under cultivation; luxury and extravagance consumed a part of the excess profits. When cotton and sugar prices fell brusquely after the war, the coastal hacendados found themselves in the impossible situation of confronting the loans they had uncontrollably accumulated to expand their crops and quadruple their expenses. A great number of coastal haciendas ended up in the hands of their creditors, the export houses that had financed our coastal agriculture, and that gave it a characteristically colonial physiognomy, regulated production according to the European and North American markets. Many coastal haciendas have become property of the export firms Grace, Duncan, Fox, etc.; more than a few *latifundistas* ended up reduced to the condition of administrators or fiduciary officers in these haciendas. In the Chicama Valley, the powerful German landowner absorbed the national agrarian businesses and even commerce in the city of Trujillo where the

Casa Grande sugar refinery processing plant developed. This business has its own port, Port Chicama, where they load and unload the ships destined to carry its imports and exports.

The exploitation of the copper and silver mines and other minerals and petroleum deposits has grown enormously. Petroleum has become the principal export product of Peru. In the department of Junín, the establishment of a large American enterprise has been announced. The Cerro de Pasco Copper Corporation, owner of the processing center in La Oroya and the Cerro de Pasco, Morococha and Goyllarisquisga mines, finds itself in such a prosperous position because of the high price of copper that it has lately agreed to a 10 percent increase in wages and salaries, which will last as long as prices stay high in the New York markets. The profits from copper and petroleum enrich foreign companies, but they do not leave anything in the country except the fiscal taxes. In Talara, the International Petroleum Company, owner of its own port and ships, imports from the United States necessary consumer goods for the population that works in the petroleum region, including foodstuffs. All the economic life of the region is found in the hands of the company, and it consequently does not drive the development of the neighboring agricultural regions.

Industry is still very small in Peru. Its possibilities for development are limited by the condition, structure, and character of the national economy, but it is even more limited by the dependency of economic life on the interests of foreign capitalism. The import firms are, in many cases, the owners or stockholders of the national factories. Logically, they are only interested in the existence of industry that because of tariffs, primary resources, or labor costs generally tends to keep Peru a consumer market for foreign manufactures or as a producer of raw materials.

Government loan policy permits the state to mitigate the effects of this situation on the general economy. The government loans are applied to the execution of some public works—to avoid a state of significant unemployment, to sustain a large bureaucracy, to balance the budget. The public works enrich a large category of speculators, who compensate the national bourgeoisie for the fall taken by the sugar and cotton *latifundistas*. The axis of our capitalism begins to be, by virtue of this process, the mercantile bourgeoisie. The landowning aristocracy suffers a visible displacement.

The Peruvian Corporation recently obtained a contract from the government that provides it with the trains it was administering. On the other hand, the Peruvian exchequer has been exonerated for the 80,000 pounds sterling annually it still has to cover, and has recovered control over the guano trade (receiving in the process a small indemnification for the difference), but has ceded the property of the railroads, valued at 18,000,000 pounds sterling. This has been an important concession to English capitalism during an epoch of increasing relations and commitment with United States capitalism.

### 3. Does the coastal economy allow for the establishment of socialist economic forms?

To the extent that it is capitalist, the economy of the coast creates the conditions for socialist production. The sugar and cotton *latifundios* cannot be divided into parcels to make way for small properties—a liberal and capitalist solution of the agrarian problem—without negatively impacting yield and its profitable functioning based on the industrialization of agriculture. The collective state management of these enterprises is, however, perfectly possible. No one disagrees that we are dealing with an agriculture that prospers vigorously under private initiative and administration. It has owed its ephemeral prosperity to the fat times of the war. The sugar industry confesses it is almost bankrupt. It does not believe it has the power to confront the crisis without state subsidies.

Today, with urgent necessity, the question of the socialization or nationalization of this branch of production is introduced. The Peruvian sugar producers have lamentably failed in their private management of the Peruvian sugar industry. The biggest sugar companies are not now nationally owned.

### 4. Since the economic structure of the coast does not allow for the formation of a proletariat with a classist orientation, is the resurgence of a liberal economic stage possible?

These problems are not resolved in theory, but in practice. What possible liberal stage anticipates the question? If we understand the liberal stage to be the capitalist stage, we are already participating in its development. Do not expect the agreement of the researchers. Capitalist policy is irrigation policy, even for its conflict with the interests of the big *civilista* sugar landowners. Sutton represents capitalist advance, with his demagogy and bold gestures. It is probable that in Peru's history his significance would be analogous to that of Meiggs.[3] If liberal policy is understood as assuring the formalization of the relations between capital and labor and the authority of the state in what is now a feudal context that guarantees the laboring masses their rights of association and culture, it is evident that this policy would normally lead to the formation of a proletariat with a classist orientation. The formation of this proletariat will not be produced without a capitalism that politically and administratively imports liberalism. As has been the case so far, the urban, industrial proletariat, that of the transportation sector, etc., has to realize its obligations of solidarity with the peasantry of the hacienda. This is the way it has happened so far, penetrating in spite of all the walls. The wall will be easier to penetrate than it has been, since automotive traffic opens a means of contact between the hacienda and the city. And has the proletariat of the haciendas not struggled to achieve its economic demands many times before? Is it not enough to remember the strikes of Chicama, which are among the most important manifestations of class struggle in Peru, to be convinced that the peasant proletariat has, if not class orientation, previously engaged in combat?

### 5. On which bases and with which socialist elements should the capitalist regime be implanted?

### 6. What characteristics will distinguish the capitalist movement?

Questions 5 and 6 are answered and thus taken care of by the previous response.

### 7. Once the liberal economic stage is achieved historically, is the advent of socialism foreordained?

The political advent of socialism does not presuppose the perfect or exact accomplishment of the liberal economic stage, according to a universal itinerary. Elsewhere, I have already said it is very possible that the destiny of socialism in Peru might be in part achieving certain tasks that are theoretically capitalist in accordance with the rhythm of history that guides us.

### NOTES

1.  A version of this interview is also found in more recent editions of *Ideología y política*, in *Obras Completas*, 3rd ed. (Lima: Biblioteca Amauta, 1971), 13: 263–274, but the actual questions are not integrated in the text.

2.  Mariátegui divided Peru into three regions, the western coast, the highland mountainous region in the Andes, which in Peru is referred to as the *sierra*, and the *montaña*, which is the Peruvian forest on the eastern side of the Andes. Indigenous peoples and customs were strongest in the sierra, which is also where the *latifundio* was strongest and most traditional.

3.  Henry Meiggs, a notorious American capitalist, was instrumental in developing Peruvian railroads.

# PART IV

# Imperialism

MARIÁTEGUI READ LENIN AS WELL AS MARX and published parts of Lenin's *Imperialism, The Highest Stage of Capitalism* in his journal *Amauta*. He was well aware of the imperial presence in Peru and Latin America and notes in his piece on anti-imperialism (IV.2): "As long as imperialist policies are able to manage the sentiments and formalities of the national sovereignty of these states, and are not forced to resort to armed intervention and military occupation, they can absolutely count on the collaboration of the bourgeoisie. Although they are dominated by the imperialist economy, these countries, or rather their bourgeoisies, will consider themselves as masters of their own destinies as do Romania, Bulgaria, Poland and other 'dependent' countries in Europe." He further noted in "Nationalism and Internationalism" (IV.1): "The boundaries between nationalism and internationalism are not yet well clarified, despite the fact that both ideas have existed for a long time." In his essay on "Yankee Intervention in Nicaragua" (IV.3), he carefully notes not only the United States imperial designs on Nicaragua, but the collaboration of the national bourgeoisie with the imperialist occupying forces. Nor does he fail to see the imperial nature of Pan-Americanism (IV.5) and how it militates against progressive forces in Latin America. The short piece on "Martial Law in Haiti" (IV.4) foretells many similar U.S. imperial actions in the Caribbean and Central America: "The methods of the United States in colonial America have not changed. They cannot change. Violence is not used in countries under Yankee administration just by accident. Three events during the past five years underscore the increasing martial tendency of U.S. policy in these countries: the intervention in Panama against a strike, the occupation of Nicaragua, and the recent declaration of martial law in Haiti. The rhetoric of goodwill is meaningless in the face of these events." Even though intellectuals such as Mariátegui condemned imperialism, the United States continued to have a heavy presence in the continent. The seeds for an increasingly strong Latin American reaction were, however, sown.

# 1—Nationalism and Internationalism

The boundaries between nationalism and internationalism are not yet well clarified, despite the fact that both ideas have existed for a long time. Nationalists categorically condemn internationalist trends. But in practice they make some concessions, sometimes hidden, sometimes explicit. Fascism, for example, collaborates with the League of Nations. At least it has not defected from this league built on pacifism and Wilsonian liberalism.

It so happens, in truth, that neither nationalism nor internationalism continues in an orthodox or intransigent line. Furthermore, one cannot exactly indicate where nationalism ends and where internationalism begins. Elements of one parallel, and sometimes intertwine, with elements of the other.

The cause of this vague demarcation in theory and practice is very clear. Contemporary history continually teaches us that the nation is not an abstraction, not a myth. Neither are civilization and humanity. Evidence shows that national realities are not necessarily in conflict with international realities. The inability to understand and acknowledge this second and higher reality is a simple myopia, a functional limitation. Dated, mechanical forms of intelligence employed in former national perspectives are incapable of understanding the new, vast, complex international perspective. They reject and deny it because they cannot adapt to it. The mechanistic nature of this attitude is the same as rejecting Einstein physics in an automatic and a priori fashion.

Internationalists, except for some extreme right-wingers and some quaint and harmless romantics, act in a less intransigent manner. Similar to relativists before Galileo's physics, internationalists do not discard the entire nationalist theory. They recognize what corresponds to reality, but only in its first approximation. Nationalists understand a part of reality, but nothing more than a part. The reality is much broader, less finite. In short, nationalism is valid as a claim, but not as a negation. The current historical setting has the same values of provincialism and regionalism as before. Nationalism is a new style of regionalism.

Why, in our time, is this feeling so exacerbated and overly stimulated that it should long ago have become a bit more passive and less passionate? The answer is easy. Nationalism is one face, one side of a vast reactionary phenomenon. The reaction is called, successively or simultaneously, chauvinism, fascism, imperialism, etc. It is not by chance that the monarchists of L'Action Française are at the same time aggressive, jingoistic, and militaristic. They currently operate in a complicated process of adjustment, of adaptation of nations and their interests in a mutually supportive manner. It is not possible that this process can be completed without meeting extreme resistance from a thousand centrifugal passions and secessionist interests. The desire to give the people an international discipline causes an exasperated erection of nationalist sentiments that, romantically and anachronistically, isolate and differentiate the interests of the nation from the rest of the world.

The accomplices of this reaction rate internationalism as a utopia. But obviously the internationalists are more realistic and less romantic than it seems. Internationalism is not merely an idea or a feeling. It is, above all, a historic event. Western civilization has been internationalized, has solidarized with the life of most of humanity. The ideas and passions spread fast, fluidly, universally.

Every day currents of thought and culture spread more quickly. Civilization has given the world a new nervous system. Transmitted by cable, Hertzian waves, newspapers, etc., any human emotion can sweep instantly around the world. Regional habits gradually decline. Life tends toward uniformity, toward unity. It has the same style in all major urban centers. Buenos Aires, Quebec, Lima—they all copy the fashion of Paris. Their tailors and stylists mimic models from Paris. This solidarity, this uniformity, is not exclusively Western. European civilization gradually attracts all peoples and races into its orbit and customs. It is a dominating civilization that does not tolerate the presence of any concurrent or rival civilization. One of its key features is its power of expansion. No culture ever conquered such a vast expanse of the earth. The English installed in a corner of Africa the phone, the car, and polo. Western ideas and emotions moved along with the machines and goods. It appears strange and unexpected to have the history and thought of various peoples so connected.

All these phenomena are absolutely and unmistakably new. They belong exclusively to our civilization that, from this point of view, does not appear like any earlier civilization. And these events are coordinated with others. European states have recently seen and recognized at a conference in London the inability to restore their economy and their respective productive capabilities without a mutual assistance pact. Because of their economic interdependence, people cannot, as before, start and stop with impunity. Not by sentimentality, but by the demands of their own interests, the victors have to renounce the pleasure of sacrificing the defeated.

Internationalism is not a brand-new current. For roughly a century in European civilization one notes the tendency to develop an international organization of humanity. Nor is internationalism necessarily a revolutionary current. There is a socialist internationalism and a bourgeois internationalism, which is not absurd or contradictory. When it finds its historical origin, internationalism is a result of emanation, a consequence of liberal ideas. The first major incubator of international organisms was the Manchester school. The liberal state emancipated industry and trade from feudal and absolutist barriers. Capitalist interests developed independently from the growth of the nation. The nation, finally, could no longer contain them within its borders. Capital is denationalized; industry began to conquer foreign markets; goods do not know boundaries and strive to move freely across all countries. The bourgeoisie becomes in favor of free trade. Free trade as an idea and as practice was a step toward internationalism in which the proletariat will recognize one of its desired ends, one of its ideals. Economic borders are weakened. This event strengthened the hope of a day to come when political borders no longer exist.

England, the only country where the liberal democratic idea has been fully realized, understood and classified as a bourgeois idea, has achieved free trade. Production, because of its lawlessness, suffered a severe crisis, which triggered a backlash against free trade measures. States once again began to close their doors to foreign production to defend their own production. This launched a protectionist period during which production was reorganized on a new footing. The dispute of markets and raw materials acquired a bitter nationalistic characteristic. But the international role of the new economy returned to find its expression. It developed new forms of capital on a huge level, of financial capital, international finance. Its banks and consortiums merged savings in various countries to be invested internationally. The world war partially tore at the fabric of economic interests. Afterward, the postwar crisis showed the economic solidarity of the countries, the moral and organizational unity of civilization.

The liberal bourgeoisie, today as yesterday, works to adapt its policies to the new forms of human reality. The League of Nations is an effort, certainly futile, to resolve the contradiction between the international economy and the nationalist politics of bourgeois society. Civilization is not resigned to die in this crash, this contradiction. It creates, therefore, every day, communication agencies and international coordination. In addition to the two worker internationals, there are various other types of internationals. Switzerland is hosting the "core" of more than eighty international associations. Not so long ago, Paris was the headquarters of an international congress of dance teachers.

The dancers discussed their problems at length, in multiple languages. They were united, across borders, by the internationalism of the foxtrot and tango.

—*Mundial*, Lima, 10 October 1924

## NOTES

Source: "Nacionalismo e internacionalismo," in *El alma matinal y otras estaciones del hombre de hoy,* in *Obras Completas*, 10th ed. (Lima: Biblioteca Amauta, 1987), 3:59–63.

# 2—Anti-Imperialist Point of View

*Mariátegui submitted this thesis to the First Latin American Communist Conference in Buenos Aires, June 1929. It is reprinted from the* El Movimiento Revolucionario Latino Americano *(Latin American Revolutionary Movement), edited by La Correspondencia Sudamericana. It also appears in Ricardo Martínez de la Torre,* Apuntes para una interpretación marxista de la historia social del Perú *(Lima: Empresa Editora Peruana, 1948), 2:414–18. Julio Portocarrero read this thesis at the conference as part of discussion topic "The Anti-Imperialist Struggle and the Tactics of the Problems of the Latin American Communist Parties." After reading the document, the Peruvian delegate said: "Comrades: So writes comrade José Carlos Mariátegui when formulating his thesis on anti-imperialism, analyzing the economic and social status of Peru"* (Obras Completas, *Eds.' Note).*

1. To what extent can the situation of the Latin American republics be likened to that of other semicolonial countries? The economic status of these republics undoubtedly is semicolonial. As their capitalism and, consequently, the imperialist penetration, grows, this characteristic of their economy is accentuated. But the national

bourgeoisie who see cooperation with imperialism as the best source of profits feel in secure enough control of political power not to worry seriously about national sovereignty. These South American bourgeoisies, who except for Panama have not yet experienced U.S. military occupation, have no predisposition to accept the need to fight for the second independence, as Aprista propaganda naively assumes.[1] The state, or rather the ruling class, does not feel the need for a greater or more secure degree of national autonomy. The independence revolution is relatively too close, their myths and symbols too alive in the consciousness of the bourgeoisie and petite bourgeoisie. The illusion of national sovereignty remains intact. It would be a serious error to assume that this social layer retains a sense of revolutionary nationalism that in other conditions would represent a factor of the anti-imperialist struggle in semicolonial countries overwhelmed by imperialism as in Asia in recent decades.

Over a year ago in our discussion with APRA leaders in which we rejected their desire to create a Latin American Kuomintang, and as part of a desire to avoid European imitations and to accommodate revolutionary action to a precise assessment of our own reality, we put forward the following thesis:

> Collaboration with the bourgeoisie, and even many feudal elements, in the anti-imperialist struggle in China, can be explained on grounds of race and national civilization that do not exist for us. The Chinese bourgeois or nobility strongly feels Chinese. They respond to white contempt for his stratified and decrepit culture with the contempt and pride of their ancient traditions. Anti-imperialism in China may, therefore, rest on sentiments and the nationalist factors. The circumstances are not the same in Indo-America. The *creole* aristocracy and bourgeoisie did not feel sympathy for the people through the bond of shared history and culture. In Peru, the white aristocratic and bourgeois despise popular and national elements. They are, above all, whites. The petit-bourgeois *mestizo* imitates this

example. The bourgeoisie in Lima fraternizes with Yankee capitalists, and even with their mere employees, at the Country Club, the Tennis Club, and in the streets. The Yankee can marry an elite girl without the inconveniences of race or religion. She, in turn, feels no nationalist or cultural misgivings in preferring marriage to an individual of the invading race. Nor does a middle-class girl feel such scruples. The "huachauita" or lower-middle-class girl who can catch a Yankee employee of the Grace Company or the Rockefeller Foundation does so with the satisfaction that she can elevate her social status. The nationalist factor, for these objective reasons that none of you can escape, is not decisive or crucial in the anti-imperialist struggle in our context. Only in countries like Argentina, which has a large and rich bourgeoisie proud of their country's wealth and power and where the national character for these reasons assumed clearer and more precise characteristics than in more backward countries, could anti-imperialism (perhaps) penetrate easily into the bourgeoisie. But this for reasons of expansion and capitalist growth, not for reasons of social justice and socialist doctrine as is our case.

The full dimensions of the betrayal by the Chinese bourgeoisie and the failure of the Kuomintang were not yet known. A knowledge of capitalism, and not just for reasons of social justice and doctrine, demonstrated how little one could trust, even in countries like China, the revolutionary nationalist sentiment of the bourgeoisie.

As long as imperialist policies are able to *ménager* [manage] the sentiments and formalities of the national sovereignty of these states, and though they are not forced to resort to armed intervention and military occupation, they can absolutely count on the collaboration of the bourgeoisie. Although they are dominated by the imperialist economy, these countries, or rather their bourgeoisies, will consider themselves masters of their own destinies, as do Romania, Bulgaria, Poland and other "dependent" countries in Europe.

This factor of political psychology must not be neglected in estimating the potential for anti-imperialist action in Latin America. Neglecting or forgetting this factor has been a feature of APRA's theory.

2. The fundamental difference between the elements in Peru that accepted APRA in principle—as a united front plan, but never as a party or even as an effective organization—and those outside of Peru who later defined it as a Latin American Kuomintang, is that the first remained faithful to the revolutionary, socioeconomic definition of anti-imperialism, and the latter explains their position by saying: "We are leftists (or socialists) because we are anti-imperialists." Anti-imperialism is therefore raised to the status of a program, to a political attitude, of a movement that is self-sufficient and spontaneously leads by some unknown process to socialism, to social revolution. This concept leads to a distorted overestimation of an anti-imperialist movement, to the exaggeration of the myth of the struggle for the "second independence," and romanticizes that we are already living in the days of a new emancipation. The result is the tendency to replace anti-imperialist leagues with a political organization. From an APRA initially conceived as a united front, as a popular alliance, as a block of the oppressed classes, APRA becomes defined as the Latin American Kuomintang.

For us anti-imperialism does not constitute, or can it constitute by itself, a political program, a mass movement capable of conquering power. Anti-imperialism, even if it could mobilize the nationalist and petite bourgeoisie to the side of the worker and peasant masses (and we have already discounted this possibility), does not annul antagonisms between classes, nor does it suppress different class interests.

Neither the bourgeoisie nor the petite bourgeoisie in power can pursue anti-imperialist policies. We have the experience of Mexico, where the petite bourgeoisie has come to an agreement with Yankee imperialism. In their relations with the United States, a "nationalist" government might use a different language than that of the Leguía government in Peru. This government is frankly and uninhibitedly Pan-Americanist and Monroeist. But any other bourgeois government would do virtually the same thing in terms of loans and concessions. The investment of foreign capital in Peru grows in close and direct relationship with the country's economic development, the exploitation of its natural wealth, with the population of its territory, with improvements of communication routes. How can the most demagogic petite bourgeoisie oppose this capitalist penetration? With nothing but words. With nothing but a temporary nationalist fix. The taking of power by anti-imperialism as a demagogic populist movement, if it were possible, would not represent the conquest of power by the proletarian masses or socialism. The socialist revolution would find its most fierce and dangerous enemy—dangerous for its confusion and demagoguery—in the petite bourgeoisie placed in power by the voices of order.

Without eliminating the use of any type of anti-imperialist agitation, nor by any means of mobilizing social sectors that can eventually contribute to this fight, our mission is to explain and demonstrate to the masses that only socialist revolution can permanently and truly oppose the advance of imperialism.

3. These factors differentiate the situation of South American countries from the situation of Central American countries where Yankee imperialism, by resorting to armed intervention without the slightest hesitation, provokes a patriotic reaction that can easily win a part of the bourgeoisie and petite bourgeoisie to anti-imperialism. APRA propaganda, led personally by Haya de la Torre, has won better results here than anywhere else in America. His confusing and messianic sermons that claim to be based on an economic struggle appeal in fact to racial and emotional factors, thereby meeting the conditions necessary to impress petite bourgeoisie intellectuals. The formation of class parties and powerful trade unions with a clear class consciousness is not destined in those countries for the same immediate growth as in South

America. In our countries class is the most decisive factor, is the most developed. There is no reason to resort to vague populist formulas behind which reactionary tendencies can only thrive. Currently APRA as propaganda is confined to Central America. In South America, as a result of the populist, strong man, petit-bourgeois diversion which defined it as a Latin American Kuomintang, it is in the process of total liquidation. Whatever the next Anti-Imperialist Congress in Paris resolves, its decisions must decide on the unification of anti-imperialist organizations and to distinguish between anti-imperialist platforms and agitation and the tasks that fall within the competence of working-class parties and trade union organizations. It will have the final say on the issue.

4. Do the interests of imperialist capitalism necessarily and inevitably coincide in our countries with the interests of the feudal and semi-feudal landholding class? Does the struggle against feudalism unavoidably and completely identify with the anti-imperialist struggle? Certainly, imperialist capitalism uses the power of the feudal class, insofar as it considers it to be the politically dominant class. But their economic interests are not the same. The petite bourgeoisie, even the most demagogic, can enter into the same intimate alliances with imperialist capitalism if it is prepared in practice to attenuate its more emphatic nationalistic impulses. Financial capital will feel safer if power is in the hands of a larger social class that meets certain demands and distorts the class orientation of the masses and is better than the old and hated feudal class to defend interests of capitalism, to be its custodian and its steward. The creation of small landholdings, the expropriation of large estates, the liquidation of feudal privileges do not run contrary to the interests of imperialism in an immediate sense. On the contrary, to the degree that the vestiges of feudalism coincide with the development of a capitalist economy, this movement of the liquidation of feudalism coincides with the requirements of capitalist growth, promoted by imperialist investments and technology. The disappearance of large estates, that instead constitutes an agrarian

economy based on what the bourgeois demagogy called "democratization" of land ownership, the old aristocracies are displaced
by a more powerful and influential bourgeoisie and petite bourgeoisie—and therefore better able to guarantee social peace—none
of this is contrary to the interests of imperialism. The Leguía
regime in Peru, even though it is timid in practice when it faces the
interests of landowners and *gamonales* that support it to a great
extent, has no problem in resorting to demagoguery in making
claims against feudalism and its privileges, in thundering against
the old oligarchies, and in promoting land distribution that will
make each farm laborer a small landowner. The Leguía regime
draws its greatest strength precisely from this type of demagogy.
The Leguía regime does not dare touch the large property owners.
But the natural movement of capitalist development—irrigation
works, exploitation of new mines, etc.—is against feudal interests
and privileges. The large landowners, as cultivated areas grow and
new sources of work emerge, lose their greatest strength: the
absolute and unconditional control of labor. In Lambayeque,
where irrigation work is presently carried out, the capitalist activity of the technical committee that leads it and over which a North
American expert, the engineer Sutton, presides, has already come
into conflict with the interests of the large feudal landowners.
These large landowners grow mostly sugar. The threat that they
will lose their monopoly of land and water, and with it the means
to control their work force, infuriates these people and drives them
toward attitudes that the government, although closely linked to
them, considers subversive or antigovernment. Sutton has the
characteristics of the North American capitalist. His mentality and
his work clash with the feudal spirit of the landowners. Sutton has
established, for example, a system of water distribution based on
the principle that ownership of them belongs to the state. The
large landowners believe that water rights are part of their land
rights. According to this view, the water was theirs; it was and is
the exclusive property of their estates.

5. And is the petite bourgeoisie, whose role in the fight against imperialism is often overestimated, as is said, for reasons of economic exploitation, necessarily opposed to imperialist penetration? The petite bourgeoisie is undoubtedly the social class most sensitive to the prestige of nationalist myths. But the economic factor that dominates the question is the following: in countries with Spanish-style pauperism where the petite bourgeoisie with its ingrained prejudices of decency resists proletarianization; where they because of their miserable wages do not have the economic power to transform themselves into the working class; where the prevailing "employment-mania," the search for a petty government job and the hunt for a "decent" salary and post; the establishment of large companies is generally favorably received by the middle class even though they greatly exploit its national staff, and always represent for this class a better paid job. The Yankee company means better pay, the possibility of promotion, emancipation from the employment mania of the state, where only speculators have a future. This reality acts with a decisive force on the conscience of the petit-bourgeois searching for or having found a job. In these countries with Spanish-style poverty, we repeat, the situation of the middle class is not the same as in countries where these classes have gone through a period of free competition and capitalist growth conducive to individual initiative and success and to the oppression of large monopolies.

In conclusion, we are anti-imperialists because we are Marxists, because we are revolutionaries, because we oppose capitalism with socialism as an adversarial system called to succeed it. In the struggle against foreign imperialism we are fulfilling our duties of solidarity with the revolutionary masses of Europe.

—Lima, 21 May 1929

## NOTES

Source: "Punto de vista anti-imperialista," in *Ideología y política,* in *Obras Completas,* 19th ed. (Lima: Biblioteca Amauta, 1990), 13:87–95.

1. Víctor Raúl Haya de la Torre founded the Alianza Popular Revolucionaria Americana (APRA, Popular Revolutionary Alliance of America) in 1924.

# 3—Yankee Imperialism in Nicaragua

Even those who ignore the events and spirit of U.S. policy in Central America can certainly take into consideration the reasons that Mr. Kellogg[1] seeks to justify the U.S. troop invasion of Nicaraguan territory. But those who remember the development of this policy over the last twenty or twenty-five years are no doubt aware of the absolute consistency of this armed intervention in the domestic events of Nicaragua and its expansionist purpose.

For many years the United States has had its eyes on Nicaragua. It has had several opportunities under similar pretexts to take control of its formal autonomy.

When President Zelaya[2] governed Nicaragua, Roosevelt, the "big game hunter," notified the country of the United States's intent to convert the San Juan River into an inter-oceanic canal, and to establish a naval base in the Gulf of Fonseca. But this plan with its stated imperialist intentions naturally met active resistance in Nicaragua. President Zelaya was unable to make any concessions to the U.S. government in this regard. The United States did not gain anything from this Nicaraguan political leader but a friendship treaty. Subsequently, U.S. agents began the task of organizing riots with the goal of creating, under the protection of Yankee guns, a government obedient to northern imperialism.

This objective was definitively achieved with the formation of Adolfo Díaz's government, which was an unconditional servant of Yankee capitalism.[3] Then as now, American troops were involved in the defense of this regime, which was vigorously repudiated by public sentiment such that its stability was seriously threatened. And the Díaz government gave the United States the treaty it so desperately wanted.

Chamorro, the foreign minister who signed the treaty, inherited power.[4] U.S. interests remained well entrenched in Nicaragua for several years. But popular sentiment continued to ferment, and eventually threw out this agent of U.S. imperialism. Since then, the United States, or rather its government, has felt the need to intervene again in Nicaragua. North American guns are now trying to impose on these people the presidency of Adolfo Díaz. Because of the resignation of the president, Sacasa, the legal vice president, represents the constitution and the Nicaraguan vote.[5]

It is very easy for the American press to depict the people of Central America in perpetual revolutionary agitation. It is indeed much harder to hide from worldview the principal participation of the Yankees in this unrest. The United States is interested in maintaining a divided and conflictive Central America. The necessary confederation of the small republics in Central America finds in the United States its greatest enemy. Yankee mechanisms were responsible for disrupting attempts six years ago to create a confederation. Nicaragua, whose government at that point was completely subjugated to U.S. policy, was at the heart of the imperialist maneuvers against the free union of the Central American states.

The emphasis on American expansionism at the moment is perfectly understandable. Europe is in a period of "capitalist stabilization." It is in the process of reorganizing its ruined empire in Africa, Asia, etc. Moreover, because of the natural momentum of its industrial and financial development, the United States is pushing its dominance over markets, roads, and centers of raw materials. If North American capitalism cannot expand its domain it will inevitably enter into a period of crisis. The United States already suffers the consequences of a plethora of gold and industrial and agricultural overproduction. Its banking and other industries have an urgent need to find larger markets. The awakening of China, which after years of moral collapse is strongly reacting against foreign domination, threatens one of the areas where U.S. imperialism gradually struggles to dislodge British and Japanese imperialism. The United States needs more than ever to turn to the Latin American continent where the [First World] War has facilitated undermining England's previously omnipotent influence.

These factors impede Latin Americans from considering the Nicaraguan conflict as a conflict foreign to its interests. Solidarity with Nicaragua, as represented and defended by the constitutional Sacasa government, is therefore unreservedly expressed.

Even more so than the excesses of U.S. imperialism, the continent's opinion condemns the betrayals of Central American local bosses who are at its service.

— *Variedades*, Lima, 10 November 1928

NOTES

Source: "El imperialismo yanqui en Nicaragua," in *Temas de nuestra América*, in *Obras Completas*, 9th ed. (Lima: Biblioteca Amauta, 1986), 12:144–47.

1.    Frank Kellogg (December 22, 1856–December 21, 1937) was the U.S. secretary of state.
2.    José Santos Zelaya (November 1, 1853–May 17, 1919) was the president of Nicaragua from 1893 until a United States–backed coup overthrew him in 1909.
3.    Adolfo Díaz (1875–1964) was president of Nicaragua after Zelaya's removal.
4.    Emiliano Chamorro (1871–1966) was a conservative politician who as Nicaragua's minister to the United States negotiated the Bryan-Chamorro Treaty in 1914 that granted the United States the rights to construct a canal across the country.
5.    Juan Bautista Sacasa (1874–1946) was a liberal politician and subsequent president of Nicaragua (1933–1936) after the withdrawal of the United States Marines in 1932.

# 4—Martial Law in Haiti

The methods of the United States in colonized Latin America have not changed. They cannot change. Violence is not used in countries under Yankee administration just by accident. Three events during the past five years underscore the increasing martial tendency of U.S. policy in these countries: the intervention in Panama against a strike, the occupation of Nicaragua, and the recent declaration of martial law in Haiti. The rhetoric of goodwill is meaningless in the face of these events.

As in other countries, the military occupation of Haiti includes a group of Haitians who claim legal representation of the majority as vested by the imperialist forces. The enemies of freedom in Haiti, the betrayers of their independence, are without a doubt the most repugnant to a free Latin American sentiment. Hispanic America has long experience with these types of things. One begins to understand that what will save it is not the admonitions of U.S. imperialism, but a thorough and systematic work of defense, conducted with firmness and dignity, by those who will have by their side the new [progressive] forces of the United States.

—*Variedades*, Lima, 13 December 1929

NOTE

Source: "La ley marcial en Haití," in *Temas de nuestra América*, in *Obras Completas*, 9th ed. (Lima: Biblioteca Amauta, 1986), 12:161–62.

# 5—Ibero-Americanism
and Pan-Americanism

## I.

Ibero-Americanism sporadically reappears in debates over Spain and Spanish America. It is an ideal or a theme that from time to time engages dialogue among intellectuals of the language (I do not think we can call them, in fact, intellectuals of the race).

But now the discussion is broader and with more intensity. Ibero-American topics have gained a conspicuous interest in the Madrid press. The approach or coordination of the Ibero-American intellectual forces, managed and advocated by some groups of writers in our America, today gives those topics a new and concrete value.

This time the discussion repudiates Ibero-American protocol in some cases and ignores it in others (Don Alfonso's official Ibero-Americanism is embodied in the Bourbon and decorative stupidity of an infant, in the courtesan mediocrity of Francos Rodríguez[1]). In the dialogue of free intellectuals, Ibero-Americanism is being stripped of all diplomatic ornament. It thus reveals its reality as an ideal of the majority of representatives of intelligence and culture of Spain and Indo-Iberian America.

Pan-Americanism, as such, does not enjoy the support of intellectuals. This abstract and unnatural category does not have any valued and sensitive supporters. It has only a few latent sympathizers. Its existence is purely diplomatic. The most obtuse minds can easily see in Pan-Americanism a robe covering U.S. imperialism. Pan-Americanism does not manifest itself as an ideal of the continent; rather, it is expressed clearly as a natural ideal of the Yankee empire (rather than a great democracy, as the apologists in these latitudes would like to classify it, the United States is a great empire). But despite all this, or rather precisely because of all this, Pan-Americanism exercises a strong influence on Indo-Iberian America. U.S. policy is not too concerned with having the ideals of the continent pass as the ideals of the empire. Nor is it bothered by the lack of an intellectual consensus. Pan-Americanism embroiders its propaganda on a solid mesh of interests. U.S. capital invades Indo-Iberian America. Pan-American trade routes are the avenues of this expansion. The currency, technology, machines, and U.S. goods are more prevalent each day in the economy of central and southern nations. It may well be, therefore, that the northern empire looks happily on a theoretical independence of the intellect and spirit of the Indo-Spanish American. Economic and political interests will gradually ensure the adhesion, or at least the submission, of most intellectuals. Meanwhile, the professors and staff of Mr. Rowe's Pan-American Union are sufficient to mobilize Pan-Americanism.

## II.

Nothing is more useless than to entertain oneself with platonic confrontations between the Ibero-American and Pan-American ideal. The number and quality of intellectual adherents little serve Ibero-Americanism. Even less does it serve the eloquence of their writers. While Ibero-Americanism rests on sentiments and traditions, Pan-Americanism is based on commercial interests. The Ibero-American bourgeoisie has much more to learn in the school of the new Yankee empire than in the school of the old Spanish nation. The Yankee model, the Yankee style, spreads through Indo-Iberia America, while the Spanish heritage is consumed and lost. The landowner, the banker, the rentier of Spanish America look much more attentively to New York than to Madrid. The exchange rate of the dollar interests them a thousand times more than the thought of Unamuno or Ortega y Gasset's *Review of the West*. For these people who govern the economy and hence the politics of Central and South America, the Ibero-American ideal has little importance. In the best of cases they are ready to join it with Pan-Americanist ideals. Travel agents for Pan-Americanism seem, on the other hand, more efficient, though less picturesque, than the travel agents—those academic choristers—of official Ibero-Americanism, which is the only thing that a prudent bourgeois can take seriously.

## III.

The new generation of Hispanic-Americans should clearly and precisely define the meaning of its opposition to the United States. They should declare themselves the enemy of the empire of Dawes and Morgan, not the people or individuals of the United States. The history of North American culture offers us many noble examples of intellectual and spiritual independence. Roosevelt is the trustee of the spirit of the empire, but Thoreau is the trustee of the spirit of humanity. Henry Thoreau, who now receives the homage of European revolutionaries, is also worthy of the devotion of the revolutionaries of our America. Is it the fault of the United States if Ibero-Americans know the thought of Theodore Roosevelt better than that of Henry Thoreau? The United States is indeed the home of Pierpont Morgan and Henry Ford, but it is also the home of Ralph Waldo Emerson, William James, and Walt Whitman. The nation that has produced the greatest masters of industrialism has also produced the best masters of continental idealism. And today the same concerns that move the Spanish American vanguard also move the North American vanguard. The problems of the new Hispanic-American generation are, with variations of place and nuance, the same problems of the new North American generation. Waldo Frank, one of the new men of the north, in his studies of our America, says things that are valid for the people of his America as well as our own.

The new men of the Indo-Iberian America can and should come to an understanding of the new men of Waldo Frank's America. The work of the new Ibero-American generation can and should be articulated in solidarity with the work of the new Yankee generation. Both generations overlap. They have different languages and races, but they communicate and bring together the same historic emotions. Waldo Frank's America is also, as in our America, an adversary of the empire of Pierpont Morgan and of petroleum.

In contrast, the same historic emotion that brings us closer to this revolutionary America separates us from the reactionary Spain of the Bourbons and Primo de Rivera. What can the Spain of Vásquez de Mella and Maura, the Spanish of Pradera and Francos Rodríguez, teach us? They teach us nothing, not even the method of a great industrialist and capitalist state. The civilization of power does not have its base in Madrid or Barcelona; it has its base in New York, in London, in Berlin. The Spain of the Catholic monarchs absolutely does not interest us. Let Mr. Pradera, Mr. Francos Rodríguez, have her.

## IV.

Ibero-Americanism needs a bit more of idealism and a bit more of realism. It has yet to be joined with the new ideals of Indo-Iberian America. It has yet to insert itself in the new historical reality of these peoples. Pan-Americanism is based on the interests of the bourgeois order; Ibero-Americanism should rely on the crowds who work to create a new order. Official Ibero-Americanism will always be an academic, bureaucratic, impotent ideal, with no roots in reality. As an ideal of the nuclei of renovators, it will instead become a militant, active, mass ideal.

—*Mundial*, Lima, 8 May 1925

NOTES

Source: "El ibero-americanismo y panamericanismo," in *Temas de nuestra América*, in *Obras Completas*, 9th ed. (Lima: Biblioteca Amauta, 1986), 12:26–30.

1.  Alfonso XIII (1886–1941), from the house of Bourbon, was the king of Spain from 1886 to 1931. José Francos Rodríguez (1862–1931) was a Spanish journalist and politician known for his books on the royal court and monarchy.

# 6—The Destiny of North America

The Dawes Plan unquestionably documents the vanity of all of the arguments between French neo-Thomists and German racists as to whether the defense of Western civilization falls to the Latin and Roman spirit or to the German and Protestant one. The payment of German reparations and the Allied debt has put the fate of Europe's economy and therefore its politics in the hands of the United States. The financial recovery of the European states is not possible without Yankee credit. The spirit of Locarno,[1] security pacts, etc., are simply the names that designate the guarantees required by U.S. capital for its significant investment in the public finance and industry of European states. Fascist Italy, which so arrogantly announced the restoration of Rome's power, forgets that its commitments to the United States placed its currency at the mercy of this creditor.

Capitalism, which in Europe displays a lack of faith in its own forces, remains endlessly optimistic about its fate in North America. And this optimism is based simply on good health. It is like the biological optimism of youth, which, noting its excellent appetite, is not worried that later arteriosclerosis will appear. North American capitalism still has growth prospects that the destruction of war irreparably harmed in Europe. The British Empire still has a formidable financial organization, but, as demonstrated by the problem of coal mines, its industry has lost skills that had ensured its primacy. The war has converted it from a creditor to a debtor of the U.S.

All these facts indicate that the seat, the axis, the center of capitalist society is now found in North America. Yankee industry is best equipped for mass production at a lower cost. The banking industry, to whose coffers flows the gold seized by the United States in wartime and postwar business, through its capital guarantees the continuous growth of industry output and the conquest of markets that must absorb their manufactured products. The illusion, if not the reality, of free competition still exists. The state, education, and laws conform to the principles of an individualistic democracy within which every citizen may freely aspire to the possession of one hundred million dollars. While in Europe working-class and middle-class individuals are feeling increasingly trapped by boundaries of class, people in the United States believe that wealth and power are still accessible to anyone who has the ambition to acquire them. And this is the measure of the existence of the psychological factors that determine their development in a capitalist society.

The North American phenomenon, moreover, is not arbitrary. North America showed from its beginning that it was predestined for the highest achievement of capitalism. Despite its extraordinary power in England, capitalist development has failed to remove all feudal remnants. Aristocratic privileges have continued to weigh on its politics and economy. The English bourgeoisie, happy to concentrate its energies on commerce and industry, did not bother to challenge the aristocracy for land. The domination of the land should be based on the exploitation of the subsoil. But the British bourgeoisie did not want to sacrifice their landlords who were destined to maintain an exquisitely refined and decorative lineage. That is why the bourgeoisie only now is discovering an agrarian problem. Only now, with industry in decline, does it miss a productive and prosperous agriculture system on land where the aristocracy have their hunting preserves. North American capitalism, meanwhile, did not have to pay any monetary or spiritual feudal dues. On the contrary, it freely and vigorously emerged from the first intellectual and moral seeds of the capitalist revolution. The New England colonizer was a Puritan expelled from Europe for a religious rebellion that was the first act of bourgeois assertion. The United States thus emerged as a manifestation of the Protestant Reformation, which was considered the purest and most original spiritual manifestation of the bourgeoisie, that is, of capitalism. The foundation of the U.S. republic signified, for its time, the definitive consecration of this fact and its consequences. "The first permanent colonies on the eastern seaboard," writes Waldo Frank, "were grounded upon conscious purposes of wealth. Their revolution against England in 1775 was one of the first clear-cut struggles between bourgeois capitalism and the old feudality. The triumph of the colonies, which gave birth to the United States, marked the triumph of the capitalistic state. And from that day to this, America has had no tradition, no articulation outside of the industrial revolution which threw it into being."[2] And this same Frank recalls Charles A. Beard's famous and concise judgment on the 1789 Constitution: "The Constitution was essentially an economic document, based upon the concept that the fundamental private rights of property are anterior to government and morally beyond the reach of popular majorities."[3]

No material or moral obstacle has hampered the energetic and free flourishing of North American capital. Unique in the world, all of the historical factors for a perfect bourgeois state, without the impediments of monarchical and aristocratic traditions, were present at its birth. On the virgin soil of America, with all Indigenous traces erased, Anglo-Saxon settlers laid the foundation of the capitalist order.

The U.S. Civil War also constituted a necessary capitalist assertion to liberate the Yankee economy from the sole defect of its infancy: slavery. With slavery abolished, the capitalist phenomenon found its path absolutely clear. The Jew, so connected to the development of capitalism, as Werner Sombart observed, not only for the spontaneous utilitarian application of his expansive and imperialist individualism but for the radical exclusion of any "noble" activity from which he was excluded in the Middle Ages, joined the Puritan in the business of building the most powerful industrial state, the strongest bourgeois democracy.

Ramiro de Maeztu has a much more solid ideological position than reactionary neo-Thomist philosophers in France and Italy when he recognized New York as the true antithesis of Moscow, and gives the United States the role of defending and continuing Western civilization as a capitalist civilization. Generally he clearly understands, within the context of his bourgeois apologetics, the moral elements of wealth and power in North America. But he reduces them almost completely to their Puritan or Protestant elements. Puritanical morality, which sanctifies wealth and regards it as a sign of divine favor is, in fact, a Jewish morality whose principles the Puritans assimilated through the Old Testament. The doctrinal relationship of Puritanism to Judaism has long been established, and the Anglo-Saxon experience with capitalism only serves to confirm it. But Maeztu, the fervent eulogist of industrial "Fordism," needs to escape, as much out of deference to Mr. Ford for his injunctions against the "Jewish international," as for his adherence to a grudge against all of the "nationalist" and reactionary movements of the world that suspect the Jewish spirit of a terrible concurrence with the spirit of its common socialist ideal of universalism.

The dilemma of Rome or Moscow, as they shed light on the role of the United States as an employer of the capitalist stabilization of Europe, whether fascist or parliamentary, will become the dilemma of New York or Moscow. The two poles of contemporary history are Russia and North America: capitalism and communism, both universalist although very different and distinct. Russia and the United States: the two peoples who are most opposed in doctrinal and political terms are, at the same time, the two closest peoples, the supreme and ultimate expression, of Western activism and dynamism. Several years ago Bertrand Russell highlighted the strange resemblance between the captains of U.S. industry and officials of the Russian Marxist economy. And that tragic Slav poet Alexander Blok greeted the dawn of the Russian Revolution with the words: "Behold the star of the New America."

—*Variedades*, Lima, 17 December 1927

NOTES

Source: "El destino de Norteamérica," in *Defensa del marxismo: polémica revolucionaria*, in *Obras Completas*, 13th ed. (Lima: Biblioteca Amauta, 1987), 5:145–50.

1.   Pact between France and Germany under the respective governments of Briand and Stresseman.
2.   Waldo Frank, *Our America* (New York: Boni and Liveright, 1919), 14.
3.   Charles A. Beard, *An Economic Interpretation of the Constitution of the United States* (New York: Macmillan, 1921), 324.

# PART V

# Politics, Organization, Peasants, Workers, and Race

. . .

JOSÉ CARLOS MARIÁTEGUI was not only a thinker and writer, he was a Marxist militant and political organizer. He very much believed in the concept of praxis and, as such, was active in the workers' movement in Peru. Indeed, one of the reasons the dictator Leguía exiled him to Europe was because of his strong support for the workers' movement in Lima. He used his Marxist-inspired understanding of the concrete conditions in Peru to enhance his writings but also to guide his political and intellectual activities. Thus he studied the economic condition of the peasants and Indigenous peoples, the intricacies of the labor movement and working conditions, and the influence of race and racial thinking on socialist and revolutionary possibilities in Peru.

In this section Mariátegui explains the place of Peru's proletariat in the world crisis (V.1), the problem of race in Latin America (V.2), the history of an Indigenous uprising (V.3), the struggle of the peasants in Huacho (which is in a region where he had spent part of his childhood) (V.4), and the orientation of the key organizational meetings of the Socialist Party of Peru (a Marxist-Leninist party whose name was later changed to Communist) (V.5). Mariátegui was the theoretician and primary organizer of the party and guided its doctrinal stance, organizational direction, and ideological orientation until shortly before his death in 1930. He was also heavily involved in union organizing, as seen in "May Day and the United Front" (V.6) and "Manifesto of the General Confederation of Peruvian Workers to the Peruvian Working Class" (V.7).

# 1—The World Crisis
## and the Peruvian Proletariat

*The following was one of a series of lectures Mariátegui present-
ed at the González Prada Popular University in Lima in 1923
and 1924 in which he contributed what he had learned during
his European sojourn to the Peruvian proletariat.*

In this conference—we will call it a conversation more than a conference—I will limit myself to explaining the subject matter of the course,
while at the same time provide some considerations about the necessity
of spreading knowledge of the world crisis to the proletariat. Peru, sadly,
is lacking an educational press that follows the development of this great
crisis with intelligence and an ideological affiliation. Similarly lacking
are university professors like José Ingenieros[1] who are capable of
becoming passionate about renovating ideas that are actually transform-
ing the world and liberating it from the influences and prejudices of
bourgeois culture and education. Also lacking are socialist and union
groups, owners of their own instruments of popular culture and consequently an aptitude to interest the people in studying the crisis. The
only course of popular education with a revolutionary spirit is this one,

developed at the Popular University. Our task is to go beyond the modest initial work plan, and introduce people to the current reality, explain to them that they are living in one of the greatest and most transcendental times in history, and infect them with a profound uneasiness that now moves the other civilized peoples of the world.

In this great contemporary crisis, the proletariat is not a spectator but an actor. The fate of the world is in the proletariat's hands. What will come from it, according to all the probabilities, is the proletarian civilization, the socialist civilization, which is destined to succeed the moribund individualist and bourgeois capitalist civilization. Now more than ever, the proletariat needs to know what is going on in the world. And it cannot know this through the fragmentary, episodic, homeopathic information from the daily news—poorly translated and even more poorly edited. It always comes from the reactionary press agencies that are charged with discrediting the revolutionary parties, organizations, and men, discouraging and disorienting the world proletariat.

The fate of all the workers of the world is in play in the European crisis. The development of the crisis ought to be of equal interest to the workers of Peru and the workers of the Far East. The crisis has Europe as the principal theater, but the crisis of the European institutions is the crisis of the institutions of Western civilization. And Peru, like the other countries of the Americas, revolves inside the orbit of this civilization, not only because politically independent countries are being dealt with, but also because they are economically colonized through links to British, United States, and French capitalism, and because both our culture and the types of institution are European. And it is precisely these democratic institutions, this culture that we copied from Europe, that come from a place that is now in a period of definitive, or even total, crisis. Above all, capitalist civilization has internationalized the life of humanity; it has created the material connections among all peoples that establish an inevitable solidarity among them. Internationalism is not only an idea, it is a historical reality. Progress makes interests, ideas, customs, the people's regimes unify and merge. Peru, like the other peoples of the

Americas, is not, then, outside the crisis, it is inside it. The world crisis has already had repercussions on these peoples. And it will, of course, continue to do so. A period of conservative reaction in Europe will also be a period of reaction in the Americas. A period of revolution in Europe also will be a period of revolution in the Americas. More than a century ago, the life of humanity was not as linked as it is today, when today's communication media did not exist, when the nations did not have the immediate, constant contact they have today. When there was no press, when we were still distant spectators of European events, the French Revolution provided the origin for the War of Independence and the creation of all these republics. Remembering this is enough for us to realize the rapidity with which the transformation of society is reflected in Latin American societies. Those who say that Peru, and Latin America in general, so far from the European revolution, have no idea of contemporary life, nor do they have even an approximate understanding of history. These people are surprised that the most advanced ideas in Europe make their way to Peru; but they are not surprised, on the other hand, at the airplane, the transatlantic ocean liner, the wireless telegraph, the radio—in sum, all the most advanced expressions of material progress in Europe. The same kind of thinking that would ignore the socialist movement would have to ignore Einstein's theory of relativity. And I am sure that it does not occur to the most reactionary of our intellectuals—almost all of them are galvanized reactionaries—that there should be a ban on studying and popularizing the new physics of which Einstein is the greatest and most eminent representative.

And the proletariat in general needs to find out about the great dimensions of the world crisis. This need is even greater in that the socialist, laborite, syndicalist, or libertarian part of the proletariat constitutes the vanguard. That part of the proletariat is most combative, conscious, and more prone to struggle and is prepared. That part of the proletariat is charged with the direction of the great proletariat actions. That part of the proletariat whose historic role it is to represent the Peruvian proletariat in the present instance. It is in that part of the proletariat, whatever its particular creed, in a word, that has class conscience, has revolutionary conscience. Above all, I dedicate my dissertations to this vanguard of the Peruvian proletariat. I do not pretend to come to this free tribunal of this free university to teach you the history of this world crisis, but to study it with you. Comrades, I do not teach you the history of the world crisis from this podium: I study it with you. In this study I do not have anything except the very modest merit of bringing three and a half years of personal observations of European life, that is, three and a half years leading up to the crisis and the echoes of contemporary European thought.

For various reasons, I especially invite the vanguard of the proletariat to study this crisis with me. I will enumerate the reasons summarily. The first reason is that the revolutionary preparation, revolutionary culture, revolutionary orientation of this proletarian vanguard has been formed on the basis of prewar socialist, syndicalist, and anarchist literature. Or at least before the culminating period of the crisis. Socialist, syndicalist, libertarian books with old data are generally what circulate among us. Here little of the classical literature of socialism and syndicalism is known and the new revolutionary literature is not known. Revolutionary culture is a classical culture, in addition to being, as you know very well, comrades, very incipient, very inorganic, very unorganized, and very incomplete. And now all this socialist and syndicalist literature is in revision. And this revision is not a revision imposed by theoreticians' caprice but by the force of events. This literature, then, cannot be used today without the benefit of an inventory. Naturally it is not that it is not being exact in its principles, in its bases, in everything external and ideal; rather, it has stopped being exact in its tactical inspirations, in its historical considerations, in everything that signifies action, procedure, means of struggle. The workers' goal continues being the same; what has changed because of the most recent historical events are the roads chosen to arrive, or, if you will, to come close to this meta-ideal. And here the study of this historical happening and its transcendence is indispensible for the militant workers and the classist organizations.

You know, comrades, that the European proletarian forces find themselves divided in two large groups: reformists and revolutionaries.

There is a reformist, collaborationist, evolutionary Workers' International and another maximal, anti-collaborationist, revolutionary Workers' International. Between the two an intermediate International has tried to surface, but it ended up making common cause with the first against the second. In one group or the other there are diverse colorings, but the groups are definitively and uncontrovertibly only two. The group of those who want to achieve socialism by politically collaborating with the bourgeoisie, and the group of those who want to achieve socialism by taking all the political power for the proletariat. Now, the existence of these two groups comes from two different conceptions, two opposed conceptions, two antithetical conceptions of the current historical moment. One part of the proletariat believes that the moment is not revolutionary, that the bourgeoisie has not yet finished with its historic function, and that on the contrary the bourgeoisie is still strong enough to maintain political power—in sum, the hour of the social revolution has not arrived. The other part of the proletariat believes that the current historic moment is revolutionary; that the bourgeoisie is incapable of reconstituting the social wealth destroyed by the war, and thus of solving the problems with the peace, that the war started a crisis whose solution cannot be anything but socialist, and that the Russian Revolution started the social revolution.

There are, then, two proletarian armies, because in the proletariat there are two opposed conceptions about the historical moment, two different interpretations of the world crisis. The numeric force of one proletarian army or the other depends on how what happens seems to confirm its respective historic conception. Because of this, the thinkers, theoreticians, the scholars of one proletarian army or the other force themselves, above all, to deepen the feeling of crisis, to comprehend its character, and to discover its significance.

Before the war, two tendencies divided proletarian predominance: the socialist tendency and the syndicalist tendency. The socialist tendency was predominantly reformist, social democratic, collaborationist. The socialists thought that the hour of social revolution was very far off and they fought for a gradual victory through legal action, with governmental or at least legislative collaboration. In some countries this political action excessively debilitated the will and revolutionary spirit of socialism. Socialism became considerably bourgeois. As a reaction against becoming more bourgeois, we had syndicalism. Syndicalism opposed the political action of the socialist parties with the direct action of the syndicates.[2] The most revolutionary and intransigent spirits of the proletariat took refuge in syndicalism. But, in essence, syndicalism was reformist and collaborationist. Also, a union bureaucracy without real revolutionary psychology dominated syndicalism. And syndicalism and socialism were seen more or less in solidarity and joined in some countries, like Italy, where the Socialist Party did not participate in the government and remained faithful to other formal principles of independence. At any rate, the more or less belligerent, similar tendencies, according to the conditions in the different nations, were two: syndicalists and socialists. The revolutionary literature of this period of struggle is what has almost exclusively informed the mentality of our proletarian leaders.

But, after the war, the situation changed. The proletarian camp is, as just noted, now not divided into socialists and syndicalists but into reformists and revolutionaries. One part of socialism has affirmed its social democratic, collaborationist orientation; the other part has followed an anti-collaborationist, revolutionary orientation, and has adopted the name communism to differentiate itself definitively from the first. The division has been reproduced in the union movement. One part of the unions support the social democrats, the other part support the communists. Consequently, the face of the European social struggle has changed radically. We have seen many intransigent prewar union activists head toward reformism. On the other hand, we have seen others follow communism. And among others, as Comrade Fonkén[3] recently reminded us, none other than the greatest and most illustrious theoretician of syndicalism, the Frenchman Georges Sorel. He gave all his support to the Russian Revolution and the men who made it, and his death has been a bitter loss for the proletariat and intellectuals of France.

Here, as in Europe, then, the proletarians must not divide into unionists and socialists—an anachronistic classification—but into collaborators and those who will not collaborate, into reformers and maximalists. But for this to be done with clarity, with coherence, it is indispensable that the proletariat knows and comprehends the broad outlines of the great contemporary crisis. Confusion is inevitable if it is done any other way.

I am of the opinion that those who believe in humanity are living in a revolutionary period. And I am convinced of the imminent demise of the social democratic theses, of all the reformist theses, of all the evolutionary theses.

Before the war, these theses were understandable, because they corresponded to different historic conditions. Capitalism was at its apogee. Production was superabundant. Capitalism could afford the luxury of making successive concessions to the proletariat. And its margins of utility were such that the formation of a large middle class, a large petite bourgeoisie that enjoyed a convenient and comfortable kind of life, was possible. The European worker got enough to eat and in some nations like England and Germany, he was given sufficient resources to satisfy some spiritual necessities. An environment, then, did not exist for revolution. After the war, Europe's social wealth was in large part destroyed. Capitalism, which was responsible for the war, needs to reconstruct this wealth at the cost of the proletariat. Consequently, this means that the socialists must collaborate with the government to strengthen the democratic institutions, though not to progress on the road to socialist accomplishments. Before, the social-ists collaborated to gradually improve conditions in the workers' lives. Now they collaborate to renounce all proletarian victory. In order to reconstruct Europe, the bourgeoisie needs the proletariat to agree to produce more and consume less. The proletariat resists one thing or the other and tells itself that it is not worth consolidating the power of a social class guilty for the war and inevitably destined to lead human-ity to an even bloodier war. The conditions that allow collaboration between the bourgeoisie and the proletariat are such that, little by lit-tle, collaborationism must lose its typical proselytizing style.

Capitalism must not make concessions to socialism. In order for the European states to rebuild, they need a regime of rigorous fiscal economy, of increasing work hours, and salary reduction: in a word, the reestablishment of economic concepts and methods that run counter to proletarian desires. Logically, the proletariat cannot consent to this rollback. All possibility of rebuilding the capitalist economy is, then, eliminated. This is the tragedy of today's Europe. In the European countries, reactionary elements cancel the economic concessions made to socialism. But, on one hand, this reactionary policy cannot be sufficiently energetic or efficient to reestablish the depleted public wealth, and on the other, a proletarian united front is being prepared. Fearful of revolution, reactionary forces thus cancel not only the economic achievements of the masses but they also attempt to defeat their political victories. This is how we arrive at a fascist dictatorship in Italy. But it is the bourgeoisie that betrays, undermines, and mortally wounds democratic institutions. And it loosens all its moral force and all its ideological prestige.

Elsewhere, in the realm of international relations, reactionary forces put foreign policy in the hands of nationalist and anti-democratic minorities. And these nationalist minorities saturate foreign policy with chauvinism. And, through their imperialist outlooks and struggles for European hegemony, they impede the reestablishment of an atmosphere of European solidarity that stimulates the states to come to an understanding about a program of cooperation and work. We see the fruit of this nationalism, this reaction, in the occupation of the Ruhr.

The world crisis is, then, an economic crisis and a political crisis. And above all, it is an ideological crisis. The affirmative, positivist philosophies of bourgeois society have been for some time undermined by a current of skepticism, of relativism. Rationalism, historicism, and positivism are declining irremediably. Indubitably, this is the most profound, most severe symptom of the crisis. This is the most definitive and profound indicator that it is just not the economy of bourgeois society that is in crisis but the whole of capitalist civilization, Western civilization, and European civilization in crisis.

Nevertheless, this is all well and good. The ideologues of the socialist revolution, Marx and Bakunin, Engels and Kropotk, in lived in the epoch of the apogee of capitalist civilization and of positivist historicist philosophy. Consequently they could not foresee that the rise of the proletariat would have to be produced by virtue of the decadence of Western civilization. The proletariat was destined to create a new type of civilization and culture. The economic ruin of the bourgeoisie was at the same time going to be the ruin of bourgeois civilization. And socialism was going to find that it had to govern not in an epoch of plenty, of wealth, of abundance, but in an epoch of poverty, of misery, of scarcity. The reformist socialists, accustomed to the idea that the socialist regime is more a regime of distribution than a regime of production, believe they see in this the symptom that the historic mission of the bourgeoisie is not yet finished and the time is not yet ripe to achieve socialism. In an article in *La Crónica,* I reported a phrase noting that the tragedy of Europe is this: capitalism cannot anymore and socialism cannot yet. This phrase, which effectively gives the feeling of the European tragedy in a reformist phrase, is saturated with an evolutionary mentality and impregnated with the idea of a slow, gradual and beatific pace, without convulsions, without shock, that moves from the individualist society to the collectivist society. And between the emergence of one and the collapse of the other, there has been, logically, a period of intermediate crisis.

We need the disaggregation, the agony of a society that is inadequate, senile, decrepit, but at the same time we need the gestation, the formation, the slow, anxious elaboration of a new society. All the men who have a sincere ideological affiliation that ties us to this new society and separates us from the old society should fix our gaze deeply on this transcendental, agitated, and intense period in human history.

NOTES

Source: *Historia de la Crisis Mundial,* in *Obras Completas,* 3rd ed. (Lima: Editorial Amauta, 1971), 8:15–25.

1.    José Ingeneiros was a noted Argentine socialist thinker, writer, intellectual, and university professor.

2.  *Syndicate* as used here means a radical syndical organization of workers in the anarcho-syndicalist tradition.

3.  Adalberto Fonkén was a descendant of Asian immigrant workers and an anarcho-syndicalist labor leader.

# 2—The Problem of Race
# in Latin America

*Mariátegui wrote the following document for discussion at the First Latin American Communist Conference in Buenos Aires in June 1929. Health reasons prevented Mariátegui from traveling to Argentina for the meeting, and he asked Dr. Hugo Pesce to attend as his personal representative and to speak in the name of the Peruvian socialist group. Upon presenting the document, Pesce opened the discussion with the following words:*

*Comrades: This is the first time an International Congress of the Communist Party has turned its attention in such a broad and specific fashion to the racial problem in Latin America. The task of our congress, to which this point refers, is to study objectively the facts and focus using Marxist methods, the problems that it entails, to order to achieve its revolutionary solution through a clear and efficient tactic, established in this particular case in accordance with the general line of the Communist International.*

*The elements that allow us to know the reality in all aspects of the racial issue are mainly of a historical and statistical nature.*

*Both have been inadequately studied and intentionally adulterated by the bourgeois criticism of all periods and the criminal disregard of capitalist governments.*

*Only in recent years have we witnessed the appearance of diligent and impartial studies to reveal the true nature of the elements that constitute among us the racial problem. Recently serious works of Marxist criticism have begun to appear that provide a thorough study of the reality of these countries, analyzing its economic, political, historical, and ethnic process, disregarding scholastic and academic molds and posing problems in relation to the fundamental fact, the class struggle. But this work has been started recently and it relates only to certain countries. For the majority of Latin American countries, fellow delegates of the respective parties have found insufficient or falsified material. This explains how the reports to this conference have necessarily shown a weak and, in some cases, a confusing character in terms of the orientation with respect to the problem of the races.*

*This report, intended to provide guidance and material for discussion in the congress, has been developed using inputs from colleagues of all of the delegations. I think, therefore, that it will reflect, to varying degrees, the identified procurement and gaps in proportion to their degree of organization in each Latin American country.*

## Considering the Issue

In bourgeois intellectual speculation, the problem of race in Latin America serves, among other things, to hide or ignore the true problems of the continent. Marxist criticism has a vital duty to establish this problem in real terms, ridding it of any sophistic or pedantic misrepresentation. Economically, socially, and politically, the problem of race, as with that of land, is fundamentally one of the liquidation of feudalism.

Because of the servitude imposed on them since the Spanish conquest, the Indigenous races in Latin America are in a resounding state of backwardness and ignorance. The interests of the exploiting class, first the Spanish and later the *creole*, has invariably tended, under various guises, to explain the condition of Indigenous races on the basis of their inferiority or primitivism. By employing this, that class has not done anything but reproduce the reasoning of the white race on the issue of the treatment and care of the colonial peoples in the national debate on this issue.

The sociologist Vilfredo Pareto, who reduces race to just one of several factors that determine the shape of the development of a society, has condemned the hypocrisy of the idea of race in the imperialist and enslaving policies of white peoples in the following terms:

Aristotle's theory of natural slavery, *Politics*, 1, 2, 3–23 (Rackham, pp. 15–31), is the theory put forward by modern civilized peoples to justify their conquests of peoples whom they call "inferior" and their domination over them. Aristotle said that some men are naturally slaves and others masters, and that it is proper for the former to obey and the others to command, which is just and of benefit to all concerned. So say the modern peoples who decorate themselves with the title "civilized." They assert that there are people—themselves, of course—who were intended by nature to rule, and other peoples— those whom they wish to exploit—who were no less intended by nature to obey, and that it is just, proper, and to the advantage of everyone concerned that they do the ruling and the others the obeying. Whence it follows that if an Englishman, a German, a Frenchman, a Belgian, an Italian, fights and dies for his country, he is a hero; but if an African dares defend his homeland against any one of those nations, he is a contemptible rebel and traitor. So the Europeans are performing a sacrosanct duty in exterminating Africans in an effort to teach them to be civilized. And there are always plenty of people to admire such work "of peace, progress, and civilization," with mouths agape! With a truly admirable hypocrisy, these blessed civilized people claim to be acting for the good of their subject races in oppressing and exterminating them; indeed so dearly do they love them that they would have them "free" by force. So the English freed the Hindus from the "tyranny" of the rajahs. So the Germans freed the Africans from the tyranny of their Black kings. So the Italians freed the Arabs from the oppression of the Turks. So the French freed the Madagascans and—to make them freer still—killed not a few of them and reduced the rest to a condition that is slavery in all but the name. Such talk is uttered in all seriousness, and there are even people who believe it. The cat catches the mouse and eats it; but it does not pretend to be doing it for the good of the mouse. It does not proclaim any dogma that all animals are equal, nor lift its eyes hypocritically to heaven in worship of the Father of us all.[1]

The exploitation of Indigenous peoples in Latin America is also justified on the pretext of serving the cultural and moral redemption of the oppressed races.

Meanwhile, as is easy to prove, the colonization of Latin America by the white race has only had a retarding and depressive effect on the lives of Indigenous races. The natural evolution of these people has been halted by the debasing oppression of whites and *mestizos*. Peoples such as the Quechuas and the Aztecs, who had reached an advanced degree of social organization, retrogressed under colonial rule to the status of scattered agricultural tribes. The elements of civilization that remain in the Indigenous communities of Peru are, above all, what survives of the ancient autochthonous organization. With a feudal agricultural system, the white civilization has not created pockets of urban life, much less industrialization and mechanization. In highland estates, with the exception of certain cattle ranches, white domination does not represent, even technologically, progress in respect to the aboriginal culture.

What we call the Indigenous problem is the feudal exploitation of the native peoples in the large agrarian landholding system. The Indian, in 90 percent of the cases, is not a proletarian but a serf. Capitalism, as an economic and political system, is unable in Latin America to build an economy free of feudal burdens. The perception of the inferiority of the Indigenous race allows the maximum exploitation of the workers of this race. Those who benefit from it are unwilling to give up this advantage. In agriculture, the establishment of wages and the adoption of machines do not erase the feudal character of the large landholdings. They simply perfect the system of exploitation of land and the peasant masses. A good part of our bourgeois and *gamonales* warmly support the idea of the inferiority of the Indian. The Indigenous problem is, in this view, an ethnic problem whose solution depends on crossing the Indigenous race with superior foreign races. The persistence of a feudally based economy stands in irreconcilable conflict, however, with an immigration movement sufficient to produce such a transformation through interbreeding. The wages paid on the coastal and highland haciendas (when the wage system is adopted in the latter) eliminate the possibility of employing European immigrants in agriculture. Immigrant farmers would never agree to work in the conditions the Indians face; they would only be attracted to this work by making them small landowners. The black slave or Chinese coolie has replaced the Indian on the coastal agricultural farms. Colonization schemes for European immigrants are, for now, only being considered for the eastern-forested region known as the *montaña*. The thesis that the Indigenous problem is an ethnic problem does not even deserve to be discussed. But it is worthwhile to note the extent to which the proposed solution is at odds with the interests and capabilities of the bourgeoisie and *gamonalismo*, among whom one finds its adherents.

For Yankee or English imperialism, the economic value of these lands would be much less if in addition to its natural resources it did not possess a backward and miserable Indigenous population that, with the assistance of the national bourgeoisie, it is possible to exploit to the extreme. The history of the Peruvian sugar industry, now in crisis, shows that their profits have rested, above all, on the cheapness of labor, that is, the misery of the laborers. Technically, this industry has not been at any time in a position to compete with other countries in the world market. The industry's distance from the consumer market burned its exports with high freight costs. But all these disadvantages were largely offset by the cheapness of labor. The work of enslaved peasant masses, housed in disgusting shanties, deprived of all freedoms and rights, subject to a backbreaking workday, placed Peruvian sugar planters in a position to compete with those in other countries who better cultivated their lands or were protected by a protective tariff or were better situated from a geographical point of view. Foreign capital uses the feudal class to exploit these peasant masses to its advantage. But sometimes the inability of these landowners (with their inherited prejudice, arrogance, and medieval arbitrariness) to fill the role as head of a capitalist enterprise is such that industry is obliged to take the administration of large landholdings and sugar mills into its own hands. This occurs particularly in the sugar industry, which an English and German company has almost entirely monopolized in the Chicama Valley.

Race has, above all, great importance in regard to the issue of imperialism. But it also has another role that prevents the struggle for national independence in Latin American countries that have a high percentage of Indigenous population from being seen as parallel to the same problem in Asia or Africa. Feudal and bourgeois elements in our countries have the same contempt for the Indians, as well as for blacks and mulattos, as do the white imperialists. The ruling class's racist sentiment acts in a manner totally favorable to imperialist penetration. The native lord or bourgeois has nothing in common with their pawns of color. Class solidarity is added to racial solidarity or prejudice to make the national bourgeoisie docile instruments of Yankee or British imperialism. And that feeling extends to much of the middle class, who imitate the aristocracy and the bourgeoisie in their disdain for the plebeian of color, even when it is quite obvious that they come from a mixed background.

The black race, imported into Latin America by the colonizers to increase their power over the Indigenous American race, passively filled their colonialist role. Spanish conquistadors reinforced the oppression of the Indigenous race through harsh exploitation. A greater degree of mixture, of familiarity, and of living with blacks in the colonial cities converted their role into an auxiliary to white dominance, notwithstanding any outburst of their turbulence or restless spirit. Blacks or mulattos, in their role as artisans or domestic servants, composed a plebeian class that was always more or less uncondition-ally disposed to the feudal class. Industry, factories, and unions redeem blacks from this domesticity. Erasing racial boundaries between proletarians has historically raised the moral level of blacks. Unions signify the definitive break with the servile habits that other-wise would keep blacks at the level of artisan or servant.

Indians are in no way inferior to the *mestizo* in their ability to assimilate with progress, with modern production techniques. On the contrary, they are generally more able to do so. The idea of racial infe-riority is too discredited at this time to honor it with a refutation. White and *creole* prejudice toward the perceived inferiority of the Indian is not based on any facts worth taking into account in a scien-tific study of the question. The coca addiction and alcoholism of the Indigenous race, quite exaggerated by commentators, are nothing more than the consequences, the results of white oppression. *Gamonalismo* promotes and exploits these vices, which in a way are fed by the need to fight against the pain that is particularly alive and active among a subjugated people. The Indian in ancient times only drank "chicha," a fermented corn drink, whereas it was whites who introduced the cultivation of sugarcane and alcoholic drinks on the continent. The production of alcohol from sugarcane is one of the more "healthy" and secure businesses of large landholders, in whose hands also lies the production of coca in the warm mountain valleys.

Some time ago the Japanese showed the ease with which peoples of races and traditions distinct from that of Europe took to Western science and adapted to the use of its productive techniques. In the mines and factories of the Peruvian highlands, the Indian peasant con-firms this experience.

And Marxist sociology has already summarily dismissed racist ideas that are products of the imperialist spirit. Bukharin writes in *Historical Materialism*:

In the first place, the race theory is in contradiction with the facts. The "lowest" race, that which is said to be incapable, by nature, of any development, is the black race, the Negroes. Yet it has been shown that the ancient representatives of this black race, the so-called Kushites, created a very high civilization in India (before the days of the Hindus) and Egypt; the yellow race, which now also enjoys but slight favor, also created a high civilization in China, far superior in its day to the then existing civilizations of white men; the white men were then children as compared with the yellow men. We now know how much the ancient Greeks borrowed from the Assyro-Babylonians and the Egyptians. These few facts are sufficient to show that the "racial" explanation is no explanation at all. It may be replied: perhaps you were right, but will you go so far as to say that the average Negro stands at the same level, in his abilities, as the average European? There is no sense in answering such a question with benevolent subterfuges, as certain liberal professors sometimes do, to the effect that all men are of course equal, that according to Kant, the human personality is in itself a final consideration, or that Christ taught that there are no Hellenes, or Jews, etc. (See for example, Khvostov, *Theory of the Historical Process*, p. 247: "It is extremely probable that ... the truth is on the side of the advocates of race equality.") To aspire to equality between races is one thing; to admit the similarity of their qualities is another. We aspire to that which does not exist; otherwise we are attempting to force doors that are already open. We are now not concerned with the question: What must be our aim? We are considering the question of whether there is a difference between the level, cultural and otherwise, of white men and black men, on the whole. There is such a difference; the "white" men are at present on a higher level, but this only goes to show that at present these so-called races have changed places.

This is a complete refutation of the theory of race. At bottom, this theory always reduces itself to the peculiarities of races, to their immemorial "character." If such were the case, this "character" would have expressed itself in the same way in all the periods of history. The obvious inference is that the "nature" of the races is constantly changing with the conditions of their existence. But these conditions are determined by nothing more nor less than the relation between society and nature, i.e., the condition of the productive forces. In other words, the theory of race does not in the slightest manner explain the condition of social evolution. Here also it is evident that the analysis must begin with the movement of the productive forces.[2]

From the prejudice of the inferiority of the Indigenous race, one begins to pass to the opposite extreme: that the creation of a new American culture will be essentially the work of autochthonous racial forces. To subscribe to this thesis is to fall into the most naïve and absurd mysticism. It would be foolish and dangerous to oppose the racism of those who despise Indians because they believe in the absolute superiority of the white race with a racism that overestimates Indians with a messianic faith in their mission as a race in the American renaissance.

The chance that Indians will raise themselves materially and intellectually depends on changes in socioeconomic conditions. They are not determined by race, but by economics and politics. Race alone has not awakened, nor will it awake, an understanding of an emancipatory ideal. Above all, it will never gain the power to impose and carry it out. What ensures emancipation on this issue is the dynamism of an economy and culture that carries the seeds of socialism in its midst. The Indian race was not defeated in the conquest wars by an ethnically or qualitatively superior race; it was defeated by technology that was superior to that of the aboriginal peoples. Gunpowder, iron, and cavalry were not racial advantages; they were technical advantages. The Spanish arrived in remote areas because they possessed means of navigation that allowed them to cross oceans. Shipping and trade later allowed them to exploit the natural resources of their colonies. Spanish feudalism superimposed itself over Indigenous agrarianism, although it did in part respect its community structures. But this very adaptation creates a static order, an economic system whose factors of stagnation were the best guarantee of Indigenous servitude. Capitalist industry breaks this equilibrium, breaks this stagnation by creating new forces and new relations of production. The proletariat will gradually grow at the expense of artisanship and servitude. The nation's

economic and social evolution enters into an era of activity and contradictions that, on an ideological level, causes the emergence and
development of socialist thought.

In all this, the influence of the racial factor is obviously insignificant in comparison to the influence of economic factors, including
production, technology, science, etc. Would it be possible to outline
the plan or the intentions of a socialist state based on the demands
for the emancipation of the Indigenous masses without the material
elements that create modern industry or, if you like, capitalism? The
dynamism of this economy, of this regime, which makes all these
relationships unstable and sets classes and ideologies in opposition,
is undoubtedly what makes possible the Indigenous resurrection.
The play of economic, political, cultural, ideological forces, not
racial ones, is what decides this reality. The greatest accusation
against the ruling class of the republic is its failure to accelerate, with
a more liberal, more bourgeois, more capitalist sense of its mission,
the process of economic transformation from a colonial to a capitalist economy. Feudalism opposed emancipation, the awakening of
Indigenous peoples from their stagnation and inertia. Capitalism,
with its conflicts and its own instruments of exploitation, advances
the thinking of the masses as they formulate their demands, forcing
a struggle in which they are materially and mentally trained to pre-
side over a new order.

The problem of race is not common to all the countries of Latin
America, nor is it always present to the same degree and with the same
characteristics. Race does not have the same level of influence in the
social and economic process in all Latin American countries. But in
countries like Peru and Bolivia, and somewhat less in Ecuador, where
most of the population is Indigenous, the demands made by the
Indian are the dominant popular and social demands.

In these countries, the race factor is compounded by the class factor, which revolutionary politics must take into account. Quechua or
Aymara Indians view the *mestizo*, the white, as their oppressor. And
among the *mestizos*, only class consciousness is able to destroy the
habitual contempt and repugnance for the Indians. It is not uncom-

mon to find prejudice against the Indian or the resistance to recognizing this prejudice as a mere inheritance or mental environmental contamination among the very urban elements who proclaim themselves to be revolutionary.

The language barrier stands between the Indian peasant masses and the white or *mestizo* nuclei of revolutionary workers. But, through Indian propagandists, the socialist doctrine, because of the nature of the demands that are generated, will readily take root among the Indigenous masses. What has been lacking until now is the systematic preparation of these propagandists. Literate Indians, corrupted by the city, commonly become accessories to the exploiters of their race. But in the city, in the environment of revolutionary workers, Indians have already begun to assimilate the revolutionary idea, to appropriate it, to understand its value as an instrument for the emancipation of their race, which is oppressed by the same class that exploits the worker in the factory, whom the Indigenous workers discover to be a class brother.

The realism of a socialist policy that is safe and accurate in assessing and using the facts on which they have to act in these countries can and should turn the race factor into a revolutionary factor. Current state structures in these countries are based on the alliance of the feudal landowning class and the commercial bourgeoisie. Once this landed feudalistic structure is defeated, urban capitalism will lack the strength to resist the rise of the workers. It is represented by a mediocre and weak bourgeoisie, formed by privilege, without a fighting and organizing spirit that is daily losing its ascendancy over the fluctuating intellectual caste.

Socialist criticism in Peru has begun a new approach to the Indigenous problem with the adamant denunciation and rejection of all bourgeois or philanthropic tendencies to consider race as an administrative, legal, moral, religious or educational problem ("The Indigenous Question" in *Seven Interpretive Essays on Peruvian Reality* by J. C. Mariátegui).[3] The findings on the economic and political terms on which this issue and the proletarian struggle to resolve it are raised in Peru, and by analogy in other Latin American countries with large Indigenous populations, in our opinion are the following:

## 1. The Socioeconomic Situation of the Indigenous Population in Peru

No recent census indicates the exact current size of the Indigenous population. It is generally accepted that the Indigenous race make up four-fifths of the total population, estimated at a minimum of 5,000,000 people. This assessment does not take into account strictly race, but rather the socioeconomic condition of the masses who constitute this four-fifths. There are provinces where the Indigenous typology shows an extensive intermixing. But in these sectors, the white blood has been completely assimilated into the Indigenous environment and the lives of the *cholos* produced by this fusion do not differ from the life of the Indians themselves.

Not less than 90 percent of this Indigenous population works in agriculture. The development of the mining industry has resulted in an increasing use of Indigenous labor in mining. But some of the mineworkers are still farmers. They are "community" Indians who spend most of the year in the mines, but return to their small plots that are insufficient for subsistence.

A regime of semifeudal or feudal labor remains in agriculture today. In highland estates wage labor, when it exists, is so nascent and deformed that it barely alters the features of the feudal regime. Indians usually receive only a minute part of the fruits of their labor. (See the chapter on "The Problem of the Land" in *Seven Interpretive Essays on Peruvian Reality* for the different systems of work employed in the highlands).[4] The soil is worked in a primitive manner on almost all the lands on these large estates. Even though those estates always keep the best lands, in many cases their yields are lower than the community's. In some regions, Indigenous communities have kept part of their land, but it is not enough to meet their needs. As a result, their members are forced to work for large landowners. These estate owners, owners of vast tracts of largely uncultivated land, in many cases have not stripped the communities of their traditional properties because if a community is attached to an estate it can then securely count on its "own" labor supply. The value of an estate is not only calculated on its landholdings, but also on its own Indigenous population. When an estate does not have this population, the owner, in accord with the authorities, resorts to the forced recruitment of poorly paid peons. Indians of both sexes, including the children, are obliged to provide free services to the owners and their families, as well as to the authorities. Men, women, and children take turns in serving the *gamonales* and authorities, not only in the hacienda house, but also in the towns or cities where they reside. The provision of free services has several times been legally banned, but the practice persists to this day, because no law can stand against the mechanics of a feudal order as long as this structure remains intact. Recently the road conscription law has accentuated the feudal structure of the highlands. This law requires all individuals to work six days every six months on the building or maintenance of roads, or the payment of a tax equal to the established wages in each region. In many cases the Indians are forced to work far from their homes, which forces them to sacrifice a greater number of days. Road conscription, which for the Indigenous masses has the character of the old colonial *mitas*, provides authorities with endless opportunities for abuse.

Wage labor prevails in the mines. In the Junín and La Libertad mines, where the two large mining companies Cerro de Pasco Copper Corporation and Northern exploit copper, the workers earn wages of 2.50 to 3.00 *soles*. These salaries are certainly high compared to the unbelievably low wages (twenty or thirty cents) that is usual on highland estates. But the companies take advantage in all forms of the backward condition of the Indigenous peoples. The existing social security legislation is almost nonexistent in the mines, where they do not observe the laws of workers' compensation and the eight-hour days, nor do they recognize the right of workers to organize. Any worker accused of attempting to organize the workers, if only for cultural or mutual purposes, is immediately fired by the company. The companies usually employ "contractors" to work in the galleries who, with a view to conducting business at the lowest possible cost, function as an instrument of exploitation of the manual laborers. The "contractors," however, typically live in austere conditions, overwhelmed by obligations to repay advances that place them in permanent debt to the companies. When a work accident occurs, the companies use their lawyers to dodge their responsibilities, abusing the misery and ignorance of the Indigenous people to deny them their rights, paying them arbitrary and miserable wages. The Morococha disaster, which claimed the lives of several dozen workers, has recently led to the denunciation of the insecurity in which the miners work. The poor state of some of the tunnels and work that almost reached the bottom of a pond, caused a collapse that left many workers buried. The official number of victims is 27, but there are reports the number is higher. The allegations of some newspapers led the company to be more respectful than usual in regard to legal compensation for the bereaved families of the victims. Finally, in order to avoid further unrest, the Cerro de Pasco Copper Corporation granted its employees and workers a 10 percent wage increase as long as the current price of copper continues to hold. The situation of miners in remote provinces such as Cotabambas is much more backward and distressing. The *gamonales* in the region are responsible for the forced recruitment of Indians, and the wages are miserable.

Industry has barely penetrated the highlands. It is represented mainly by the textile factories of Cuzco, which produce excellent-quality wool. The personnel of these factories are Indigenous, except for the managers and bosses. Indians have been perfectly assimilated to mechanization. They are careful and sober operators whom the capitalist skillfully exploits. The feudal atmosphere of agriculture extends to these factories, where a certain patriarchalism exists, using the protégés and wards of the owners as tools for the subjugation of their colleagues and to oppose the formation of class consciousness.

In recent years, the rise of Peruvian wool prices in foreign markets has initiated a process of industrialization on southern agricultural estates. Several landowners have introduced modern technology, importing foreign bulls that have improved the quantity and quality of production, shaking the yoke of commercial intermediaries, and establishing mills and other small industrial plants next to their ranches. Apart from this, in the highlands there are no other industrial plants and crops except those used for the production of sugar, molasses, and liquor for regional consumption.

Highland Indigenous labor is used to a considerable extent for the operation of coastal estates where the population is insufficient. Large sugar and cotton farms use *enganchadores* [labor recruiters] to supply the necessary laborers for their agricultural activities. These laborers earn wages that, though always very little, are much higher than those typically paid in the feudal highlands. But in return they suffer from strenuous work in a warm climate, a diet inadequate for the job, and malaria, which is endemic in coastal valleys. It is hard for highland peons to avoid malaria, which forces them to return to their region, often with an incurable case of tuberculosis as well. Although agriculture on these estates is industrialized (they work the land with modern methods and machines and they process the products in well-equipped sugar mills), the environment is not that of capitalism and wage labor in urban industry. Estate owners retain their feudal spirit and practice it in how they treat their workers. They do not recognize the rights that the labor law stipulates. On these estates, the only law is that of the owner. Not even the slightest trace of a workers' association is tolerated. Supervisors refuse entry to individuals who, for whatever reason, the owner or administrator distrusts. During the colonial period, these estates were worked with African slaves. Once slavery was abolished, they brought Chinese coolies. The traditional landowner has not lost the habits of the slave or feudal lord.

In the forests, agriculture is still nascent. It uses the same *enganche* system as laborers in the highlands, and to some extent used the services of savage tribes familiar with whites. But in terms of a labor regime, the *montaña* has a much grimmer tradition. The most barbarous and criminal slavery procedures were employed in the exploitation of rubber when this product had a high price. The crimes of Putumayo, sensationally denounced in the foreign press, constitute the blackest page in the history of rubber workers. It is alleged abroad that these crimes have been greatly exaggerated and fantasized, and that even an attempt at blackmail lies at the origin of the scandal, but the truth is well documented by investigations and testimony from officials of the Peruvian justice system, such as the judge, Valcárcel, and the prosecutor Paredes, who proved the slaving and bloody methods of the Araos overseers. And not even three years ago, an outstanding official, Dr. Chuquihuanca Ayulo, a great defender of the Indigenous race, an Indigenous person himself, was relieved of his duties as prosecutor in the department of Madre de Dios as a consequence of denouncing the slave-like methods of the most powerful company in that region.

This summary description of the socioeconomic conditions of the Indigenous population in Peru establishes that alongside a small number of wage-earning miners and a still incipient agricultural working class a system of servitude exists. In the distant *montaña* regions, aboriginals are still frequently subjugated to a system of slavery.

### 2. *The Indigenous Struggle against* Gamonalismo

When talking about the attitude of the Indians toward their exploiters, the impression is generally that degraded and oppressed Indians are incapable of any form of struggle or resistance. The long history of Indigenous insurrections and mutinies, and the resulting massacres and repression, is sufficient in itself to dispel this impression. In the majority of cases, the Indian rebellions originated with a violent incident that forced them to revolt against an authority or a landowner. But other cases have not had this character of a local mutiny. The rebellion followed a less incidental agitation, and spread to a more or less extensive region. To repress the uprising, the government had to appeal to substantial forces and true massacres. Thousands of Indian rebels have sown terror among the *gamonales* in one or more provinces. Major Teodomiro Gutiérrez, a highland *mestizo* with a high percentage of Indigenous blood who called himself Rumimaqui and identified himself as the savior of his race, led one of the recent uprisings that assumed extraordinary proportions. The government of Billinghurst had sent Major Gutiérrez to the Puno department, where *gamonalismo* carried out exploitation to an extreme, to conduct an inquiry into Indigenous allegations and report back to the government. Gutiérrez came into intimate contact with the Indians. When the Billinghurst government was overthrown, he believed that any prospect of legal redress had disappeared and thus launched a revolt. Several thousand Indians followed him, but, as always unarmed and defenseless before the troops, were condemned to death or dispersal. Following this uprising came those of La Mar and Huancané in 1923 and other smaller ones, all bloodily suppressed.

In 1921, delegations from various community groups attended an Indigenous congress held under government auspices. The purpose of the congress was to formulate the demands of the Indigenous race. In Quechua, delegates delivered strong accusations against *gamonales*, authorities, and priests. They created a Tawantinsuyu Indigenous Rights Committee. They held annual congresses until 1924, when the government persecuted the revolutionary Indigenous elements, intimidated the delegations, and distorted the spirit and purpose of the assembly. The 1923 congress, which voted for conclusions that were disturbing for *gamonalismo,* such as calling for the separation of church and state and repeal of the law of road service conscription, revealed the danger of conferences in which groups of Indigenous communities from different regions came into contact and coordinated their action. That same year Indians formed the Regional Indigenous Workers Federation with the intent to apply anarcho-syndicalist principles and methods to its organization. It was not destined to be more than an attempt, but it nevertheless represented a revolutionary orientation of the Indigenous vanguard. With two Indian leaders of this movement banished and others intimidated, the Regional Indigenous Workers Federation was soon reduced to just a name. And in 1927 the government dissolved the Tawantinsuyu Indigenous Rights Committee under the pretext that its leaders were mere exploiters of the race they had sought to defend. This committee never had more importance than that attached to its participation in the Indigenous congresses and was composed of elements that lacked ideological and personal valor, and that on many occasions had made protests in adherence to government policy, considering them to be in favor of the Indians. But for some *gamonales* it was still an instrument of agitation, a remnant of the Indigenous congresses. The government, moreover, directed its policies in the direction of associating with statements in favor of the Indians, promises of redistributing land, etc. This was a resolute act against any agitation among the Indians by revolutionary groups or those susceptible to revolutionary influence.

The penetration of socialist ideas and the expression of revolutionary claims among Indigenous peoples have continued despite such vicissitudes. In 1927, a pro-Indigenous action group called Grupo Resurgimiento [Resurgence Group] was founded in Cuzco. It was composed of several intellectuals and artists, along with some Cuzco workers. This group published a manifesto denouncing the crimes of *gamonalismo* (see *Amauta*, no. 6). Soon after its creation, one of its key leaders, Dr. Luis E. Valcárcel, was captured in Arequipa. His imprisonment lasted only a few days, but meanwhile, the Grupo Resurgimiento was definitively dissolved by the Cuzco authorities.

### 3. Conclusions on the Indigenous Problem and the Tasks Involved

The Indigenous problem is identified with the land problem. Ignorance, backwardness and misery of the Indigenous peoples are, we repeat, only the result of their servitude. Feudal estates maintain the exploitation and absolute domination of the Indigenous masses by the landowning class. The Indian struggle against the *gamonales* invariably lies in the defense of their lands against absorption and dispossession. Therefore, Indigenous peoples have an instinctive and deep demand: the demand for land. Giving an organized, systematic, defined character to their demand is the task we have a duty to perform.

The communities that have demonstrated a truly amazing persistence and resistance under the harshest conditions of oppression represent in Peru a natural factor for the socialization of the land. The Indian has an ingrained habit of cooperation. Even when community property passes to individual ownership, cooperation is maintained and the heavy work is shared. This is true not only in the highlands, but also on the coast where a higher level of mixing acts against Indigenous customs. With minimal effort, the community can become a cooperative. Awarding large estate lands to the communities is the solution to the agrarian problem in the highlands. On the coast, where large landholders are also omnipotent but where communal owner-ship has disappeared, the inevitable tendency is to the individualiza-tion of land ownership. The harshly exploited tenants known as *yana-conas* should be supported in their struggles against the landowners. The natural demand of these *yanaconas* is to own the land they work. The struggle is different on large estates that owners exploit directly with peon labor they recruit partly in the highlands among those who lack a link to the land. The demands for which they must work are: freedom of association, abolition of *enganche*, wage increases, the eight-hour day, and enforcement of laws protecting labor. Only when the peons on these estates have won these demands will they be on the path toward final emancipation.

It is very difficult for information from unions to penetrate the estates. Each estate, on the coast as in the highlands, is a fiefdom. No association is tolerated that does not accept the patronage and pro-tection of the owners and management, and only sport or recreation associations are found on estates. But the increase in automobile traffic is slowly opening a gap in the barriers that previously closed the estates to outside influence. This points to the importance of organizing and actively mobilizing transportation workers in the class movement in Peru.

When the peons on the estates know that they have the fraternal solidarity of the unions and understand the value of them, a will to fight that today is missing but that more than once they have proven exists will easily be aroused in them. The nuclei of labor union mem-bers that are gradually formed on the estates will have the function of explaining rights to the masses, to defend their interests, in fact to rep-resent them in any demand and to take advantage of the first opportu-nity to shape their organization to the degree circumstances permit.

For the progressive ideological education of the Indigenous mass-es, the workers' vanguard has at its disposal those militant elements of the Indian race who, in mines or particularly in urban centers, come into contact with trade union and political movements. They assimilate its principles and receive training to play a role in the emancipation of their race. Workers from an Indigenous milieu often return temporarily or permanently to their communities. Their language skills allow them to carry out an effective mission as instructors of their racial and class brothers. Indian farmers will only understand individuals who speak their own language. They will always distrust whites and *mestizos*, and, in turn, it is very difficult for whites and *mestizos* to carry out the hard work of coming to the Indigenous milieu to bring class propaganda.

Methods of self-education, regular reading of the periodicals and pamphlets of the labor and revolutionary movement in Latin America, and correspondence with comrades in urban centers will be the means by which the Indigenous masses will successfully complete their educational mission.

Indigenous members of our movement must always take a principal and leading role in various activities with the dual objective of giving a serious direction to the class orientation and education of Indigenous peoples and avoiding the influence of misleading elements (anarchists, demagogues, reformers, etc.). Activities also include the coordination of Indigenous communities by region, aid for those who suffer persecution from the courts or police (*gamonales* prosecute Indigenous peoples who resist or whose lands they wish to take with common crimes), defense of communal property, the organization of small libraries and study centers.

In Peru, the organization and education of the mining proletariat is, together with that of the agricultural proletariat, one of the most pressing issues. The mining centers, the largest of which (La Oroya) is on track to become the largest processing center in South America, are points where class propaganda can advantageously operate. Apart from representing themselves in substantial proletarian concentrations with conditions similar to wage earners, Indigenous day laborers work alongside urban industrial workers who bring the class spirit and principles to those centers. Indigenous peoples in the mines are still largely peasants, so therefore any adherents won among them are also elements won among the peasant class.

This undertaking, in all of its aspects, will be difficult. But its progress will fundamentally depend on the ability of the activists who carry it out, and their precise and specific assessment of the objective conditions of the Indigenous question. The problem is not racial but rather social and economic. But race has a role in it and the methods of confronting it. For example, only militants who come from the Indigenous milieu can, because of their mentality and language skills, achieve an effective and immediate influence over their companions.

A revolutionary Indigenous consciousness will perhaps take time to form, but once Indians have made the socialist idea their own, they will serve it with a discipline, a tenacity, and strength that few other proletariats from other milieus will be able to surpass.

The reality of grounded and precise revolutionary politics in which the appreciation and utilization of the circumstances on which one must act in countries where the Indigenous or black population has an important size and role can and must convert the racial factor into a revolutionary factor. It is essential to provide the Indigenous or black proletariat movement, whether agricultural or industrial, a clear orientation as a class struggle. "One must give Indigenous or enslaved black populations," said a Brazilian comrade, "the certainty that only a government of workers and peasants of all races who inhabit the territory will truly emancipate them, since only that will terminate the rule of large estate owners and the industrial capitalist system, and definitively liberate them from imperialist oppression."

NOTES

Source: "El problema de las razas en América Latina," in *Ideología y política*, in *Obras Completas*, 19th ed. (Lima: Biblioteca Amauta, 1990), 13:21–86.

1.  Vilfredo Pareto, *The Mind and Society: A Treatise on General Sociology* (New York: Harcourt Brace, 1935), 626–27.

2.  Nikolai Ivanovich Bukharin, *Historical Materialism: A System of Sociology* (New York: International Publishers, 1925), 127–28.

3.  This note by Mariátegui indicates that the above section is taken from chapter 2, "The Problem of the Indian," in the *Seven Essays*.
4.  This note is by Mariátegui and draws attention to chapter 3, "The Problem of the Land," in the *Seven Essays*.

# 3—Preface to *The Amauta Atusparia*

The most significant new feature of contemporary Peruvian historiography is certainly the interest in social history events that previously had been ignored or neglected. Peru's republican history has been almost invariably written as a political history in the narrowest and most *creole* meaning of this term. Its conception and presentation has suffered the limitations of a sense of "court," a spirit of bureaucratic capital that converts political history into a chronicle of changes of government, public administration, and crises and events that most directly and visibly influence one or another of these issues. As always happens, it is due to outside forces that our social history has begun to be written as a scientific discipline. And it is no wonder, then, that the task is not reserved exclusively for professional historians.

Ernesto Reyna, author of this chronicle of the 1885 Indigenous uprising, is not a historian but a narrator, a journalist. *The Amauta Atusparia* is more like a story or news report than a historical essay.[1] I know that Reyna, a hard worker and passionate man, has scrupulously documented his work. The information collected for this booklet reflects a lengthy search for information. But before searching the National Library for newspaper collections, Reyna interviewed survivors of the uprising, survivors of the Indigenous terror and the reactionary terror. He traveled, searching for their dark and disappearing tracks and the road to insurrection until he fell in love with their difficult scene and was able to understand their language. In short, he gained a deep sympathy for his subject. Reyna gives a vital explanation in a few brief lines in the epilogue to the story in which he explains his methodology. He expresses solidarity with the Indians who in 1925 protested against their conscription to work on a road in Huaraz: this republican labor draft placed a new type of exploitation on the backs of the Indigenous population that is no less odious than the previous "personal tax." The weight of a road policy, devoid of economic and technical acumen, led Reyna to place it in a historic and sentimental context. In the same way that these Indians agitated and complained in 1885 against the work of the republic and personal taxes, the violence of church leader provoked a revolt. For Reyna, the church leader Martin Miranda's flogging in 1925 for inciting the Indigenous masses to protest had similarities to the beatings of the protagonists who had been jeered in the 1885 insurrection. "I felt the flogging given to comrade Martin as if I had received them." I find this sentence reflects the wellspring of the deepest human spirit!

We need to identify with Reyna's sentimental theme because of his gifts as a storyteller, and even more because of his tendency to idealize and romanticize the episode and its characters. Life and emotion surround this story. In an era in European literature in which the biographical novel, without any literary or historical concern, thrives, Reyna found a novelized story to be the best way to revive the Atusparia revolt. The jealous sentries who remain outside of erudition and data would complain about the introduction of imaginary elements into the realm of history. But in this case it really adds something to history. Furthermore, this account reads like a novel, not so much for its style as for the novelty of the topic, and its "dramatis personae" that creates mental images of Peruvian history. Atusparia? Ushcu Pedro? How unusual and novelistic they seem from this distance, through the fog that separates us from the events! Colonel Callirgos, Counsel Mosquera, *The Sun of the Incas*, are indispensable as mediators, as points of reference, to ensure the historical drama.

Reyna has written, I repeat, a novelized version of the Atusparia insurgency. Perhaps, at the current stage of the writing of our social history, it was not possible to reconstruct the event differently. Afterward a critical historical study will come that will explain the significance of this revolt to the struggle of the Indigenous population of Peru against their oppressors.

The Indian, so easily accused of cowardice and submission, has not ceased to rebel against the semi-feudal regime that continues to oppress under the republic, the same as it did during the colonial period. Peru's social history records many events similar to those of 1885. The Indigenous race has had many Atusparias, many Ushcu Pedros. Officially only Túpac Amaru is remembered as a precursor to the independence revolution, that was the work of another class and the triumph of other demands. A chronicle of this centuries-long struggle is already being written. The materials are being discovered and organized.

The defeat of Atusparia and Ushcu Pedro is one of many defeats suffered by the Indigenous race. The Indians at Ancash rose up against the whites, protesting against the work demands of the republic, against personal taxes. The uprising had a clear economic and social motivation. And not the least of Reyna's merits is highlighting this at the beginning of his story. But when the revolt aspired to become a revolution, it was left powerless due to lack of rifles, a program, and a doctrine. The imagination of the journalist Montestruque, a romantic *creole* and mimic, sought to remedy this with the utopia of a return: the restoration of the empire of the Incas. The opportunism of the attorney Mosquera, a Cacerist, alcoholic, and cheater, wanted to incorporate the Huaraz uprising into the process of the Caceres revolt.[2] The direction of movement ranged between a tropical fantasy unleashed by Montestruque and the pragmatic prefectural of Mosquera. With an ideologue such as Montestruque, and a *tinterillo* [informal lawyer] such as Mosquera, the 1885 Indigenous insurrection could not have had better luck. The plan for a romantic return to the Inca empire was as anachronistic as the types of weapons used to defeat the republic. The movement's program was as old and helpless as its military park. The Huaraz insurrection, without the agenda of *The Sun of the Incas*, was one of many Indigenous uprisings that overwhelmed a community's resignation and patience. The capture of Huaraz, its spread over a vast territory, would not be enough to distinguish it from other instinctive and desperate uprisings. Ushcu Pedro, a terrifying guerrilla, would be more representative of the movement than Atusparia. The leadership of Atusparia and its historic mission, which Montestruque assigned, placed in motion a series of aristocratic and racist movements that positions it in the context of Independence and the Túpac Amaru movements. *Kurakas* [Indigenous leaders], who were descendants of the ancient Indigenous nobility, led insurrections that failed to trigger a mass movement with a program that extended beyond an ill-timed and impossible attempt to restore a distant past. Survivors of a wounded and defeated class, the heirs of the old Indian aristocracy, could not successfully undertake the business of revolution.

Peasant demands will not succeed against European feudalism as long as they are only expressed as "*jacqueries*."[3] It triumphed with the liberal bourgeois revolution, which transformed them into a program. In our Spanish America, still semifeudal, the bourgeoisie has failed to fulfill its tasks of liquidating feudalism. Struggling beside the descendants of Spanish settlers, it was impossible to take and articulate the demands of the peasant masses. This business touches on socialism. Socialism is the only doctrine that can give a modern, constructive orientation to the Indigenous cause, which, in its true social and economic terrain, and elevated to the level of a creative and realistic policy, accounts for the performance of this undertaking with the will and discipline of a class that today makes its appearance in our history: the proletariat.

## NOTES

Source: "Prefacio a *El Amauta Atusparia*," *Ideología y política*, in *Obras Completas*, 19th ed. (Lima: Biblioteca Amauta, 1990), 5:184–88.

1. Ernesto Reyna, *El amauta Atusparia: la sublevacion indigena de Huaras en 1885* (Lima: Ediciones de Amauta, 1930).

2. Andrés Avelino Cáceres was a Peruvian army commander during the 1879–83 War of the Pacific with Chile who went on to wage a campaign of guerrilla warfare against the Chilean occupation after Peru's defeat. Cáceres also served as Peru's president from 1886 to 1890, and again briefly in 1894.

3. Named after a peasant uprising in France during the Hundred Years War in the 1300s, the *jacqueries* was a peasant revolt that was usually local and often bloody. Eds.

# 4—Huacho Peasants Defend Their Irrigation System: An Institution Deserving Respect

The small owners and tenants of the countryside around Huacho have, since the time of their aboriginal ancestors, retained not only the common ownership of land, but also many habits of mutuality and communal practices that demonstrate just how, even on the coast, the socialist sentiments of the native farmer still remain. The transformation of property and customs has not destroyed reciprocal assistance in the tasks of planting and harvesting. The farmers in each village are noted for their spirit of solidarity. And their survival is not explained, as some might imagine, merely as a conservative impulse. On the contrary, the countryside around Huacho has invariably exhibited trends toward progress and renovation. The area exhibits a spirit and atmosphere favorable to class theory. The first manifestations of a proletarian ideology promptly found propagandists and proselytes among the farmers of Huacho. Their struggles for an 8-hour day and against the increasing cost of basic commodities places the farmers of Huacho at the forefront of our social movement.

But the issue now is not the unique histories of the Huacho peasants, but to publicize and support the demands of the Huacho peasants who have organized to increase the distribution of water in the countryside of Huacho. They maintain water outlets and channels through their irrigation committees. Seven council members and seven constables appointed by the community keep the system running smoothly, and they do this without payment. Weekly community service sessions execute all necessary tasks, without any cost to the community. So far the government has respected this institution that the farmers so jealously defend. On one occasion several years ago the government of Pardo attempted to pass control from the peasant union to the Water Board, as has happened elsewhere. The peasant union, however, protested against the measure, which would have altered this system. The Water Board, therefore, formed a commission in Huacho to study how the farmers' system of communal administration worked, and decided that it worked perfectly. As a result, they formally authorized its continuance.

Lately there have been moves to change the exceptional system that has survived in the Huacho countryside. The farmers have been surprised by the notice that henceforth a "technical expert" will exercise the authority that they themselves currently hold through their union. Furthermore, they must pay a tax of three hundred pounds per dry season. The community has unanimously decided to fight against this decision and defend its own administration at any cost. There is no reason why a system that the farmers established and maintained and continues to function, without any cause for complaint, should be replaced by another, totally unnecessary system that will be in conflict with the ideas and interests of the farmers. Furthermore, such a system will cost them several thousand *soles* annually. The farmers see the hand of large landowners behind this move. Those landowners have never forgiven the peasants of the Huacho countryside for their pride, their independence, their spirit, their agitation, and their class spirit.

The strong union of the Huacho peasantry is a sure guarantee of victory in the struggle for these demands and for a vigilant sense of proletarian solidarity.

NOTES

Source: "Los campesinos de Huacho defienden su sistema de riegos: Una institución que debe ser respetada," *Labor: Quincenario de información e ideas* 1/10 (September 7, 1929): 7.

# 5—The Herradura Beach Meeting

*These notes from Mariátegui and Martínez de la Torre record the essence of two meetings that Mariátegui organized. They laid the basis for the formation of a Socialist Party of Peru that later became the Peruvian Communist Party. The first was held in a beach area near Lima and the second in a small resort town close to Lima.*

To avoid confusion we remember a meeting on the Herradura beach. The comrades for this meeting were chosen with a determined scrupulousness for their solvency, responsibility, and capability of giving a solid direction for the party that they were trying to found.

This meeting took place halfway along the road to the Herradura beach on Sunday, September 16, 1928. There were seven people present: four workers, Julio Portocarrero, Avelino Navarro, Hinojosa, and Borja; an insurance employee, Ricardo Martínez de la Torre; a street vendor, Bernardo Regman. José Carlos Mariátegui was unable to attend, but Martínez de la Torre presented his point of view.

The decisions taken were:

1. Constitute the initial cell of the party, which would be affiliated with the Third International, whose name would be the Socialist Party of Peru, under the direction of consciously Marxist elements.

2. Help the labor opposition cell that Julio Portocarrero had organized to carry out the directives from the Fifth Congress of the Red International of Labor Unions (Profintern).

3. The Executive Committee of the Socialist Party will be formed by the "secret cell of the seven."

4. Convene a new meeting in which others would be included.

### The Barranco Meeting

The second meeting was held on Sunday, October 7, at the home of Avelino Navarro, in Barranco. José Carlos Mariátegui attended, as well as Avelino Navarro, Borlas, Hinojosa, Portocarrero, Martínez de la Torre, Regman, Luciano Castillo, and Chávez León.

The agreements reached were:

1. Form a group to organize the Socialist Party of Peru.

2. Mariátegui was appointed Secretary General; Labor Secretary, Portocarrero; Secretary of Propaganda, Martínez de la Torre; Treasurer, Bernardo Regman. Navarro and Hinojosa were added to the Labor Secretariat.

3. Adoption of the following motion, drafted by Mariátegui:

    The undersigned declare that they have formed a committee to work among the masses of workers and peasants according to the following:

    1. The classist organization of workers and peasants is the object of our effort and our propaganda and at the base of the struggle against imperialism abroad and the national bourgeoisie.

2. To defend the economic interests of workers in the city and countryside, the Committee will actively promote the establishment of labor unions in factories and on haciendas, etc. The unions will form federations at the level of industry, as well as a confederation at a national level.

3. The political struggle requires the creation of a class-based party, whose training and orientation will work hard to advance its revolutionary class views. According to the current conditions in Peru, the Committee will establish a socialist party, based on the organized masses of workers and peasants.

4. To guard against the demoralizing effects of repression and persecution, labor unions and small farmers will apply for recognition by the Section of Labor. In its statutes, its statement of principles will be limited to asserting its class character and its duty to contribute to the establishment and maintenance of a general confederation of labor.

5. The union organization and Socialist Party for which we are striving will contingently accept a tactic of building a united front or alliance with petite bourgeoisie organizations or groups as long as they effectively represent a mass movement with concrete, specific objectives and demands.

6. The Committee shall undertake the organization of committees throughout the republic, and of cells in all workplaces, established with strict discipline.

And so was officially laid the first stone of the proletarian revolutionary movement in Peru. Since that time, there was an active effort to organize cells, both in factories and workshops, as well as in the rest of the country.

This work was done amid the greatest of difficulties. The members had to outwit police repression, enter into the very active work of ideological clarification, fighting not only against the backward politics of the workers but also against anarcho-syndicalist leaders, against intellectuals, and even worse against the confusing work of Haya de la Torre. In addition, the distribution of labor for the completion of these tasks was reduced to only a few people, since Luciano Castillo, Chávez León, and Teodomiro Sánchez first limited their activity to Committee meetings and later left the party without having performed a single act in favor of the working-class cause.

NOTE

Source: "La reunión en la playa de la Herradura; La reunión del Barranco," in *Apuntes para una interpretación marxista de la historia social del Perú*, ed. Ricardo Martínez de la Torre (Lima: Empresa Editora Peruana, 1947), 2:397–98.

# 6—May Day and the United Front

The First of May is a day of revolutionary proletarian unity all over the world, a date that binds all organized workers in an immense international united front. On this day the unanimously obeyed and respected words of Karl Marx resound: "Workers of the world, unite." On this day all the barriers that differentiate and separate the political vanguard into different groups and different schools come down.

May Day does not belong to one International: it is the date for all Internationals. Today, socialists, communists, anarchists of all stripes merge and mix in one army that marches toward the final struggle.

In sum, this date is an affirmation and an answer that the united proletarian front is possible and practicable and that there is no present interest or exigency that would stand in its way.

This international day invites many reflections. But for the Peruvian workers the most pressing, the most timely, is that which concerns the need and the possibility of a united front. Recently there have been some secessionist attempts. And it is important to understand, in order to stop these attempts from prospering, to make sure they do not betray and undermine the nascent proletarian vanguard in Peru.

My attitude, since my incorporation into this vanguard, always has been that of a convinced supporter, that of a fervent advocate for the united front. I remember having declared it in one of my first conferences in my course on the world crisis.

Responding to the first signs of resistance and apprehension from some old and hierarchical anarchists, more worried about dogmatic rigidity than the efficacy and fruitfulness of the action, I said from the speaker's stand at the Popular University: "We are still too few to divide ourselves. We should not worry about labels or titles."

After that I have repeated these or analogous words. And I will not tire of reiterating them. The classist movement, between us, is still incipient, too limited for us to think of fractionizing it and splitting it. Before the perhaps inevitable hour of a division, it is up to us to complete much common work, much shared labor. We have to set off on many long days of work together. It is up to us, for example, to be the cause of class consciousness and class feeling in the majority of the Peruvian proletariat. This task belongs equally to socialists and syndicalists/unionists, to communists and anarchists. We all have the obligation to sow the seeds of renovation and to spread classist ideas. We all have the obligation of distancing the proletariat from the yellow assemblies and the false "representative institutions." We all have to fight against reactionary attacks and repression. We all have to defend the speaker's platform, the press, and proletarian organization. We all have the obligation of sustaining the vindications of the enslaved and oppressed Indigenous race. In accomplishing these historic tasks, these elementary obligations, we can be sure that our way and our paths will merge together, whatever our ultimate goal.

The united front does not annul the personality, does not annul any of those who make it up. It does not signify confusing or amalgamating all of the doctrines into a single doctrine. It is a contingent, concrete, practical action. The program of the united front only considers the immediate reality, outside of any abstraction and of any utopia. Recommending the united front is not, then, recommending any ideological confusion. Inside the united front everyone should keep his own affiliation and his own ideology. Everyone should work for his own credo. But all should feel united by class solidarity, bound together by the struggle against the common adversary, tied by the same revolutionary will, and the same renovating passion. To form a united front is to have an attitude of solidarity before a concrete problem, before an urgent necessity. It is not to renounce the doctrine that each one follows or the position that each one occupies in the vanguard. The variety of tendencies and the diversity of ideological shades are inevitable in this immense human legion that is called the proletariat. The existence of tendencies and precise, defined groups is not something bad; on the contrary, it is the sign of an advanced period in the revolutionary process. What is important is that these groups and tendencies know how to understand each other before the concrete reality of the day. They are not mired in byzantine reciprocal confessions and excommunications. They do not distance themselves from the masses of the revolution by pursuing meaningless complaints. They do not use their weapons or squander their time in wounding one another, but rather to combat the social order, its institutions, its injustices, and its crimes.

We try to feel the historic tie that unites all of us in the vanguard, to all those who reinvigorate the process. The examples that come to us from the outside each day are innumerable and magnificent. The most recent and moving is that of Germaine Berthon. Germaine Berthon, an anarchist, accurately shot her revolver at an organizer and leader of the white terror to avenge the assassination of the socialist Jean Juarès. In this way, the notably elevated and sincere spirits of the revolution perceive and respect, beyond any theoretical barrier, the historical solidarity of their efforts and actions. They belong to the base, horizon-less, wingless/earthbound spirits, to the dogmatic mentalities that want to petrify and immobilize life in a rigid formula of incomprehension and egoistic sectarianism.

Fortunately for us, the proletarian united front is a decision and an evident longing by the proletariat. The masses call for unity. The masses want faith. And because of this their souls reject the corrosive, thin, pessimistic voice of those who deny, of those who doubt, and instead seek the optimistic, cordial, youthful, and fruitful voice of those who affirm and those who believe.

JOSÉ CARLOS MARIÁTEGUI: AN ANTHOLOGY

NOTE

Source: "El Primero de May y el Frente Unico," in *Ideoloía y política,* in *Obras Completas*, 19th ed. (Lima: Editorial Amauta, 1990), 5:107–10.

# 7—Manifesto of the General Confederation of Peruvian Workers to the Peruvian Working Class

The creation of the Central Federation of the Peruvian Proletariat ends a series of working-class attempts to give life to a United Federation of the workers' organizations. In 1913 the Maritime and Terrestrial Federation appeared, headquartered in Callao, with a sub-committee in Lima that after waging different struggles disappeared in 1915. In 1918, on the occasion of the struggle for the eight-hour workday, the "Pro Eight Hours" Committee was created and led the movement to culmination. The next year the Committee "Pro Price Reduction of Basics" was created, coming out of the committee "Regional Peruvian Federation," which convened the First Workers Congress in October 1921. In 1922, this federation was transformed to the "Local Labor Federation of Lima," an organization that, even though the name seemed directed to the laborers of Lima, was concerned with the problems of the workers in the provinces, planning protests for the workers of Huacho and peasants of Ica who showed concern for the massacre in Parcona, just as it did for massacres of Indigenous peoples in Huancané and la Mar. The anarcho-syndicalist inheritance that prevailed in the organization provided efficiency in its activities as they organized serious conflicts for ideological supremacy that culminated in the Local Labor Congress of 1926. This Congress . . . approved a resolution to transform the Local into the "United Peruvian Union." This resolution . . . would have produced a great advance in the union movement but could not be put into practice . . . and ended the Congress and the Local Federation. . . . [Mariátegui follows with descriptions of struggles in Ica, Puno, and Trujillo, and a call to create a Central.] The birth of our Central is not a work of happenstance but of a whole process that the Peruvian Proletariat has followed in its efforts for vindication. The popular assemblies of April 30 and May 1, held in the local of the Lima chauffeurs, approved the following conclusions for the creation of our Central:

1. Fight for the creation of a united labor front without any distinction as to political tendencies in a United Proletariat Central.

2. Fight for the creation and continuation of a Proletarian Press.

3. Fight for the freedom of association, of assembly, of press, of the speaker's platform.

4. Defend and ensure that the laws that refer to the worker are respected, laws that today are so grossly violated by reactionary capitalist forces.

Until now, activists have spoken of an organization but only in a general sense, without workers realizing the kind of class organization that would work to defend their interests. The "General Confederation of Peruvian Workers" encompasses this problem, laying out in general terms the form of organization for which the confederation will struggle incessantly. The overall situation of the country, with incipient industrial development in the cities and feudal latifundism on the coast and in the mountains, has until now impeded the classist development of the proletariat. The artisans have gone to their mutual aid societies, seeing in them the only possible kind of labor association. But today when large concentrations of the proletarian masses are operating in the mines, ports, factories, sugar refineries, plantations, etc., this type of organization, which corresponded to the artisan stage, declines, making way for the union system. What are the advantages of union organization? In the first place, union organization allows grouping together all the workers who work in the same business, industry, without distinction as to race, age, sex, or belief, in order to fight for their economic betterment, for the defense of their class interests.

Second, union organization gets rid of the bureaucratism established by the mutualist system that puts all the management direction in the hands of the president, who in many cases is not a worker. Third, it brings workers to manage their interests by themselves, educating and developing their class spirit, and exiling the intermediary, who almost always turns out to be a political opportunist. And fourth, being an organization of economic defense, a union resolves all the workers' economic problems with the very carefully monitored formation of mutual funds, cooperatives, etc., that are nothing more than sections of the union, as is the worker sports section, culture section, that of solidarity, art, union library, etc. These are the fundamental (though not all the) advantages of union organization....

Union organization is born as a force of the proletariat itself, which has to confront and resolve multiple class problems, among which are the following:

### Problems of the Industrial Proletariat

#### RATIONAL ORGANIZATION

Financial capital does not find any better way of prospering than the incessant exploitation of the working class. The current system of industrial organization shows us how the bourgeoisie organizes its system of exploitation. We find this exploitation in the big companies (we mention among others Fred T. Levy and Company), which to bet-

ter their development wipe the slate clean of all rights that help workers, using the piecework and "contractor" system. These intermediaries get their day's work, which is endangered by "professional" competency, by getting workers who agree to the lowest salary to work for
9 or 10 hours a day. . . . To combat this problem, there is nothing else
to do but organize the exploited masses in solid unions. . . .


### THE CHILD LABOR PROBLEM

Until now the child labor problem has not been raised among us; moreover, many do not give it importance. But if we take a minute to study it,
we see conclusively that it cannot be neglected and that the organization
of youth will give us a more active force for our struggles. We have to
consider the young apprentices who work in the workshops, factories,
etc., and see how they are exploited by the *patron* [boss] from the
moment they arrive. . . . The workday for apprentices is 10 hours in the
best of cases, but there are workshops where they work until 10 or 11 in
the evening, that is to say, they work 14 hours a day. The initial day's pay,
if we dispense with those who work without receiving anything, is 80
cents or a sol, a daily wage that will not vary until the apprentice is official in the eyes of the boss; that is, when a young person becomes official he can replace the operator and compete with him at a pay rate of
50 or 60 percent. . . .

In the mines and businesses we find that youths are exploited
equally or worse than in workshops or orchards. But where the
exploitation of the youth reaches new heights is undoubtedly in the
very homes of the bourgeoisie. There they are found carrying out all
the functions of messenger, dry-nurse, cook, laundress, that is, all the
functions of "servants," working from six in the morning until ten or
eleven at night. . . . Conscious workers, that is, those who are union-
ized, have to confront this problem, since the problems of the youth
are the problems of all those who are exploited. . . .

## THE WOMAN PROBLEM

If the juvenile masses are so cruelly exploited, proletarian women suffer the same or worse exploitation. Until very recently proletarian women had their labor circumscribed to domestic activities in the home. With the advance of industrialization she enters the workplace to compete with workers in the factory, workshop, business, etc., overcoming the prejudice that kept her locked in a conventional life. However, if women advance in democratic-bourgeois terms on their road to emancipation, this act supplies cheap capitalist labor that seriously competes with that of the male worker. Thus we see women in textile and cookie factories, laundries, bottle factories, factories that manufacture containers, cardboard boxes and soap, in which they perform the same functions as male workers, from handling a machine to the most minimal occupation, yet they earn 40 to 60 percent less than the male. . . . We have capitalists . . . who have not been afraid to consider that if a female worker was about to be a mother it was a "crime," and a "crime" that occasions her violent sacking. . . . This accumulation of "calamities" that weighs on exploited women cannot be resolved if it is not done so on the basis of immediately organizing women; in the same way that the unions have to construct their youth groups, they should create women's sections where our future militants will be educated.

## THE AGRICULTURAL PROLETARIAT PROBLEM

The living conditions of the great masses of agricultural workers also require more attention. In empirical treatment, this issue is confused with the peasant problem, which is something that needs to be separated so as not to commit the same errors. Who forms the agrarian proletariat? The great masses of workers who provide their efforts in haciendas, orchards, small farms, plantations, etc., the authority of the *patron* exercised by an army of foremen, stewards, supervisors, and administrators, paid by day or task, living in miserable dens—these are the agricultural laborers. These workers who from four in the morning must pass muster, who work until the sun sets . . . [are paid] from 60 cents for women and youths, to 2.20 *soles* for adults, have not, with rare exceptions (the haciendas of Santa Clara, Naranjal, Puente Piedra), enjoyed organizations that watch out for their class interests. For the agricultural worker it is as though the laws of eight-hour workdays, work accidents, protection of women and child labor did not exist. . . .

The formation of union groups made up of agricultural workers is necessary to give birth to Hacienda Committees, to the "Unions of Agricultural Workers."

## THE PEASANT PROBLEM

The peasant problem has a certain objective similarity to the agricultural problem because of the task it represents; it also is identified with the Indigenous problem because it is a problem of the land, and because of this requires special treatment. Different types of peasants exist in the country: the sharecropper or coworker who works the land to share its products and harvests with the *patron*; the *yanacona* who leases the land (the majority of *hacendados* require payment in *quintales* [hundredweights] of cotton); and the owner of small parcels of land inherited from his ancestors, etc. There are different types of peasants but they have common problems to resolve. In our milieu there are peasant organizations like the one that exists in Ica, the "Federation of Peasants in Ica," and in Lima, the "General Federation of *Yanaconas*," and moreover, small societies of irrigators exist in the coast. But the great masses of peasants are disorganized; they have multiple problems to resolve. The most outstanding, most immediate are: the fall in yield from the land, a lack of freedom to plant the best seeds, equitable division of water for irrigation, rapid denigration of the land, the right to be paid for crops in national money. In order to focus and resolve these problems, it is necessary to organize and educate the masses as to their class role, and to gather them in peasant leagues and peasant communities that lead to the creation of the "National Federation of Peasant Leagues."


## THE INDIGENOUS PROBLEM

If the agrarian and peasant problems require a great deal of attention, the Indigenous problem cannot be left behind. As we delve more deeply into this problem, we see the connection with agrarian, peasant, mining, and other problems. So to deal with this problem from the union point of view, it must be done on the basis of class organization and education. The Indigenous problem is linked to the problem of the land, and its solution cannot advance if it is not based on organizing the Indigenous masses. The Indian in our mountainous regions works from 6 to 7 months of the year, the time it usually takes for planting and harvesting the products. In the remaining months, he dedicates himself to working in the mountain *latifundios* and mines, or one or another of the haciendas on the coast, thereby making himself an agricultural laborer. From the union point of view, this form of seasonal migration reinforces the need to pay all necessary attention to these issues. The agricultural and mining proletariat bear a heavy responsibility for the tasks imposed by the seasonal flow of these Indigenous masses, and educating them through a union, when little class awareness exists, will also be more difficult. A great effort, then, is necessary in the communities, *ayllus*, etc., where organizers should establish libraries, educational institutions that fight against illiteracy (it could be said that illiteracy is a social scourge for the Indigenous race), sports sections, etc. These activities should be run by prepared comrades who can develop an active teaching role that allows workers to fully comprehend their class role, explain their condition of exploitation, their rights and the means for vindication. This way, the Indian will be a militant in the union movement, that is, a soldier who fights for the social liberation of his class. The objective of communities will then be to realize the full potential of their capabilities, and to bring the federation of all the communities into a single common defense front.

## THE IMMIGRATION PROBLEM

The ever-greater influx of immigrant workers demands that we do not leave this problem aside in union organization. The union organizations cannot be imbued with false nationalist prejudices, because those prejudices wholly favor capitalism; organizations will always encounter docile elements among our immigrant brothers, and use them against the "native" workers, making them carry out the work of scabs and strikebreakers. Since we group ourselves under principles that tell us "workers of the world unite," we should proceed to make room in our unions for all the Asian, European, Latin American, or African workers, who acknowledge their condition of exploitation, see in the union their organism of representation and defense. It is necessary that the unions set up commissions of militants who, seeing commonalities with the "foreign" workers, study their living conditions and needs, and introduce them to the unions that will in turn defend the rights of these brothers and sisters, incorporating them in the statement of demands presented to the companies.

## THE SOCIAL LEGISLATION PROBLEM

Up to now the Peruvian worker has not been protected by effective social laws. The 1919 decree on eight-hour workdays, the work accident law, and the protection of women and children law are weak attempts at this type of legislation. The solidarity force of the proletariat in the capital led to the eight-hour decree in 1919. Up to now it has only been obeyed in certain sectors, in one factory or another where the workers' organizational power had prevented violations. Subsequently, however, all employers have ignored its stipulations, beginning with the small factories that exist in Lima, like bottling, cardboard boxes, shoes, soap, laundries, dressmaking, bakery branches, etc., and going to the largest businesses. With the process of the organization of industry, this farce is made even less effective. Recently, Associated Electrical Businesses adopted the contract system (and not just this company because we have seen that others also employ it), in order to establish a price scale for different kinds of work that has been presented to the most skilled and longest-serving workers, who are faced with the dilemma of accepting it or facing immediate termination of their labor. The workers who accept this rate in fact become contract workers, losing their seniority and the few benefits that the legislation provided at the same time. . . . The Work Accident Law is not violated any less than the eight-hour law. . . .

### Conclusions

When the fundamental problems of our organization are summarily studied, it is helpful to mention the question of the legality of the type of organization we advocate and promote. The conditions of exploitation and semi-slave regime that exist in nine-tenths of Peru make workers think of this question as they organize. Our bourgeoisie has always seen in worker organization the "ghost" that would put an end to their regime of exploitation and randomly create false stories around it. The government of Peru, as signatory to the Treaty of Versailles, has recognized the right for workers to organize into unions. Moreover, the Ministry of Development has established a section in charge of the recognition of institutions. The "General Confederation of Peruvian Workers" argues the principle that the only thing necessary for a union to exist legally and juridically is the agreement of its members. . . . The Confederation demands the right to legal existence and the necessary juridical personhood for labor organizations in all the industries and areas of labor in order to represent and defend proletarian interests. For the rest, the problems of the working masses cannot be resolved or even known if it is not by means of an organization, or an organism that expresses its necessities, studies the deficiencies of our social regime, that expounds and supports the claims of all the workers of Peru. The objective of the creation of a Central Federation of the Peruvian proletariat, on top of its historical justification, is that of the genuine representation of the exploited class of our country. It is not born of random caprice; it is born through the experience acquired in past struggles and as the exploited Peruvian masses' organic necessity. . . . Representation of the national worker corresponds to a Central Federation formed from top to bottom, that is, by organizations born in factories, workshops, mines, sea and land enterprises, by the agricultural workers and peasants, by the grand masses of exploited Indians. A Central that counts on these elements, which houses in its breast the country's labor unions, will be the only one that will have the right to speak in the name of the workers of Peru. Supported by the proletarian masses defending their interests, the "General Confederation of Peruvian Workers," meeting its stated function, specifies the immediate objectives for which it will fight:

- Respect the implementation of the eight-hour day for the worker in the city, countryside, and mine.

- A 40-hour workweek for women and minors younger than 18 years.

- Full rights of labor organization.

- Liberty of print, press, of assembly, and of workers' speaking platforms.

- Prohibition of non-paid employment for workers or apprentices.

- Equal rights to work, equal treatment and salary for all workers, adults, youth, without distinction as to nationality, race, or color, in all industries and businesses.

- The General Confederation of Peruvian Workers, having shown in its process of creation, and in the objectives for which it would fight, recommends to all the workers, to the representatives of labor organizations, that over the following days they contact this Central, providing it with their addresses, explaining problems that need to be resolved, and agreeing to join at the same time. It also recommends the discussion and vote on the regulatory project (published in No. 9 of *Labor*).

The provisional address of the Central is Calle de Cotabambas No. 389, Lima; Post Office Box 2076, Lima.

LONG LIVE THE ORGANIZATION
OF CITY AND COUNTRY WORKERS!

LONG LIVE THE RIGHT TO ORGANIZE, OF A SPEAKERS'
PLATFORM, OF PRESS, OF ASSEMBLY!

LONG LIVE THE EFFECTIVE UNION OF THE WORKERS OF
PERU!

LONG LIVE THE "GENERAL CONFEDERATION
OF PERUVIAN WORKERS"!

—The Executive Committee

NOTE

Source: "Manifesto de la Confederación de Trabajo del Perú," in *Ideología y política,* in *Obras Completas*, 19th ed. (Lima: Editorial Amauta, 1990), 13:137–55.

# PART VI

# Women

. . .

JOSÉ CARLOS MARIÁTEGUI was very much a feminist. Progressive thinkers and activists of his time, including Rosa Luxemburg, whose work he published in *Amauta*, and Russian feminists such as Alexandra Kollantai influenced his views. Indeed, the Marxist egalitarianism of the Russian Revolution helped shape many of his feminist attitudes:

> The woman in Russia votes and stands for office. Under the constitution, all workers, regardless of gender, nationality or religion, enjoy equal rights. The Communist state does not distinguish or differentiate by gender or nationalities, it divides the society into two classes: bourgeoisie and proletariat. And within its class dictatorship, proletarian women may exercise any public function. In Russia countless women work in the national administration and communal administrations. Women are also often called to be part of the Tribunals of Justice.

And further, in this same piece, "Women and Politics" (selection VI.1), he adds, "And not just in Russia does the feminist movement appear strongly identified with the revolutionary movement. Feminist demands have found strong support from the Left in all countries. In Italy, socialists have always advocated women's suffrage. Many socialist organizers and agitators come from the ranks of the suffrage movement. Once the battle for suffrage was won, Sylvia Pankhurst, among others, enlisted in the extreme left of the British proletariat." He looked to feminism to help bring about socialism.

In "Feminist Demands" (selection VI.2), Mariátegui argues that the subject of feminism is vast and that "This movement should not and cannot feel strange or indifferent to men who are sensitive to the great emotions of the time. The feminine question is a part of the human question. Women must be included as part of a move for human liberation."

Mariátegui eulogized many women writers, political activists, and poets. He especially promoted the poet Magna Portal in the pages of his journal *Amauta*, and also in the chapter on literature in *Seven Essays*, part of which we include in selection VI.3. Mariátegui was quick to realize that Portal was writing as a woman and bringing precisely that perspective to her verse: "Not only compassion and tenderness—but all the intensity of a woman who lives passionately and vehemently, set afire by love and longing, and tortured by truth and hope, are found in her poetry." To wit:

> Come, kiss me . . . your lips,
> Your eyes and your hands . . .
> Later . . . nothing
> And your soul? And your soul?

# 1—Women and Politics

One of the substantial accomplishments of the twentieth century is the acquisition of men's political rights by women. Gradually, we arrived at legal and political equality of both sexes. Women have entered politics, in parliament and in government. Their participation in public affairs has ceased to be exceptional or extraordinary. In the ministry of Ramsay MacDonald's Labour government a portfolio has been assigned to a woman, Miss Margaret Bondfield, who comes to government after a diligent political career representing England in the International Labor Conference in Washington and Geneva. And Russia has given its diplomatic representation in Norway to Alexandra Kollontai, ex-Commissar of the People in the government of the Soviets.

Miss Bondfield and Mme. Kollontai are, on this occasion, two very current figures on the world stage. The figure of Alexandra Kollontai, above all, is not just part of today´s headlines, she is a figure who for some years has attracted European attention and curiosity. And though Margaret Bondfield is not the first woman to hold a state ministry, Alexandra Kollontai is the first woman to head a legation.

Alexandra Kollontai is a leader of the Russian Revolution. When the Soviet regime began, she already had a high-ranking position in

Bolshevism. The Bolsheviks moved her up almost immediately, a Commissary of the People, that of Hygiene, and on one occasion gave her a foreign policy mission. In his memoir of Russia that emotionally chronicles the historic days of 1917 to 1918, Captain Jacques Sadoul calls her the "Red Virgin of the Revolution."[1]

The history of the Russian Revolution is indeed very connected to the history of the achievements of feminism. The Soviet constitution gives women the same rights as men. The woman in Russia votes and stands for office. Under the constitution, all workers, regardless of gender, nationality, or religion, enjoy equal rights. The Communist state does not distinguish or differentiate by gender or nationalities; it divides the society into two classes: bourgeoisie and proletariat. And within its dictatorship of the working class, proletarian women may exercise any public function. In Russia countless women work in the national administration and communal administrations. Women also are often called to be part of the Tribunals of Justice. Several women, Krupskaya and Menjinskaia, for example, assist in Lunatcharsky's educational work. Others, for instance, Angelica Balabanoff, are conspicuously involved in the activity of the Communist Party and the Third International.

The Soviets esteem and greatly encourage female collaboration. The reasons for this feminist policy are well known. Communism found a dangerous resistance in women. The Russian woman, primarily the peasant woman, was an element who was randomly hostile to the revolution. Because of their religious superstitions, Russian women viewed the work of the Soviets as impious, absurd, and heretical. The Soviets understood from the outset the need for a clever educational strategy and revolutionary adaptation for women. They mobilized, for this purpose, all their adherents and supporters, among whom were, as we have seen, some highly capable women.

And not only in Russia does the feminist movement appear strongly identified with the revolutionary movement. Feminist demands have found strong support from the Left in all countries. In Italy, socialists have always advocated women's suffrage. Many Socialist organizers and agitators come from the ranks of the suffrage movement. Once the battle for suffrage was won, Sylvia Pankhurst, among others, enlisted in the extreme left of the British proletariat.

The victory of feminism demands, in reality, is the realization of a late stage of the bourgeois revolution and a final chapter of liberal ideology. Formerly, women's relationships with politics were morganatic. The women in feudal societies only influenced the progress of the state exceptionally, irresponsibly, and indirectly. But at least women of royal blood could reach the throne. Females and males could inherit the divine right to rule. The French Revolution, however, inaugurated a system of political equality—for men, not women. Human rights could have been called, rather, the Rights of the Male. Within the bourgeoisie, women were far more removed from politics than they were within the aristocracy. Bourgeois democracy was exclusively male. Its development had to be, however, strongly favorable to the emancipation of women. Capitalist civilization gave women the means to enhance their capacity and improve their position in life. It enabled and prepared them to make demands to have men's political and civil rights. Today, finally, women have acquired these rights. This fact, hastened by the advanced gestation of the proletarian socialist revolution, is still an echo of the individualistic and Jacobin revolution. Political equality, before that, was not complete; it was not total. Society was not only divided into classes but also divided into sexes. Gender conferred or denied political rights. Such inequality disappears now that the historical path of democracy reaches the end of its trajectory.

The first result of the political equalization of men and women has been the entry of some women of the vanguard into politics and the management of public affairs. But the revolutionary importance of this event has to be much greater. Troubadours and lovers of female frivolity are right to worry. The kind of woman produced by a century of capitalist refinement is doomed to decline and be left behind. An Italian scholar, Pitigrilli, classifies this type of modern woman as a type of "luxury mammal." And thus, this luxury mammal will gradually be depleted. As the socialist system replaces the individualistic system, feminist luxury and elegance will decline. Paquín[2] and socialism are incompatible enemies. Humanity will lose some luxury mammals, but it will gain many women. In the future a woman's dresses will be less expensive and sumptuous, but the condition of the woman will be more dignified. And the axis of feminine life will move from the individual to the social. Fashion no longer consists of imitations of Mme. Pompadour adorned by Paquín. It will consist, perhaps, of an imitation of Mme. Kollontai. A woman, in sum, will cost less, but will be worth more.

Writers who are enemies of feminism fear that the beauty and grace of women will be affected because of feminist victories. They believe that politics, academia, the courts, will turn women into less amiable beings, and even make them unfriendly. But this belief is unfounded. Biographers of Mme. Kollontai tell us that in the dramatic days of the Russian Revolution the illustrious Russian had time and the spiritual disposition to fall in love and marry. The honeymoon and being a Commissar of the People did not seem at all incompatible or antagonistic.

Various advantages have been perceived from the new education women receive. Poetry, for example, has been greatly enriched. These days, women's literature has a feminine accent it did not have before. In the past, women's literature did not have gender. Generally, it was not masculine or feminine. It represented at most a genre of neutral literature. Today, the woman begins to feel, think, and speak as a woman in her literature and art. A specifically and essentially feminine literature appears. This literature will reveal unknown rhythms and colors. Do not the Countess de Noailles, Ada Negri, and Juana de Ibarbourou[3] sometimes speak a strange language; do they not reveal a new world?

Félix del Valle[4] in an essay submits the naughty, original notion that women are displacing men of poetry. They have replaced them in essays, and also seem close to replacing them in poetry. Poetry, in short, has begun to be a women's profession.

But this perspective is, in truth, a humorous view. It is not certain that masculine poetry is being extinguished, but that for the first time one is hearing a distinctly feminine poetry. And this makes it, temporarily, a very advantageous development.

—*Variadades*, Lima, 15 March 1924

## NOTES

Source: *Temas de Educación,* in *Obras Completas* (Lima: Editorial Amauta, 1970): 14:123–28.

1.  Jacques Sadoul, *Notes sur la révolution bolchevique (Octobre 1917–Janvier 1919)* (Paris: Éditions de la Sirène, 1919).
2.  Jeanne Paquin (1869–1936) was a well-known French fashion designer.
3.  The Countess de Noailles, Ada Negri, and Juana de Ibarbourou were popular French, Italian, and Uruguayan poets of Mariátegui's time.
4.  Félix del Valle (1892–1950) was a Peruvian journalist who, together with Mariátegui and César Falcón, founded *Nuestra Época* in 1918.

# 2—Feminist Demands

The first feminist concerns are gestating in Peru. There are some cells, some nuclei of feminism. The proponents of nationalism, of extremism, probably think: here is another exotic idea, another foreign idea that is injected into the Peruvian mind.

We reassure these apprehensive people a little. We must not see feminism as an exotic idea, a foreign idea. We must see it simply as a human idea. It is an idea that is characteristic of a civilization and peculiar to an era. And thus it is an idea with citizenship rights in Peru, as in any other segment of the civilized world.

Feminism has not appeared in Peru artificially or arbitrarily. It has appeared as a result of the new forms of intellectual and manual labor of women. Women with real feminist alliances are women who work, women who study. The feminist idea thrives among women who do intellectual work and among women who do manual work: university professors, laborers. They find an environment conducive to feminism's development in the university classroom, which attracts a growing number of Peruvian women, and in the labor unions, which women from factories join and organize, enjoying the same rights and obligations as men. Apart from this spontaneous and organic feminism, which draws its adherents from the various categories of women's work, there is here, as elsewhere, a dilettante feminism, which is a bit pedantic and a bit mundane. Feminists in this category convert feminism into a simple literary exercise, a mere sport of fashion.

No one should be surprised that not all women unite in a single feminist movement. Feminism necessarily has different colors, different trends. One can distinguish three main trends in feminism, three substantive colors: bourgeois feminism, petit-bourgeois feminism, and proletarian feminism. Each of these feminisms made their demands in a different way. Bourgeois women are in feminist solidarity with the interest of the conservative class. The proletarian woman consubstantiates her feminism with a faith in the revolutionary masses to create a future society. The class struggle, made historical fact and not theoretical assertion, is reflected in feminist terms. Women, like men, are reactionary, centrist, or revolutionary. Thus they cannot fight the same battle together. In the current human panorama, class differentiates individuals more than sex.

But this plurality of feminism does not depend on the theory itself. Rather it depends on its practical distortions. Feminism, as a pure idea, is essentially revolutionary. The thinking and attitudes of women who feel at the same time feminist and conservative lack, therefore, a logical coherence. Conservatism works to maintain the traditional organization of society. The organization denies women the rights women want to acquire. The bourgeois feminists accept all the consequences of the existing order, less those that are opposed to women's demands. Tacitly. they argue the absurd thesis that the only reform society needs is a feminist reform. The protest of these feminists against the old order is too exclusive to be valid.

True, the historical roots of feminism are in the liberal spirit. The French Revolution contained the first seeds of the feminist movement. For the first time it raised, in precise terms, the question of the emancipation of women. Babeuf, the leader of the conspiracy of equals, asserted feminist demands.[1] Babeuf harangued his friends this way: "Do not impose silence on this sex that does not deserve disdain. Enhance rather the most beautiful part of yourself. If you count for nothing to the women in your republic, you will make them little lovers of the monarchy. Their influence will be such that they will restore it. If, on the contrary, you count for something, you will make them Cornelius and Lucretius. They will give you Brutuses, Gracchi, and Scevolas." Polemicizing with the anti-feminists, Babeuf speaks of "the tyranny of sex that men have always wanted to annihilate, of this sex that has never been useless in revolutions." But the French Revolution did not want to remind women of the equality and freedom advocated by these Jacobean or egalitarian voices. The Rights of Man, as I wrote once, could rather have been called Rights of the Male. Bourgeois democracy has been an exclusively male democracy.

Born in the liberal womb, feminism could not be started during the capitalist process. It is now, when the historical path of democracy comes to an end, that the woman acquires the political and legal rights of the male. And it is the Russian Revolution that has explicitly and categorically granted women the equality and freedom that for over a century the French Revolution, Babeuf, and egalitarian advocates have called for in vain.

But if bourgeois democracy has not achieved feminism, it has unwittingly created the conditions and assumptions for the moral and material premises of its realization. It has been valued as a productive element, an economic factor, by making use of women's work more extensively and more intensely every day. Work radically moves the feminine mentality and spirit. The woman acquires, by virtue of work, a new notion of herself. Formerly, the society destined the woman for marriage or concubinage. Presently, they are destined above all to work. This fact has changed and has raised the position of women in life. Those who challenge feminism and its progress with emotional or traditionalist arguments claim that women should be educated only for the home. But practically this means that women should only be educated for gendered roles as a female and mother. The defense of the poetry of the home is actually a defense of women's servitude. Instead of ennobling and dignifying the role of women, domesticity diminishes and decreases it. The woman is more than a mother and a female the way the man is more than a male.

The kind of woman to produce a new civilization must be substantially different from the one who formed the civilization that is currently in decline. In an article on women and politics, I have examined some aspects of this theme:

> The troubadours and lovers of female frivolity are right to worry. The kind of woman produced by a century of capitalist refinement is doomed to decline and be left behind. An Italian scholar, Pitigrilli, classifies this type of modern woman as a type of "luxury mammal."
>
> And thus, this luxury mammal will gradually be depleted. As the socialist system replaces the individualistic system, feminist luxury and elegance will decline. Paquín and socialism are incompatible enemies. Humanity will lose some luxury mammals, but it will gain many women. In the future, a woman's dresses will be less expensive and sumptuous, but the condition of the woman will be more dignified. And the axis of feminine life will move from the individual to the social. Fashion no longer consists of imitations of Mme. Pompadour adorned by Paquín. It will consist, perhaps, of an imitation of Mme. Kollontai. A woman, in sum, will cost less, but will be worth more.

The subject is vast. This brief article tries only to note the character of the first manifestations of feminism in Peru and presents a very brief and rapid interpretation of the appearance and spirit of the global feminist movement. This movement should not and cannot feel foreign to men who are sensitive to the great emotions of the time. The feminine question is a part of the human question. Besides, feminism seems to me also a more interesting and historically transcendent subject than a hairpiece. Although feminism has some significance, the wig is but anecdote.

—*Mundial*, Lima, 19 December 1924

NOTES

Source: *Temas de Educación*, in *Obras Completas* (Lima: Editorial Amauta, 1970): 14:129-33.

1.  Babeuf advocated an uprising of equals and was executed by his fellow French revolutionary leaders. He is credited with originating many of the egalitarian ideas that later influenced anarchist and communist thought.

# 3—Magda Portal

Magda Portal is another notable asset in the process of our literature. With her appearance Peru has its first poetess. Until now we had only women of letters, of which one or another had an artistic or more specifically literary temperament, but we have not exactly had a poetess.

One should understand the term *poetess*. The poetess is, to some extent in the history of Western civilization, a phenomenon of our time. The previous eras produced only masculine poetry. Women's poetry was the same, content with being a variation of the same lyrical songs or philosophical reasonings. The poetry that did not show a masculine mark did not carry that of a woman either—virgin, female, mother. It was an asexual poetry. In our time, women finally put their own flesh and spirit into their poetry. The female poet is now one that creates a feminine poetry. And since women's poetry has been emancipated and differentiated spiritually from that of men, the female poets have acquired high regard in the literary catalogue. The existence of women's poetry became clear and interesting from the moment it began to be different.

In the poetry of Hispanic America, two women, Gabriel Mistral[1] and Juana de Ibarbourou,[2] have received more attention than any other poet of their time. Delmira Agustini[3] has a noble and long lineage in her country and Latin America. Blanca Luz Brum has brought her message to Peru. And we are not dealing with solitary, exceptional cases. Rather, we are dealing with a much wider phenomenon that is common to all types of literature. Poetry, grown a little old in men, is reborn and rejuvenated in women.

Félix del Valle, a writer of brilliant intuition, said to me one day, responding to the multiplicity of poetesses in the world, that the scepter of poetry had passed to women. With his humorous wit he put it this way, "Poetry is turning into a female profession." This is without doubt, an extreme thesis; but it is certain that poetry by men tends toward a nihilist, sporting, skeptical attitude, whereas in the female poets it has fresh roots and white flowers. Their accent suggests more *élan vital*, more biological force.

Magna Portal is not yet well known in Peru or Hispanic America. She has only published one book of prose: *El Derecho de Matar* [The Right to Kill] (La Paz, 1926) and one book of verse: *Una Esperanza y el Mar* [One Hope and the Sea] (Lima, 1927). *El Derecho de Matar* presents only one of her sides: a rebellious spirit and revolutionary messianism that, in our time, are indisputable testimony to the historical sensitivity of an artist. Besides this, in Magna Portal's prose one always finds a shred of her magnificent lyricism. Three poems from this volume—"El Poema de la Cárcel," "La sonrisa de Cristo," and "Círculos violent"—have Magda's clarity, passion, and exalted tenderness. But her book is not characterized or defined by *El Derecho de Matar,* an anarchistic and nihilist title that does not reflect Magda's spirit.

Magda is essentially lyric and human. In terms of personal autonomy, her compassion is similar to the compassion of Vallejo.[4] This is the way she is presented to us in the verses of "Anima absorta" and "Una Esperanza y el Mar." And surely this is the way she is. She does not exhibit any touch of nineteenth-century decadence or paradox.

In her early verses, Magda Portal is, almost always, the poetess of tenderness. And in some her lyricism is revealed in her humanity. Exempt from megalomaniac egoism or romantic narcissism, Magna Portal says to us: "Small am I . . . "!

Not only compassion and tenderness, but all the intensity of a woman who lives passionately and vehemently, set afire by love and longing, and tortured by truth and hope, are found in her poetry.

In the frontispiece of one of her books, Magda Portal has written these lines of Leonardo da Vinci: "The soul, the first spring of life, is reflected in all that it creates." "The true work of art is like a mirror that reflects the soul of the artist." Magda's fervent adherence to these principles of creation is an integral part of her artistic sense that her poetry never contradicts and always ratifies.

In her poetry, Magda gives us, above all else, a clear version of herself. She does not obscure, she does not mystify, she does not idealize. Her poetry is her truth. Magda does not offer us an image aligned with her soul all made up for the ball. We can open one of her books without trepidation, without ceremony, sure that no simulation is waiting for us, and that we will not be ambushed. The art of this pure, deep lyricist, reduces to the minimum—almost to zero—the proportion of the artificial that is necessary to be art.

This is for me the best proof of Magda's great value. In this epoch of decadence in the social order—and consequently in its art—the most imperative obligation of the artist is truth. The only works that will survive this crisis will be those that are a confession and a testimony.

The perennial and dark contrast between two principles that govern the world—that of life and that of death—is always present in Magda's poetry. In Magda, one feels an anguished longing to finish, and not to be, and a desire to create and be at the same time. Magda's soul is an agonistic soul. And her art fully and entirely translates the two forces that tear and drive it forward. At times the principle of life triumphs; at other times the principle of death triumphs.

The dramatic presence of this conflict in Magda's poetry gives it a metaphysical depth easily reached by the spirit via the route of lyricism, without need of the crutch of any philosophy.

It also gives her work a psychological depth that permits it to register all the contradictory voices of her dialogue, her struggle, her agony.

The poetess achieves an extraordinary force of her own expression in these admirable verses:

Come, kiss me! . . .
What does it matter that something dark
Is gnawing at my soul
With its teeth?

I am thine and you are mine . . . kiss me! . . .
I do not cry today, I choke on joy,
A strange joy
That comes from I know not where.

You are mine . . . Are you mine? . . .
A door of ice
Is between you and me:
Your thought!
That that gets you in the brain
And whose hammering
Escapes me . . .

Come, kiss me . . . What does it matter?
The heart called you all night,
And now that it is you, your flesh, and your soul
Why do I have to remember what you did yesterday? . . .
          What does it matter!

Come, kiss me . . . your lips,
Your eyes and your hands . . .
Later . . . nothing.
And your soul? And your soul?

This poetess of ours, whom we should salute as one of the best poetesses of Indo-America, does not descend from Ibarbourou. She does not descend from Agustini. She does not even descend from Mistral, with whom, because of a certain affinity of accent, she feels closer to than any other. She has an original and unique temperament. Her secret, her word, her force, were born with her and are in her.

NOTES

Source: "El proceso de la literatura," in 7 *Ensayos de interpretación de la realidad Peruana,* in *Obras Completas,* 26th ed. (Lima: Editorial Amauta, 1973), 1:322–26.

1.  Gabriela Mistral (April 7, 1889–January 10, 1957) was a Chilean poet, educator, diplomat, and feminist.
2.  Juana de Ibarbourou (1892–1979) was a Uruguayan poet.
3.  Delmira Agustini (October 24, 1886–July 6, 1914) was a Uruguayan poet.
4.  César Vallejo, Peruvian vanguardist poet.

# PART VII

# Myth and the Optimism
of the Ideal

JOSÉ CARLOS MARIÁTEGUI WAS A BELIEVER. He strongly believed in socialism and saw it as the animating force of his day. The Russian Revolution and other socialist movements like Rosa Luxemburg's Spartakusbund inspired him. He had read the French philosopher Henri Bergson and was much taken with his concept of élan vital, the vital life force. He read and cited Georges Sorel's *Reflections on Violence* and thought Sorel's concept of the revolutionary myth was relevant for revolutionary unionism and the socialist movement, and helped to distinguish revolutionary socialism from evolutionary socialism. Mariátegui's affirmative approach to thought, politics, and Marxism was at least in part a result of his upbringing by his mother and maternal family. His mother had an almost mystical commitment to the Catholic faith. Mariátegui seems to have acquired this mystical conception of religion and other belief systems from her. He maintained it throughout his life, was never antireligious, and even interjected his mystical-religious feelings into his conception of Marxism and revolution.[1] Although some orthodox Marxists criticized him and some writers misunderstood him, this imbued Mariátegui's belief system with an ardent passion that fueled his socialist commitment. It was precisely this type of commitment that paved the way for the Peruvian priest and theologian Gustavo Gutiérrez to incorporate aspects of Mariátegui's Marxist analysis and socialism into liberation theology.[2]

The following selections allow for an appreciation of Mariátegui's orientation in this area. As he says in "Myth and Man" (VII.1), man, "as philosophy defines him, is a metaphysical animal. He does not live productively without a metaphysical conception of life. The myth moves man in history. Without myth, the history of humanity has no sense of history. History is made by people possessed and illuminated by a higher belief, by a superhuman hope; others are the anonymous chorus of the drama. The crisis of bourgeois civilization appeared obvious from the moment that this civilization displayed its lack of myth." And later, he adds, "The religious, mystical, metaphysical character of socialism has been established for some time. Georges Sorel, one of the highest representatives of French thought of the twentieth century, wrote in his *Reflections on Violence* that 'a new analogy has been discovered between religion and the revolutionary socialism which aims at the apprenticeship, preparation, and even reconstruction of the individual. This is a gigantic task. But Bergson has taught us that it is not only religion that occupies the profounder region of our mental life; revolutionary myths have their place there equally with religion.'" For Mariátegui, these voluntarist notions of human actions were key to determining the course of history.

All selections in this section are taken from a compilation published during Mariátegui's lifetime under the symbolic title *El Alma Matinal* (The Morning Soul). The essays represent faith in a new, revolutionary belief system that would inspire men and women to create socialist revolutions. This view of politics and political action was a strong motivating force for the Peruvian Marxist. In *Defensa del Marxismo*, he recalls Lenin's reputed answer to someone who was criticizing him for his revolutionary efforts because they went against reality: "So much the worse for reality."[3] Mariátegui believed in a new and better reality.

1. Harry E. Vanden, *National Marxism in Latin America, José Carlos Mariátegui's Thought and Politics* (Boulder, CO: Lynne Rienner Publishers, 1986), 116.
2. See Gustavo Gutiérrez, *A Theology of Liberation: History, Politics, and Salvation* (Maryknoll, NY: Orbis Books, 1988). Mariátegui's youngest son, Javier, and Gutiérrez were schoolmates and frequently conversed about the elder Mariátegui's thought. Harry E. Vanden, interviews with Javier Mariátegui and Gustavo Gutiérrez, Lima, Peru, April 1994.
3. *Defensa del marxismo*, in *Obras Completas*, 3rd ed. (Lima: Editorial Amauta, 1967), 5:56. Mariátegui takes this reference from Miguel de Unamuno's *La Agonía del Cristianismo* (The Agony of Christianity).

# 1—Man and Myth

## I.

All modern intellectual investigations on the global crisis lead to a unanimous conclusion: bourgeois civilization suffers from a lack of myth, of faith, of hope. Missing is the expression of its material bankruptcy. The rationalist experience has had the paradoxical effect of leading humanity to the disconsolate conviction that reason cannot offer a way forward. Rationalism has only served to discredit reason. Mussolini has said that demagogues killed the idea of freedom. More accurate, undoubtedly, is that rationalists killed the idea of reason. Reason has eradicated the residue of old myths from the soul of bourgeois civilization. Western man for some time has placed Reason and Science at the altar of dead gods. But neither Reason nor Science can be a myth. Neither Reason nor Science can meet the need of the infinite that exists in man. Reason itself has been challenged, demonstrating to humanity that it is not enough. Only Myth possesses the precious virtue of satisfying its deepest self.

Reason and Science have eroded and dissolved the prestige of the ancient religions. Eucken in his book on the meaning and value of life clearly and accurately explains the mechanism of this solvent.[1]

Creations of science have given humanity a feeling of power. Humanity, previously overwhelmed with the supernatural, has suddenly discovered an exorbitant power to correct and rectify Nature. This feeling has removed the roots of the old metaphysics from its soul.

But man, as philosophy defines him, is a metaphysical animal. He does not live productively without a metaphysical conception of life. Myth moves man in history. Without myth, the history of humanity has no sense of history. History is made by people possessed and illuminated by a higher belief, by a superhuman hope; others are the anonymous chorus of the drama. The crisis of bourgeois civilization appeared obvious from the moment that this civilization displayed its lack of myth. Renan, once proud of positivism, melancholically highlighted the decline of religion, and was disquieted about the future of European civilization. "Religious people," he wrote, "live in a shadow. On what will those who come after us live?"[2] The despairing question still awaits an answer.

Bourgeois civilization has fallen into skepticism. The war seemed to revive the myth of the liberal revolution: Liberty, Democracy, Peace. But the bourgeoisie's allies soon sacrificed them to their interests and grudges at the conference of Versailles. The rejuvenation of these myths nevertheless served to fulfill the liberal revolution in Europe. Its invocation sentenced to death the residue of feudalism and absolutism that still survives in Central Europe, Russia, and Turkey. And above all, the war proved once more in vivid and tragic fashion the value of myth. The people who were capable of victory were those capable of a massive myth.

II

Modern man feels the urgent need for myth. Skepticism is infertile, and humanity is not satisfied with infertility. An exasperated and at times impotent "will to believe," so sharp in postwar people, was already intense and categorical in prewar people. A poem by Henri Frank, *Dance in Front of the Ark*, is a document I keep on hand regard-

ing the mood of literature in the prewar years. A great and deep emotion beats in this poem. For this, above all, let me quote him. Henri
Frank tells us of his deep "will to believe." As an Israelite, he tries first
to illuminate his soul with faith in the god of Israel. The attempt is
futile. The words of the god of his fathers sound strange at this time.
The poet does not understand them. He declares himself deaf to their
meaning. As a modern man, the word from Sinai cannot move him. A
dead faith cannot be resurrected. It is buried under twenty centuries.
"Israel has died from having given a god to the world." The voice of
the modern world proposes its fictional and precarious myth: Reason.
But Henri Frank is unable to accept it. "Reason," he says, "is not the
universe."

> *La raison sans Dieu c'est la chambre sans lampe.*[3]

The poet leaves in search of God. He is urgent to satisfy his thirst
for infinity and eternity. But the pilgrimage is unsuccessful. The pilgrim wanted to make do with the illusion of daily life.

> *¡Ah! sache franchement saisir de tout moment—*
> *la fuyante fumée et le sue éphémère.*[4]

He finally thinks that the "truth is enthusiasm without hope." The
man carries truth within himself.

> *Si l'Arche est vide oú tu pensais trouver la loi,*
> *rien n'est réel que ta danse.*[5]

## III

Philosophers give us a truth similar to that of poets. Contemporary
philosophy has swept away the positivist mediocre edifice. It has clarified and demarcated the modest confines of reason. It has formulated
the current theories of Myth and Action. It is useless, according to

these theories, to search for an absolute truth. The truth of today is not the truth of tomorrow. A truth is only valid for a period of time. We should be content with a relative truth.

But this relativist language is not accessible or intelligible to the common people. Common people are not so subtle. Humanity is reluctant to follow a truth that it does not believe to be absolute and supreme. It is futile to recommend the excellence of faith, of myth, of action. We must propose a faith, a myth, an action. Where will we find the myth able to revive the spirit of the declining order?

The question annoys the intellectual and spiritual anarchy of bourgeois civilization. Some souls are striving to restore the Middle Ages and the Catholic ideal. Others work to return to the Renaissance and the classical ideal. Fascism, in the words of its theorists, has been given a medieval and Catholic mentality. They think they represent the spirit of the Counter-Reformation; but on the other hand, they claim to embody the idea of Nation, a typically liberal idea. The theory seems to take pleasure in inventing the most affected sophistry. But all attempts to resurrect myths are doomed to failure. Each era wishes to have its own sense of the world. There is nothing more sterile than trying to revive a dead myth. Jean R. Bloch, in an article published in the journal *Europe*, writes words of profound truth on this topic. In the Cathedral of Chartres, he felt the wonderfully faithful voice of the distant Middle Ages. But he warns how much that voice is foreign to the concerns of this time. "It would be crazy," he writes, "to think that the same faith would repeat the same miracle. Look at your surroundings: somewhere a new, active mysticism capable of miracles, is able to fill the miserable with hope, raise martyrs, and transform the world with promises of goodness and virtue. When you have found it, designated it, appointed it, you will absolutely not be the same man."

Ortega y Gasset speaks of the "disenchanted soul." Romain Rolland speaks of the "enchanted soul." Which of the two is right? Both souls exist. The "disenchanted soul" of Ortega y Gasset is the soul of a decadent bourgeois civilization. The "enchanted soul" of Romain Roland is the soul of the framers of the new civilization. Ortega y Gasset only sees the sunset, the twilight, *tramonto, der*

*Untergang*. Romain Rolland sees the sunrise, the dawn, *der Aurgang*. What most clearly and obviously differentiates them in this era of the bourgeoisie and the proletariat is myth. The bourgeoisie no longer has any myths. It has become incredulous, skeptical, nihilistic. The reborn liberal myth has aged too much. The proletariat has a myth: the social revolution. It moves toward that myth with a passionate and active faith. The bourgeoisie denies; the proletariat affirms. The bourgeois intellectuals entertain themselves with a rationalist critique of the method, theory, revolutionary technique. What a misunderstanding! The strength of revolutionaries is not in their science; it is in their faith, in their passion, in their will. It is a religious, mystical, spiritual force. It is the force of myth. The revolutionary excitement, as I wrote in an article on Gandhi, is a religious emotion.[6] Religious motives have been displaced from the heavens to earth. They are not divine; they are human, social.

The religious, mystical, metaphysical character of socialism has been established for some time. Georges Sorel, one of the highest representatives of French thought of the twentieth century, wrote in his *Reflections on Violence* that "a new analogy has been discovered between religion and the revolutionary socialism which aims at the apprenticeship, preparation, and even reconstruction of the individual. This is a gigantic task. But Bergson has taught us that it is not only religion that occupies the profound region of our mental life; revolutionary myths equally have their place with religion." Renan, as Sorel himself recalls, notes the religious faith of the socialists, showing their resistance to any disappointment: "After each abortive experiment they recommence their work: the solution is not yet found, but it will be. The idea that no solution exists never occurs to them, and therein lies their strength."[7]

The same philosophy that teaches us the necessity of myth and faith is usually incapable of understanding the faith and myth of modern times. It is the "Poverty of Philosophy," to quote Marx. Professional intellectuals will not find the path of faith; the masses will find it. It will later fall to the philosophers to codify the thought that emerges from this great mass achievement. Were the philosophers of

Roman decadence able to understand the language of Christianity?
The philosophy of bourgeois decadence can have no better future.

—*Mundial*, Lima, 16 January 1925

NOTES

Source: "El hombre y el mito," *El alma matinal y otras estaciones del hombre de hoy*, in *Obras Completas*, 10th ed. (Lima: Biblioteca Amauta, 1987), 3:23–28.

1.    Rudolf Christoph Eucken (January 5, 1846–September 15, 1926) was a German philosopher and writer.
2.    Ernest Renan, *Feuilles détachées faisant suite aux Souvenirs d'enfance et de jeunesse*, 2nd ed. (Paris: Calmann Lévy, 1892), 17–18.
3.    "Reason without god is a room without a lamp."
4.    "Ah! To know to boldly seize each moment—the fleeting hope and the ephemeral essence."
5.    "If the Ark is empty where you hoped to find the law, nothing is real but your dance."
6.    José Carlos Mariátegui, "Gandhi," in *La escena contemporánea*, 14th ed. (Lima: Biblioteca Amauta, 1987), 193–99.
7.    Georges Sorel, *Reflections on Violence* (New York: Collier Books, 1950), 52.

# 2—The Final Struggle

## I.

Madeleine Marx, one of the most restless women of letters and most modern in contemporary France, has gathered her impressions of Russia in a book bearing this title: *C'est la lutte finale. . . .*[1] The sentence of singer Eugene Pottier[2] acquires a historical highlight. "It is the final struggle!"

The proletarian revolution in Russia welcomes this cry—the ecumenical cry of the worldwide proletariat. The massive battle cry and hope that Madeleine Marx heard in the streets of Moscow, I have also heard in the streets of Rome, Milan, Berlin, Paris, Vienna, and Lima. It embodies all of the excitement of an era. Revolutionary crowds believe in engaging in the final struggle.

Is the final struggle truly engaged? For those skeptical creatures of the old order this final struggle is just an illusion. For the ardent fighters of the new order it is a reality. *Au-dessus la Melée,*[3] a new and enlightened philosophy of history, suggests otherwise: illusion and reality. The final struggle of Eugene Pottier's stanza is both a reality and an illusion.

We are engaging, in effect, the final struggle of an era and a class. Progress, or human process, is accomplished in stages. Therefore humanity has always felt the need to be close to a goal. Today's goal is surely not the goal of tomorrow; however, for the theory of human progress, it is the ultimate goal. The messianic millennium will never come. People arrive only to leave again. It cannot, however, dispense with the belief that a new day is the final day. No revolution ever foresees the revolution that comes next, even though it contains the seeds of it. For people, as subjects of history, nothing exists but their own personal reality. They are not interested in an abstract struggle, but rather a concrete struggle. The revolutionary proletariat thus lives the reality of a final struggle. Humanity, meanwhile, from an abstract point of view, lives the illusion of a final struggle.

## II.

The French Revolution had the same idea of its own importance. Its men also wished to inaugurate a new era. The convention wanted to be burned forever in time, to be the beginning of the republican millennium. Its members thought that the Christian era and the Gregorian calendar could not contain the republic. The anthem of the revolution hailed the dawn of a new day: "*Le jour de gloire est arrivé.*"[4] The individualistic and Jacobin republic appeared as the supreme desideratum of humanity. The revolution felt it was final and insurmountable. It was the final struggle. The final struggle for freedom, equality, and fraternity.

Less than a century and a half has been enough to make this myth antiquated. "La Marseillaise" is no longer a revolutionary song. The "glory day" has lost its supernatural prestige. The very instigators of democracy are disenchanted by the presence of the parliament and universal suffrage. Another revolution is fermenting in the world. A collectivist regime is struggling to replace an individual regime. The revolutionaries of the twentieth century are about to summarily judge the work of eighteenth-century revolutionaries.

Proletarian revolution, however, is a consequence of the bourgeois revolution. The bourgeoisie has created more than a century of rapid capitalist accumulation, the spiritual and material conditions of a new order. The first socialist ideas were nested within the French Revolution. Later, industrialism gradually organized armies of the revolution at its plants. The proletariat, previously confused with the bourgeoisie on the same plane, then made their class demands. The fat breast of capitalist well-being increased socialism. The fate of the bourgeoisie is that it supplies ideas and people to the revolution against its power.

## III.

The illusion of the final struggle is both a very ancient and extremely modern illusion. Every two, three, or more centuries this illusion reappears with a different name. And, as now, it is always the reality of an innumerable human phalanx. It possesses people to renew it. It is the motor of all progress. It is the star of all rebirths. When the great illusion sinks, it is because it has already created a new human reality. People then rest with their eternal concerns. It closes a romantic cycle and it opens a classic cycle. In the classic cycle it develops, stylizes, and degenerates a form that, fully realized, cannot contain the new forces of life. Only in cases where people's creative power is weakened does life sleep, stuck within a rigid, decrepit, outdated form. But the ecstasy of these people or societies is not unlimited. The sleepy lagoon, the swampy quiet, is about to bubble up and overflow. Life then recovers its energy and momentum. India, China, and contemporary Turkey are living examples of these rebirths. The revolutionary myth has the potential to shake and revive these peoples in collapse.

The East awakes ready for action. Hope was reborn in its ancient soul.

## IV.

Skepticism was satisfied with contrasting the unreality of large human illusions. Relativism does not comply with the same negative result and infertility. It starts by teaching that reality is an illusion, but it concludes by recognizing that the illusion is, in turn, a reality. It denies that there are absolute truths, but it realizes that people must believe in their relative truths as if they were absolute. People have a need for certainty. What difference does it make if the certainty people feel today is not the certainty of tomorrow? Without a myth people cannot live fruitfully. Relativistic philosophy proposes, therefore, to obey the law of myth.

Pirandello,[5] a relativist, offers the example of adhering to fascism. Fascism seduces Pirandello because while democracy has become skeptical and nihilistic, fascism represents a religious and fanatic faith in the hierarchy and the Nation (Pirandello is a petit-bourgeois Sicilian who lacks mental fitness to understand and follow the revolutionary myth). The writer of exasperated skepticism does not love political doubts. He prefers violent, categorical, passionate, brutal assertions. The crowd, who is even more skeptical than the philosopher, more than the relativistic philosopher, cannot dispense with a myth, cannot dispense with a faith. It is not possible to distinguish the subtle truth of the true past or future. All that exists for the myth is the truth. Absolute, unique, eternal truth. And, according to this truth, their struggle is really a final one.

The vital impulse of people answers to all the questions of life before the philosophical investigation. Illiterate people do not care about the relativity of this myth. It would not even be possible for them to understand it. But generally they do a better job of finding their own way than the writer or philosopher. Because they must act, they act. Since they must believe, they believe. Since they must fight, they fight.

Nothing is known about the relative insignificance of their efforts in time and space. Their instinct is to deviate from sterile questions. They have no more ambition than what everyone should have: to carry out their work and do a good job.

—*Mundial*, Lima, 20 March 1925

NOTES

Source: "La lucha final," in *El alma matinal y otras estaciones del hombre de hoy,* in *Obras Completas,* 10th ed. (Lima: Biblioteca Amauta, 1987), 3:29–33.

1.  English version: Magdeleine Marx, "This Is the Final Fight," in *The Romance of New Russia* (New York: T. Seltzer, 1924).
2.  Eugène Pottier was a French worker-poet and author of the famous proletarian song "L'Internationale" that became the anthem of the Soviet Union.
3.  Romain Rolland, *Au-dessus de la Mêlée* (Paris: Ollendorff, 1915) (Above the Mêlée) was a pacifist manifesto against World War One.
4.  The day of glory has arrived.
5.  Luigi Pirandello (1867–1936) was an Italian dramatist, novelist, and short-story writer.

# 3—Pessimism of the Reality, Optimism of the Ideal

## I.

It seems to me that José Vasconcelos[1] has found a formula on pessimism and optimism that not only defines the feeling of the new Ibero-American generation in the face of the contemporary crisis, but also corresponds to the absolute mentality and sensibility of an era in which, despite the thesis of José Ortega y Gasset on the "disenchanted soul" and "the twilight of revolutions," millions of people are working with mystical courage and a religious passion to create a new world. "Pessimism of reality, optimism of the ideal," is Vasconcelos's formula.

"Do not ever conform, always be above and beyond the moment," writes Vasconcelos. "Reject reality and fight to destroy it, not for a lack of faith but by an excess of faith in human capabilities and the firm conviction that evil is never permanent nor justifiable, and that it is always possible and feasible to redeem, purify, improve the collective condition and the private conscience."

The attitude of people who intend to correct reality is certainly more optimistic than pessimistic. They are pessimistic in their protest and in their condemnation of the present, but they are optimists in their hope for the future. All great human ideals have started with a denial, but they also have been an affirmation. Religions have always perpetually represented this pessimism of reality and optimism of the ideal that this Mexican writer is now preaching to us.

We are not content with mediocrity, let alone do we settle for injustice. We are often described as pessimistic, but, in truth, pessimism dominates our spirit much less than optimism. We do not believe that the world should be fatal and eternally as it is. We believe that it can and should be better. The optimism we reject is the easy and lazy Panglossian optimism of those who think we live in the best of all possible worlds.


## II.


There are two kinds of pessimists, just as there are two kinds of optimists. The exclusively negative pessimist is limited to gestures of helplessness and hopelessness, the misery of things and the vanity of effort. That person is nihilistic and melancholy, waiting for the final disappointment. As Artzibachev said, "The extreme limits." Fortunately, this kind of person is not common. This type belongs to a strange hierarchy of disenchanted intellectuals who are also a product of a period in decline or of a people in collapse.

Among the intellectuals, it is not uncommon that a simulated nihilism is a philosophical excuse for refusing to cooperate in any great effort of renovation or as a means to explain their disdain for any mass work. But the fictional nihilism of this type of intellectual is not a philosophical attitude. It is reduced to a hidden and artificial disdain for the great human myths. It is an unacknowledged nihilism that does not dare to come to the surface of the work or life of a negative intellectual, who approaches this theoretical exercise as a solitary vice. The intellectual, nihilistic in private, is likely to be a public member of an anti-alcohol league or a protector of animals. Their nihilism is only intended to guard and defend themselves from the great passions. In the face of petty ideals, the false nihilist behaves with the most vulgar idealism.

## III.

It is with pessimistic and negative spirits of this nature that our optimism of the ideal refuses to let us be confused. Negative attitudes are absolutely sterile. Action is made of negations and affirmations. The new generation in our America and around the world is, above all, a generation that shouts its faith, sings its hope.

## IV.

A skeptical mood prevails in contemporary Western philosophy. This philosophical attitude, as its critics so pervasively stress, is a gesture peculiar to a civilization in decline. Only in a decadent world would a disillusioned sense of life flourish. But not even this contemporary skepticism or relativism has a relationship, or any affinity, with the cheap and fictitious nihilism of the impotent, nor with the absolute and morbid nihilism of the suicidal madmen of Andreiev and Artzibachev. Pragmatism, which so effectively moves people to action, is in fact a relativistic and skeptical school. Hans Vainhingher, the author of *Philosophie der Als Ob*, has been justifiably classified as a pragmatist. For this German philosopher, there are no absolute truths. But there are relative truths that govern people's lives as if they were absolute. "Moral principles, just like aesthetic ones, legal criteria, just like those upon which science operates, the very foundations of logic, have no objective existence. They are our fictitious constructions that serve only as regulatory precepts for our actions, which are conducted as if they were true."[2] Thus the Italian philosopher Giuseppe Renssi defines the philosophy of Vainhinger in his *Lineamientos de Filosofía escéptica,* which, as I see in a bibliographic note in Ortega y Gasset's journal, has begun to attract interest in Spain and hence in Spanish America.

This philosophy, therefore, does not call us to abandon action. It only seeks to deny the Absolute. But it recognizes in human history the relative truth, the temporal myth of each time, the same value and the same effectiveness as an absolute and eternal truth. This philosophy proclaims and confirms the need of the myth and the usefulness of the faith. Although it then entertains the thinking that all truths and all fictions, in the final analysis, are equivalent. Einstein, a relativist, behaves in life as an optimist of the ideal.

## V.

The desire to overcome skeptical philosophy burns in the new generation. It is made in the contemporary chaos from the materials of a new mysticism. The world in birth will not put its hope where conceited religions placed it. "The strong strive and struggle," says Vasconcelos, "in order to anticipate somewhat the work of heaven." The new generation wants to be strong.

—*Mundial*, Lima, 21 August 1925

### NOTES

Source: "Pesimismo de la realidad y optimismo del ideal," in *El alma matinal y otras estaciones del hombre de hoy*, in *Obras Completas*, 10th ed. (Lima: Biblioteca Amauta, 1987), 3:34–37.

1.    José Vasconcelos (February 28, 1882–June 30, 1959) was a Mexican writer, philosopher, and secretary of public education.
2.    Guiseppe Rensi, *Lineamenti di filosofia scettica*, 2nd ed. (Bologna: Nicola Zanichelli, 1921).

# 4—Imagination and Progress

Luis Araquistáin writes that "the conservative spirit, in its most disinterested form, if it is not born of a low selfishness but from fear of the unknown and uncertainty, ultimately shows a lack of imagination."[1] To be a revolutionary or reformer is, from this point of view, a consequence of being more or less imaginative. The conservative rejects any idea of change because of a mental incapacity to conceive and accept it. This applies, of course, to a pure conservative, because the attitude of a practical conservative who accommodates ideas for their usefulness and comfort undoubtedly has a different genesis.

Traditionalism and conservatism are defined as a simple spiritual limitation. The traditionalist has no ability except to imagine life as it was. The conservative has no ability except to imagine how it is. The progress of humanity, therefore, is fulfilled in spite of traditionalism and despite conservatism.

Several years ago Oscar Wilde, in *The Soul of Man under Socialism*, said, "Progress is the realisation of Utopias."[2] In a parallel to Wilde's thought, Luis Araquistáin adds that "without imagination there is no progress of any kind." And, in truth, progress would not be possible if human imagination suddenly suffered a collapse.

History always gives right to imaginative people. In South America, for example, we just commemorated the life and work of the organizers and leaders of the independence revolution. These men seem to be real geniuses. But what is the first condition of being a genius? Undoubtedly, it is a strong power of imagination. The liberators were great because they were, above all, imaginative. They were insurgents against the limited reality, the imperfect reality, of their time.

They worked to create a new reality. Bolívar had futuristic dreams. He imagined a confederation of Indo-Spanish states. Without this ideal, it is likely that Bolívar would not have come to fight for our independence. The fate of the independence of Peru thus depended in large part on the imaginative ability of the Liberator. To celebrate the centennial of the victory of Ayacucho is to celebrate, in fact, the centennial of the victory of the imagination. The sensible reality, evident reality, in the time of the independence revolution was certainly not republican or nationalist. The value of the liberators consists in seeing a potential reality, a higher reality, an imaginary reality.

This is the story of all great human events. Progress has always been made by imaginative people. Posterity has invariably accepted their work. The conservatism of a later era has never had more defenders, more proselytizers than a few quirky romantics. Humanity, with rare exceptions, estimates and studies the men of the French Revolution much more than those of the monarchy and feudalism they defeated. Louis XVI and Marie Antoinette seemed to many people, above all, as unfortunate. No one sees them as great.

On the other hand, imagination is generally less free and arbitrary than is often assumed. The poor have been very much maligned and distorted. Some believe them to be more or less crazy; others see them as limitless and infinitely so. In fact, imagination is quite modest. As with all human things, imagination has its limits. All people, from the most brilliant to the most idiotic, are conditioned by circumstances of time and space. The human spirit reacts against contingent reality. But just when one reacts against truth, is when one is more dependent on it. People struggle to change what they see and what they feel, not what they ignore. Later, the only utopias that are valid are those that could be called realistic. Those utopias are born out of the same entrails as reality. Georg Simmel[3] once wrote that a collectivist society is moving toward ideals of individualism, and conversely, an individualistic society is moving toward socialist ideals. Hegelian philosophy explains the creative force of an ideal as a result, at the same time, of the resistance and impulse that it found in reality. One could say that people do not foresee or imagine more than that which is already germinating, maturing in the dark entrails of history.

Idealists need to rely on the concrete interests of a broad and conscious social strata. The ideal will not prosper unless it incorporates broad interests. It needs to acquire, in short, useful and convenient characteristics. A class needs to become an instrument of its realization.

In our time, in our civilization, utopias have never been too daring. Modern people have almost always predicted progress. Even the fantasies of novelists many times have been overtaken by reality in a short period of time. Western science has gone faster than what Jules Verne dreamed.[4] The same has happened in politics. Anatole France predicted the Russian Revolution for the end of this century, and a few years later the revolution opened a new chapter in the history of the world.[5]

Anatole France used omens to predict the future in his novel *The White Stone*.[6] He shows how culture and wisdom confer no privileged power over the imagination. Galion, his character in an episode of Roman decadence, was exemplary as a cultured and wise man of his time. This man, however, was completely unaware of the decline of his civilization. Christianity seemed to him to be an absurd and stupid sect. Roman civilization, in his view, could not sink, could not perish. Galion conceived of the future as a mere extension of the present. For this reason, we find his speeches ridiculously sad and lacking in inspiration. He was a very intelligent, very knowledgeable, very refined man, but he had the great misfortune not to be an imaginative man. Hence his attitude toward life was mediocre and conservative.

This thesis about imagination, conservatism, and progress could lead to very interesting and original conclusions. Conclusions could move us, for example, not to categorize people as revolutionaries and conservatives, but as those who are imaginative and those who are not. Distinguishing them as such means perhaps committing the injustice of flattering the vanity of the revolutionaries and, ultimately and with respect, offending a bit the vanity of the conservatives. In addition to academic intelligence and methods, the new classification will seem rather arbitrary, quite unusual. But obviously it is very boring to always classify and qualify people in the same way. And above all, if humanity has not yet found a new name for conservatives and revolutionaries it is also, undoubtedly, due to a lack of imagination.

—*Mundial*, Lima, 12 December 1924

### NOTES

Source: "La imaginación y el progreso," in *El alma matinal y otras estaciones del hombre de hoy*, in *Obras Completas*, 10th ed. (Lima: Biblioteca Amauta, 1987), 3:44–47.

1.   Luis Araquistáin (1886–1959) was a Spanish socialist and political leader. Mariátegui may here be citing from his *Vida y resurrección* (Madrid, 1922).
2.   Oscar Wilde, *The Soul of Man under Socialism* (Boston: John W. Luce, 1910).
3.   Georg Simmel (March 1, 1858–September 28, 1918) was a pioneering German sociologist.
4.   Jules Verne (February 8, 1828–March 24, 1905) helped pioneer the science-fiction genre with novels such as *Twenty Thousand Leagues under the Sea* (1869–1870) and *Around the World in Eighty Days* (1873).
5.   Anatole France (1844–1924) was a French poet, journalist, and novelist.
6.   Anatole France, *The White Stone* (London, New York: John Lane, 1910).

PART VIII

*Aesthetics*

. . .

JOSÉ CARLOS MARIÁTEGUI WAS NOT NARROW, rigid, or dogmatic, nor were his interests limited to one area of human endeavor. He had transcended the small town where he was born, another town at the foothills of the Andes where he was raised, and had also transcended the traditionalism and conservatism of Lima, the city where he came of age. He read widely from a young age, and perused a wide variety of works and articles in Spanish, Italian, and French throughout his life. He experienced the fullness of the world through literature, cinema, theater, travel, living with the masses and rubbing shoulders with workers, revolutionaries, and societal and political elites as he worked as a journalist and militant, and as he lived as an expatriate in Europe. Although he is best known for his social and economic analysis, he was equally interested in literature, art, cinema, and even literary criticism. The whole world of ideas was his, and aesthetics were of great importance. In his famous "Presentation" of *Amauta*, Mariátegui indicated the breadth of his interests: "We will study all the great movements of political, philosophical, artistic, literary and scientific renovation. All that is human is ours."[1] As he wrote in "Literature on Trial" in *Seven Essays*, "Man's spirit is indivisible and it must be so to achieve plenitude and harmony. I declare without hesitation that I bring to literary exegesis all my political passions and ideas, although in view of the way this word has been misused, I should add that my politics are philosophy and religion." Mariátegui adds, "This does not mean to say that I consider the literary or artistic phenomenon from extra-aesthetic points of view, but that my aesthetic conception is united, in the intimacy of my conscience, with my moral, political and religious conceptions, and that, without ceasing to be strictly aesthetic conceptions, I cannot operate independently or differently from them." Indeed, earlier in that essay he advised the reader that his writing was informed by a point of view: "My criticism renounces any pretense of impartiality, agnosticism—if indeed any criticism can be so—which I absolutely do not believe. All criticism is informed by philosophical, political, and moral concerns."[2]

Mariátegui also appreciated art in its purest forms. This is reflected in his laudatory treatment of the "pure poetry" of the Peruvian José María Eguren, who writes innocent of any political, social, or class affiliation.[3] In a 1929 introductory essay to a number of his poems in *Amauta*, Eguren writes of poetry: "The line is emotion and beauty: simple and paradoxical. It is happy when it is ascending and it suffers when it turns and inclines downward. The line is the form that contains the spirit."[4] In a special section dedicated to the reconsideration of his friend Eguren, Mariátegui writes: "To his brilliant gift for creation, Eguren always unites the purity of a poetic life. He never profited from his verses; he did not demand official or academic laurels for them. It is difficult in Peru to be so true to a vocation and a destiny. Knowing this, Eguren seems to us even more exemplary and unique." Mariátegui further notes that "the evasion of reality has kept him pure. Much like a child, he has maintained his poetic innocence intact."[5]

This issue of *Amauta* and those that followed in 1929 contained Mariátegui's essays on "The Defense of Marxism," essays by Lenin and Marx (a critical essay on Kant, and an essay on Spartacus, respectively), and by Rosa Luxemburg, Peruvian and world art criticism and even images from Peruvian *matés*, the famous hand-carved, decorated dried gourds. Equally significant for understanding Mariátegui's aesthetics is not only his criticism of the art and literature linked to bourgeois interest and taste, but his appreciation for the self-effacing cinema of Charlie Chaplin. Like many intellectuals, he wrote in the Marxist tradition, before Stalin's narrow aesthetic vision circumscribed it—and here we think not only of luminaries such as Rosa Luxemburg or Leon Trotsky but also socialist, nay Marxist-Leninist, thinkers such as Henri Barbusse of France, the Hungarian Georg Lukács, and Antonio Gramsci.

NOTES

1. "Presentación de *Amauta*," *Ideología y Política*, in *Obras Completas*, 18th ed. (Lima: Editorial Amauta, 1988), 13:239.
2. José Carlos Mariátegui, *7 ensayos de interpretación de la realidad peruana* (Lima: Editorial Amauta, 1967), 182.
3. See Mariátegui's extensive and highly favorable treatment of Eguren in the essay on literature in *7 ensayos*.
4. José María Eguren, "Linea. Forma. Creacionismo." *Amauta* 28 (January 1930): 1.
5. José Carlos Mariátegui, "Poesía y verdad, preludio del renacimiento de José María Eguren," *Amauta*, (February–March 1929): 11.

# 1—Maxim Gorky and Russia

Maxim Gorky is the novelist of the vagabonds, the pariahs, those who are miserable. He is the novelist of the lower depths, of lives gone wrong, of hunger. Gorky's work is a special, spontaneous representative of this century of the masses, the Fourth Estate, and the social revolution. Many contemporary artists draw themes and characters from the plebeian strata, the lower classes. The bourgeois soul and passions are somewhat out of date. They are overexplored. In the proletarian soul and passions, on the other hand, new shades of meaning and unusual threads of inquiry can be found.

The plebeian of Gorky's novels and dramas is not the Western plebeian. But he is authentically the Russian plebeian. And Gorky is not just a narrator of the Russian romance, but one of its protagonists. He did not make the Russian Revolution, he has lived it. He has been one of its critics, one of its chroniclers, and one of its actors.

Gorky has never been a Bolshevik. Intellectuals and artists habitually lack the necessary faith to enroll themselves as factional, disciplined, and sectarian members of a party. They tend toward a personal, particular, and arbitrary attitude in life. Gorky, meandering, disquiet, and heterodox, has not rigidly followed any program or political confession. In the early days of the revolution, he published a revolutionary socialist daily, *Novaia Zhizn*. This paper regarded the Soviet regime with distrust and enmity. It accused the Bolsheviks of being theoreticians and utopians. Gorky wrote that the Bolsheviks were carrying out an experiment useful to humanity, but mortal for Russia. But the source of Gorky's resistance was more recondite, intimate, and spiritual. It was a state of mind, a basic counterrevolutionary spirit common to the majority of intellectuals. The revolution watched and treated them as latent enemies. And they became ill- humored that the revolution, so boisterous, so impetuous, so explosive, discourteously disturbed their dreams, research, and discourse. Some persisted in this state of mind. Others were infected and inflamed by revolutionary faith. Gorky, for example, did not take long in moving closer to the revolution. The Soviets charged him with the organization and directorship of the House of Intellectuals. This institution, chosen to safeguard Russian culture from the revolutionary tide, sheltered, nourished, and provisioned Russia's men of science and culture with the rudiments of research and labor. Gorky, given over to the protection of Russia's scholars and artists, thereby became one of the essential collaborators of Lunacharsky, the Commissar of Public Education.

Days of drought and scarcity came to the Volga region. An unexpected poor harvest totally impoverished various provinces already weakened and emaciated by long years of war and blockade. Many millions of people were left without bread for the winter. Gorky felt his duty was to move, to arouse humanity about this immense tragedy. He sought the collaboration of Anatole France, Gerard Hauptmann, George Bernard Shaw, and other great artists. He left Russia, now more distant and alien than ever, to tell Europe of it firsthand. But he was no longer the vigorous vagabond, the robust nomad, of earlier times. His old case of tuberculosis attacked him along the way and forced him to stop in Germany and take shelter in a sanatorium. A great European, the explorer and sage [Fridtjof] Nansen, crisscrossed Europe demanding help for the famished provinces. Nansen spoke in London, in Paris, in Rome. With the guarantee of his indubitable and apolitical position, he stated that this was not communism's responsibility, but a scourge, a cataclysm, a misfortune. Russia, blockaded and isolated, could not rescue all its starving people. There was no time to lose. The winter was approaching. Not to not aid the hungry immediately was to condemn them to death. Many generous spirits responded to this call. The working masses gave their coins. But the moment was not propitious for charity and philanthropy. The atmosphere in the West was too charged with rancor and anger against Russia. The major European press gave Nansen's campaign a disinterested response. The European states, insensitive, poisoned by emotion, were not dismayed by Russia's affliction. Help was not given in proportion to its magnitude. Some millions were saved, but other millions perished. Gorky, despondent over this tragedy, cursed Europe's cruelty and prophesied the end of European civilization. The world, he said, had just witnessed a weakening of the moral sensibility of Europe. This weakening is a symptom of the decline and degeneration of the Western world. European civilization had not only been respected for its technical and material wealth, but also for its moral wealth. Both had given it authority and prestige before the East. Once in decline, nothing could defend European civilization from the assaults of barbarism.

Gorky hears a subconscious, internal voice announcing the ruin of Europe. This same voice tells him the peasant is an implacable and fatal enemy of the Russian Revolution. The revolution is the work of the urban working class and a socialist ideology that is essentially urban. The peasants supported the revolution because it gave them land. But other sections of its program are not equally intelligible to agrarian minds and interests. Gorky despairs that the egoist and sordid peasant psychology cannot assimilate itself to the ideology of the urban worker. The city is the center, the home, of civilization and its creations. The city is civilization itself. The psychology of the city person is more altruistic and disinterested than the psychology of the country person. This can be observed not only among the peasant masses, but also among the peasant aristocracy. The temperament of the agrarian *latifundista* is much less elastic, active, and comprehensive than that of the industrial *latifundista*. The rural magnates are always on the extreme right; the magnates of finance and industry prefer a centrist position and tend to make agreements and compromises with the revolution. The city adapts humanity to collectivism, the country savagely stimulates their individualism. And because of this, the final battle between individualism and socialism could perhaps break out between the city and the country.

Various European statesmen share Gorky's preoccupation. Caillaux,[1] for example, looks with disquiet and apprehension at the tendency of the peasants of Central Europe to free themselves from urban industrialism. Rural, small-scale industry is on the rise in Hungary. Peasants are again spinning their own wool and forging their own tools. They are attempting to resurrect a medieval, primitive economy. Gorky's intuition and vision coincide with the certainty, the verification, of men of science.

I spoke of this and other things with Gorky in December of 1922 in the Neue Sanatorium in Saarow Ost, Germany. His quarters were closed to all extraneous and unexpected visitors. But Maria Feodorowna, Gorky's wife, opened their doors to me. Gorky speaks only Russian. Maria Feodorowna speaks German, French, English, and Italian.

At that time, Gorky was writing the third volume of his autobiography and beginning a book about Russians.

"Russian people?"

"Yes. People I saw in Russia, people I have known—not famous people, but interesting ones."

I questioned Gorky about his relationship with Bolshevism. Some newspapers claimed that Gorky was distancing himself from its leaders. Gorky denied the story. He intended to return to Russia soon. His relations with the Soviets were good, normal.

There is something of the old vagabond, the old pilgrim, in Gorky: his sharp eyes, his rustic hands, his body a bit doubled over, his Tatar mustache. Gorky is not physically a metropolitan man; rather, he is a rural and peasant type. Yet, unlike Tolstoy, he does not have a patriarchal and Asian soul. Tolstoy preached a peasant and Christian communism. Gorky admires, loves, and respects Western machinery, technology, and science, all those things that Tolstoy's mysticism found

repugnant. This Slav, this vagabond, is secretly and subconsciously a
devotee, a supporter, a lover of the West and its civilization.

And under the lindens of Saarow Ost, where neither the rumors of
communist revolution nor the chants of fascist reaction arrive, his sick
and hallucinating eyes saw with anguish the coming twilight and death
of a marvelous civilization.

## NOTES

Source: "Maximo Gorki y Rusia," in *La escena contemporanea*, in *Obras
Completas*, 4th ed. (Lima: Editorial Amauta, 1970), 1:173–77.

1.    Joseph-Marie-Auguste Caillaux, a major French politician of the time, was
      leader of the Radical Party.

# 2—A Balance Sheet on Surrealism

None of the vanguard literary and artistic movements of Western Europe had, contrary to what appearances suggest, the significance or historical content of Surrealism. Other movements were limited to the affirmation of some aesthetic postulates, to experimentation with some artistic principles.

The Futurist Italian was, without doubt, certainly an exception to the rule. Marinetti[1] and his henchmen intended to represent not only artistically, but also politically and sentimentally, a new Italy. But the Futurist, when viewed from a distance, makes us smile this side of his histrionic megalomania; perhaps more than any other he has entered the "order" and the academy: Fascism has digested him effortlessly, which does not credit the assimilative power of the Black Shirts' regime, but rather the innocence of the Futurists. Futurism has also, to some extent, the virtue of persistence. But, in this respect, the Futurist's was a case of longevity, not continuity or development. In each recurrence, one recognizes the old prewar Futurism. The wig, makeup, tricks, did not prevent one from noticing the cracked voice, the mechanized gestures. Marinetti, unable to obtain a continuous, dialectic presence of Futurism in Italian literature and Italian history, saves it from being forgotten through noisy *rentrées*. Futurism, in the end, was certainly flawed by its so-Italian affinity for the spectacular, the histrionic, and perhaps that would be the excuse an honest critical review could concede, condemning Marinetti to a life behind the proscenium, in an entrancing, fictional, declamatory role. The fact that one cannot speak of Futurism without the use of theatrical terminology confirms this dominant feature of its character.

Surrealism has another kind of life. It is truly a *movimiento*, an *experiencia*. It is not where they left it two years ago, for example, when those watching it hoped that it would fade or be pacified. Anyone who imagines understanding Surrealism with a formula, or a definition of one of its stages, does not know it. Even at its inception, Surrealism was distinguished from other trends and artistic and literary programs. Not born perfectly assembled and perfect in the head of its inventors, it has been a process. Dada is the name of its childhood. If we follow its development carefully, one may discover a crisis of puberty. Upon reaching adulthood, it has felt its political, civil duties, and has enrolled in a party; it has joined a doctrine.

And, at this level, Surrealism has behaved very differently from Futurism. Instead of launching a program of political Surrealism, it accepts and supports the specific program of the concrete, current revolution: the Marxist program of proletarian revolution. It does not occur to Surrealism to subordinate politics to artistic rules and taste. Just as in the fields of physics, there is no objection to the data of science; in the realms of politics and economics it is deemed puerile and absurd to attempt original speculation based on artistic data. The Surrealists did not exercise their right to nonsense, absolute subjectivism, except in art; in all other respects they behave wisely and this is another thing that sets them apart from the scandalous variety of romantic and revolutionary precedents in the history of literature.

But Surrealists do not reject anything as much as voluntarily limiting themselves to pure artistic speculation. Autonomy of art, yes, but not the closure of art. Nothing is stranger to them than the formula of art for art's sake. The artist who, at any given time, does not comply with the duty of throwing a *flic*[2] by M. Tardieu into the Seine, or to interrupt a speech by Briand,[3] is a poor devil. Surrealism denies the

VIII.2—A BALANCE SHEET ON SURREALISM

right to rely on aesthetics to not feel the repugnant, that which is hateful from Mr. Chiappe's work,[4] or of the oral anesthetics of pacifism of the United States of Europe. There have been some dissidents, some defections from the original conception of the unity of man and artist. Noting the departure of Robert Desnos,[5] who at one time made numerous contributions to the notebooks of *La Révolution Surréaliste*, André Breton says, "He thought he could indulge with impunity in one of the most dangerous activities, journalism, and accordingly not respond to a small number of serious demands that Surrealism confronted as it advanced: Marxism or anti-Marxism, for example."[6]

It will be hard and perhaps impossible for those in this tropical America who imagine Surrealism as licentiousness to admit this affirmation: that it is a difficult, painful discipline. I can temper it, moderate it, replace it with a scrupulous definition: that is the difficult, painful search for a discipline. But I absolutely insist on the rare quality—unavailable and forbidden to snobbery, to simulation—of the experience and work of Surrealism.

*La Révolution Surréaliste* has reached its twelfth number and its fifth year. An evaluation of some of its operations opens issue 12; André Breton titles it: "Second Manifesto of Surrealism."

Before commenting on this manifesto[7] I wanted to establish in a few paragraphs the scope and value of Surrealism, a movement I have followed with attention, reflected more than once, not just episodically, in my articles. This attention, nourished by sympathy and hope, ensures the loyalty of what I write, arguing with the Surrealist text and intentions. About issue 12, I would add that its text and tone confirm the nature of the Surrealism experience and the magazine that displays and translates it. An issue of *La Révolution Surréaliste* is almost always an examination of conscience, a new question, a risky attempt. Each number accuses a new grouping of forces. The editing of the magazine, in its functional or personal sense, changed several times until it was taken over by André Breton, who gave it continuity. Such a magazine could not have an exact regularity in its publication. All expressions must be true to the troubled, dangerous, challenging line of its research and experiments. . . .

André Breton, in the "Second Manifesto of Surrealism," puts the writers and artists who have participated in this movement but have more or less openly reneged, on trial. In this respect, the manifesto is something of an indictment, and violent reactions have not been slow in coming, brought against the author and his cohorts. But in this indictment there is the least possible of the personal. The process of apostasy and defection tends, especially in this polemic piece, to insist on the difficult and courageous spiritual and artistic discipline that the Surrealism experience brings. Breton writes:

> It is noteworthy, moreover, that when they are left to their own devices, and to nothing else, they have been immediately forced to resort to the most miserable expedients in order to reingratiate themselves with the defenders of *law and order*, all proud partisans of leveling via the head. This is because unflagging fidelity to the commitments of Surrealism presupposes a disinterestedness, a contempt for risk, a refusal to compromise, of which very few men prove in the long run to be capable. Were there to remain not a single one, from among all those who were the first to measure by its standards their chance for significance and desire for truth, Surrealism would continue to live.[8]

Breton barely mentions the notorious and former dissidents in this manifesto but, in contrast, rigorously examines the behavior of those who have strayed from Surrealism in recent times. He is extreme in his personal aggression against Pierre Naville, who so strongly stood out, next to Marcel Fourrier, in the liquidation of *Clarté* and its replacement by *La Lutte des Classes*. Naville is presented as the upstart son of a millionaire banker in a desperate search for fame, and whom the demon of ambition has guided on his journey, from editing the Surrealist magazine to *La Lutte des Classes*, *La Venté*, and the Trotskyite opposition.

In Naville I think there is something much more serious. And I do not exclude the possibility that Breton would reconcile with him—if Naville corresponds to my own hope—with the same nobility that, after a long quarrel, he recognized Tristan Tzara's daring effort and strenuous work.

The same honesty, the same scruples, lead us into the balance of surrealism, stating:

> More than anything else, Surrealism attempted to provoke from the intellectual and moral point of view, *an attack of conscience*, of the most general and serious kind, and that the extent to which this was or was not accomplished can alone determine its historical success or failure.[9]

Breton says:

> From the intellectual point of view, it was then, and still is today, a question of testing by any and all means, and of demonstrating at any price, the meretricious nature of the old antinomies hypocritically intended to prevent any unusual ferment on the part of man, were it only by giving him a vague idea of the means at his disposal, by challenging him to escape to some meaningful degree from the universal fetters.[10]

It is not possible to justly approve—for the very reasons that one accepts this definition, to specifying Surrealism as experiential in the phrases that follow:

> Everything tends to make us believe that there exists a certain point of the mind at which life and death, the real and the imagined, past and future, the communicable and the incommunicable, high and low, cease to be perceived as contradictions. Now, search as one may, one will never find any other motivating force in the activities of the Surrealists than the hope of finding and fixing this point.[11]

The spirit and the program of Surrealism are not expressed in these or other ambitious phrases of ultraist and *epatante* [astounding] intention. Perhaps the best passage of the manifesto is one which, with

JOSÉ CARLOS MARIÁTEGUI: AN ANTHOLOGY

a historical sense of Romanticism, is a thousand times more clear than the often banal inquiries of the erudite scholars of the Romanticism-Classicism question. André Breton affirms the Romantic affiliation of the Surrealist revolution:

> But, at a time in history when the officials in France are getting ready to celebrate grotesquely the hundredth anniversary of Romanticism with public ceremonies, we say, and insist on saying, that this Romanticism which we are today willing to consider as the tail, *but only then as an amazing prehensile tail,* by its very essence remains unmitigated in its negation of these officials and these ceremonies, and we say that to be a hundred is for it to be still in the flower of youth, that what has been wrongly called its heroic period can no longer honestly be considered as anything but the first cry of a newborn child which is only beginning to make its desires known through us, and which, if one is willing to admit that what was thought "Classical" before it came into being was tantamount to good, undeniably wishes *naught but evil.*[12]

But phrases with a Dadaist flavor are not lacking in the manifesto, in passages such as "I ask for the profound, veritable occultation of Surrealism," "no concession to the world," etc.—an infantile intonation that is no longer possible to excuse, given the experience and research that have given the movement its historical moment.

—*Variedades*, Lima, 19 February and 5 March 1930

## NOTES

Source: "El Balance de Suprarealismo," in *El Artista y la Época*, in *Obras Completas*, 12th ed. (Lima: Biblioteca Amauta, 1987), 6:45–56.

1.	Filippo Tommaso Emilio Marinetti (December 22, 1876–December 2, 1944) was an Italian poet, initiator of the Futurist artistic style, and a Fascist activist.
2.	A Parisian nickname for the police.

3. Aristide Briand (March 28, 1862–March 7, 1932) was a prime minister of France during the Third Republic.

4. Jean Baptiste Pascal Eugène Chiappe (May 3, 1878–November 27, 1940) was a conservative French civil servant.

5. Robert Desnos (July 4, 1900–June 8, 1945) was a French surrealist poet.

6. See André Breton, *Manifestos of Surrealism,* trans. Richard Seaver and Helen R. Lane (Ann Arbor: University of Michigan Press, 1969), 65. Andre Breton's influence was wide and left an impact on psychoanalysis and feminism through Jacques Lacan, on politics via Herbert Marcuse, and on criticism through Roland Barthes.

7. André Breton, "Second Surrealist Manifesto," *La Révolution surréaliste* 12 (December 15, 1929). Mariátegui promised the readers of *Variedades* his comments on this Manifesto and on *Introduction 1930* that Louis Aragon published in the same issue, but he died before he was able to do so.

8. Ibid., 129.

9. Ibid., 123.

10. Ibid.

11. Ibid., 123–24.

12. Ibid., 153.

# 3—Art, Revolution, and Decadence

It is convenient to hasten the elimination of a mistake that disorients some young artists. To correct certain hasty definitions, it should be established that not all new art is revolutionary, nor is it really new. Two spirits coexist in the modern world, that of revolution and that of decadence. Only the presence of the first gives a poem or painting value as new art.

We cannot accept as new any art that merely brings us a new technique. This would mean amusing ourselves with one of the most fallacious modern illusions. No aesthetic can reduce artistic work to a question of technique. New technique should also correspond to a new spirit. If not, the only things that change are the parameters, the decorations. And an artistic revolution does not content itself with formal conquests.

Distinguishing between these two contemporaneous categories of artists is not easy. Decadence and revolution, as they coexist in the same world, also coexist in some individuals. The artist's consciousness is the agonistic circle of struggle between these two spirits. The understanding of this struggle almost always escapes the artists themselves. But in the end, one of the two spirits prevails. The other is left strangled in the arena.

The decline of capitalist civilization is reflected in the atomization, the dissolution, of its art. Art has, above all, lost its essential unity in this crisis. Every one of its principles, every one of its elements, has demanded autonomy. Secession is art's most characteristic result. Schools multiply infinitely, because only centrifugal forces are at work.

But this anarchy in which the spirit of bourgeois art is dying, irreparably split and divided, is the prelude and preparation for a new order. It is the passage from the darkness on one side of the mountain to dawn. In this crisis, the elements of the art of the future are being elaborated. Cubism, Dadaism, Expressionism, etc.—as these announce a crisis, they also announce a reconstruction. Separately, each movement does not bring a formula, but together they all contribute to its construction, each bringing an element, a value, a principle.

The revolutionary aspect of these contemporary schools or tendencies does not lie in their creation of a new technique. Nor is it the destruction of the old technique. It is the repudiation, the removal, the mockery of the bourgeois absolute. Consciously or not, art is always nourished by the absolute of an epoch. The contemporary artist, in most cases, has an empty soul. The literature of decadence is a literature without an absolute. But one can only take a few steps in this way. Humanity cannot advance without a faith, because to lack faith is to lack a goal. To proceed without a faith is to skate in place. The artist who most desperately considers himself the most skeptical and nihilistic is generally the one most desperately in need of a myth.

The Russian Futurists have affiliated with communism; the Italian Futurists have affiliated with Fascism. What better historical demonstration that artists cannot escape the pull of politics? Massimo Bontempelli[1] says that in 1920 he felt himself nearly a communist, and in 1923, the year of the March on Rome, felt himself nearly a Fascist. Now he seems all Fascist. Many have mocked Bontempelli for this confession. I defend it; I find it sincere. The empty soul of poor Bontempelli had to adopt and accept the myth that Mussolini laid at his altar (the Italian vanguardists are convinced that Fascism is the revolution).

Vicente Huidobro claims that art is independent of politics.[2] The reasoning and motivation of this assertion are so ancient and lacking in reason and motive that I cannot imagine even an ultraist poet holding to it, if one considers the extent to which ultraist poets discourse on politics, economics, and religion. Since for Huidobro politics is exclusively that of the Palais Bourbon,[3] it is clear we can grant his art all the autonomy he desires. But the truth is, as Unamuno says, that for those of us who raise it to the category of a religion, politics is the very plot of history. In Classical eras, or at the height of any order, politics can be simply administration and parliament. In Romantic eras, or in those of crisis, politics occupies the primary dimension of life.

Louis Aragon, André Breton, and their comrades at *La Révolution Surréaliste*—the greatest spirits of the French vanguard—proclaim this with their actions on their march toward communism. Drieu La Rochelle, who was so near to this mood when writing *Mesure de la France* and *Plainte contre inconnu*, has been unable to follow them. But, as he has been also unable to escape from politics, he has declared himself to be vaguely Fascist and clearly reactionary.

In the Hispanic world, Ortega y Gasset is partially responsible for this error about the new art. He did not distinguish between schools or tendencies, and at least in modern art, did not distinguish the revolutionary elements from the decadent elements. The author of *The Dehumanization of Art* did not give us a definition of the new art. But he took characteristics that typically correspond as much to decadence as those of a revolution. This led him to claim, among other things, that "the new inspiration is always, unfailingly, cosmic." His picture of the symptoms is generally correct, but his diagnosis is incomplete and wrong.

Procedure is not enough. Technique is not enough. Paul Morand, despite his imagery and modernity, is a product of decadence.[4] One breathes an atmosphere of dissolution in his writing. Jean Cocteau, after having flirted for a time with Dadaism, now leaves us with his *Call to Order*.[5] We should illuminate the issue until the last ambiguity vanishes. It is a difficult job. It takes a lot of work to understand many points. Images of decadence are often present in vanguard art until it sets truly revolutionary goals, overcoming the subjectivism that weakens art at times. Hidalgo, situating Lenin in a poem of many dimensions, says that "Salome breasts" and "boyish hair" are the first steps toward the socialization of women. And this should not be surprising. There are poets who think the jazz band is a herald of the revolution.

Fortunately, there are still artists like George Bernard Shaw who are able to understand that "art has never been great when it has not facilitated an iconography for a living religion, and it has only been fully abject when imitating this iconography after the religion has become a superstition." This latter path seems to be the one that various new artists have taken in French and other literatures. The future will laugh at the silly stupidity with which some critics of their era called them "new" and even "revolutionary."

*—Amauta*, November 1926

### NOTES

Source: *El Artista y la Epoca,* in *Obras Completas*, 2nd ed. (Lima: Editorial Amauta, 1964), 6:18–21.

1.    Massimo Bontempelli (1878–1960), Italian writer and poet.
2.    Vicente Huidobro (January 10, 1893–January 2, 1948) was a Chilean poet.
3.    The Palais Bourbon was the palace where the Chamber of Deputies met in France.
4.    Paul Morand (March 13, 1888–July 24, 1976) was a French diplomat, novelist, playwright and poet.
5.    Jean Cocteau (July 5, 1889–October 11, 1963) was a French poet.

# 4—*Cement* and Proletarian Realism

## I.

I have repeatedly heard that reading Fedor Gladkov's novel *Cement* is not edifying or encouraging for those outside the revolutionary ranks looking for the image of the proletarian revolution. According to this view, the spiritual adventures and moral conflicts Gladkov describes are not apt to feed the illusions of the hesitant and wondrous souls who dream of a rosewater revolution. The residue of an ecclesiastical family education based on the ineffable beatitudes and myths of the kingdom of heaven and the promised land reverberates a lot more in their subconscious than these comrades can imagine.

First, it should be noted that *Cement* is not a work of propaganda. It is a realist novel in which Gladkov has absolutely not proposed the seduction of those, near or far from Russia, who hope the revolution would show its smiling face so that they could decide to follow it. Bourgeois pseudo-realism, including that of Zola, has accustomed readers to a certain idealization of characters representing goodness and virtue. In the end, bourgeois realism in literature does not renounce the spirit of Romanticism against which it seemed to react as irreconcilable and antagonistic. Its innovation was a procedural innovation, of decor, of dress. The bourgeoisie in history, philosophy, politics that has refused to be realistic clings to its habit and its principle of idealizing or disguising its motives and cannot be realistic in literature. True realism comes with the proletarian revolution when, in the language of literary criticism, the term "realism" and the artistic category it connotes are so discredited that there is  an urgent need to counter with the terms "surrealism," "infrarealists," etc. The rejection of Marxism, similar in origin and process, and the rejection of Freudianism, as noted by Max Eastman in *The Science of Revolution*— which is so wrong in other respects—is for the bourgeoisie a logical, instinctive attitude that does not allow its literature the consciousness to free itself from the tendency to idealize characters, conflicts, and outcomes. The serial in literature and cinema obeys this tendency that strives to maintain the hope of the petite bourgeoisie and the proletariat in a final bliss won through resignation rather than struggle. The Yankee cinema has led this optimistic and rosy petit-bourgeois pedagogy to its most extreme and powerful industrialization. But the materialist conception of history had to cause the abandonment and repudiation of these wretched recipes in literature. Proletarian literature tends naturally to realism, such as is the case in socialist politics, historiography, and philosophy.

*Cement* belongs to this new literature, which in Russia has precursors in Tolstoy and Gorky. Gladkov has not been emancipated from the most mesocratic taste for newspaper and magazine serials that brings a robust painting of the revolution where another would have worried about softening its colors and lines for reasons of propaganda and idealization. The truth and the power of his novel—artistic, aesthetic, and human truth—lie precisely in its stringent effort to forge a revolutionary heroic expression of what Sorel called "the sublimely proletarian," without omitting any of the failures, disappointments, or spiritual tears through which this heroism prevails. The revolution is not an idyllic apotheosis of Renaissance angels, but a terrible and painful battle of one class to create a new order. No revolution, neither of Christianity nor of the Reformation, nor of the bourgeoisie, is fulfilled without tragedy. The socialist revolution, which moves men into battle without otherworldly promises, urging their extreme and unconditional commitment, cannot be an exception to this inexorable law of history. The anesthetic, paradise-like revolution has yet to be invented and it is indispensable to say that man will never reach the top of his new creation except through a difficult and painful effort in which pain and joy are equal in intensity. Gleb, the worker in *Cement*, would not be the hero he is if fate saved him from sacrifice. The hero always arrives at his objective, bloody and torn, and only at this price does he reach the fullness of his heroism. The revolution had to test in the extreme Gleb's soul, senses, and instincts. A sweet haven, his wife, his home, his daughter, his bed, his clean clothes could not wait for him, secured against storms. And Dasha, for serious Dasha, whom we know in *Cement*, should in turn overcome the most terrible trials. For the revolution to take control over her completely and ruthlessly could only make Dasha a hard and strong militant. And in this process the wife, the mother, the housewife had to succumb; everything, absolutely everything had to be sacrificed to the revolution. It is absurd, childish, to want a heroine like Dasha, human, very human, but before receiving justice as a revolutionary, it requires a certificate of marital fidelity. Dasha, under the rigor of civil war, knows all the world of danger, all degrees of distress. She sees her comrades whipped, tortured, shot; she herself only escapes death by chance; on two occasions she experiences preparations for her own execution. In the tension of this struggle, waged while Gleb is far away in battle, Dasha is outside of any code of sexual morality: she is only a militant and should only be held accountable as such. Her extramarital love has no sinful pleasure. Dasha fleetingly and sadly loves the soldier for her cause who goes off to battle, who may not come back, who needs his lover's touch as a ration of joy and pleasure in his stark, icy daily labor. She always resists Badyn, the man to whom all the women give in and who wants her like no other. And when she gives in to him—after a day in which the two have been about to perish at the hands of the Cossacks as they complete a risky mission, and Dasha has a noose around her neck, already strung from a tree on the road, and thus she feels the spasm of strangulation—it is because, for an instant, both life and death have united for a moment stronger than themselves.

## II.

*Cement* by Fedor Gladkov and *Manhattan Transfer* by John Dos Passos, a Russian book and a Yankee book. Life in the U.S.S.R. is contrasted to life in the U.S.A. (The two super-states of current history, alike and opposed to each other as large enterprises are too big to be expressed in a word, so they use an abbreviated name, their initials.) (See Luc Durtain's *L'autre Europe.*) *Cement* and *Manhattan Transfer* appear outside the petit-bourgeois panorama of those in Hispanic America who, daily reciting the vanguard creed, reduce the new literature to a Western European scenario, with the boundaries formed by Cocteau, Morand, Gómez de la Serna, Bontempelli, etc. Without any doubt, this confirms that they come from the poles of the modern world.

Spain and Hispanic America do not obey the taste of the petit-bourgeois vanguardists. Among its instinctive predilection is that of the new Russian literature. And from now on we can predict that *Cement* will soon reach the same circulation as Tolstoy, Dostoevsky, Gorky.

Gladkov's novel is better than those that have preceded it in translation, in that it reveals like no other the revolution itself. Some novelists of the revolution move in a world outside it. They know its reflexes, but not its conscience. Pilnyak, Zotschenko, even Leonov and Fedin, described the revolution from outside, foreign to its passion, oblivious to its momentum. Others, such as Ivanov and Babel, discover elements of the revolutionary epic, but their stories are contrary to the bellicose, military aspect of Bolshevik Russia. *The Red Cavalry* and *Armored Train* belong to the chronicle of the campaign. You could say that in the greater part of these works one finds the drama of those who suffer from the revolution, not of those who make it. In *Cement* the characters, the scenery, the feeling, are those of revolution, felt and written from within. There are novels close to it among those already known, but none brings together so naturally and beautifully concentrated the primary elements of individual drama and the massive epic of Bolshevism. . . . [1]

Gladkov, then, is not simply a witness to the revolutionary work done in Russia between 1905 and 1917. During this period, his art matured in a climate of hope and heroic effort. After the days in October he was counted among the authors of the revolution. And later, none of the intimate adventures of Bolshevism escaped him. Therefore, in Gladkov the revolutionary epic is represented by more than the emotions of armed struggle; it is represented by feelings of economic reconstruction, by the vicissitudes and hardships of building a new life.

Tchumalov [Gleb], the protagonist in *Cement,* returns to his village after three years of combat in the Red Army. And his most difficult, most awful battle is the one that awaits him in his village, where the years of danger and war have disorganized everything. Tchumalov finds the large cement factory where, before he fled—repression had chosen as a victim—he had labored as a worker. Goats, pigs, weeds invading the courtyards; stagnate inert machines, and cable cars, which brought down the stone from the quarries lie motionless since the cessation of movement in this factory where thousands of workers once moved. Only the diesels, because of the care by a worker who has remained in place, shine, ready to revive the collapsed pile. Tchumalov does not recognize his home. In the three years Dasha, his wife, has become militant, the cheerleader of the Women's Section, the most tireless worker in the local soviet. Three years of struggle, first beset by ruthless repression, later totally committed to the revolution, have made Dasha a new woman. Niurka, their daughter, is not with her. Dasha had to put her in the House of Children, to whose organization she earnestly contributed. The party has won a hard, energetic, intelligent militant, but Tchumalov has lost his wife. There is no longer a place in Dasha's life for her marital and maternal past; she has entirely sacrificed herself to the revolution. Dasha has an autonomous existence and personality; she is no longer a thing Tchumalov owned nor will she be again. In Tchumalov's absence, she has, under the pressure of inexorable fate, known other men. She has remained intimately honorable, but that shadow comes between her and Tchumalov, a dark presence that torments the jealous male instinct. Tchumalov suffers, but in turn, tightly caught up by the revolution, he cannot let his personal drama monopolize him. He makes it his duty to revive the factory. To win this battle he has to overcome sabotage by technical specialists, the resistance of the bureaucracy, the silent counterrevolutionary backlash. There is a moment when Dasha seems to return to him. But it is only for a moment that their fates come together, to separate once again. Nurka dies. And that breaks the last sentimental link that held them together. After a struggle which reflects the entire process of the reorganization of Russia, all the reconstructive work of the revolution, Tchumalov revives the factory. It is a day of victory for him and the workers, but is also the day when he feels distant, strange, lost forever to Dasha, and left with his angry and brutal jealousy.

In the novel, the conflict between them is intertwined and confused with a multitude of other beings, in horrible tension, in furious agony. Tchumalov's drama is but a fragment of the drama of revolutionary Russia. All the passions, all the impulses, all the pains of the revolution are in this novel. All types of destinies—the most opposed the most intimate, the most diverse—are justified. Gladkov manages to express, in pages of powerful, rugged beauty, the new force, the creative energy, the human wealth of the greatest contemporary event.

NOTES

Source: *El Alma Matinal*, in *Obras Completas*, 4th ed. (Lima: Editorial Amauta, 1970), 3:165–73.

1.    A short biographical section on Gladkov is omitted here.

# 5—On Explaining Chaplin

The theme of Chaplin seems to me, in any explanation of our era, no less significant than that of the themes of Lloyd George or that of [Ramsay] MacDonald (if one looks for equivalents in Great Britain only).[1] Many agree with the assertion by Henri Poulaille that *The Gold Rush* is the best contemporary novel. But always placing Chaplin in his country—I think that in any case the human resonance of *The Gold Rush*[2] largely surpasses Mr. H. G. Wells's *The Outline of History* and Bernard Shaw's theater. This is a fact that Wells and Shaw would surely be the first to recognize. (Shaw exaggerates it in an extremely bizarre way, and Wells attributes something melancholy to the deficiency of secondary education.)

Chaplin's imagination chooses for his works matters no less important than the return of Methuselah or the vindication of Joan of Arc: gold, the circus. And he effectively develops his ideas more artistically: the regulatory-bound intellectualism of the guardians of the aesthetic order will be shocked by this proposition. The success of Chaplin is explained, as are their mental formulas, just as that of Alexander Dumas or Eugene Sue. But without recourse to the reasons for Bontempelli on the novel of intrigue or subscribing to their revaluation of Dumas, this simplistic view is disqualified as soon as one remembers that Chaplin's art is liked, with the same relish, by those with doctorates and by illiterates, by writers, and by boxers. When one speaks of the universality of Chaplin, one is not appealing to popularity. Chaplin has all the votes: majority and minorities. His fame is both rigorously aristocratic and democratic. Chaplin is a true type of elite, for those who do not want to forget that elite means elect.

The search, the seizure of gold, the Gold Rush was the romantic chapter, the bohemian phase of the capitalist epoch. The capitalist epoch begins the instant Europe renounced the theory of gold to look for real gold, the physical gold. The discovery of America is, above all, intimately and essentially attached to its history (Canada and California are major stops in its itinerary). Without doubt, the capitalist revolution was primarily a technological revolution: its first great victory is the machine, its greatest invention financial capital. But capitalism has never managed to free itself from gold, despite the tendency of the productive forces to reduce it to a symbol. Gold has continued to snare its body and its soul. Bourgeois literature, however, has almost totally neglected this theme. In the nineteenth century, only Wagner expresses it in his own grand, allegorical way. The novel about gold appears in our time: *L'Or* by Blaise Cendrars, *Tripes d'Or* by Crommelynk, are two distinct but related specimens of this literature. *The Gold Rush* also belongs legitimately to it. In this case, Chaplin's thought and the images that show it are born of a great contemporary intuition. The creation of a great satire on gold is imminent. It is already anticipated. Chaplin's work grasps something that vividly stirs in the subconscious of the world.

Chaplin incarnates the bohemian in the cinema. Whatever his disguise, we always imagine Chaplin in the vagabond role of Charlot. To attain the deepest and most naked humanity, the purest and most mysterious drama, Chaplin absolutely needs the poverty and hunger, the bohemianism, the romanticism, and the insolvency of the Little Tramp. It is difficult to define the bohemian precisely. Francis of Assisi, Diogenes, and Jesus himself are the sublimation of this spiritual type; Navarro Monzo says that the bohemian is the antithesis of the bourgeois.[3] The Little Tramp is anti-bourgeois par excellence. He is always ready for adventure, for change, for departure. No one imagines him with a savings account. He is a little Don Quixote, God's juggler, humorist, and beggar.

It is thus logical that Chaplin would interest himself in that bohemian and romantic capitalist enterprise, the search for gold. The Little Tramp leaves for Alaska, enrolled in that greedy and miserable phalanx that takes off to discover gold with their own hands in the rugged and snowy mountains. He cannot stay and make it with capitalist cunning in commerce, industry, or the stock market. This was the only way to imagine the Little Tramp getting rich. The ending of *The Gold Rush*—which some find vulgar, because they would prefer the Little Tramp to return to his shirtless bohemia—is absolutely just and accurate. It does not even minimally obey the rationale of Yankee technology.

The whole work is insuperably constructed. The sentimental, erotic element intervenes with mathematical precision, with rigorous artistic and biological necessity. Jim McKay finds the Little Tramp, his old comrade in poverty and vagrancy, at the exact moment the Little Tramp, in romantic tension, decides in a burst of energy to accompany him in search of a huge lost mine. Chaplin, the author, knows that erotic arousal is a propitious state for creation and discovery. Like Don Quixote, the Tramp must fall in love before undertaking his daring voyage. In love, vehemently and bizarrely in love, it is impossible for the Tramp not to find the mine. No power, no accident can stop him. It would not matter if the mine did not exist. It does not matter that Jim McKay, his mind dulled by a blow that erases his memory and makes him lose his way, has misled him. The Little Tramp will surely find the fabulous mine. His pathos gives him surreal powers. The avalanche, the storm, are impotent to defeat him. On the edge of a precipice, he will have abundant energy to fight off death and take an acrobatic leap over it. He must return from this trip a millionaire. And, considering the contradictions in his life, who would be his logical comrade in this victorious adventure? Who but Jim McKay, this ferocious, brutal, imperious gold miner who, mad from hunger in the mountains, one day wanted to kill the Tramp and eat him? McKay has the rigorous and completely perfect constitution for a gold miner. The ravenous, insane ferocity that Chaplin attributes to him is not overblown or a fantasy. McKay could not have been the consummate hero of this story if Chaplin had not portrayed him as having decided, in an extreme case, to eat a comrade. The first duty of a gold miner is to live. His logic is Darwinian and cruelly individualistic.

In this work, then, Chaplin has not only brilliantly seized upon an artistic idea of his time, but has expressed it in strictly scientific psychological terms. *The Gold Rush* confirms Freud. As myth, it descends from the Wagnerian tetralogy. Artistically and spiritually, it transcends the theater of Pirandello and the novels of Proust and Joyce.

The circus is bohemian spectacle, the bohemian art par excellence. On the one hand, the circus has its first and most profound relationship with Chaplin. On the other, the circus and the cinema have a visible bond in the context of their technical and essential autonomy. Despite their distinct manner and style, the circus, like the cinema, is the movement of images. Notwithstanding the effort to make cinema speak, pantomime is at the source of circus art, which is silent par excellence. Chaplin comes out of pantomime, or rather, from the circus. Cinema has killed the theater as bourgeois theater. Theater has been unable to do a thing against the circus. The spirit of the circus— all the living bohemian, romantic, nomadic sense of the circus—has freed Chaplin, the film artist. Bontempelli has summarily dismissed the old, literary, wordy bourgeois theater. The old circus, though, is alive, active, and unchanged. Whereas the theater needs to remake itself by returning to the medieval "mystery," the plastic spectacle, the agonistic or circus techniques, or approximate the cinema with the synthetic action of the movable stage, the circus needs only to continue; it finds all the elements necessary for its development and continuation within its own tradition.

Chaplin's latest film is subconsciously a sentimental return to the circus, to pantomime. Spiritually, it shows much Hollywood-style evasion. It is significant that this has not upset, but rather favored, the finished cinematographic manifestation. I have encountered objections to *The Circus* as an artistic work in a seasoned vanguard journal. I think exactly the opposite. If the cinematographic represents what is artistic in the cinema above all else, Chaplin has hit the target as never before in *The Circus*. *The Circus* is purely and absolutely cinematic. Chaplin in this work has succeeded in expressing himself solely in images. The subtitles are reduced to a minimum. And they could be totally eliminated without losing any of the spectacle's expressed comedic power.

According to the official version of his biography, Chaplin comes from a family of clowns, circus artists. In any event, he himself was a clown in his youth. What power could have taken him from this art, so consonant with his bohemian soul? To me, the attraction of the cinema, of Hollywood, seems neither the only nor the most decisive reason. I prefer historical, economic, and political explanations, and even in this case I think it possible to attempt one that is perhaps more serious than humorous.

The English clown represents the highest degree of evolution of clowns. It is the farthest possible from those quite vicious, excessive, strident Mediterranean clowns we are accustomed to finding in traveling circuses. He is an elegant, measured, mathematical mime who exercises his art with a perfectly Anglican dignity. Great Britain has come to produce this human type as it does the racing or hunting thoroughbred—in conformity with a rigorous and Darwinian principle of selection. The laugh and visage of the clown is an essential classic mark of British life, a cog in the magnificent machine of empire. The clown's art is a ritual, his comicality absolutely serious. The metaphysical and religious Bernard Shaw is, in his country, nothing more than a clown who writes. The clown is not a type, but rather an institution, as respectable as the House of Lords. The clown's art signifies the domestication of the wild and nomadic buffoonery of the bohemian in accord with the taste and needs of a refined capitalist society. Great Britain has done the same thing with the clown's laugh as it has done with the Arabian horse: trained it through capitalist art and zoo technology as a Puritan recreation for the Manchester and London bourgeoisie. The clown notably illustrates the evolution of the species.

No clown emerging in the era of a persistent and regular British ascendancy, not even the great genius Chaplin, could have deserted

his art. The discipline of the tradition, the mechanics of its undis-
turbed and unshaken customs, would have been enough to automatically inhibit any impulse to escape. In a normal period of British evolution, the spirit of rigid, corporate England was enough to maintain
fidelity to the profession, to the trade, but Chaplin entered history at a
moment when the axis of capitalism was silently shifting from Great
Britain to North America. The disequilibrium of the British machine,
recorded early on by his ultrasensitive spirit, acted on his centrifugal
and secessionist impulses. His genius felt the attraction of the new
capitalist metropolis. The pound sterling, humbled by the dollar, the
crisis of the coal industry, the silencing of Manchester's looms, the agitation for autonomy in the colonies, Eugene Chen's communication
on Hankow—all these symptoms of the weakening of British power
were anticipated by Chaplin, an alert receptor of the most secret mes-
sages of the era. The Little Tramp, the film artist, was born from the
rupture of the internal equilibrium of the clown. The gravitational pull
of the United States, in the midst of rapid capitalist development,
would not have been able to draw Chaplin from the destiny he would
have normally fulfilled as a clown without a series of failures in the
high-tension current of British history. How different Chaplin's destiny would have been in the Victorian age, even if the cinema and
Hollywood had already lit their searchlights!

But the United States has not spiritually assimilated Chaplin.
Chaplin's tragedy and humor receive their intensity from an intimate
conflict between the artist and North America. The prosperity, the
energy, the élan of North America hold and excite the artist, but its
bourgeois puerility, its upstart prosiness, are repugnant to the bohemian, who is romantic at heart. North America, in turn, does not love
Chaplin. As is well known, Hollywood's bosses consider him subversive, antagonistic. North America feels there is something in Chaplin
that escapes them. Among the neo-Quakers of Yankee finance and
industry, Chaplin will always be linked to Bolshevism.

One of the greatest and purest modern artistic phenomena feeds
from this contradiction, this contrast. The cinema allows Chaplin to
assist humanity in its struggle against sorrow with a breadth and

simultaneity that no artist has ever achieved. The image of this tragically comic bohemian provides a daily ration of joy across five continents. In Chaplin, art achieves the maximum of its hedonistic and liberating function. He alleviates the sadness of the world with his pained smile and hurt expression. And he contributes more to the miserable felicity of humanity than any of its statesmen, philosophers, industrialists, or artists.

—*Variedades*, 6 and 13 October 1928

NOTES

Source: *El Alma Matinal*, in *Obras Completas*, 4th ed. (Lima: Editorial Amauta, 1970), 3:55–62.

1. David Lloyd George (January 17, 1863–March 26, 1945) was a leader of the Liberal Party, and Ramsay MacDonald (October 12, 1866–November 9, 1937) became the first British Labour prime minister in 1924.
2. Mariátegui parenthetically inserts here: "'In Search of Gold,' or 'The Chimera of Gold' are only approximate translations of the title."
3. Julio Navarro Monzo (1882–1943) was an Argentine writer.

# PART IX

# Latin America

. . .

Like so many of Latin America's thinkers and intellectuals, Mariátegui thought in hemispheric terms. As he observes in the first essay in this section on the unity of Latin America, "These peoples are really not only brothers rhetorically, but historically. They come from a single womb. The Spanish conquest destroyed the Indigenous cultures and groups, and homogenized the ethnic, political, and moral physiognomy of Hispanic America. The Spaniards' methods of colonization unified the fate of its colonies." Mariátegui was quite clear on how the nations of the region developed differently over time.

Mariátegui avidly followed events in Mexico and in Nicaragua, where Augusto César Sandino was waging his popular people's guerrilla war against the U.S. Marines and the elitist Nicaraguan politicians who were collaborating with them.[1] The Mexican Revolution inspired thinkers, activists, and intellectuals throughout Latin America and much of the rest of the world, so it is little wonder that Mariátegui applied his powerful intellect to understanding and analyzing events in the post-revolutionary period. His essay on "Mexico and the Revolution" gives a succinct overview of the revolutionary process. The other two essays in this section, "Portes Gil Against the CROM"[2] and "The New Course of Mexican Politics as Seen from the Margins," provide a cold-eyed analysis of the developing politics of post-revolutionary Mexico, and have proven remarkably prescient: "The historical experiment begun in Mexico with Madero's insurrection and the overthrow of Porfirio Díaz provides the observer with an accurate and unique collection of proofs of the inevitable attraction toward capitalism and the bourgeoisie of all political movements led by the petite bourgeoisie, with all its particular ideological confusion." Mariátegui's close attention to political developments in Mexico indicates the importance he placed on hemispheric unity.

## NOTES

1. See, for example, Augusto César Sandino, "Mensaje de Sandino," *Amauta* 3/16 (July 1928): 1; Augusto C. Sandino, "Mensajes: Sandino y la libertad de los pueblos," *Amauta* 4/20 (January 1929): 95; letter from Augusto César Sandino to José Carlos Mariátegui, May 20, 1928, in *José Carlos Mariátegui: Correspondencia* (Lima: Biblioteca Amauta, 1984), 2:380; and selection IV.3 in this volume, "Yankee Imperialism in Nicaragua."

2. Emilio Portes Gil (Oct. 3, 1891–Dec. 10, 1978) was a Mexican political leader who served as provisional president of Mexico after the assassination of President-elect Alvaro Obregón from December 1, 1928, to February 3, 1930.

# 1—The Unity of Indo-Hispanic America

The people of Spanish-speaking America all have the same orientation. The solidarity of their historical destinies is not an illusion of Latin American literature. These people are really not only brothers rhetorically, but historically. They come from a single womb. The Spanish conquest destroyed the Indigenous cultures and groups and homogenized the ethnic, political, and moral physiognomy of Hispanic America. The Spaniards' methods of colonization unified the fate of its colonies. The conquistadors imposed their religion and feudalism on the Indigenous populations. Spanish blood mixed with Indian blood. The Spanish thereby created the nuclei of *creole* populations, the germ for future nationalities. Thereafter, identical ideas and emotions stirred the colonies against Spain. The process of formation of the Indo-Hispanic peoples had, in short, a uniform trajectory.

The liberators' generation felt this South American unity intensely. A united continental front opposed Spain. These leaders did not obey a nationalist ideal, but a Latin American one. This attitude corresponded to a historic necessity. Moreover, there could be no nationalism where there were not yet nationalities. The revolution was not a movement of the Indigenous populations. It was a movement of the *creole* populations, among whom the reflections of the French Revolution had generated a revolutionary spirit.

But succeeding generations did not continue the same way. Emancipated from Spain, the former colonies remained pressed by the tasks necessary for national formation. The Latin American ideal, superior to the contingent reality, was abandoned. The independence revolution had been a great romantic act, its leaders and inspirers exceptional men. The idealism of this act and these men had allowed them to ascend to a height unattainable by less romantic actions and men. Absurd fights and criminal wars rent the unity of Indo-Hispanic America. At the same time, some former colonies developed more securely and quickly than others. Immigration fertilized those nearest to Europe. These benefited from greater contact with Western civilization. Hispanic-American countries began to differentiate themselves in this way.

Presently, though some nations have liquidated their fundamental problems, others have not progressed too much toward their solution. While some nations have come to have a normal democratic organization, deep residues of feudalism remain in others. The process of development in all these nations proceeds in the same direction, but is more rapidly achieved in some than in others.

But what separates and isolates the Hispanic-American countries is not this diversity in their political timetables. It is the impossibility that incompletely formed nations, the majority of which have scarcely been outlined, can agree to and articulate an international system or conglomeration. In history, the commune precedes the nation. The nation precedes any society of nations.

The insignificance of Hispanic-American economic ties appears as a specific cause of this dispersion. Hardly any commerce or exchange exists between these nations. All of them are, more or less, producers of raw materials and foodstuffs that they send to Europe and the United States, for which they receive in exchange machinery, manufactured goods, etc. They all have a similar economy and analogous trade. They are agricultural countries and trade, therefore, with industrial countries. There is no cooperation among the Hispanic-

American peoples; on the contrary, at times there is competition. They do not need, do not complement, and do not seek after each other. Economically, they function as colonies of European and North American industry and finance.

Despite the lack of credit afforded the materialist conception of history, it is not possible to ignore the fact that economic relations are the main agent of communication and articulation among peoples. Perhaps the economic fact is neither anterior nor superior to the political fact. But at least the facts are consubstantial and mutually reinforcing. Modern history teaches this at every step. (German unity came through the *Zollverein*.[1] This tariff system, which removed the borders among German states, was the motor force of this unity, which defeat, the postwar period, and the maneuvers of the Poincarists have been unable to break.[2] Austria-Hungary, despite the heterogeneity of its ethnic makeup, has also constituted one economic organism in recent years. The nations that came about from the peace treaty that divided Austria-Hungary are a little artificial, despite the evident autonomy of their ethnic and historical roots. Living together in the Austro-Hungarian Empire had finally welded them together economically. The peace treaty gave them political autonomy, but has not been able to give them economic autonomy. These nations have had to seek a partial restoration of their unitary functioning through tariff pacts. Lastly, the politics of international cooperation and assistance that are being attempted in Europe develop from the reality of the economic interdependence of the European nations. These policies are not driven by abstract pacifist ideals, but by concrete economic interest. The problems coming from peace have shown the economic unity of Europe. The moral unity, the cultural unity of Europe, is not less evident but is less valid in convincing Europe to pacify itself.)

It is true that these young national formations find themselves scattered over an immense continent. But, in our time, economics is more powerful than space. Its fibers, its nerves, suppress or abolish distances. The exigencies of communication and transportation in Indo-Hispanic America are a consequence of the exigencies of economic relations. A railroad is not tendered to satisfy a spiritual or cultural need.

For practical purposes, Spanish-speaking America finds itself divided, split, and Balkanized. Nevertheless, its unity is not a utopia, it is not an abstraction. The people who make Hispanic-American history are not dissimilar. There is no appreciable difference between the Peruvian *creole* and the Argentine. The Argentine is more optimistic, more affirmative than the Peruvian, but each is irreligious and sensual. Between them, there are more differences of hue than of color.

Things differ from one region of Spanish America to another; the landscape differs but the people hardly differ at all. And the subject of history is, above all, people. Economics, politics, religion are forms of human reality. Their history is, in its essence, the history of humanity.

The identity of Hispanic-American people finds one expression in intellectual life. The same ideas, the same emotions, circulate through all of Indo-Hispanic America. All powerful intellectual personalities have an influence on the continental culture. Sarmiento, Martí, and Montalvo do not belong exclusively to their respective countries; they belong to Hispanic America. The same that can be said of these thinkers can be said of Darío, Lugones, Silva, Nervo, Chocano, and other poets. Rubén Darío is present throughout Hispanic-American literature. Currently, the ideas of Vasconcelos and Ingenieros are having continental repercussions. Vasconcelos and Ingenieros are the teachers of an entire generation of our America. They are the guides for its thought.

It is absurd and presumptuous to speak of a properly and genuinely Latin American culture that is germinating and developing. The only evident fact is that there is a vigorous literature that already reflects the Hispanic-American mentality and spirit. This literature— poetry, fiction, criticism, sociology, history, philosophy—is not yet connected to the peoples; but it is connected, if only partially and weakly, to the intellectuals.

Our time has finally created a more vivid living and extensive communication, which has established a revolutionary emotion in Hispanic-American youth. More spiritual than intellectual, this communication recalls one that united the generation of independence. Now as then, a revolutionary spirit unites Indo-Hispanic America.

Bourgeois interests are competitive or rival; the interests of the masses are not. All of America's new men are in solidarity with the Mexican Revolution, its fate, its ideals, and its people. Timid diplomatic toasts will not unite these peoples. In the future, the historical choices of the multitudes will unite them.

—*Variedades*, 6 December 1924

### NOTES

Source: "La unidad de la América Indo-Española," *Temas de Nuestra América*, in *Obras Completas*, 1st ed. (Lima: Editorial Amauta, 1960), 12:13–17.

1.   Customs agreement.
2.   Poincarism was a political movement named after Raymond Poincaré (August 20, 1860–October 15, 1934), a conservative French leader committed primarily to political and social stability.

# 2—Mexico and the Revolution

The dictatorship of Porfirio Díaz produced a situation of superficial economic well-being but also deep social malaise in Mexico. While in power, Porfirio Díaz was an instrument, proxy, and prisoner of the Mexican plutocracy. During the reformist revolution and the revolution against Maximilian, the Mexican people attacked the feudal privileges of the plutocracy. With Maximilian brought down, the large landowners took control of one of the generals of this liberal and nationalist revolution, Porfirio Díaz. They made him the leader of a bureaucratic military dictatorship designated to suffocate and repress these revolutionary demands. Díaz's policies were essentially plutocratic ones. Cunning and deceitful laws dispossessed Mexican Indians of their land to the benefit of national and foreign capitalists. *Latifundia* absorbed the *ejidos,* the traditional lands of the Indigenous communities. The peasant class was totally proletarianized as a result. The plutocrats, the *latifundistas,* and their hired clientalist lawyers and intellectuals constituted a faction, structurally analogous to *civilismo* in Peru, that dominated a feudalized country with the support of foreign capital. Portirio Díaz was its ideal gendarme. This so-called *cientifico*[1] oligarchy feudalized Mexico. The oligarchy marshaled a large praetorian guard to protect it. It extended special rights to foreign capitalists who were treated with special favor. It encouraged lethargy and desensitization among the masses, temporarily deprived of an animator, a leader. But a people who had so stubbornly battled for their right to the land could not resign themselves to the existence of this feudal regime and renounced its demands. Moreover, the growth of factories was creating an industrial proletariat to which foreign immigration was bringing pollen laden with new social ideas. Small socialist and syndicalist nuclei appeared. Flores Magón, from Los Angeles, injected a dose of socialist ideology into Mexico. And, above all, he fomented a bitter revolutionary feeling in the countryside. A leader, an incident, could ignite and inflame the country.

As Porfirio Díaz's seventh term was ending, the leader appeared: Francisco Madero. Madero, who until that time was a farmer of no political import, published a book against Díaz's reelection. An indictment of the Díaz government, the book found an immense popular response. At first Porfirio Díaz, with the vain confidence in his own power that blinds waning despots, was not worried over the commotion that Madero and his book aroused. He judged Madero's personality to be inferior and powerless. Madero, acclaimed and followed like an apostle, nevertheless aroused a powerful current against Diaz's reelection. And finally, the dictatorship, alarmed and upset, felt the need to combat that campaign violently. Madero was jailed. The reactionary offensive dispersed the anti-reelectionist party, the *científicos* reestablished their authority and power, Porfirio Díaz won for the eighth time, and the celebration of Mexico's centenary was the splendid apotheosis of his dictatorship. Such successes filled Díaz and his band with optimism and confidence. The end of his government was nevertheless near. Madero, released conditionally, fled to the United States, where he devoted himself to organizing the revolutionary movement. Orozco joined the first insurrectionist army shortly thereafter. And the rebellion spread quickly. The *científicos* tried to attack it with political weapons. They declared themselves ready to satisfy revolutionary aspirations. They passed a law blocking another reelection. But this maneuver could not contain the movement on the way. The antireelection campaign was only a passing phase. Around it had gathered all the discontented, all the exploited, all the idealists. The revolution did not yet have a program, but it was beginning to be outlined. Its first concrete demand was for the land usurped by the *latifundistas*.

The Mexican plutocracy, with the sharp instinct for self-preservation of all plutocracies, pushed to negotiate with the revolutionaries. It thereby kept the revolution from bringing the dictatorship down by force. In 1912 Porfirio Díaz handed the government over to De la Barra, who oversaw an election. Madero came to power through a compromise with the *científicos*. He consequently accepted their collaboration. He maintained the old parliament. These transactions and deals weakened and undermined him. The *científicos* sabotaged the revolutionary program and isolated Madero from the social strata from which he had recruited his converts, and at the same time prepared their own reconquest of power. They lay in wait for the moment to remove a weakened and ruined Madero from the presidency of the republic. Madero rapidly lost his popular base. Now came the insurrection of Félix Díaz, and then the betrayal of Victoriano Huerta, who stormed the government over the bodies of Madero and Pino Suárez. The "scientific" reaction appeared victorious. But the pronouncement of a military chief could not stop the march of the Mexican Revolution. All the roots of this revolution were still alive. General Venustiano Carranza took up the banner of Madero and, after a period of struggle, expelled Victoriano Huerta from power. The demands of the revolution were sharpened and better defined, and Mexico revised and reformed its fundamental charter in accordance with these demands. Article 27 of the constitutional reform of Queretaro declares that the land belongs originally to the nation and orders the breakup of the *latifundia*. Article 123 incorporates various aspirations of the workers into the constitution: a maximum length for the working day, a minimum wage, health and retirement insurance, compensation for accidents on the job, and profit sharing.

But the conditions did not exist to realize the revolution's program once Carranza was elected president. His character as a landlord and his commitments to the landowning class hindered him in carrying out the agrarian reform. The division of the land promised by the revolution and ordered by the constitutional reform did not occur. The Carranza regime gradually became petrified and bureaucratized. In the end, Carranza claimed the right to designate his successor. The country, constantly aroused by the revolutionary parties, rose up against this idea. Carranza, virtually abandoned, died at the hands of an irregular band. Victoriano Huerta's provisional presidency carried out elections that brought General Obregón to the presidency.

The Obregon government has taken a resolute step toward satisfying one of the deepest desires of the revolution: it has given land to the poor peasants. A collectivist regime has flourished under its protection in the state of Yucatan. Its prudent and well-organized policies have normalized Mexican life, and it has persuaded the United States to recognize the Mexican regime.

But the most revolutionary and transcendent activity of the Obregón government has been its work in education. José Vasconcelos, one of the most outstanding men in modern Latin America, has led an extensive and radical reform of public education. He has used the most original methods to decrease illiteracy; he has opened up the universities to the poorer classes; he has spread the works of Tolstoy and Romain Rolland to all the schools and libraries like a modern evangelist; he has incorporated into the Law of Public Education the state's obligation to support and educate orphans and the children of the disabled; and he has sown the immense and fertile lands of Mexico with schools, books, and ideas.

—*Variedades*, 5 January 1924

NOTES

Source: "México y la revolución," *Temas de Nuestra América*, in *Obras Completas*, 1st ed. (Lima: Editorial Amauta, 1960), 12:39–43.

1.     Literally a "scientist," but here referring to a group of positivist advisers to Díaz.

# 3—Portes Gil against the CROM

There is no longer any possible doubt about the reactionary tendency of the provisional president of Mexico's policies. The offensive against the Confederación Regional Obrera Mexicana [CROM: Mexican Regional Workers Confederation], though its real motives are concealed with demagogic language, proposes nothing less than beating down or diminishing the political power of the working masses. This is an unequivocally counterrevolutionary objective that no rhetoric can hide or disguise.

Portes Gil does not have the responsibility and initiative for these policies; in his management he obeys factors greater than his personal judgment. Here is another fact that is no less certain. Portes Gil has not changed the government's attitude toward CROM because of a sudden inspiration. His selection as provisional president was decided by the forces opposed to CROM that have grown in the governmental bloc in recent years. The incubation process of this government began when the boldest enemies of CROM accused its leader, Morones, of being the Machiavellian instigator of the assassination of General Obregón. From that moment, the popular front that governed Mexico in the name of the principles of the revolution was definitively broken. The rise to power of the so-called

Obregónistas had to lead to the revolution, the crisis, that we are currently witnessing.

During Obregón and Calles's governments, the stabilization of the revolutionary regime had been obtained by virtue of a tacit pact between the insurgent petite bourgeoisie and the worker and peasant organizations to collaborate on a strictly reformist basis.[1] This could be pursued using radical phraseology against reactionary attacks, aimed at keeping alive the masses' enthusiasm. But in reality all radicalism had to be sacrificed to a politics of normalization and reconstruction. The revolutionary conquests could only be consolidated at this price. CROM arose and grew under revolution's leadership—its baptism was at the workers' convention of Saltillo in 1918—and lacked the capacity and ambition to dominate the government materially and intellectually, both at the time of the first election of Obregón and the time of Calles's election. In 1926, its adherents, which at the Saltillo convention had not added up to seven thousand, were reduced to only five thousand. The whole process of development of CROM had occurred under the governments of Obregón and Calles, which they supported, while receiving the indispensable guarantees for its work of organizing the worker and peasant masses in its ranks. At the moment of its greatest mobilization, CROM calculated its membership at two million. Its political function—despite its representation in the government—was not related to its social power. But it would not have been able to build and increase it in so little time without the help of an exceptional situation, like that of Mexico and its government after long years of victorious revolutionary agitation.

Under this regime, not only have the workers' forces developed, channeled in a reformist direction, but also the forces of capital and the bourgeoisie. The most unskilled energies of the reaction had been consumed in the attempt to attack the revolution from the outside. The wisest operated inside the revolution, waiting for the hour of Thermidorian reaction to sound.

The Mexican state was not a socialist state in theory or in practice. The revolution had respected the principles and forms of capitalism.

What was socialist about this state consisted of its working-class political base. However moderate its politics, CROM, as a class organization, had to accentuate its program of socialization of wealth day by day. But at the same time that this was going on with the working class the capitalist class solidified in the context of the regime created by the revolution. And they had in their favor a greater political maturity. The petit-bourgeois elements, the military *caudillos* of the revolution, placed between these two influences, had to regularly give way to capitalist influence.

In this way the road was laid for the conflict that exploded, albeit somewhat precipitously, with the assassination of the president-elect, General Obregón, the only *caudillo* who, after Calles, had been able to prolong the compromise between the two rival forces.

CROM entered into combat under unfavorable conditions and at an unfavorable moment. Its reformist general staff—Morones and his lieutenants—could not go from a pacifist, legal, evolutionist practice to the struggle against power. Morones gave ardent and polemical speeches at the last CROM convention, but he did not affirm the right and will of the working class to take the government into its hands as soon as its situation and strength would allow. It can be clearly seen that Morones is not renouncing his opportunism, and that he trusts more in the possibility of exploiting the divisions and rivalries among the *caudillos* than in the possibility of leading the working masses to a genuinely revolutionary politics. The recourse of bringing Calles to the convention was a maneuver of this strategic type.

For this reason, the efforts of various workers' organizations independent of CROM to establish a united proletarian front, which includes all the active sectors, through a national peasant assembly, have great consequence and significance. The daily cry of the Communist Party and the worker and peasant groupings that follow it is: "Long live CROM! Down with its Central Committee!" All the workers' forces are called to aid CROM in its struggle against the reactionary offensive. All intransigent inclinations to give birth to a new confederation are condemned. It is understood that CROM constitutes a starting point that the proletariat should not lose.

The revolution faces its gravest test. And Mexico is today, more than ever, the site of a revolutionary experience. Class politics in this country is entering its most interesting phase.

—*Variedades*, 19 January 1929

NOTES

Source: "Portes Gil Contra la CROM," *Temas de Nuestra América*, in *Obras Completas,* 1st ed. (Lima: Editorial Amauta, 1960), 12:56–59.

1.    Emilio Portes Gil (October 3, 1890–December 10, 1978) was provisional president of Mexico for fourteen months after a religious fanatic assassinated president-elect Álvaro Obregón (February 19, 1880–July 17, 1928) in the midst of a widespread and violent religious war known as the Cristero Rebellion. Portes Gil served under the guidance of the de facto Mexican ruler Plutarco Elías Calles (September 25, 1877–October 19, 1945). Calles was president of Mexico from 1924 to 1928, but he continued to be the de facto ruler from 1928 to 1935.

# 4—The New Course of Mexican Politics as Seen from the Margins

The careful observation of Mexican events is destined to clarify, for the theoreticians and practitioners of Latin American socialism, the questions that frequently muddle and disfigure the dilettantish interpretations of tropical super-Americanists. Both in times of revolutionary flow and reactionary ebb, and perhaps more precisely and neatly in the latter, the historical experiment begun in Mexico with Madero's insurrection and the overthrow of Porfirio Díaz provides the observer with an accurate and unique collection of proofs of the inevitable attraction toward capitalism and the bourgeoisie of all the political movements led by the petite bourgeoisie, with all its particular ideological confusion.

Mexico made these pressured and overdrawn apologists conceive the tacit hope that its revolution would provide Latin America with a patron and method for a socialist revolution governed by essentially Latin American factors, with the most sparing use of European theorizing. The facts have put the stop to this tropical, messianic hope. And no circumspect critic would today risk subscribing to the hypothesis that the leaders and projects of the Mexican revolution are leading the Aztec people toward socialism.

Luis Araquistain, in a book written with obvious sympathy for the work of the political regime he studied in Mexico two years ago, feels himself obliged, by his most elemental duty of objectivity, to undo the legend of "socialist revolution." This is also the more specific and systematic object of a series of articles by the young Peruvian writer Esteban Pavletich, who has been in direct contact with the people and events of Mexico since 1926. The writers who are followers or allies of the regime admit that, for the moment, the policies of the regime do not tend toward creating a socialist state. Froylán C. Manjarrez, in a study appearing in the journal *Crisol,* claims that for the stage of gradual transition from capitalism to socialism life "now offers us this solution: between the capitalist state and the socialist state, there is an intermediate state: the state as regulator of the national economy, whose mission corresponds to the Christian idea of property, today triumphant, which assigns it social functions."

Without being teleological or deterministic, the Italian Fascists arrogate to themselves the role of creating precisely this type of national and unified state. The class state is condemned in the name of a state above class interests, a state that conciliates and arbitrates these interests, depending on the case. It is not strange that this eminently petit-bourgeois idea, particularly supported by Fascism in the context of its unequivocally and unmistakably counterrevolutionary activities, now appears incorporated in the ideas of a political regime that is the consequence of a revolutionary surge. The world's petites bourgeoisies are similar, though some go back to Machiavelli, the Middle Ages, and the Roman Empire, and others dream of a Christianity that assigns property a social function. The regulatory state of Froylán C. Manjarrez is none other than the Fascist state.[1] It matters little that Manjarrez prefers to see this regulation in the German state as it appears in the Weimar constitution.

Neither the Weimar constitution nor the presence of the Socialist Party in the government has freed the German state of its character as a class state, a bourgeois-democratic state. The German Socialists, who drew back from the revolution in 1918—an attitude that has a formal expression precisely in the Weimar constitution—do not propose anything more than the slow, prudent transformation of this state, which they know capitalist interests dominate. As reformist leaders like the Belgian Vandervelde explain, ministerial collaboration is necessary because of the need to defend the interests of the working class from inside the government against the predominance of capitalism and because of the importance and responsibilities of the Socialist parliamentary faction. On the other hand, incidents such as the removal of the Social Democrat Hilferding, the finance minister, from the government because of his conflict with Schacht, the dictator of the Reichsbank and the trustee of the big financial bourgeoisie, should be enough to make the German Socialists remember the real power of capitalist interests in the government and the practical circumstances of Social Democratic collaboration.

What does categorize and classify the German state is the degree to which it realizes bourgeois democracy. Germany's political evolution is not measured by the Weimar constitution's vague designs for the nationalization of industry, but by the effectiveness of its bourgeois-democratic institutions: universal suffrage, parliamentarism, the right of all parties to exist legally and propagate their ideas, etc.

The regression in Mexico in the period after Obregón's death, the rightward march of the Portes Gil and Ortiz Rubio regimes, can similarly be judged by the suspension of the democratic rights of the previously accepted extreme left forces. Persecuting the militants of the United Mexican Union Confederation [CSUM], the Communist Party, Workers Aid, and the Anti-Imperialist League for their criticism of its abdications before imperialism and for their propagation of a proletarian program, the Mexican government disowns the true mission of the Mexican Revolution: substituting the despotic and semifeudal Porfirista regime with a bourgeois-democratic regime.

The regulatory state, the intermediary state, defined as an organ of the transition from capitalism to socialism, appears as a concrete regression. Not only is it not capable of ensuring proletarian political and economic organizations the guarantees of bourgeois-democratic legality, but it assumes the task of attacking and destroying them when it feels the least bit bothered by its most elementary manifestations. It proclaims itself the absolute and infallible repository of the revolution's ideals. It is a state with a patriarchal mentality that, without professing socialism, opposes the proletariat—the class historically charged with fulfilling this duty—when it affirms and exercises its right to fight for it, independent of all bourgeois and petit-bourgeois influences.

None of these arguments call into question the social depth of the Mexican revolution or its historical significance. The political movement that defeated Porfirismo in Mexico, in all that the movement meant as an advance and victory over feudalism and its oligarchies, has nourished mass sentiment, found support in its strength, and has been driven by an indisputably revolutionary spirit. It is an extraordinary and instructive experience in all these aspects. But the character and objectives of this revolution, considering the men who have led it, the economic situation from which it arises, and the nature of its development, are those of a bourgeois-democratic revolution. Socialism cannot be brought on without a class party. It can only be the result of socialist theory and practice. The intellectual supporters of the regime grouped around the journal *Crisol* have taken upon themselves the task of "defining and illuminating the ideology of the revolution." They thereby recognize that it is neither defined nor illuminated. The latest repressive acts, directed in the first place against foreign political refugees—Cubans, Venezuelans, etc.—indicate that this illumination is coming slowly. The Mexican Revolution's politicians, while otherwise quite different from one another, show themselves less and less disposed to conduct a bourgeois-democratic revolution. They have already started to move the revolution backwards. And in the meantime its theoreticians are serving up theories of the regulatory state, the intermediary state, with Latin American eloquence, and it all seems piece for piece like the Fascist theory of the state.

—*Variedades*, 19 March 1930

## NOTES

Source: "Al margen del nuevo curso de la política mexicana," *Temas de Nuestra América*, in *Obras Completas*, 1st ed. (Lima: Editorial Amauta, 1960), 12:66–70.

1.    Froylán C. Manjarrez was a representative to the 1917 Mexican Constitutional Convention that created the juridical underpinnings of the post-revolutionary Mexican state.

# Glossary

AYLLU
Kinship forms of social organization in Andean Indigenous areas.

CACIQUE
Taíno word for Indigenous leaders in the Caribbean. The Spanish brought the term to the Andes, where it referred to local power brokers.

CAUDILLO
A charismatic and often authoritarian political leader common in nineteenth-century South America, often translated as "strongman."

CHOLO
Peruvianism for a *mestizo*, a person of mixed European and Indigenous heritage.

CIVILISMO, CIVILISTA
Refers to a Peruvian political movement of the late nineteenth and early twentieth centuries, led by those who opposed military control of the government (*civilistas*).

CREOLE
American-born descendants of the Spanish conquistadors, often used in a derogatory sense to indicate something that is second-rate compared to the Spanish.

CURACA (KURAKA)
A hereditary leader in the Andes.

ENCOMIENDA, ENCOMENDERO
In colonial times, the *encomendero*, traditionally a conquistador, ran the *encomienda*, which was land given to him by the Spanish crown. *Encomenderos* were charged with incorporating the land into the crown's domain, making it productive, and Christianizing the population. In return they could use the land's Indigenous inhabitants as they saw fit.

ENGANCHE
Forced recruitment of indentured labor through a system of debt peonage. *Enganchadores* were the labor recruiters.

GAMONALISMO, GAMONAL
Derogatory Peruvianism that refers to a system of large landed estates (*latifundia*) under the control of a local landowner or local boss (*gamonal*); similar to *cacique*.

HUACO
An antiquity or ritual object, often in the form of a ceramic vessel.

INDIGENISMO, INDIGENISTA
Defense of the rights of Indigenous peoples by elite, educated outsiders (*indigenistas*).

LATIFUNDIA/LATIFUNDIO, LATIFUNDISTA
Large landed estates under the control of a wealthy local landowner (*latifundista*).

MESTIZO
A person of mixed European and Indigenous heritage.

MINGA
Communal work party in Indigenous communities.

MITA
System of mandatory work periods under Spanish colonizers that forced Indigenous peoples to perform for weeks to months at a time.

MONTAÑA
Peru's eastern forested region.

PONGAZO, PONGOS
Domestic service that subordinated Indigenous servants (*pongos*) performed.

SOLES
Peruvian unit of currency.

TAWANTINSUYU
Quechua name for the Inca Empire.

YANACONAZGO, YANACONA
Sharecropping system (*yanaconazgo*); sharecroppers, a harshly exploited tenant worker (*yanacona*).

# Index